Economics of Agriculture: Challenges and Strategies for Development

Economics of Agriculture: Challenges and Strategies for Development

Dr. Ashok Purohit

RANDOM PUBLICATIONS
NEW DELHI (INDIA)

Economics of Agriculture: Challenges and Strategies for Development

ISBN 978-93-5111-811-4

Published in 2016 in India by

RANDOM PUBLICATIONS

4376-A/4B, Gali Murari Lal, Ansari Road
New Delhi-110 002
Phone : +9111-43580356, 011-23289044, 011-43142548
e-mail: sales@randompublications.com,
info@randompublications.com, randomexports@gmail.com

Reprinted 2021

Type Setting by : Friends Media, Delhi-110089
Digitally Printed at: Replika Press Pvt. Ltd.

Preface

Agricultural economics arose in the late-19th century, combined the theory of the firm with marketing and organization theory, and developed throughout the 20th century largely as an empirical branch of general economics. The discipline was closely linked to empirical applications of mathematical statistics and made early and significant contributions to econometric methods. In the 1960s and afterwards, agricultural economists were drawn to the development problems of poor countries, to the trade and macroeconomic policy implications of agriculture in rich countries, and to a variety of production, consumption, and environmental and resource problems." Agricultural economics or agronomics is an applied field of economics concerned with the application of economic theory in optimizing the production and distribution of food and fibre - a discipline known as agronomics. Agronomics was a branch of economics that specifically dealt with land usage. It focused on maximizing the crop yield while maintaining a good soil ecosystem. Throughout the 20th century the discipline expanded and the current scope of the discipline is much broader. Agricultural economics today includes a variety of applied areas, having considerable overlap with conventional economics. Agricultural economists have made substantial contributions to research in economics, econometrics, development economics, and environmental economics. Agricultural economics influences food policy, agricultural policy, and environmental policy.

– Author

Contents

1

Development of Modern Agriculture

FARM MANAGEMENT

PRIMITIVE AGRICULTURE

Historical writers agree that in early days, the inhabitants of the earth gained a livelihood by hunting and fishing. When the population of a region became so dense as to deplete the supplies of food to be gained in this way, the more enterprising ones tamed and domesticated some of the wild animals for their own use. These animals were given protection and provided with food so that they multiplied rapidly. In this way a supply of meat was insured for those who cared for and protected them. From hunting and fishing the people turned to such pursuits as grazing and herding, and gave much of their time to caring for animals. This was known as the pastoral stage of subsistence. It was more reliable than hunting and fishing for several reasons. By protecting the domesticated animals from the beasts of prey and driving away the less useful animals, larger numbers of useful animals were enabled to live in a given region. Food supplies of meat were therefore more plentiful and certain.

This custom of providing food supplies for animals led to the discovery that certain plants were better adapted for food than others. To raise these desirable plants in abundance it became necessary to destroy other plants that were not so useful, but which contended with the useful plants for possession of the soil. This may be said to be the beginning of agriculture. At least it was the first indication of the organization of nature's forces to meet the needs of man. The demand for land for grazing and tilling purposes led to mutual agreements for territory which should be used for such purposes by certain persons or tribes, and is the first suggestion of land allotment or ownership.

BRITISH AGRICULTURE

The agriculture of England has passed through many different stages. Because of scarcity of agricultural labourers between 1350 and 1375, many of the owners of large estates were forced to change their system of farming.

Previous to that time most of the tillable land had been devoted to grain raising, bread being the chief article of food. Then the land was changed into pasture, and sheep and cattle raising took a prominent place in British agriculture.

The greatest development came about the middle of the seventeenth century with the introduction o fclover and turnips as field crops. The chief advantage in these crops was the increased amount of feed, which enabled the farmer to keep more cattle on his land. Keeping of cattle gave manure that was applied to the land and resulted in better handling of the farms. The turnips took the place of bare fallowing which had previously been practiced, thus enabling the farmer to use all of his land each year.

Improved methods of tillage followed rapidly. About the first of the eighteenth century Jethro Tull started the practice of drilling the grain in rows, later advocating tillage between the rows, and inventing implements for the work. Lord Townshend, about the same time began the rotation of crops, greatly improving the producing power of his land thereby. Another notable man in British agriculture is Coke of Holkham, who like his predecessors grew turnips and clover, but who also studied economical management of his farm. He reduced the number of horses used in plow teams and increased greatly the efficiency of his live stock. Following the work of these three men, farming became a gentleman's profession in England and progress since has been rapid. The development and improvement of live stock has received so much attention at the hands of British breeders that the whole world practically has been drawn to their markets for foundation stock.

AMERICAN AGRICULTURE

The agriculture of America has been developed largely from the methods followed on the British Isles. The American colonists brought with them the customs of the British farmers and have since gone frequently to the mother country for improved seeds, for live stock, and even for men to do certain parts of the farm labour, as for instance, caring for the more valuable imported stock.

The development of agriculture during colonial days was slow and full of hardship. The British and European methods of agriculture required re-adapting to the new conditions. The people were forced to live a new kind of life, to clear land of trees and stones, and to learn by experience what crops were adapted and what methods of tillage would succeed. From the Indians they learned how to grow corn and tobacco, which have ever since been two of our important crops. From them also they learned many of the secrets of soil and climate. The agricultural development proceeded along two lines.

In the South large plantations with negro slaves as labourers were established. Such establishments were practically self-sustaining because they supplied nearly all articles of food and clothing. In the North the family farm was developed largely and the labour of the farm was performed mainly by the farmer and his family. The conditions existing in the North encouraged the cooperative spirit and developed sociability among the people. Land in either section was abundant and the greatest problem in the management of farms waws that of economizing labour.

The colonial development was along the eastern sea coast. Following the Revolutionary war, settlement moved westward beyond the Alleghany Mountains and into the Great Central Basin. The invention of the cotton gin about 1793, and the development of the cotton industry, changed rapidly the systems of farming in the South. Slavery became greatly extended to provide cheap labour for the cotton fields, and probably had much to do with the rapid settlement of the southern states.

Cotton and tobacco growing were the leading industries in these states and agricultural improvement was slow because labour was cheap as compared with that in the northern states and the use of improved machinery was not so imperative. Migration westward was encouraged by the opening of the Northwest Territory in 1785. A liberal land policy on the part of the National Government and the discovery of gold in California served to stimulate the movement westward and aided the rapid settlement and development of the great prairie regions of the Mississippi Valley. The invention and perfection of farm machinery, begun about 1825 to 1830 and continued to the present time, has also been a great factor in the development of agriculture in America. The reaper, invented, the thresher, perfected about 1850, and steel plows for turning the soil, manufactured since 1840, have had a great influence on the agriculture of the northern states which were especially interested in grain and corn raising.

Live stock raising was followed to some extent in the northern states also, but received great impetus about 1839 by the importation of the English thoroughbred stallion "Denmark" into Kentucky. Percheron draft horses from France were also introduced soon after. Corn raising on the western prairies stimulated greatly the growing of hogs. Cattle raising on the vast prairies also was greatly extended during this period. Dairying began to develop about 1850. The improvement of machinery and the increase in stock and grain raising went on steadily in the northern states, not being interrupted seriously even by the Civil War. In the South where cotton and tobacco grown on large plantations by slave labour were the main crops, agriculture was seriously demoralized by the war which set free the slaves, thus destroying the source of cheap labour. Several years were required to build up a new system of agricultural production and to adjust labour problems, but the agriculture of the South is now on a much better basis.

During the past twenty-five years agricultural development has been particularly rapid. The establishment of experiment stations in 1888 in every state in the Union, through the passage by Congress of the Hatch Act in 1887, and the development of Agricultural schools and colleges has led to a systematic application of science to agriculture. Crop growing has become much more certain and live stock growing has been largely developed. The occupation and settlement of the prairie lands, the perfection of machinery, and extended opportunities for agricultural education, have been large factors in improving conditions for farming. In the days of abundant land, large holdings were secured by many farmers. The tendency in later years is to reduce somwhat the size of farms and to take up more intensive forms of agriculture. Greater efficiency is demanded in the management of farms in order that greater profits may be realised by the tiller of the soil.

FARMING MUST BE ORGANIZED

During the period of cheap land and comparatively cheap labour, many crops were raised which do not under existing conditions, yield a profit. Methods of tilling the land and handling the crops that were followed during that period would not now give large enough yields to support the farmers and their families. Crops and methods of tillage must be readjusted to meet the changed economic conditions and satisfy the demands of the rapidly growing population for food stuffs. The practice of grain raising so prevalent in many portions of the United States must give way to live stock raising, fruit and vegetable growing and other more intensive systems of agriculture. A great variety of crops and a larger supply of all food stuffs and clothing material is required by the present population. The value of the agricultural products in the United States in 1910 was $8,694,000,000. The total value of all live stock on farms in the United States in 1910 was $4,925,000,000. The demand is constantly increasing. The future supply of these commodities is a matter demanding the most serious consideration.

It is important that the old soil robbing types of farming be superseded by more conservative methods; that the land be so tilled that it will bring the largest crops at the least expense of soil fertility; and that these crops be used or fed as near as possible to the land upon which they were grown, the manures and crop residues being returned to the soil.

It is important also that the farmer receive a fair compensation for his labour. Crops must be selected that pay the best profits. These will differ in different years and localities. The farmer, therefore, must learn to select wisely and manage well so as to make a reasonable profit on his labour and investments.

The business of farming is constantly becoming more complex. The keen demand for land, the scarcity of labour, the desire for financial gain and the call of the city residents for supplies are acting as a spur for still greater effort. To meet these demands a new science is being developed which aims to correlate the various factors entering into the farmers' business so that it will be certain and remunerative. An effort is being made to organize the business of farming so that it may provide for the needs of the present generation without exhausting the source of supplies for generations yet to come. This new science is called *Farm Management*.

BUSINESS SIDE OF FARMING

FARMING AS A BUSINESS

Farming has not usually been considered a business. The diversity of the duties of the farmer, the area over which the operations of the farm extend and the complexity of the records required, combine in making difficult the organization of the details of farming into business form. The successful financial operation of a farm presents quite as complex problems and calls for at least as much business ability and judgment as is required in operating a store with the same investment. Farming, therefore, should be considered as a business, and the man who can produce his crops and products at the lowest cost and sell them at the highest price, investing the proceeds to the best advantage, should be considered the best farm manager. The man who knows the details of the cost of production and operation, and whose records show the profitable and unprofitable lines of production, thus enabling him to eliminate those that do not yield a profit, may be counted as the best business man.

A farmer should know the elements of soil fertility. He must understand the principles of the movement of soil water, and the action of soil bacteria. He should understand the nature of plant growth and be familiear with varieties and species of plants and with the effect of one crop on the crop following. He must also be familiar with animals and their habits and know how to feed and care for them. In addition, he must know how to buy and sell to advantage, make contracts, and plan his buildings and his farm so as to necessitate a light expenditure for labour, also that he may distribute his labour to advantage over the various farm enterprises. And he should know how to keep accounts.

The farmer in organizing his business could well follow the example of the merchant. The merchant first takes an inventory of his stock. He studies the demand for his goods, both present and prospective. He notes the supply, the cost, and the demand for each article. He calculates the labour required to operate his business and such other items of expense are considered as may be legitimately charged against the business. He regulates his purchases and his prices according to the cost of securing his goods and putting them on the market. In conducting a large store business, it is customary to organize it into departments, putting some competent person in charge of each department and having the labour and accounting charges so systematized and recorded as to show the profit or loss from each department and from the business as a whole.

The farmer should likewise take an inventory of his capital, stock, and equipment. He should consider the type of farming to which the soil and climate are adapted. He should consider the fertility of the soil and the demand that will be made upon it by the crops grown. He should consider, in connection with the soil fertility, the sources from which it may be renewed and at what cost. He must study the markets, the transportation, and the demand for such crops as he grows; also the cost of producing each of the crops and the probable net profit that will be returned. His labour likewise should be charged against the various crops or enterprises and distributed to the best advantage.

In studying the problems of farm organizations, interest on investment, taxes, insurance, and other expense must be included as they affect the financial result. As in a large store business, it is frequently necessary to organize the large farm into departments, keeping accounts with the dairy, with the swine, the grain crops, the garden, and other similar enterprises.

Where the business is large enough, it is well to put an expert in charge of each large branch or group of enterprises, thus enabling one to use cheaper labour for performing the work or making the labour more effective by closer supervision. Where the farming is conducted as an organized business, and accounts are kept with the various lines of work, it is possible at the end of the year, to make a business statement which will show which lines have been profitable. The manager then can change his methods or drop out those lines that prove to be unprofitable and the business as a whole may be put on a better basis.

INVESTMENT

The investment of money in land, buildings, and equipment demands careful consideration. It is possible to pay so much for a farm that it will be impossible to produce sufficient revenue to meet the expense of operation and to pay a normal rate of interest on the money invested. This is particularly true where low-priced products are produced. A farm may be highly productive but so located that it will be impossible to market the produce on a profit bearing basis. One should study closely the market facilities of the neighbourhood and raise supplies which can be successfully marketed locally, or which can be transported to a market that pays well for such produce. Unless the produce of the farm is well related to the market, the farm is likely to be operated at a loss.

PROPORTION IN REAL ESTATE

It is a mistake for one to invest all of his capital in the real estate itself. Sufficient capital should be reserved for operating the farm. The hunger for land has induced many farmers to buy more land that they can equip and operate well. Such farmers are said to be land poor. They would secure greater profit from a medium sized farm, well tilled and managed, than from a large one which is insufficiently equipped and poorly operated. Rarely should more than 50 or 60 per cent of the capital be tied up in the land. The size of the farm and the amount of equipment are closely related to the possible profits. A farm of forty or eighty acres devoted to diversified crops and live stock, cannot be so economically equipped per acre as a larger farm. The investment per acre in machinery will be higher as the cost will be spread over fewer acres than the machinery has capacity to handle. Investment in other equipment will also be correspondingly high. Often the labour on such a farm is not fully employed and loss results from inactivity of labour and equipment. A medium to large sized farm, when well organized, fully equipped, and with sufficient capital reserved to operate it well, will pay a much better labour income than a small farm.

PROPORTION OF INVESTMENT IN MACHINERY

Investments in machinery are worthy of quite as much consideration as investments in land. Machinery is looked upon as one of the means of reducing the cost of production. The wise use of machinery saves time and labour and enables the farmer to handle large acreages. In this light, the use of ample machinery is wise. The fact remains, however, that investments in machinery are often poorly made and that many farmers are embarrassed by debts for machinery. Frequently, farmers purchase machinery because it is fashionable or because a neighbour has it, rather than because carefully made calculations show that a certain machine can be used profitably. A safe rule is to buy no machine until carefully made calculations show that the cost of production of a certain crop or product will be reduced sufficiently by the purchase to cover the cost of the machine. That machinery investments can be studied from a business standpoint is quite plain. The following example, showing the relative cost of cutting corn with a machine versus cutting by hand, will illustrate:

The original cost of a corn binder is $125. The annual depreciation, as shown by statistical records covering ten years' work with farmers in Minnesota, is $12.50. The interest on the investment at the average value of the binder throughout its life will be $4.12. Repairs, shelter, and insurance will cost $2 annually. The total annual cost for the use of the binder, therefore, will be $18.62. If only twenty acres of corn are grown each year, the annual cost an acre for the corn binder will be $.93. The cost of cutting corn would be as follows: It will be noted that a twenty-acre corn field can be more economically harvested by hand where labour is available.

On a ten-acre field, the difference in expense would be still greater in favour of the hand harvesting, as the cost of machinery per acre would be doubled. The scarcity of labour, however, and the necessity of harvesting corn quickly to save it from frost, would often warrant the expenditure for the machine, even though it does slightly raise the cost of harvesting per acre. The greater the acreage, the more useful the machine becomes in harvesting, and the less the expense per acre for machinery use. Calculations similar to this should be made before purchasing a machine for any purpose. If it can be shown that the cost of performing the labour may be reduced by the machine, and that the labour can be performed in a more satisfactory and efficient manner with the use of it, then the purchase may be warranted. In many cases, however, calculation will show that the purchase is not warranted and that it would be better to hire labour and rent the machine, or to buy in partnership with some one else.

COST OF MOTIVE POWER

Another factor that should receive consideration is the cost of motive power in use on the farm. Horses usually furnish the farm motive power, though tractors are used to advantage in some cases. Auto trucks and automobiles can often be used to advantage in marketing dairy, fruit and garden products and the cost of using them, when it can be ascertained, should be compared with the cost of horse power. It costs from $40 to $100 per year to keep a work horse, depending on the locality and on the price of feed stuffs; also on the work that the horse does. The average cost a year of keeping a horse in Minnesota for the years 1904 to 1907, varied from $75.07 at Halstad, to $90.40 at Northfield.

Often a large number of horses are kept because the farm has been devoted to grain raising and the horses are needed at seeding and harvest times. They run in the pasture during the summer and are idle during the winter months. They must be fed and cared for during this time. The money invested in them would be drawing interest if invested somewhere else. Farmers should reduce the horses kept to the number actually required to do the work, unless the surplus are colts growing in value as one of the market products of the farm. The work of a farm can often be lessened by adopting a good crop rotation and using such crops as do not demand large amounts of horse labour at the same time. In this way a farm of 160 to 240 acres can often be worked with four to six horses, whereas eight to ten are frequently kept. The support of two or three extra horses per year would amount to $200 to $250 and is an item well worth saving.

INVESTMENT IN BUILDINGS

Investment in buildings, fences, and other items of equipment should be considered in the same business-like way. A barn costing $4,000 and providing shelter for forty head of cattle would carry with it an annual cost of $440. This annual cost is made up from the interest on the investment, insurance, depreciation, paint, and repairs. It will be about 11 per cent on the total investment. If the same forty cattle could be housed in a barn costing $2000 the total annual cost would be only $220, charging the same interest and expense rates as in the first instance, and assuming that the rate of depreciation would be the same.

While the $4000 barn would undoubtedly be a better barn, it would not add to the production of the cows housed, unless it was much more comfortable. It would not add to the net profit from the investment unless the labour of doing the chores and caring for the cows would be considerably reduced by greater convenience. The cost of horse barns, swine barns, and other buildings can be similarly calculated. One should not erect a building unless it is going to add to the efficiency of the live stock, shelter hay or machinery, or lessen the labour of doing the chores. It is wiser to invest money in drainage or in better tillage of the soil, than to invest it in buildings that shelter unproductive stock, or that add nothing to the earning power of the farm.

COST OF LABOUR

The employment, organization and direction of labour demands considerable study. The value of a good farm manager lies quite as much in his abilitiy so to select and direct labour as to yield a profit, as it does in his ability to drive a good bargain or sell his crops well. The only reason for employing labour is to increase the product and consequent profit. If a farmer can, by employing a man eight months in the year at $40 per month, increase the product of his farm by $500, he will be warranted in employing the labour. If, however, the $320 invested in labour should yield an increase of only $200 in the products of the farm, employment would be at a loss.

FACTORS OF PRODUCTION

Three primary factors are necessary in agricultural production. These are capital, land, and labour. The adjustment of these three factors is an important part of the business of the farm owner or manager, and determines largely the profits that may be made from the individual farm. Capital, as commonly understood, includes the money value represented in the investment of the farm property, no matter what the form may be. Implements, live stock, teams, buildings, and othe rarticles of equipment, ar each a part of the capital of the farm. Cash for operating is also included.

*Good buildings and fences and a well kept farm often help in attracting customers for stock, seed grain or other products. As an advertisement they may increase the earning power of the farm indirectly. The satisfaction of owning good buildings and their influence in keeping the young folks on the farm or in enabling one to keep hired help should also be considered. The reputation of a farm in this respect may become a business asset. Land represents the larger part of capital on most farms, and demands special consideration because the amount of land available for agricultural purposes is limited. Farmers have for this reason, regarded it wise to secure large quantities in localities where it was cheap, anticipating a rise in value. Location and demand for land in particular sections has led to much speculation, and land values fluctuate frequently.

The proportionate investment in each of the three forms,—circulating capital, land, and labour—bears a vital relation to the profits possible from the farm, and must be given the most careful consideration by the person who is buying and equipping a farm.

CAPITAL CLASSIFIED

There are two forms of capital in common use. They are known as fixed or invested capital, and circulating or working capital. The fixed capital properly includes all forms of permanent equipment, such as investment in land, buildings, implements, teams, and other articles that are used continuously. In land it includes the natural value and the value of the improvements that have been made upon it. Picking stones from a rough section of land adds to its value and increases the capital invested. Clearing trees from the land has the same effect. Wells, drainage, roads, fences, and other forms of improvement which are permanent and which become part of the land, also add to the natural value and become a part of the fixed capital. Buildings also are looked upon as part of the fixed capital. Strictly speaking, only those buildings which add to the producing power of the farm should be included in the capital invested in the farm.

The dwelling house, while commonly added to the investment in the farm, is really intended for the personal use of the farmer and his family. Except in so far as it shelters the help employed on the farm, it can add but little to the returns from it. So far as making a statement of the business of the farm is concerned, it would be better were the farm-house inventoried separately from the other buildings and regarded as a personal expense to the farmer, just as the house of the banker in the city is separated from the business of the bank. All other buildings including silos, corn cribs, granaries, and buildings for sheltering the stock and necessary in conducting the farm business, should be included in the inventoried capital of the farm. Equipment in the way of teams for work purposes; implements; live stock, such as cows, brood sows, sheep and poultry, that are kept for live stock products, are all a part of the permanent equipment, since they are permanently employed and if sold are replaced by other animals for the same purpose. The circulating or working capital, includes such items of equipment as are frequently changing. Seed grain, household and farm supplies that are immediately used or marketed, live stock, such as fattening steers, and money for hired labour, are examples of circulating capital. The classificiation intends tha the term “circulating capital” shall include only those items that are used once and disappear. If sold for cash, the cash may be invested in other forms of working capital which in turn disappear. Needless to say, the amount of working or circulating capital varies greatly in accordance with the type of business done, with the market, and with the tastes of the farmer. No rule can be given for the exact adjustment of capital for these reasons.

PRODUCTION LIMITED BY DEFICIENT FACTOR

It is a common experience that the production on a farm is limited by the minimum amount of the one deficient factor. Difficulty is experienced in securing profitable production on a limited land area. In such a case, labour will not be fully employed or the equipment cannot be used effectively. On the other hand, a large land area and large equipment cannot be used to advantage without a plentiful supply of labour. Again, neither land nor labour can be used to the best advantage if the equipment is inadequate. It therefore stands to reason that these three factors must be carefully considered and proportioned in accordance with the needs of the business.

In purchasing and organizing a farm with limited capital, it is believed best to make the investment in about the following proportions:

- 45% for land investment
- 20% in buildings, provided they are to shelter productive live stock or market products;
- 22% in work animals and live stock;
- 8% in implements and tools;
- 5% reserved as working capital.

In buying a farm and equipping it with new machinery, the land investment will run lower than above indicated and the implements and tools investment will run higher. The machinery, however, will depreciate in value while the land is more likely to increase in value. As the farm becomes older and the land is improved, the proportion of investments will gradually change. On old farms near city markets, the machinery investment may become comparatively insignificant.

EXERCISES FOR PUPILS

Farm Inventory

Have the pupils take inventories of their fathers' farms, providing a form similar to the following. The inventory may be taken on the regular weekly holiday. Prices should be checked over by the proprietor of the farm and brought to class for discussion and completion. The teacher should, if possible, go with the class to some farm and take an inventory, with the help of the proprietor, before starting the class members on their individual work. Allowing for any withdrawals of or additions to capital, the difference between the totals of two successive inventories will be the gain.

Proportion of Investment

Have the pupils find the total investment and the per cent of the capital invested in each of the forms of equipment used in classifying the inventory.

Cost of Shelter

Have the pupils learn the cost of the barns on their fathers' farms. Ask them to calculate the interest at the prevailing rate. Determine the amount of depreciation on each barn at 5%. Learn the cost of insurance and repairs for the year. Include the interest, depreciation, insurance, and repairs in one sum called the "Annual Cost." Divide this annual cost by the number of animals sheltered and learn the cost of sheltering one head on each of the farms. Where different animals are kept, they may be reduced to a comparative basis by estimating the weight and considering 1000 pounds as a unit.

2

What is Agricultural Economics

Agricultural economics is the study of applying economic management principles to food farming. The result, ideally, is anagriculture industry that better understands efficiency, sustenance and market demand. The field of agricultural economics looks at all elements of food production and applies rational thought and planning as a whole. From crops, livestock, land usage and soil content, all aspects of farm life are examined, including how its connection to one another can be strengthened. Many times, this involves learning about the latest technology to help crops or livestock, but it also might require a knowledge of what has and has not worked in the past.

Agricultural economics is a relatively new field, considering the countless years that people have been farming. Interest began to mount in the early 1900s, when many economic thinkers around the globe began focusing attention to agriculture. Noting that the act of planting, harvesting and distributing crops and livestock was inefficiently performed, academics believed thatfarms around the world could see greater yields and profits with a change of thought. Additionally, many universities and colleges opened agricultural economics programmes with the intent of preparing students for a career in this field. Careers in economical agriculture are as wide ranging as the crops produced around the world. The principles of farm economics, agricultural production and management can be directly applied to being a successful farmer, but there are a multitude of other options. Seed and chemical companies utilize agricultural economic thought in their production and development, grain elevator companies and equipment manufacturers must understand the economic landscape for each crop in order to stay relevant, and salesmen use agricultural economics to better serve their clients with the products they demand.

Since its inception, agricultural economics has helped further the science behind farming, too. Advances in food preservationand shipping techniques have allowed a myriad of fruits, vegetables and meats to reach grocery stores. Currently, many economists see the implementation of microcomputers in agriculture as another step towards streamlining farmland economics.

Agricultural economics is not a term that fits neatly within a single definition. It is the accumulation of many schools of thought on practically every aspect of agriculture, from planting a seed to serving food on a dinner table. It contains many different careers and needs that are constantly evolving as technology and economic thought grow.

THE PROGRAMME

The agricultural economics programme emphasizes decision making, technical expertise and communication with a focus on agriculture and the food industry. Students are trained to be decision makers through course work and practical experience in agriculture, analytical and communication skills, team building, economic theory and agricultural policy.

The agricultural economics programme is flexible. Students may complement required courses with classes from within the Department of Agribusiness and Applied Economics, as well as from other programmes across campus. Students planning careers in production agriculture are encouraged to enroll in courses in crop and livestock sciences, agricultural systems or other production–oriented courses within the college. Students wanting careers in the food industry may select courses in food science and food safety, transportation or business.

Students wishing to work in agricultural education, communication or extension can add courses in production agriculture, education or communication to their programmes. Regardless of the students' selection of elective courses, the agricultural economics programme contains a common core of classes introducing students to economic theory, farm management, agricultural finance, crop and livestock marketing, quantitative methods, and laws and policies important to agriculture. The Department of Agribusiness and Applied Economics also offers majors in agribusiness and in economics and offers a minor in agribusiness and economics.

THE FACULTY

The department has 20 faculty involved in teaching, research and extension. Our faculty have received numerous prestigious teaching and research awards including the Burlington Northern Foundation Faculty Achievement Award; the Fargo Chamber of Commerce Distinguished Professorship Award; the Chancellor's Award for Academic Leadership; the Western Agricultural Economics Association's Outstanding Educator Award; the Premier Forecaster Award; the Eugene R. Dahl Excellence in Research Award, Senior Faculty; and the Teaching Award of Merit from the National Association of Colleges and Teachers of Agriculture. Faculty expertise varies across a wide range of specialties including agricultural marketing, production, natural resource management, economic development, trade, finance, cooperatives and agricultural law.

CAREER OPPORTUNITIES

Agricultural economics graduates have become loan officers; managers of farm supply, equipment firms and grain elevators; sales representatives with chemical, seed, feed and fertilizer companies; economists with state and federal agencies; and commodity merchandisers. About 30% of the graduates choose to farm and ranch. While many graduates remain in North Dakota or Minnesota, others begin careers throughout the nation and the world.

FINANCIAL AID AND SCHOLARSHIPS

Several $500 scholarships are available to outstanding freshmen who enter the programme fall semester. Contact area high schools or the department for an application form. Scholarships also are available for transfer students. The department annually awards $50,000 in scholarships (ranging from $500 to $1,000) to agricultural economics and agribusiness majors. Contact the department for information and application forms. The College of Agriculture, Food Systems, and Natural Resources awards additional scholarships each year. Contact the Office of the Dean, College of Agriculture, Food Systems, and Natural Resources, NDSU, for information and application forms. Student loan, grant and work–study information is available from the NDSU Office of Student Financial Services.

UNEQUAL TRADES IN AGRICULTURE

From the perspective of winning trade wars, the United States has an insurmountable advantage in agriculture. However, sales of most U.S. agricultural products are not only unnecessary, they are morally wrong. While multiplying exporters GDP, these exports destroy native agriculture by usurping their local markets.

The smaller level of circulating money within the economy (the sabotage of the multiplier factor) due to paying for imported food limits the development of, or even destroys industries in, other sectors of the economy. Overseas markets are developed for U.S. farmers because they must sell, not because others must buy:

A lot of attention is being paid these days to the developing world as a prime growth market for American farmers.... The United States has become more dependent on the developing world with more than 58 per cent of total agricultural exports going to these countries in 1986–87.... Virtually every trade analysis by the USDA stresses the potential sales among developing nations in Latin America, Africa and Asia....

Agriculture Secretary Richard E. Lyng said he most wanted freedom for farmers "to produce what they want to produce" and that to accomplish that would involve solving international trade problems....James R. Donald, chairman of the department's World Agricultural Outlook Board, emphasized "The developing countries likely will continue to increase global grain imports and could be a source of expansion for U.S. agricultural exports."

One of the most sacred illusions of America is that its agriculture is above all reproach. Not only is the United States the "breadbasket of the world," but the developing world is somehow incapable of emulating America's productive farming methods. There is one thing Americans are sure about, without their food and generosity, much of the rest of the world would starve. Yet 40% of the developing world that was once plagued by severe food shortages-China, Guinea – Bissau and-until impoverished by embargoes-Cuba and North Korea produced and distributed the 2,300–to–2,400 calories per day required to sustain an adult. India has finally achieved and maintained self–sufficiency. Angola, Mozambique, and Nicaragua had also achieved self–sufficiency, but their economic infrastructures were sabotaged by anti–government rebels organized, trained, and armed by U.S. or allied intelligence services.

The countries that are newly self–sufficient in food production have far less cultivable land per person than most of the countries still suffering from chronic food shortages. China, for example, has only.13 hectares of arable land per person; the former North Vietnam had.10; and North Korea (self sufficient before devastation by the Korean War and the embargo) has.07. Despite having more arable land per person, their neighbours are unable to feed themselves. Pakistan has.40 cultivable hectares per person; Bangladesh has.16; and Indonesia has.15 hectares.

The best–known example of a country that is continually faced with hunger is Bangladesh, where "two–thirds of the population suffers from protein and vitamin deficiencies." Yet the country exists on a fertile plain blessed with plenty of water, and "grows enough in grain alone to provide everyone in the country with at least 2,600 calories a day." It is obvious that nature has provided this country with the ability to feed more than the present population.

The reasons for such anomalies become clearer when one studies Africa and South America, the two continents with the hungriest populations. The United Nations Food and Agriculture Organization estimates that only 60% of the world's arable land is farmed. In Africa and South America, the figure averages 20%, and their grain yields are only one–half that of industrialized countries. Brazil, for example, is burdened with a large hunger problem, but, even without the destruction of more rainforests, it has cultivable acres per person.

In Brazil, as well as most of South and Central America, one–half the acres being farmed—invariably the best land—currently grows crops for feeding cattle or for export. The masses are unable to feed themselves because their land is subtly monopolized. Brazil has ranches with up to 250,000 head of cattle (that one owned by the Rockefellers) which monopolizes land capable of feeding hundreds of millions of people. Latin Americans and Africans, despite rampant hunger, consume only a small percentage of their land's agricultural potential while a substantial share is exported.

The remaining hungry nations, mostly in Southeast Asia, have such large populations that the land's capacity to feed the people entails a much smaller margin of safety. Yet, if they controlled their land, these nations could also produce an adequate supply of food. China, probably the best example of rational land reform, now adequately feeds 1.3–billion people. But when the population was one–third w hat it is today and the land was monopolized, there were massive famines. Fifteen of the poorest countries in the world raise and export more agricultural products than they keep for their own use. Some of these countries, the exported crops, and the percentage of farmland thus removed from local consumption include: Guadeloupe—sugar, cocoa, and bananas, 66%; Martinique—bananas, coffee, cocoa, and sugar, 70%, and Barbados—sugar cane, 77%. Guatemala plants cotton for export in blocks of 50,000 acres. These are all familiar developed world consumer items imported from these impoverished countries.

In 1973, the United States imported 7% of its beef, much of it from the Dominican Republic and Central America. Costa Rica alone exported 60–million pounds to the United States in 1975, even though its own per–capita beef consumption dropped from 49 pounds per year in 1950, to 33 pounds in 1971.

If Costa Ricans had not exported this increased production, their per–capita consumption would have been 3–times as high, or 98 pounds per year. While the United States imports all this beef, two–thirds of the grain it exports is used to feed livestock and much of the rest is distilled into liquors, both for elite consumption. In addition, it requires 40–cents' worth of imported oil to produce and transport every $1 worth of agricultural exports. "To produce and distribute 'just one can of corn containing 270 calories' consumes 2,790 calories of energy."

During 1992, U.S. food imports are estimated to have been $22–billion and exports $40–billion. Economists teach that there must be balanced trade and, from the perspective of maintaining the status quo, this may be true. However, the status quo reflects the unequal distribution of political and economic power in the world; the "geography of world hunger" is specifically the consequence of entire populations having lost control of their land, and thus their destiny. The impoverished world does not need America's, or Europe's, surplus food.

They only need the right to control their own land, the right to industrial capital, and the right to grow their own food. Given those rights, they will not generally be hungry. However, because only the affluent have money to purchase this production, monopolization of land diverts the production of social wealth to those already well off. "The world can simply produce more than those who have money to pay for it can eat."11 The results are small well–cared–for elite groups, primarily in the developed world, and hunger for the dispossessed.

HUNGER IS DETERMINED BY WHO CONTROLS THE LAND

The often–heard comment that, "There are too many people in the world, and overpopulation is the cause of hunger," is the same myth expounded in 16th–Century England and this *social–control–paradigm ("framework of orientation")* has been revived continuously since.

Through repeated parliamentary acts of enclosure, the peasants were pushed off the land so that the gentry could raise more wool for the new and highly productive power looms. They could not have done this and allowed the peasants to retain their historical entitlement to a share of production from the land. Massive starvation was the inevitable result of this expropriation.

There were serious discussions in learned circles that decided peasant overpopulation was the cause of poverty. This was the accepted reason because social and intellectual elites were doing the rationalizing and they controlled the educational institutions that studied the problem. Naturally the conclusions (at least those published) absolved the wealthy of any responsibility for the plight of the poor. The absurdity of suggesting that England was then overpopulated is clear when one realises that "the total population of England in the sixteenth century was less than in any one of several present–day English cities."

The hunger in undeveloped countries today is equally tragic and unnecessary. The European colonizers understood well that ownership of land gives the owners control over what a society produces. Military power is the foundation of all law and the more powerful colonizers redistributed the valuable land titles to themselves, eradicating millennia–old traditions of common use.

If rights in common had ever been reestablished, the "rights" of the new owners would have been reduced. For this reason, much of the land was unused or under–used until the new owners could do so profitably. Profits meant selling primarily to the developed world, the local populations, being far underpaid, had no buying power to purchase from each other (short–circuiting the multiplier factor).

This pattern of land use characterizes most developing world countries today. What causes hunger is external control guiding agricultural production to the wealthy developed world, instead of internal control managing production for indigenous use. These conquered people are kept in a state of relative impoverishment. Permitting them any meaningful share of social wealth would negate the historical reason for conquest, which is ownership of that wealth.

THE MARKET ECONOMY GUIDES THE WORLD'S PRODUCTION TO IMPERIAL–CENTERS–OF–CAPITAL

Currently the purchasing power of the poor keeps falling further and further behind that of the wealthy and powerful. André Gorz, in his book Paths to Paradise, explains why a market economy can only work efficiently when the purchasing power of the poor is increased: This is what we have to understand—growing soya for our and other wealthy nations' cows is more profitable for the big landowners of Brazil than growing black beans for the Brazilian masses. Because our cows' purchasing power has risen above that of the Brazilian poor, soya itself has got so expensive in Brazil that a third of the population can no longer afford to buy either its beans or oil. This clearly shows that it is not enough to ensure the developing world gets 'a fair price' for its agricultural exports. The relatively high prices that we would guarantee might merely aggravate hunger in the developing world, by inciting the big landowners to evict their shareholders, buy agricultural machines, and produce for export only. Guaranteed high prices have positive effects only if they can be effectively used to raise the purchasing power of the poor.

Thus the market guides the world's production to those with money. The defeated, dispossessed, dependent, and impoverished have no money because their labour is far underpaid, and historically there has been no serious intent to let them have agricultural and industrial capital to produce their own wealth and pay themselves well. The world's natural wealth automatically flowed to the money–center countries where these basic commodities were processed into consumer products by high–paid industrial labour to produce both consumer products and buying power which is the essence of a wealthy society.

The industrialized world is the prime beneficiary of this well–established system. Great universities search diligently for "the answer" to the problem of poverty and hunger. They invariably find it in "lack of motivation, inadequate or no education," or some other self–serving, social–control–paradigm. They look at everything except the cause; the powerful own the world's social wealth.

The major beneficiaries have much to gain by perpetuating the myths of overpopulation and cultural and racial inferiority. The real causes of poverty must be ignored; how else can this systematic siphoning away of others' wealth through inequality of trades be squared with what people are taught about democracy, rights, freedom, and justice? If people have rights to their own land and the industrial capital to produce the tools to work it, every region in the world could feed itself.

This access would have to be permanent and consistent. Any alienation of land rights, or underselling of regional agricultural production with cheap imports, disrupts food production, retards industrial development, and ensures hunger and poverty.

With capital and undisturbed access to their land, the developing world would have little need for the surplus food of the United States. Consequently, there would be no reason to plant the one–quarter of U.S. crops that are for export. The current U.S. agricultural export multiplier of possibly $100-billion (60% of $50-billion in exports which go to the developing world times an estimated multiplier of 3.5) would then be working its magic in developing countries as they produced, processed, and distributed their own food as well as other consumer products for which the increased buying power would create a market.

STEVIA: SWEETER THAN SUGAR

Subsidies, acreage permits, and import restrictions to protect the developed world's beet and cane sugar industries are well–recorded history. But the Indians of South America have known of the leaves of a plant today called Stevia which is 30-times swe eter than sugar and it does not require expensive processing as does sugar beets and sugar cane. Needing only harvesting, drying, and grinding into powder or squeezing out the oils, the labour costs of raising and processing Stevia are minimal.

Requiring one–thirtieth as much to sweeten foods even as it costs roughly 10% as much to raise and process, this natural sweetener would sell for a fraction of the cost of sugar. Scientifically tested for safety and used extensively in Japan, Brazil, and China, Stevia is kept out of American markets by classifying and regulating this beneficial leaf as an herb.

Besides the elimination of substantial amounts of unnecessary labour spent producing sugar, sugar is undoubtedly the primary cause of most developed world health problems (diabetes, overweight). Through replacing sugar with Stevia here would be a huge savings to the world's health care industry while simultaneously increasing the quality of life. Where many monopolies are hard to bypass, the sugar monopoly is not. Using Stevia (or a couple of other similarly sweet plants in Africa) as a sweetener throughout the world would quickly raise the quality of life both by being able to simultaneously enjoy sweet foods and good health.

BEEF: "A PROTEIN FACTORY IN REVERSE"

In Diet for A Small Planet, Frances Moore Lappé teaches that:

- The human body can manufacture all the 22 amino acids that are the building blocks of protein, except eight (some say nine)—these are called the essential amino acids;
- These nutrients are found in grains, vegetables, and fruits but not all eight (nine) amino acids exist in any one non–meat food;
- If any essential amino acid is missing or deficient in a person's diet, that sets the limit on the human body's ability to build protein; when consuming vegetables, grains, and fruits that include all eight (nine) essential amino acids in adequate amounts, the body builds its own protein; to fulfill the need for human protein, an amino acid is an amino acid whether it is in meat or vegetables; and
- Chemically there is no difference between an essential amino acid, such as lysine, whether the source is meat, vegetables, grains, or fruits.

Ms. Lappé points out that vegetables, grains, and fruits—properly balanced for amino acids—can provide more protein per acre than meat. Each 16 pounds of perfectly edible human food in the form of grain fed to cattle produce only one pound of beef. This is "a protein factory in reverse." Lappé's calculation is conservative; prime–fed cattle have 63% more fat than standard grade, and much of it is trimmed off, cooked away, or left on the plate. Even the fat that is eaten is usually not wanted. Subtracting the unwanted fat demonstrates that it requires more than 16 pounds of grain to produce one pound of meat.

Cattle are ruminants with multiple stomachs that efficiently convert roughage (grass) into muscle. But they are inefficient converters of grain to meat and, in that effort, consume large amounts of this human food. If the grains fed to cattle were consumed directly by the world's hungry, the available protein from those foods would increase by 16–times, 1,600%. But when fed to cattle, the overwhelming share of grain is converted into worthless fat, bone, intestines, and manure. Professor David Pimentel of Cornell University estimates that the grain now fed to livestock worldwide would feed 1–billion people.

While cattle are efficient consumers of roughage, the grain fed to them is subtracting from, not adding to, the already short supply of protein. With a digestive system designed by nature for that purpose, if cattle were fed only roughage, and the high–quality grains they once consumed were consumed by the human population, hunger would be eliminated while reducing the pressure on the environment. If the developed world returned to the practice of growing cattle on roughage and feeding grain for only a short time before slaughter, the quality of the beef would be higher (measured by leanness, not by marbling) and the quantity available only slightly reduced. At 1991 prices, just eliminating the last 2 weeks of cattle feeding (finishing) would have saved American consumers at least 40–cents per pound.

Counting the grain required to produce the meat they eat, the consumption by the well to do of 8,000–to–10,000 calories per day is a major cause of world hunger. Global production exceeds 3000 calories of food per day for each person, while the daily need is only 2,300–to–2,400 calories, and the potential world calorie production could be raised much more by planting high–protein, high–calorie, crops. On the average, the proper combination of leafy vegetables produces 15–times more protein per acre than grain–fed beef, while peas, beans, and other legumes produce 10–times more, and grain produces only five–times more. By ignoring the multiplier factor and subsidies, highly mechanized farms on large acreages can produce units of food cheaper than even the poorest paid farmers of the developing world.

When this cheap food is sold, or given, to the developing world, their local farm economy is destroyed. If the poor and unemployed of the impoverished world were given access to land, access to agricultural tools, access to industrial tools, and protection from cheap imports, they could plant high–protein, high–

calorie, crops and become self–sufficient in food. Consumers would buy their food from local producers, those farmers would spend that money in the community, and the producers of those products and services would spend it on their needs.

Purchasing of local production multiplies by however many times that money circulates within an economy. Although the multiplier factor varies, for simplicity, 350% is a good figure to use. Because the circulation of money energizes production and creates wealth, reclaiming their land and utilizing the unemployed would cost these societies almost nothing, feed them well, and save far more money than they now pay for the so–called "cheap" imported foods.

CONCEPTUALLY REVERSING THE PROCESS OF FREE FOOD

If American farmers were undersold by subsidized agricultural surpluses from another society or that imported food was given to American consumers, U.S. farmers could not sell their crops.

They would go bankrupt, the tractor and machinery companies would go bankrupt, the millions of people depending on these jobs would be without work, resources and production of remaining industries would have to be sold to other societies to pay the import food bill, and America would quickly become impoverished.

In a country not yet industrialized, the natural resources must be sold to pay for food and consumer products from the industrialized world and debt traps are put in place to maintain that dependency.22 This process is currently at work in Mexico. As their food imports rose to 60% of their needs, wages fell drastically, industrial production shrunk substantially, and debts increased dramatically.

Many believe that the developing world "does not understand and will never change." But they do not consider that massive subsidies permitting underselling of regional agricultural production shatter already weak economies. Thus sincere, but misinformed, people go on producing for others what they could produce for themselves if permitted the technology. This process siphons the wealth from the already poor and perpetuates their poverty.

Because they do not have industrial capital to produce manufactured wealth from their natural wealth, undeveloped countries have much bigger problems. To pay for their "cheap" imported food, their natural resources must be sold to pay for that food and other consumer products from the industrialized world and trade rules and debt traps have been put in place to maintain that dependency. Once those monopolies are in place, "free trade" is simply a method to siphon the wealth of the periphery, or even defeated powerful nations to the victorious imperial–centers–of–capital. Witness what happened to the former Soviet federation whose resources are now pouring into the West to feed their industries.

THE PERIPHERY OF EMPIRE IS A HUGE PLANTATION PROVIDING FOOD AND RESOURCES TO THE IMPERIAL CENTER

That the periphery of empire functions as a huge plantation system providing agricultural products and resources to the imperial center can be determined by analyzing who consumes those agricultural products and resources. While Somoza was kept in power in Nicaragua by America, 22 – times more farm land was utilized to produce crops for exports than was used for domestic consumption and 90% of all agricultural credits financed those agricultural exports. Running the same statistical analysis on the agriculture of many countries on the periphery of empire will expose similarly high percentages of their land providing food for the imperial center. The same analysis on natural resources (timber, iron, copper, diamonds, *et al.*) on the periphery will show an even higher level of consumption by the imperial center and lower level of consumption by the periphery.

World hunger and poverty exists because:

- Colonialism, mercantilism and neo–mercantilism (now transposed into corporate imperialism) dispossessed hundreds of millions of people from their land. The current owners are the new plantation managers producing for the mother countries.
- The low–paid undeveloped countries sell to the highly–paid developed countries because there is no local market—the defeated, dispossessed, and underpaid have no money. Thus it is highly unequal pay for equally–productive work that creates invisible borders guiding the world's wealth to imperial–centers–of–capital.
- And—as the periphery producing food and resources for the developing world requires exports to the center to pay for those imports—cheap, subsidized, agriculture exports from the wealthy world is part of the process of stripping the natural wealth from the impoverished world to provide exotic foods, lumber, minerals, and—so long as the developed world financiers and intermediaries still maintain control of the direction of the flow of money—even manufactured products for the imperial center. To eliminate hunger:
  - There must be equalizing managed trade to protect both the developing world and the developed world, so the dispossessed can reclaim use of their land. The simplest reclamation of those rights would be society collecting the landrent. Under that Henry George philosophy only the most productive would own that land and absentee ownership would disappear.
  - The currently underfed people can then produce the more labour–intensive, high–protein, high–calorie, crops that contain all eight essential amino acids.
  - And those societies must adapt dietary patterns so that

vegetables, grains, and fruits are consumed in the proper amino acid combinations, with small amounts of meat or fish for protein and flsvour. Though population control must be practiced so as to take the pressure off of dwindling resources and the environment, with similar dietary adjustments among the wealthy, there would be increased, improved, and adequate food for everyone.

With highly–subsidized food exported from the wealthy world to the impoverished world leading to typically 40% to 70% of their food being imported and their local agriculture impoverished, developing world farmers and common labour understand well that, through the multiplier factor running in reverse, every hundred dollars of imports subtracts several hundred dollars from their economy and, through that multiplier factor in forward motion, adds several hundred dollars to the exporting nation's economy. They also recognize that this is true of every commodity produced. For a healthy economy, every nation or region requires, on balance, sovereignty over their food supply, their fibre, their shelter, and consumer products. Sovereignty can only be attained through equal sharing of resources, technology, and markets, and equal pay for equally productive labour.

AGRICULTURAL ECONOMIC POLICY

INTRODUCTION

The analysis of the effects of price and price distorting policies on the agricultural sector has received a great deal of attention in the economic literature pertaining to Sub–Saharan Africa. This literature suggests that inappropriate price and price–related policies have been the key impediment to agricultural growth and development in most Sub–Saharan countries. This finding appears to have had a significant influence on the design of structural adjustment programmes (SAPs) in which getting the structure of relative prices right was considered to be the leading operational objective. Liberalization of input, output and service prices, marketing and trade, privatization of most public enterprises, devaluation of local currencies and disengagement of the state from most support services were primarily meant to achieve this objective.

With respect to privatization of parastatals, policy reforms implicitly assumed that the private sector will take over all the functions performed by these parastatals in a more efficient and cost–effective manner. It is, however, important to observe that the advocates of reforms appear to have paid little attention to some key questions related to the privatization process. Little attempt was made to identify functions that are best performed by government agencies and those that are best handled by the private sector or to assess the private sector base in each country concerned.

The failure to examine these and other related key questions has made it difficult for the designers of the structural adjustment reforms to propose appropriate policy measures and actions that could help strengthen and foster the development of the private sector in order to enable it to effectively handle various functions that were previously carried out by parastatals in the economy. In addition, these policy reforms also failed to be specific about the timing and sequencing of the privatization process in order to avoid the disruption of agricultural and other economic activities.

Furthermore, structural adjustment programmes appear to have paid limited attention to reforming government public goods, institutional and human capital development policies. These policies are even more central to the long–term development process of the economy than the stabilization and adjustment policies that have been the focus of the structural adjustment programmes in Sub–Saharan Africa. Since the main objective of SAP was to get the structure of relative prices right, a question one may wish to address is did these policy reforms achieve this operational objective. What is clear here is that limited attention was paid to the impact of external factors on the structure of relative prices. The whole SAP package seems to have over–estimated the magnitude of leverage national governments in Sub–Saharan Africa have to affect the domestic agricultural terms of trade and hence the growth of agricultural output and income.

In fact, the failure of structural adjustment programmes to improve the economic situation in Sub–Saharan Africa is now recognized both explicitly and implicitly by the opponents and designers of this policy reform package. As one of the most seasoned African economists put it "the continent" (Sub–Saharan Africa) has the dubious distinction of being the only developing region of the world that experiences zero average per capita growth over the last thirty years, including negative growth rates over the last two decades (Elbadawi 1995). Embedded in the last two decades of the negative per capita growth is more than ten years of implementation of structural adjustment programmes in most of Sub–Saharan Africa. After such a period of time, it is now appropriate to assess the impact these policy reforms have had on the agricultural sector.

This chapter attempts to evaluate the impact of economic policies undertaken since the 1970s including structural adjustment policy reforms on domestic terms of trade of major tradable agricultural commodities and in so doing to establish the extent of leverage governments in Sub–Saharan Africa have to affect the structure of relative prices facing their economies. More specifically, the examines the movements of domestic agricultural terms of trade and its major components in the light of economic policy reforms initiated in Sub–Saharan Africa; assesses the impact of external factors and domestic policy variables on the real exchange rate, one of the key components of the domestic terms of trade of tradable commodities; and finally estimates the contribution of external factors and domestic policies to change in the domestic terms of trade of agricultural tradables.

This study is based on historical data. Three West African countries, Côte d'Ivoire, Niger, and Senegal, were selected for the study. As can be seen, this sample of countries is made up of one coastal non–sahelian country (Côte d'Ivoire), one coastal sahelian country (Senegal), and one landlocked sahelian country (Niger). These countries are all members of the West African Economic Monetary Union (WAEMU) They have the same currency that is linked to the French franc by a fixed nominal exchange rate. This exchange rate which was pegged at 50 CFA francs for one French franc since the 40's was changed on January 11, 1994 to 100 CFA francs for one French franc. This policy change has been one of the major macro–economic policy reforms initiated collectively by these and other countries of the Union. The following crops are selected for the study, cocoa, cotton and rice in Côte d'Ivoire and, groundnut, cotton and rice in Senegal and Niger. It should also be observed that in Niger cotton and groundnut are the major export crops, while rice is the main importable food crop. Likewise in Côte d'Ivoire, cocoa is the major export commodity and cotton is an important raw material for local textile industry, while rice is the major importable food crop. Despite its decline, groundnut still remains a leading export crop in Senegal, while cotton, a relatively new export crop, presents significant potential for growth. With respect to rice in Senegal, it is not only the most important importable commodity, but a leading food crop.

The second section reviews the economic policies followed during the last two decades. The third section develops the analytical framework. The fourth section analyses the movement of domestic terms of trade of selected agricultural tradables. The fifth section evaluates the impact of external factors and domestics variables on these terms of trade. Finally, the last section provides some policy implications and concludes the study.

ECONOMIC POLICIES IN THE STUDY COUNTRIES

Côte d'Ivoire: The agricultural sector has played and continue to playa leading role in Côte d'Ivoire's economic development and the sector's rapid growth in the 1960s was the basis of what has been called the "Ivorian economic miracle." Although the Ivorian economy is relatively diversified, it remains dependent on agriculture, which contributes almost one–half of GDP and employs about 54 per cent of the economically active population. Two major crops dominate this sector: coffee and cocoa.

Coffee contributes about 50 per cent of the country's export revenue and Côte d'Ivoire was the second largest African producer in 1992 after Ethiopia. Coffee farms are 98 per cent small in size and the robust type dominates production. Cocoa production doubled in the 1970s and Côte d'Ivoire became the world's largest producer in 1977–1978 when its production over–took

Ghana's. A state marketing agency, the *Caisse de Stabilization et de Soutien des Price des Productions Agricoles (CAISSTAB)* traditionally purchased all coffee and cocoa production before its privatization in early 1990s. Furthermore, Côte d'Ivoire has managed to diversify production in rice, cotton and rubber and the country has achieved self–sufficiency in almost all the food crops, except rice.

Cote d'Ivoire has experienced four episodes during the 1965–93 period. The 1965–73 sub–period was marked by high rate of growth of agricultural output and gross domestic product. The government development strategy was based on external borrowing and extraction of agricultural surplus to increase investments in basic infrastructure and other sectors. The CAISSTAB played a major role in this area by paying producer prices which were below the international level.

The 1974–78 sub–period was marked by various policy developments. The most notable development was the proliferation of state–owned companies. The sub–period was also characterized by an unprecedented boom in primary commodity prices and subsequent increasing export earnings. The latter helped the country to enlarge its industrial base in the areas of energy (Kosson dam), agro–based industries (sugar, palm oil, coffee and cocoa processing). In the agricultural domain, the country decided to diversify production into new crops (cotton, rubber, sugar) and extending export and food crops out of the cocoa belt. The 1973–74 oil shock did not force Côte d'Ivoire to reduce investment expenditure, instead the country resorted to heavy external borrowing in order to maintain high investment rate. At the end of this sub–period, the country started to experience difficulties to service its heavy external debt.

This sub–period was characterized economic and financial crisis which prompted the country to apply austerity measures. Incapacity to reimburse external debt was one of the factors which led Côte d'Ivoire to negotiate an economic recovery programme in 1980 with the IMF. This helped the country to obtain its first series of debt rescheduling in 1983, 1984 and 1986. But new adverse developments in export revenues led to further deterioration of economic and financial situations. The occurrence of drought in 1983 and 1984 caused production reduction in agriculture with coffee being one of the most affected.

Furthermore, a prolonged collapse of primary commodity prices on international markets led to a severe decline in export revenues. Despite this, Côte d'Ivoire decided to increase producer prices in mid–1980s and the replanting programme was maintained. Faced by shrinking export revenues, the government reacted to world price collapse by attempting to stockpile cocoa production. This unsuccessful attempt led to further erosion of the country's financial liquidities and subsequent increase in domestic and external debt arrears. Therefore, the country has no choice but to adopt the structural adjustment programme.

The 1989–93 sub–period was marked by government's efforts to apply structural adjustment programmes and a reverse producers' price policy was adopted. The structural adjustment policies focused on extended financial stabilization measures and structural reforms in order to create a competitive environment for the country. Stabilization measures were reflected in public investment and public employment reduction. Other structural measures included, inter alia, the liberalization of external trade, reduction of corporate tax and reduction of government role in the productive sectors. The latter led to the privatization of some of the largest public enterprises such as water and electricity utilities, opening of private participation in CAISST AB.

With regard to producer prices, further deterioration in world prices for primary commodities led to reducing coffee and cocoa producer prices by half, while the government encouraged producers to increase food crop production in areas where self–sufficient was yet to be achieved. Despite these measures, improvement in leading economic indicators including the level of the country's competitiveness was rather limited. This led the country to accept along with other member countries in the WAMEU to devalue their commonest currency the CFA in January 1st, 1994.

AGRICULTURE AND RURAL DEVELOPMENT

Stabilization and Structural Adjustment Policies (SAPs) have been pursued in Sub–Saharan Africa (SSA) since the early 1980s to restore internal and external equilibria by controlling aggregate demand, and by liberalizing markets to reinstate the role of the price mechanism in efficient resource allocation.

Within the SAP framework, financial sector reform/restructuring consisted of:

- Liberalization of nominal interest rates from a fixed controlled regime to a market–determined regime, to mobilise savings and allocate loanable funds to projects with the highest returns on investment;
- Removal of credit allocation quotas and interest rate ceilings to particular sectors, including agriculture, to allow financial services to flow to the most productive uses;
- Privatizing parastatal banks and other financial institutions, to remove administrative inefficiencies and bankruptcy due to government bureaucracy, political interference and rent–seeking activities; and
- Tightening of banks supervision to ensure profitability by enforcing the recovery of non–performing assets, and solvency by increasing the equity base and tightening prudential regulations.

Implemented as such, financial sector restructuring was expected to promote long–term economic development. Since the relationship between financial sector restructuring and economic development has been examined by five papers sponsored under the research network, "African Perspectives on Structural Adjustment," it will not be re–examined here. In this financial sector restructuring is affecting long–term agricultural development and off–farm activities in the rural sector, which is the largest single sector in the SSA economies. An evaluation of the World Bank's early experience over the period by Jayarajah and Branson reveals that the approach to financial sector restructuring is practically *independent* of agricultural sector reform. Within agriculture, the reforms focused upon: decontrol of producer prices, removal of the implicit tax on agricultural exports by liberalizing the nominal exchange rate; dismantling state marketing monopolies; and inflation control to improve the rural/urban terms of trade.

For financial sector restructuring, the reforms concentrated on: removing financial repression; rehabilitating the formal banking system; and getting capital markets started. While it was acknowledged by Jayarajah that "Financial sector reform in many developing countries is more a process of development than reform" this *development element* was not explicitly incorporated into the restructuring of the financial sector in order to meet the development needs of the single largest real sector of the SSA economies.

In the World Bank Report covering the most recent period, *Adjustment in Africa: Reforms, Results, and the Road Ahead*, agriculture and financial sector restructuring do not show any change in the direction of the World Bank's policy thrust. Whereas the need for adequate availability of credit, to sustain the SAPs price–based incentives to promote agricultural sector growth, is acknowledged, in the second volume *Adjustment in Africa: Lessons From Country Case Studies*, the how to provide the needed credit is neither elaborated nor linked to financial sector restructuring.

Meanwhile, Montiel's review covering seven SSA countries: Ghana, Gambia, Kenya, Nigeria, Malawi, Tanzania and Uganda, is sounding a discordant note. The experience to–date in these countries, according to the review, suggests that the process of financial sector restructuring has not achieved much success: " financial liberalization, though recently undertaken in various countries of the region, has been tentative, and has thus far not appeared to be very successful." The key researchable issue, therefore, is whether the way in which this process is being conducted can promote long–term economic development, while omitting the largest rural sector, that is, "The issue confronting policy makers in sub–Saharan Africa is not whether further financial liberalization is desirable, but rather when and how it should be brought about." The purpose of this is to examine this issue systematically with respect to agriculture and off–farm activities in the rural sector, taking Uganda as a case study.

Uganda is chosen because it is lately considered the most successful implementer of the SAPs on the SSA continent by the Institutions. The macro–economic success indicators over the period include: a real GDP growth rate of 5–6% p.a., a slashed inflation from over 300% to just around 10% p.a., and a parallel market exchange rate premium of over 300% reduced to zero, for example. The Uganda economy is basically rural. Agriculture provides over 60% of rural household income, with the rest coming from a wide range of off–farm activities: brewing local beer, fishing, handicraft, brick and charcoal making, construction and maintenance of owned–occupied dwellings etc. The Agricultural sector employs around 80% of the entire active labour force: this contributed 45% to real GDP in constant 1991 prices in 1996/97, and 90% to exports revenue. Agriculture is 90% organised by scattered small holders; estates are confined to tea and sugar production.

Amid the successful macroeconomic achievements, Uganda started financial sector restructuring in 1993 to remove financial repression, strengthen the banking system, and open a capital market. Yet the review of this financial sector restructuring programme by the Republic of Uganda, Agricultural Policy Committee states that this programme has no special action to help development of the rural financial market.

In fact, the rationalization of the branch network and liberalization of credit allocation can have a negative impact on the role of the banks in rural credit. The liberalization of credit allocation has had the tendency of*crowding out agriculture* from the banks' loan portfolio.

Faced with this brewing crisis by 1996, three years after the start of restructuring the financial sector, a number of proposals and studies are on the table debating how to provide rural financial services. "The challenge facing the banking system is therefore how to expand and broaden the financial intermediation in rural areas since the agricultural sector is crucial for economic development. This is a serious ongoing debate addressing a major defect in the design of the SAPs.

This is set out to contribute to the debate as follows:

- First, it describes the importance of financial services for the economic development of the rural sector, which must be appreciated first, in order to put the gravity of the omission of these services in financial sector restructuring into proper perspective.
- Second, it outlines the peculiar characteristics of rural SSA, including Uganda, which must be taken into account to deliver financial services effectively; these characteristics put a limit on how much can be learned as relevant lessons from elsewhere in Asia and Latin America with different rural settings.
- Third, it reviews the theoretical literature and best practices in rural finance to promote economic development; presents the Uganda case study; with a critical evaluation of the likely adequacy and relevance of the current proposals being debated to address the financial needs of Uganda's rural sector.

RURAL FINANCIAL SERVICES AND ECONOMIC DEVELOPMENT

Rural financial services are needed for three purposes: to provide *rural credit* for productive activities and allied services; to provide a *savings facility* for the rural population; and to provide a *payments mechanism* to transfer purchasing power between economic agents within the rural sector itself, and between the rural sector and the rest of the economy.

RURAL CREDIT

Within agriculture, credit is needed for *direct production* activities: for *short–term* periods up to one year, to purchase variable inputs and meet working capital requirements; *for medium–term* needs for investments of 3 to 5 years to purchase productive assets and invest in land improvements; and for *long–term needs* 10 to 15 years to establish shambas, irrigation schemes, and other long–term farm infrastructure, etc.

Indirect Agricultural Credit is Needed: *To finance the distribution of inputs* on a timely basis, by wholesalers and retailers; to provide *crop finance* for the purchase, storage, processing and marketing of agricultural produce; and export credit to facilitate international shipments. *Non–agricultural credit* is needed for both the short and medium term to facilitate micro enterprises that provide*consumer goods and services* to rural areas (*e.g.*, radios, bakeries), and *off–firm employment*, which is particularly important in the utilization of off–season labour, and the diversification of rural income sources.

A RURAL SAVINGS FACILITY

The bulk of the literature that stresses the need for rural credit overlooks that of a savings facility, with the result that the rural sector is forced to save in kind (in animals, birds, etc), or in idle cash in pots, within the informal sector mechanism, which may not bear interest. *To Promote Economic Development, the Rural Sector Needs a Savings Facility*: To earn interest in order to accelerate accumulation; to meet a wider range of contingencies and respond to investment opportunities without the delay caused by looking for a customer to translate savings in kind into cash; and to generate internal loanable funds for credit schemes, rather than rely on donors and governments for continuous injection of funds into these schemes, which is not sustainable.

PAYMENTS MECHANISM

The rural sector is often inconvenienced by having to carry large sums of cash for payments of school fees, bulky purchases, crop–finance, transfer payments of pension schemes, facilitation of NGO operations, etc. Often this cash is stolen on the way, or poorly counted at the expense of the rural customer. The rural sector needs a payments mechanism to facilitate all the enumerated transactions.

THE PECULIAR PROBLEMS OF THE RURAL SECTOR IN SSA FOR THE PROVISION OF FINANCIAL SERVICES

The provision of rural financial services has three peculiarities in the SSA environment to contend with.

Risk

Agriculture is the single most important sector in SSA economies accounting for between 30% and 60% of real GDP and dominating the rural sector as a source of income and employment, food security, exports, tax revenues, and raw materials for the agro–allied import–substitution industries. Most SSA agriculture is rainfed and yields depend on variation in weather, turning out to fluctuate over wide margins. Second, there is no effective technology to fight pests and diseases; this opens room for large losses. Institutions for crop and livestock insurance or credit guarantee are particularly hard to manage since they have to cover a wide area of varied climates in order to avoid covariant risk.

These institutions hardly exist in SSA, and where they are attempted there is a danger to go bankrupt when all customers fail to repay their loans for no fault of their own. Third, the best hedge against risk is individual land title of ownership. In many parts of SSA, however, land is communally owned.

Seasonality

A rural financial institution must be able to manage the large cash *in–flow* as farmers sell their harvest, the preceding equally large cash *out–flows* as traders borrow for crop finance, as well as the demand for *financing inputs* pr-ocurement at the time of planting. What makes the management of seasonality even more difficult is the thin or practical absence of financial integration; the rural financial institutions are cut off from their urban counterparts which could have provided the large cash needs for crop finance, and gainfully utilized the large inflows of savings from farmers as they market their harvest.

The Scattered Low–Income Populations

The SSA household settlement patterns are highly scattered, unlike the dense populations of Asia and parts of Latin America. Shifting cultivation or/ and transhumance are still practiced. This makes the collection of information on customers to identify bankable projects, supervise and collect loans, and servicing of small deposits, particularly expensive. Also the required modem physical plants, such as bank offices, computers, etc., to serve customers efficiently become impractical to operate since they have to stay idle or under–utilized in certain migration seasons or have to handle very small businesses where populations are thin, making it impossible to benefit from economies of scale.

Rural infrastructure is particularly thin in SSA, with adverse consequences on the provision of financial services. The high cost of transport due to poor feeder roads lowers profitability and competition, leading to low farm–gate prices, a retreat into subsistence with only a small marketable surplus to meet contingencies, and a retreat by men from Agriculture altogether, leaving food production to women. The reduced volume of business exasperates rural poverty and increases the cost of banking in the rural sector. According to the Food and Agricultural Organization of the United Nations (FAO) Training Manual, farmers in SSA receive only 30% –60% of the market price for their produce because of the thinner and poorer road network, compared with their colleagues in Asia whose share is 75% –90%. Over two–thirds (66.1%) of the difference between the consumer and producer prices in SSA is explained by transport costs 39.1% and 27.0% by transaction costs.

The different needs for credit, saving facility and payments mechanism to match the peculiarities of rural SSA are analysed later when we examine the criteria for best–practice in providing financial services.

Financial Sector Restructuring and Economic Development: An Evaluation of the Literature from the Standpoint of Its Relevance to Promoting Long–term Economic Development in Rural SSA A vast literature sprung up in the mid–1980s and early 1990s regarding the relationship between financial sector restructuring and economic development in rural areas.

THE PRO–KENYESIAN PERSPECTIVE

According to the pro–Keynesians, moderately expansionary but regulated financial policies are what promotes higher and more stable economic growth and employment. Under such policies, *institutional finance for Agriculture and rural development should be expanded through the participation of the public sector, along with the private sector*, to increase the *volume* of business in rural areas, *lower transaction costs* and reap benefits from*economies of scale*; lower the *risk of default* by making the environment more conducive to collecting *information*; provide a *variety of forms* of organization and types of service to meet the *rural customers' multiplicity of needs*.

Along this reasoning, the following six organizational principles were proposed:

- *Promoting Multiples of RFIs:* That is, more than one RFI for a given service area;
- Encouraging a variety of forms of organization of these institutions;
- Ensuring vertical organization of the structure of RFIs from local to regional and national levels;
- Encourage high geographical density of the field–level offices of the RFIs;
- Ensuring that a high proportion of rural clients are reached by them; and

- Romoting diversified and multiple functions that horizontally integrate the agricultural production, input distribution, marketing and processing systems for the benefit of their clients and themselves. (Desai and Mellor 1993:3)

Capital and reserve requirements should be modest, interest rates should have a ceiling and credit should be targeted to socially desirable sectors and projects which cannot attract it on their own from the open market (small holder agriculture, for example).

The development rationale underlying the pro–Keynesian hypotheses were:

- That lower interest rates would stimulate investment demand, since the real interest rate is a cost, *and investment is inversely related to the real interest rate*;
- That low interest rates would facilitate the financing of government expenditure for infrastructural and para statal investments, this being particularly relevant for rural development;
- That credit ceilings, by sector, would assist in the transfer of resources to *sectors with a higher positive social compared to private rate of return*, such as small holder agriculture, which would otherwise be "rationed out" of the credit market because of risk, rurality, and seasonality;
- That overall growth would promote savings from higher incomes.

EVALUATION OF THE PRO–KEYNESIZAN PERSPECTIVE

A major contribution of the Pro–Keynesian School was to identify the organisation principles for the desirable institutional structure. The *multiplicity of institutions* was to ensure competition; the *variety of forms* were to meet the multiplicity of needs of rural customers; the *density of coverage* was to ensure an adequate volume of business to reap economies of scale, and to lower information costs; the *multiplicity of functions* was to promote the emergence of linkages and structural change of the rural economy, with the vertical linkages to facilitate the payments mechanism and to integrate the rural and urban financial sectors into a unified structure to reduce dualism.

Unfortunately, the pro–Keynesians underestimated the negative effects of public involvement, using fixed interest rates and credit quotas, on rural financial institutions. According to Adams, fixing interest rates led to financial institutions bankruptcy because they could not charge rates that would cover the cost of the services; the same fixed interest rates made financial institutions unsustainable because they could not raise voluntary savings and had to rely on donor or budgetary injections for loanable funds.

Political interference led to the award of credit as patronage or rents to supporters with no seriousness to pursue loan repayment: this led to the accumulation of non–performing assets.The *rural poor* in whose favour public involvement was supposed to distribute credit were instead *rationed out of the credit market* since they lacked political connections and clout. The adherence to political criteria destroyed the *incentive to develop professionalism* in the running of rural financial institutions.

What the Keynesians sought was a supply–driven policy of making rural financial services available to stimulate economic development. Unfortunately the methods of implementation, particularly the political involvement into rural sector finance, had so many negative effects that they prevented the emergence of viable and sustainable rural financial institutions; they also excluded the poor rural clients. Because of both of these defects, the pro–Keynesian approach became regarded as a failure in promoting long–term economic development.

However, the development content of *the pro–Keynesian contributions still remain valid* to the SSA context. Financial sector development has to ensure *horizontal and vertical integration* of the entire national financial structure to promote inter–sectoral and inter–seasonal movement of resources to cope with risk and seasonality. *A critical density of financial institutions* is also still required to reduce market failure by increasing information flow, and to reduce unit costs by increasing the volume of business. We shall return to these contributions when we evaluate the Ugandan proposals in the concluding section.

THE NEOCLASSICAL PERSPECTIVE

The neo–classical economists, in refuting the pro–Keynesian perspective, focused particularly on the problems created by the repressed interest rates:

- They encouraged *investment* in low–net return projects, thus misallocating scarce capital and reducing potential growth;
- They discouraged the *mobilization of savings,* to finance investment, since savers were not compensated for parting with their liquidity; under inflation and fixed nominal rates, real interest rates were negative;
- *They Distributed Income Against Small Economic Agents*: these were unable to borrow because the cost of collecting information on small loans exceeded the income to be earned from the low fixed interest rates; the small economic agents also earned practically nothing on their savings, which were on–loan to larger economic units.

The overall emerging reaction was for liberalization of the *entire financial sector,* which went beyond the de–regulation of nominal interest rates, to include lifting credit allocation controls to specific sub–sectors, including agriculture, privatization of parastatal rural banks and other financial institutions. The most provocative neo–classical work that provided the theoretical framework for the financial sector restructuring policy package under the SAPs is edited by Adams, Graham, Pinske; it argues that *rural development should not be undermined with cheap credit!*

The Limitations of the Price Mechanism in Providing Rural Financial Services for Economic Development The liberalized interest rate, as a price for financial services is essential for viability and sustainability of the financial sector generally since it enables financial institutions to charge a price that is sufficient to cover the direct cost of their services and the opportunity cost of loanable funds.

However, the role of the interest rate under the liberalized SAPs framework while necessary, is not sufficient to ensure the provision of rural financial services. The experience of many SSA countries, reviewed in the work edited by Frimpong–Ansah and Barbara Ingham indicates the following problems:

- Whereas repressed interest rates "crowded out" small economic agents, especially in rural areas, the liberalized interest rates regime, in an overall deregulated environment, is likely to "crowd out" the rural sector even more severely. Commercial banks are no longer required to operate rural: either to collect savings; or provide credit; or administer the payments mechanism.

Instead, commercial banks concentrate on urban and peri–urban sectors, particularly trade and commerce where higher interest rates can be charged, where loan collection can be done at shorter gestation periods than in agriculture subject to seasonality, and where there is no risk from weather, pests and diseases.

Privatization of the parastatal–banks led to closure of rural branches. This raised the risk of rural finance by reducing inter–bank information flow; it also raised the unit cost of doing business and reduced the gains from economies of scale by lowering the overall volume of rural business. In other words, liberalization introduced a private financial institutions' response that run counter to the six organizational principles of rural finance outlined by the pro–Keynesians (Desai and Mellor 1993), with the development content thrown out.

Higher interest rates did not appear to lead to an increase in the volume of financial saving either. Paying interest rates on small deposits is a cost to commercial banks which carefully avoid *it* by raising minimum deposit requirements. The small savers, with fewer formal financial institutions to turn to, continue to save in kind, perpetuating economic dualism. Investment did not benefit from higher interest rates either. *The pro–Keynesian hypothesis remains valid, investment is inversely related to the real interest rate.*

Banks that attempted to expand investment in productive sectors hurt the economies in two ways: first, by undertaking riskier projects from which they expected to earn a higher interest rate, without careful evaluation of risk; this has made the financial sector less stable. Second, the new projects paying higher interest rates in an imperfectly competitive setting, by passing on this cost to their customers, contribute to "cost–push inflation." In the midst of the above criticisms, *the excess demand for credit for productive rural investments, has remained;* the high interest rates under the SAPs have failed to clear the market for loanable funds.

THE STRUCTURALIST PERSPECTIVE

According to the structuralists, *the role of the interest rate in cleaning rural credit markets is over–stated by the neoclassical school.*

The rural credit market is dualistic: the formal segment provides credit from donors and government sources at below market interest rates; the informal segment relies on credit from private individuals who include, for example, professional money lenders, traders, landlords, friends and relatives (Hoff and Stiglitz 1993).The informal credit market uses direct rationing to solve the *screening* and *enforcement* problems by lending to only those clients from whom it can collect information and over whom it can exert sanctions to recover the loans. This is to say: the trader lends to those farmers from whom produce can be collected at harvest time to pay the loans; the friend and kin lend within the known circles where information on credit worthiness is available, and within which peer pressure can be exerted to repay the loans..

The professional money lender cultivates loyalty from the customers to repay the loans, and collects information on their creditworthiness. Given the direct mechanisms for screening and enforcement, *informal credit is available to only limited segments of the population: the ability of the lenders to charge high interest rates* does not clear the market.In the formal credit market, the interest rate is used for screening and enforcement, but only up to a point. Charging higher interest rates increases the profitability of lending: simultaneously, however, *as interest rates go up, the risk of default increases.* It follows that a formal financial institution will only lend up to a point where profitability exceeds the risk of default. Beyond this, the rising demand for credit, as reflected in rising interest rates, will not lead to credit expansion; instead the financial institution will ration out the extra customers by non–price mechanisms such as excessive paper work. *The disequilibrium in the credit market persists despite deregulated interest rates.*

A rise in interest rates in the formal financial market should attract savings from the informal sector, which is not rewarding savers: this movement of resources was expected to increase the volume of loanable funds in the economy to finance investment, according to the prediction from the neo–classical school. However, the literature summarized by Simmons indicates that unless the funds from the informal sector are "idle", their flow into the formal sector reduces investment in the informal sector; and, at the margin, there may not be any net expansion in overall investment in the economy.Owen and Solis–Fallar have argued that the movement of funds from the informal to the formal financial sector should expand investment, on the grounds that the latter allocates these funds more efficiently in a competitive environment, unlike monopolistic competition in the informal financial market. However, this critique does not address the problem of risk aversion which prevents rural formal credit markets from clearing.

THE CONTRIBUTION OF THE STRUCTURALIST CRITIQUE

The focus of the structuralist perspective on market segmentation, persistent disequilibrium and credit rationing, has contributed the following: Liberalization of interest rates will not by itself lead to the integration of rural financial markets to equilibrate demand and supply for financial services. The problems of *screening* and enforcement, related to risk aversion due to insufficient information, must be tackled *directly*. The neoclassical view has not been able to resolve this contention. Public sector involvement will not eliminate the excess demand for rural financial services either, unless it too addresses the information problem directly. Given the possible adverse effects of such involvement, the emerging view from the literature is that public involvement would be more useful if it addressed the structural obstacles to rural finance directly, such as:

- Improve *rural infrastructure* to increase farm–gate prices and farm income by lowering transaction costs: as income increases, the risk of default diminishes;
- Promote *technological change* through research and extension, which too in turn increases agricultural profitability and farm income, and lowers the risk of default;
- Improve the *legal framework*, especially the definition and enforcement of property rights, so that collateral can be used more.

3

Agriculture, Industry and Services

INTRODUCTION

According to PROUT, agriculture is the basis of an economy and, as such, it is given a very high status. We advocate developing as many essential products as possible from organic materials in order to maximally use local resources, reduce toxicity and increase the efficiency of recycling waste.

This means that agriculture will provide food as well as household items, building materials, fuels, industrial materials etc. Agriculture is to be developed in accordance with principles of economic democracy, decentralization, balanced economy, and other relevant factors. In essence, PROUT advocates a revolution in the agrarian sector based upon cooperative, integrated farming, using the most advanced biological techniques.

The first step to enacting a Proutist agricultural system is to address the division of land. Lands must be evaluated according to their fertility, and subsequently classified as economic or uneconomic holdings. Economic holdings are ones which are economically viable–*i.e.* the cost of all the factors which go into production is less than the market price of the output.

An economic holding should be neither too large nor too small, the exact size depending on many agricultural factors. Many farmers in the world have insufficient land to provide subsistence (much less a reasonable living standard), while large farms leave much land poorly utilized. An economic holding should contain land of similar type and fertility, and have sufficient irrigation water available. The size of an economic holding may increase with advances in farming techniques–but the difference between the largest and smallest holdings in an area should be limited.

Uneconomic holdings may be developed and made economical using advanced farming techniques. Each block will, of course, contain numerous agricultural holdings. Block divisions should be adjusted so that lands with similar levels of productivity are grouped together to facilitate planning. A given block should have a certain level of agricultural uniformity, otherwise many unrelated plans will have to be developed for only a small area.

SCIENTIFIC ACCOUNTING IN AGRICULTURE

Under PROUT, agricultural accounting will be the same as that used in industry. That is, the pricing of goods will adequately reflect raw material and labour costs, capital, equipment investments, production rates, depreciation, interest on loans, maintenance costs, etc.–all the factors considered in industry. An industry would never price items below their production costs, while farmers are often forced to sell at low prices under the pressure of circumstances. Often in farming families, everyone is working–but is there any calculation of their labour value in pricing? Enacting this reform will ensure stability in the lives of farmers.

This will necessitate changes in the economic system, but will have tremendous benefits for the small farmer. This change in economic emphasis recognizes the importance of farmers and their livelihood. Though food prices may rise in proportion to industrial goods, this does not mean that purchasing capacity will be less. Pre and post–production agricultural industries (agrico and agro industries) must also be treated in a similar way. This will ensure the stability of the agricultural economic sector and pave the way for all–round economic prosperity based on a solid agricultural foundation.

AGRICULTURAL COOPERATIVES

PROUT recognizes the cooperative system as ideal for agriculture. It has been noted that the cooperative system was a failure in communist countries. The large cooperatives in the Soviet Union and especially China had very low rates of production and resulted in drastic food shortages. These state–run communes, however, are not the cooperatives envisioned by PROUT. Their defects were many. Most importantly, they failed to create a sense of worker involvement by denying private ownership and not providing incentives. Secondly, planning was made by central authorities and the local people had no say over their own work. Forceful coercion, including death, was used to implement the commune system.

PROUT does not advocate the seizing of agricultural land or forcing farmers to join cooperatives. Rather, it is recognized that various factors are required for the success of such a cooperative system. For example, it requires an integrated economic environment, common economic needs and a ready, local market. Furthermore, a phase–wise implementation process is also needed. In the first phase, an evaluation of economic holdings would be made. Those farmers owning profitable land would maintain the rights of private ownership if desired, while those with insufficient or deficient land (uneconomic holdings) would be encouraged to join cooperatives.

They would also retain the ownership of their land. Those who work as employees on privately owned farms would be entitled to a percentage of net produce or profits as well as salary. For cooperatives, compensation would be a combination of ownership and labour, with roughly equal emphasis on both–*i.e.* shares would be based upon labour and upon the percentage of land owned within the cooperative. There would also be a bonus system based upon profits.

Hence people's inherent desire for ownership and self–determination would not be violated. There would also be a system of elected management with remuneration for outstanding skills. The following chart gives an example of percentages of profit that accrue to members in a cooperative, based upon their investment and/or labour, depending upon productivity.

	Acres Owned	Per cent of Total Yield	Shares	Labour	Percentof Profit
Farmar A	2	7.4%	7.4%	33%	9.86%
Farmer B	5	14.8%	14.8	33%	19.73%
Farmer C	10	33.3%	33.3	33%	44.39%
Farmer D	15	44.4%	44.4	0%	26.02%

One of the immediate benefits of cooperatives would be the utilization of land currently used for boundaries. In areas where agricultural land is limited or where population density is high, a good amount of land is wasted on boundary fences and underutilized borders. Another major benefit would be the collective purchasing of farm equipment currently beyond the means of the individual farmers. Through collective capital or loans, irrigation facilities, dams, and other modern equipment can also be purchased or developed. Collective planning can also take place for the development of previously infertile land.

In the second phase of forming cooperatives, all would be requested to join them on a voluntary basis as there would be many successful examples and obvious benefits. In the third phase, there would be re–evaluation and rational distribution of land. The minimum amount of land necessary for an agricultural family to earn a decent living, and the capacity of the people involved to utilize land will determine ownership. In the ideal stage, ownership of land will be less of a consideration as a true collective spirit develops. This can be achieved only by phase–wise implementation along with all–round human development.

IDEAL AND INTEGRATED FARMING

PROUT recommends a system of integrated farming techniques for increased production, higher produce quality, and environmental sustainability. Insofar as PROUT advocates that each block should be self–sufficient, especially in food production, it is best if farming projects integrate many different products. Monocrop agro–industry is viable only with a massive and wasteful distribution system–not to mention its environmental damage and low–quality produce. What is needed is decentralized, integrated farming that will incorporate all types of agricultural production and cottage industries. Only then can real self–sufficiency and sustainability develop. Integrated farming could include many areas such as agriculture, horticulture (orchards), floriculture (flowers), sericulture (silk), lac culture (for ceramics), apiculture (bee–keeping), dairy farming, animal husbandry, pisciculture (fish), pest control, fertilization, and related areas. It is best if the processing of any agricultural products takes place locally for maximum efficiency and self–sufficiency. If energy production (bio–gas, solar, wind, etc.), water management, and developmental research take place locally, self–sufficiency and sustainability will certainly be possible.

The maximum utilization of land is one of the main objectives of integrated farming. The mass breeding of animals for slaughter is both cruel and from a food perspective, inefficient. Land that could easily feed many people on a vegetarian diet can feed only a few people if it is used for rearing animals for slaughter.

There is increasing awareness of the ill health effects of meat–based foods in the present age, and growing recognition of the damage caused by mass cattle rearing. From this standpoint alone, PROUT suggests that as far as possible, society should reduce and finally eliminate the usage of meat. While advocating this goal in principle, it is necessary to recognize that people's psychology can be changed only through inner conviction, rather than imposition.

To achieve maximum utilization of land, three main crop systems are recognized: mixed cropping, supplementary cropping, and crop rotation. Mixed cropping involves the selection of complementary crops for simultaneous growth. This technique can improve space utilization, reduce erosion, conserve water, and utilize the natural complementary plant relationships. For example, one plant uses nitrogen while another replenishes it.

Plant groups may include many interrelationships. In supplementary cropping, one plant is considered main and another minor or supporting. Crop rotation is the alternation of crops that have different suitable growing seasons. Crop rotation results in less soil depletion, and ensures that land is productive year round, depending upon climate.

PROUT advocates a system of sustainable agriculture and ecological balance. As far as possible, organic fertilizers should be used which maintain soil fertility. Advanced composting and plant combination techniques, along with a strong focus on research, will create considerable harmonious progress in agriculture.

Many independent groups and individuals are developing and implementing techniques and systems such as organic and bio–dynamic farming, permaculture, microbial composting, radionics, and much more.

Decentralized agriculture is much more conducive for such techniques. Water management is a key issue in sustainability. Riverside and lakeside tree planting, mass afforestation, desert afforestation, rainfall capturing, artificial pond and reservoir creation, and other techniques would be implemented in a Proutistic agricultural framework. As far as possible underground water reserves would be conserved to maintain ecological balance.

RURAL DEVELOPMENT: AGRO AND AGRICO INDUSTRIES

Rural poverty is a major problem facing most areas of the world. Under capitalism, little attention has been given to the development of rural economies. Industrialization has proceeded in a centralized manner, draining the populations of rural areas and creating ever–expanding urban centers. These cities, especially in third–world nations, give rise to numerous social and ecological problems, and in many respects, fail to provide a decent quality of life to their inhabitants.

There also seems to be no immediate solution to the rural exodus and global urbanization crisis in the current economic setup. Hence, measures are needed to develop rural economies and provide incentives for the diffusion of urban populations into smaller, more sustainable and humane communities.

While the long term solution to urbanization and rural poverty is an integrated, decentralized economy, the creation of pre– and post– agricultural production enterprises (agrico and agro industries) is an important step to rural economic vitalization. In most impoverished rural economies, production or extraction of raw materials is the primary source of income, whether food production, plant fibre production or mining. What is needed is to bring all industries related to the processing and production of these resources to the rural areas themselves.

This will create a demand for skilled labour in rural areas and raise the living standards. Food preservation and processing, the production of finished fabric from raw materials, oil production, milling, fertilizer manufacturing, tool manufacturing, etc can all be accomplished in rural areas. Combined with educational efforts and the introduction of non–agricultural cottage industries, this will diversify and vitalize the economies and make a decent living standard possible. Combined with modern communications technologies and information accessibility, the possibility of decentralized economies and smaller communities emerges.

INDUSTRY

DECENTRALIZATION AND SELF–SUFFICIENCY

According to PROUT, economic planning has to begin at the grassroots level in order to make use of and develop the experience and expertise of the local population. This implies that the optimal form of an economy is a decentralized one, rather than the centralized form which is present in both capitalist and socialist countries.

Decentralization is preferred as it is the system which best allows local people to retain power over their own economic destiny. And as previously discussed, decentralization is a crucial ingredient for economic democracy. In order for decentralization to exist successfully, there must be a cooperative economic structure. In such a structure the profit motive would be replaced by the desire to produce goods to meet the needs of the local people.

The desire for profit is often at odds with this idea of production for consumption. Capitalists start industries only where favourable conditions for production and sales exist. They therefore often ignore the real needs of a population insofar as profits are often made at the expense of local people and the local eco–systems. Under the cooperative economic structure, self–supporting economic units will be the norm. Such units must be nurtured and strengthened. This requires a decentralized approach to industry as well as agriculture. Self–sufficiency does not mean only the local production of food–the industrial sector is highly important as well, and cannot be neglected. Hence PROUT advocates the existence of a full range of industries, mostly on a small scale, for every socio–economic unit.

THREE–TIERED OWNERSHIP AND ECONOMIC DEMOCRACY

Under the Proutist economic system there are three different scales on which industry can be organized: key industries, cooperatives and private enterprises. The largest of these are the key industries, followed by cooperatives and then individual businesses. Key industries are those which require large capital investment and are on a large scale. Examples might be the railway system or steel mill. Key industries may also function on different levels of decentralization. While the railway system may be administered at the federal level, energy production or raw material extraction would be administered by a local government.

It would be difficult to operate key industries on a cooperative basis due to size constraints or their central role in economic production. As such the government needs to control these industries on behalf of the population. These key industries should be operated on a no–profit, no–loss basis, while providing enough worker incentive to maximize efficiency, quality, and worker happiness.

It is a basic right in an economic democracy for workers to be involved in management. As in agriculture, this is best accomplished through the cooperative system. Producer and consumer cooperatives form the mainstay of a PROUT economy. They are involved in the production and distribution of clothing, housing, food, medicines, appliances, personal transportation, etc. To serve the larger producer cooperatives, many smaller satellite cooperatives should be formed. For example, many of the component parts needed in automobile manufacturing can be produced by a satellite cooperative, and then shipped off to the car manufacturing plant for final assembly. In this way, highly decentralized, specialized industries can be developed on a small scale. There is a high degree of autonomy and individual franchise in such a system.

Entrepreneurs or small businesses form the third tier of a PROUT economy. These may be involved in the production of non–essential or luxury goods and services. Goods such as handicrafts or jewelry, and services such as restaurants might be appropriate for this. If anyone is privately employed in such an enterprise, there will be incentive for the owner to compensate well and provide incentive, for at any time the employees could leave to join a cooperative arrangement. And if a private industry becomes too large it will be required to make a transition to cooperative management.

RATIONALIZATION (SCIENTIFIC PLANNING AND DEVELOPMENT)

Under a capitalist system, the benefits of scientific advancement in an industry usually accrue only to the stockholders and often results in a loss of jobs. This is due to the outlook that profits are to be maximized and that human beings are nothing more than another capital input. Since the goal of PROUT is to satisfy the needs of the people instead of maximizing profits, any invention that increases productivity will either lead to an increase in the workers' compensation or increased leisure time without a resultant loss in income. A reduction in working hours, however, would depend not only on increased production, but also on demand for the product and the availability of labour.

We have seen a call for a reduction of the average working hours from time to time in the industrially developed countries. Under PROUT such measures would be built–in. PROUT strongly advocates regional self–sufficiency, yet it is clear that not all regions are blessed with equal resources. Advances made in science, however can help deficient areas to overcome a lack of natural resources. This will come about through advances in the production of synthetic raw materials, and through new methods of utilizing existing resources.

SERVICES

TAXATION AND THE BANKING SYSTEM

Instead of taxing income, as is customary at the present time, PROUT proposes that taxes be levied at the point of production. Essential commodities would be tax free. Hence, there would be less bureaucratic involvement, reducing government expenditure, and the government's income would accurately reflect the activity in the economic sector.

The banking system would be under the control of cooperatives. There would, however, also be a central bank controlled by the government. Two points are important to remember in regards to the banking system; the first is that banks exist to serve the people, not to increase the wealth of a few select individuals. As such, careful regulations must exist concerning the income of banks.

This problem is also partially solved by using the cooperative or credit union system. Secondly, in the Proutist banking system, money will not be printed unless there is sufficient bullion in the governmental treasury. To do otherwise contributes greatly to the spiral of inflation and all of its attendant problems.

Banks will lend money to agricultural or industrial cooperatives and possibly individuals for productive enterprises–*i.e.* only for such endeavors which promise to generate revenue. The maxim of a Proutist banking system is, "Keep money rolling." The more that money circulates the greater its productivity. Idle money makes no contribution to keeping an economy vital. It is, in fact, one of the causes of economic depressions. Therefore, let purchasing and investment be ever increasing, with money moving more and more quickly. The more it changes hands, the more it increases the purchasing capacity of the people and economic vitality. The only factor that should curb the speed of the circulation of money is the sustainability of the biological diversity of the region.

SERVICE AND BUYERS' COOPERATIVES

Service cooperatives are considered very important in PROUT. Service providers, such as doctors, dentists, plumbers, etc., may decide to join forces and form cooperatives in the cases where the individual service provider is unwilling or unable to open their own practice. Thus, there is the scope for certain services to be offered either by private business or by the cooperative system. Buyer's cooperatives would be responsible for the distribution of most essential commodities. As far as possible, PROUT seeks to eliminate middle men who take profits but do not contribute to productivity. In a decentralized economy, buyer's cooperatives become very practical and important. Food cooperatives have become quite popular in many places already, and this success should be extended to other aspects of the basic necessities.

QUALITY THEORIES

With agricultural products it is particularly clear that quality is important in determining price and even market structure, and for this reason agricultural economics was the first to develop the economics of quality, starting with the hedonic approaches following from Waugh. Most of these theories are based on the realities of agricultural products in agricultural markets. There is, however, another set of theories which is based on the assumption of rational economic man (REM) making optimal choices between goods on the basis of the objective characteristics of these goods, with perfect knowledge about the level of these characteristics and their prices. Some REM theories, such as the characteristics approach, come directly from the agricultural economists' normative models for mixing animal feeds, using them as descriptions of how rational economic man behaves. There are now well over 10,000 papers in this research tradition which depend crucially on the fundamentals laid down in the seminal papers even though additional assumptions and a long chain of logic means that the theory may look very different at first glance. These dominate the mainstream economics approach to quality and are also important in agricultural economics and marketing. In this paper the REM theories are examined at a fundamental level in order to identify weaknesses common to the whole REM research programme. Repeated reference is made to Lancaster because he provided the logical foundation for the research programme and his analysis is detailed, clear and rigorous. His work is the most cited in the economics of quality and, indeed, his 1966 paper is one of the most cited in economics.

It will be shown here that the fundamental assumptions are not simplifications but conflict with observed reality. The boundary assumptions and *ad hoc* assumptions are so restrictive as to forbid any real life situations. Conceptual and logical errors mean that the conclusions do not follow from the assumptions. It is formally impossible to test the theories by their predictions and no attempt has been made to do so. This combination of weaknesses is fatal under any of five very different epistemological approaches used by economists. These weaknesses are at a very basic level so they affect all theories and models sharing this common basis of assumptions, concepts and logic.

This paper does not present any alternative to REM theories of quality, because there are already many established and in general use. There are, for instance, the hedonic approach, compensatory models, perceived quality, behavioural, behaviourist and heuristics approaches and the composite and complex approaches of agricultural marketing economics (*e.g.* Bowbrick, 1992) and the new mainstream economics (*e.g.* Earl 1986). One may weed the garden without first breeding new orchid hybrids.

FUNDAMENTAL ASSUMPTIONS

In agricultural economics it is normally held that theory must be based on assumptions that are both realistic and non–trivial. Some simplification is necessary and, indeed, desirable, but assumptions contrary to observed reality are not acceptable.

If trivial or unrealistic assumptions are used, an infinite number of theories can be generated, and it would be absurd to test the predictions of all such theories, as there is no reason to believe that they will be good predictors. Such theories are not normally included in the canon of agricultural economics. (Some less common epistemological approaches are discussed in the final section of this paper). The fundamental assumptions are ones that cannot be changed without reworking the theory from the beginning. In the seminal papers that set out the foundations for the research programme, it is not possible to get beyond the first stage of the analysis if these assumptions are changed.

With those papers published today, which build a long chain of analysis from these fundamental assumptions, the conclusions can be changed radically if there is even the slightest change to the fundamental assumptions–'for the want of a nail a kingdom was lost'.

It is not necessary to drop the assumption or change it radically The common fundamental assumptions of the REM research programme are on,

- Consumer preferences,
- Characteristics space,
- Supply price and
- Objectivity.

Theories develop in many different directions from these fundamental assumptions, with different further assumptions, boundary assumptions and *ad hoc* assumptions.

Assumptions on Consumer Preferences

REM theory is concerned with 'characteristics', which are the objective properties of goods. A good is a unique mixture of characteristics, so one combination of colour, seedlessness, juiciness, sugar and acids makes the 'good' Washington Navel Orange. Oranges in general are a 'group of goods'. The theory is not concerned with an individual's subjective preference or 'attributes'.

The research programme assumes that each consumer always prefers a good with more of at least one characteristic, so that an indifference curve between two characteristics in characteristics space looks like the traditional indifference curve between two goods in goods space.

This fundamental assumption has been formalized by Lancaster who shows that it is necessary to assume transitivity, completeness, continuity, strict convexity, non–satiation and all characteristics positively desired, in order 'that the consumer's preferences can be expressed in terms of an ordinal utility function of the neo–classical kind with all its first order partial derivatives positive'. The intention is to 'simply carry over traditional preference theory, applying it to collections of characteristics instead of collections of goods'.

A basic conceptual error arises here, as a result of applying theory appropriate to *goods* to a completely different situation, *characteristics*. In standard economics we are talking of two goods which may be bought separately to be consumed separately, steak and ice cream, or bread and wallpaper, for instance. When we are talking of quality, the characteristics are necessarily bought together and usually consumed together. One does not buy the creaminess, the sweetness and the flavour of an ice cream separately, one buys ice cream. Figure shows an extreme example, chosen to be favourable to REM theory. Here two characteristics of a good are consumed together. The pleasure the consumer gets from more peppermint flavouring in the ice cream is independent of the amount of vanilla flavouring.

The consumer buys a premixed product and can buy different goods (flavours of ice cream) but cannot change them once bought. In this example it is assumed that marginal utility first increases with the level of the characteristic, then becomes constant, then falls. The result is that when there is increasing marginal utility, the indifference curve is concave to the origin, rather than convex as REM theory demands. People prefer to have all one characteristic or all the other.

As quantities increase, a bull's eye appears, surrounding the optimum product mix. In order to get indifference curves like those of Figure, it is necessary to assume that there is a positive but declining marginal utility for all products at all levels and that this is true for all characteristics at all times. This is contrary to observed reality.

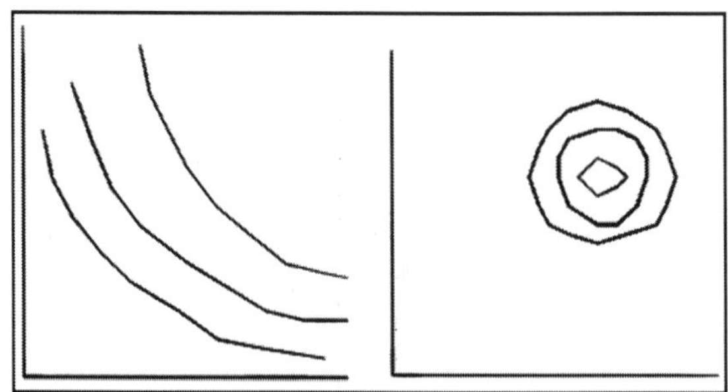

In practice, consumers seldom value quality characteristics independently. The preferred amount of peppermint in ice cream depends on the level of other flavours, on the cream and sugar content and so on. The utility obtained from one characteristic depends on the level of other characteristics, so ratio and proportion of characteristics are important. This can be seen in Figure which shows a consumer's preferences for the characteristics 'sugar' and 'acid' in an orange. This consumer prefers an orange that is medium sweet, medium acid, so the highest indifference curve is at the centre of a bull's eye. If it is more acid, it will be perceived as sour, if less acid as bland, and either way it will be on a lower indifference curve. This is in stark contrast to the theories of Lancaster, Rosen and others in the REM research programme, which imply that consumers will always prefer the orange with the maximum amount of acid and sugar.

It also raises the possibility of buying fewer oranges of a preferred characteristics mix, which these models do not allow. The fundamental assumptions of strict convexity, non–satiation, and all characteristics positively demanded clearly do not hold. In the previous example, it was shown that indifference curves like those could be obtained when there was a positive but declining marginal utility, when the characteristics were valued independently. Here it has been shown that this is not usually so when the characteristics are valued together. A wide range of indifference curves can be expected in practice. There is one utility peak for medium–acid, medium–sugar dessert apples and another one for high–acid, high–sugar cooking apples like Bramleys. The two peaks occur because there are two end uses, but the claimed advantage of REM models based on objective characteristics is that they work regardless of end uses and consumer perceptions. Multiple–peak indifference surfaces are common and some are caused by the laws of physics, not by idiosyncratic consumer preferences. For example, a chord consisting of two notes as characteristics gives most utility when the notes are identical or an octave apart, and less utility at the discords in between. These multiple peak surfaces conflict with all the fundamental assumptions of REM theory.

All agricultural products may be contaminated. Milk is valuable when pure, but less so when contaminated by insecticides, manure, kerosene, etc. The contaminants themselves may be valuable when 'pure' and not mixed with milk. Obviously, anyone who buys a bottle of milk must consume the milk with the contaminants–it is not possible to extract the insecticides or kerosene at this stage.2 If no contamination is acceptable, and pure milk and pure diesel are valued, the indifference curves consist of points where the axes meet the diagonal. Since contamination is a problem with all agricultural products, curves like this will occur between some axes of all products.

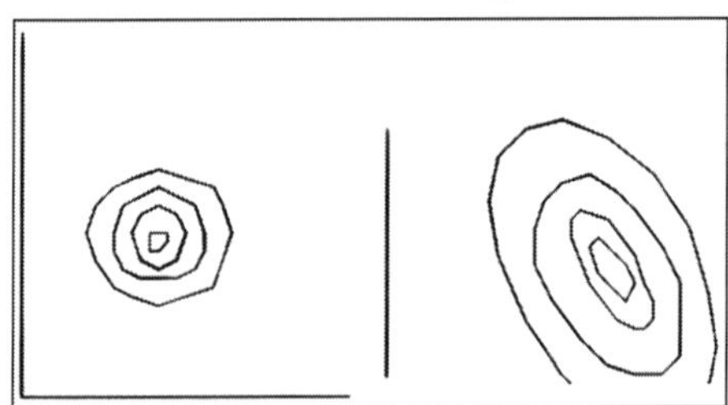

FUNDAMENTAL ERRORS ON CHARACTERISTICS SPACE

REM theories of quality consist of analysis in 'characteristics space' with axes of the form 'Level of Characteristic A' and 'Level of Characteristic B'. Conceptual and logical errors in the fundamental assumptions on characteristics space invalidate the theory. There is not, in fact, one single characteristic space of this form. Clearly any analysis that is valid for one of these characteristics spaces is invalid for any other.

Lancaster uses up to fourteen such spaces interchangeably:

- Total amount of characteristic in total consumption. This requires the assumptions of linearity and additivity. It appears to be the characteristics space used for the basic paradigm case.
- Total amount of characteristic in the diet.
- Total amount of characteristic in a single unit of a good. This is the space used for the automobile example.
- One axis being 'Cleaning power per dollar' for goods in the product group detergent This conflates two characteristics and introduces

concepts like value for money. It does not appear in Lancaster.

- Level of characteristic obtained from one or more goods in one product group. This appears to be the characteristics space used for most of the analysis, including that which at first sight uses the paradigm case.
- Characteristics per unit of a good.
- A space with a 'normalized' efficiency frontier, implying some kind of 'normalized' definition of characteristics. This is used for his second paradigm case. In fact different 'normalized' spaces may be created starting from any of the six previous spaces and be related to total consumption, to an automobile etc. so there are many more than seven spaces used.[3]

It is not possible to proceed to Lancaster's second paradigm case of 'normalized characteristics' without the boundary assumptions of linearity, additivity, perfect knowledge etc. which are discussed below.

FUNDAMENTAL ASSUMPTIONS ON SUPPLY

The supply assumptions of REM theory are also fundamental, as they are necessary for the first stage of the analysis, determining an individual's optimum purchase. The fundamental assumption is that the supply functions for all characteristics of every good are of the same form. It will be shown here that there are few products for which this is true of all or even most characteristics. In traditional analysis based on separate goods it was reasonable to assume that all goods were positively priced and that one could get more of a good by paying more for it. REM quality theory carried this assumption over, assuming that characteristics were positively priced. One could only get a good with more of one characteristic by paying more (and the origin of the theory in agricultural economics stock feed mixing models is obvious here). These assumptions are no longer reasonable when dealing with a good whose characteristics are necessarily supplied together. Why should it cost any more to buy a good just because it has more of one characteristic? REM theory would require for instance that an orange with more acid content necessarily costs more. The constant outlay curves are highest around a medium–sweet, medium acid orange, as market demand is concentrated on these. The very acid and very sweet oranges are cheaper.

This bull's eye constant outlay curve is very different to the curve assumed by REM theory. The indifference curve of one individual, also a bull's eye, is shown next to this set of constant outlay curves. This individual's optimum choice is clearly made at a point where both constant outlay curve and indifference curves are concave to the origin and there will be a trade off between quantity and quality. This is contrary to the whole of REM theory which assumes that the acid in oranges is always positively required, and is always positively priced so that the most acid oranges are preferred and are the most expensive. It also has an optimum choice where the indifference curve is convex to the origin. Most agricultural markets are price taking, and prices are determined by demand in the short run, so preferences like those will lead to prices quite unlike those assumed by REM theory. Similarly, when input characteristics are different from the output characteristics, as in art, agriculture and most industry, there is no obvious reason why it should cost more to produce a good with a higher level of one characteristic. With many agricultural products those farmers with the skill to produce 'higher quality' from the same inputs earn an economic rent.

Price making markets seem more promising at first sight. If a good is made by mixing ingredients and those ingredients are characteristics (as with feedstuffs), then the assumptions appear to hold. However, it is not possible to operate such price–making markets under the REM assumptions that all buyers perceive the same characteristics in each good and are perfectly informed on price etc. It is not possible to plot an individual's multidimensional indifference surface from observed purchases, especially in cases. This would require a very large number indeed of purchases in directly comparable situations–with all other factors, including prices of alternative goods, held constant. It is seldom that an individual makes even a dozen purchases that would meet this criterion.

FUNDAMENTAL ASSUMPTIONS ON SUBJECTIVE OR OBJECTIVE QUALITY

REM theories of quality are attractive because the analysis is based on objective characteristics, and ignore psychology, subjective preferences and so on. The approaches promise to be much cheaper and easier as a result.

The fundamental assumptions of most such theories are:

- A good has objective characteristics, and consumers' decisions are made solely on these;
- All individuals see the same characteristics in each good and perceive them identically;
- Individuals may value the characteristics differently. The REM theories explicitly ignore subjective attributes and may ignore characteristics which are difficult to measure.

These assumptions are rejected by the whole of marketing and market economics and many branches of economics including information economics, the economics of advertising and the theory of monopolistic competition.

One approach used widely in marketing but inconsistent with the REM approach is that:

- Quality is in the mind of the consumer, and
- Consumers value a good purely for the characteristics they attribute to it subjectively.

Choices are not made on the objective characteristics but on subjective attributes. The characteristics may or may not be related to the attributes, but advertising, brand image etc. Means that the relationship is seldom simple. Even if the consumers can see some characteristics, they may or may not use them as a proxy for characteristics. Hedonic theory is usually based on assumptions incompatible with REM theory. One formulation is 'I, the researcher, subjectively perceive that the goods on the market have certain attributes (that is to say I have no objective knowledge of which are characteristics as defined by REM theory and, accordingly, no way of measuring them). Regression shows that goods with more of attributes A, B and C get a higher price. I predict that if the marginal producer switches to producing a product with a higher level of A, B or C, then he or she will get a higher price.' This can produce accurate predictions when consumers use something akin to the researcher's attributes as cues or proxies for their own, possibly very different, attributes.

It is not necessary that the researcher knows the characteristics as defined in REM theory, or that the consumer values them. Another common formulation is 'Market research shows that consumers ascribe certain levels of attribute to each good in this product group. Regression analysis shows that the goods with the highest level of attributes X, Y and Z fetch the highest price. It is predicted that if the marginal producer can increase the level of X, Y or Z, whether by changing production specifications or by changing the brand image, then he or she will get a higher price. This formulation does not require any knowledge of objective characteristics by the researcher or anyone else. If the assumption of objectivity is dropped, then REM theory falls away. 'If different individuals were to "see" the same goods in fundamentally different ways, there would be little point in devising an analysis to take account of the objective properties of goods. For then either it is meaningless to speak of "objective" properties, or those properties which are objective are irrelevant to people's relationship to goods.'.

The REM approach can only work if it is possible to plot the indifference curves of all individuals on the same set of axes, and if each individual faces the same supply.

This is not possible under any of the following conditions: individuals:

- Perceive different characteristics in a good,
- Perceive nonexistent characteristics like dietary fibre in beef,
- Ignore 'objectively important' characteristics like dangerous food additives,
- Perceive a different set of a good's characteristics as being relevant,
- Value the same set of characteristics but perceive and measure them in different ways–even with perfect knowledge of an automobile's power, for instance, individuals might perceive it in terms of engine

capacity, top speed, acceleration from a standing start or ability to pull a trailer.

In all these cases, neither the preferences of different individuals nor the supply facing them can be plotted on the same diagram.Consumer preference for an attribute, like'refreshing' for an orange may be linear and positive even when the preference for objective characteristics like acids, sugars and juiciness is not. This makes hedonic theory more applicable for attributes than with REM theory.

A further set of constraints arises because subjectivity implies that people do not perceive characteristics correctly. In principle an individual could plot his or her own indifference curve, against attributes like 'My perception of attribute A' or even 'My perception of characteristic B'. If these diagrams are brought together onto another diagram with axes like 'Perceived level of Attribute A' or 'Perceived level of Characteristic B', the difference in perception means that a single good will occupy many different positions, perhaps as many as there are individuals. Similarly, price and budget lines will occupy different positions, depending on the 'quality' they are perceived to apply to.

If a researcher were to replot the diagrams against his or her own perceptions, so that the same point always applied to the same good, the shapes of the indifference curves would change. The smooth indifference curves presented here would become very jagged, showing that someone thought that two boxes of brand X were equivalent to one box of brand Y with identical ingredients, for instance. In this case, none of the REM assumptions of strict convexity, transitivity, completeness, continuity, non–satiation and all characteristics positively desired, can be expected to apply.

One of the biggest attractions of REM theory is that it claims to predict sales when the objective characteristics of a product are changed. In practice, attributes may change while characteristics remain constant because of advertising etc., or brand image may remain constant through repeated re–formulations of the product.

This analysis confirms Lancaster's belief that REM theory cannot work if subjectivity is allowed. It is not possible to reach even the basic paradigm case where the preferences and decisions of different individuals are compared on the same diagram. In practice even those who work within REM theory find it very difficult to avoid using attributes, which suggests that the theory has no practical application.

BOUNDARY ASSUMPTIONS

Boundary assumptions set out the domain in which a theory is intended to work, and each of the REM theories has different boundaries. Surprisingly, these are seldom made explicit. The example of Lancaster is used here as he sets out his boundary assumptions and other assumptions rigorously and completely, as his formulation remains the paradigm case and as it is the dominant theory of quality today.

Among the assumptions are:

- One unit of characteristic gives the same satisfaction whatever good it is part of. Chilli powder gives the same satisfaction in ice cream as in chilli con carne.
- It is the level of characteristic in total consumption that determines the satisfaction achieved: the level in any good is irrelevant. It does not matter whether the chilli powder is eaten neat, by the pound, or as a seasoning to many dishes.

None of his optimization or aggregation procedures apply where these assumptions do not hold. These assumptions are wrong if they are self–contradictory or if, as he admits is true of his 1975 paper, they rule out all reality. These assumptions limit the application of his theory to situations like the perfectly informed farmer mixing chicken rations, (ignoring most of the constraints) and this is the theory from which REM theory evolved.

It cannot be used elsewhere. Hendler, Ladd and Zober and Lucas strongly criticized this theory for its over restrictive boundary assumptions but, worryingly, only 1.5% of the people who have cited Lancaster in recent years have cited these criticisms.

AD HOC ASSUMPTIONS

Ad hoc assumptions are ones added to a theory because the theory will not work otherwise. They are not to be confused with fundamental assumptions, boundary assumptions or realistic assumptions made to fit a theory into a model of a real world situation. Typically each *ad hoc* assumption is an unrealistic assumption that limits the number of real life situations the theory can apply to.

Each explicit *ad hoc* assumption introduces implicity assumptions. The more *ad hoc* assumptions there are, the less likely it is that the theory will apply to any real world situation. Lancaster is one of the few writers attempting to make his assumptions explicit.

There are 40–60 explicit *ad hoc* assumptions in *Consumer Demand* with sixteen in Some are It is not possible to determine whether or not the assumptions apply in any case, to determine an individual's transformed indifference curves in specification–quantity space for instance. Formally, they are no different from assumptions about how many angels can dance on the end of a pin.

Surprisingly, Lancaster in *Variety, Welfare and Efficiency* draws from these assumptions a wide range of conclusions on 'welfare, variety and the GNP', 'intra industry trade between identical economies', 'variety in capital goods', 'the optimal division of labour', and 'variety and economic development'.

Two Stage Models

Lancaster's two–stage model was abandoned as unworkable in his later work. It had the infinitely more restrictive assumption that characteristics are derived from consumption activities in which goods, singly or in combination are the inputs. It can only work if, for instance, all consumers eating meals prepared from a shopping basket perceive the same output characteristics, regardless of which set of meals is prepared from it, or who cooks them.

HEDONIC PRICES

In the preceding sections reference has been made to hedonic analysis which goes back to Waugh, which was market based, not REM based. This was established 35 years before most REM theory and is logically independent of it. Nevertheless Rosen is an attempt to justify Waugh from a REM standpoint and Lancaster is sometimes seen to have the same objective. Rosen's fundamental assumptions are close to Lancaster's, though the analysis develops in a different direction.

The failings of REM theory discussed above mean that this support is invalid. In addition, however, REM theory uses different prices from that used in hedonic theory.[7]Hedonic prices are defined as the implicit prices of attributes and are revealed to economic agents from observed prices of differentiated products and the specific amount of characteristics associated with them. Econometrically, implicit prices are estimated by the first–step regression analysis (product price regressed on characteristics) in the construction of hedonic price indexes.

If most transactions had taken place in the SW quadrant, the prices of both characteristics would appear to be positive, if in the NE both would appear to be negative. If most transactions were in the SE or NW, one characteristic would be positively priced, one negatively. There would be a poor fit if transactions were scattered randomly. Yet this is a situation where there is a clear, consistent and logical relationship between the price of goods and the level of their characteristics.

Why would a consumer with a price list wish to know the regressions or the 'price of each characteristic'? Market research suggests that people are more likely to rank goods by their characteristics or attributes and then by their prices and after this make a choice. REM theories and hedonic theories deal with different types of prices so REM theory can neither support nor refute hedonic theory.

CAN PREDICTIONS BE TESTED

It is not possible to test economic theories directly, as they are not presented in a way that applies to the real world. Instead they must be tested indirectly. Do models of real world situations and markets using Theory A predict better than models, otherwise identical, using Theory B? This test is possible if and only if there is no doubt that all the assumptions of the theory apply. If this were not so, inaccurate predictions could be taken as evidence that the assumptions did not hold in this case, rather than that it was bad theory. It is no criticism of a theory that it does not work outside its boundaries.

It has been shown above that there is a strong reason to believe that the assumptions do not hold in any real situation. It is further shown that it is not possible to determine in any market that most individuals have the preferences assumed (though it may be easy to show that they do not). Accordingly it is not possible to say in any case whether a prediction was wrong because the assumptions of the REM theory did not hold, or.

Hedonic prices are defined as the implicit prices of attributes and are revealed to economic agents from observed prices of differentiated products and the specific amount of characteristics associated with them. Econometrically, implicit prices are estimated by the first–step regression analysis (product price regressed on characteristics) in the construction of hedonic price indexes. The REM analysis is confusing: Rosen appears to assume that the set of prices facing buyers is at the same time:

- A market clearing price.
- An average equilibrium price at the end of a day's trading.
- The price facing each buyer and each seller at all periods through the day.

Whether a good prediction occurred precisely because a bad theory was used in the wrong place. Some of the epistemologies discussed below do not require realistic assumptions or correct logic: they require only that the predictions of a theory have been tested repeatedly and have been found to be consistently good predictors.

This may be modified to the statement that they have been found to be good predictors in X% of cases, which requires that a much greater sample has been tested.

It would be extremely difficult and expensive to carry out such a programme of tests in the necessary systematic fashion. Several extensive literature searches have failed to show any evidence of such a programme for any one of the REM theories or their variants.

Even if a programme had been attempted, it is doubtful whether meaningful results would have been obtained as there are well–recognized problems identified by the Victorians,8 Hutchinson, Machlup and 'sophisticated falsificationists' (including Popper) in refuting a theory in this way.

Very few uses of the theory have been designed as tests: rather researchers have used the theory as a tool to make a prediction. The situations chosen have not been selected as random samples of a specific type of situation from a known population, and very few of the uses are reported–some gave 'negative' results and are unpublishable and others are commercial secrets. One cannot therefore, comb the literature and show that Theory X gives a better prediction in y% of cases.

HOW SERIOUS ARE THESE WEAKNESSES

The following weaknesses have been identified:

Fundamental Assumptions

- The fundamental assumptions on preferences are wrong. They are contrary to observed fact. They are not simplifications of reality. It is improbable that any individual will have preferences like those assumed for any product group.
- Serious logical errors arise from confusions about characteristics space.
- The fundamental assumptions on supply are wrong in most cases. They may apply in price making markets but here other REM assumptions do not apply.
- The REM theories depend crucially on assumptions of objectivity. Most economists and market researchers think it essential to include subjectivity in any analysis.

Other Assumptions

- Boundary assumptions rule out most of the real world.'The ingenuity of these nineteenth century writers knew no bounds when it came to giving reasons for ignoring apparent refutations of an economic prediction, but no grounds, empirical or otherwise, were ever stated in terms of which one might reject a particular theory' Blaug.
- The large number of *ad hoc* assumptions means that the theories do not apply to any real world situation.

Do the Assumptions Apply

- It is not possible to say in any situation that the fundamental, boundary or *ad hoc* assumptions apply, though it may be possible to say they do not. It is not possible to plot a multi dimensional indifference surface for an individual, or in practice the prices facing an individual. Accordingly, bad predictions may arise because the theory is operating outside its domain, not because it is a bad theory.

Has the Theory Been Tested

- There has been no programme of crucial tests on any of the REM theories or their variants.

ARE THESE WEAKNESSES FATAL

REM theory fails in its own terms: all REM theory is constructed in the belief that there is a special virtue in applying strict logic to stated assumptions. Agricultural economists usually believe that there is a virtue in working from what we know–observed facts about agricultural markets–to what we do not know–predictions. Many can expect to lose their jobs if they make patently false assumptions, that beef grows on trees, for instance, however accurate the predictions of the resulting model. From this epistemological viewpoint the REM theories must be rejected because they conflict with observed reality.

The idiosyncratic belief that theories can only be tested by their predictions, and that assumptions are irrelevant, is strange in a discipline where it is easy to test assumptions and very difficult to test predictions. Even under this epistemology, the lack of testing means that we have no reason to prefer these theories to any of an infinite number of possible alternatives. Even under Friedman's approach, accepted by some economists, the fact that assumptions are contrary to observed reality makes these the least attractive of the untested theories.

AGRICULTURAL AND ANIMAL SCIENCES

INTRODUCTION

Agriculture is the mainstay of the Indian economy. The agricultural sector today provides livelihood to about 64 per cent of the labour force, contributes nearly 26% of Gross Domestic Product and accounts for abut 18% share of the total value of the country's exports. It supplies bulk of wage goods required by the non–agricultural sector and raw materials for large sections of industry. It is but natural, therefore, that facilities for agricultural education are expanding at various levels.

The Government had also created a Department of Agricultural Research and education (DARE) in the Ministry of Agriculture to coordinate educational and research activities. As an apex body of the National Agricultural Research System (NARS), the Indian Council of Agriculture Research (ICAR) located in this Department is entrusted with national agricultural research agenda.

Education in the area of Agricultural and Animal Sciences covers Agricultural Sciences, Veterinary Science and Animal Husbandry (which along with Animal Product Technology such as Dairying is now known as Animal Science), Fisheries, Horticulture, Sericulture, and Forestry and Wild Life. Home Science is also considered a part of agricultural education and, therefore, most of the Home Science Colleges are affiliated to Agricultural Universities. In addition, Food Science and

Technology is also treated as a subject allied to agricultural science. When India attained Independence in 1947, there were about 15 institutions in the country providing agricultural and veterinary education with a total intake capacity of around 1500 students. These institutions were established by the State governments and were managed by the respective departments of agriculture and animal husbandry of the concerned States.

In 1954, the Government of India appointed a Joint Indo–American Team to make a comparative study of the institutions dealing with agricultural education research in the United Stated and India. The Team which submitted its report in 1955, made recommendations, among others, the adoption of the pattern of higher education as in Land Grant Colleges of American Universities. This recommendation led to the establishment of separate agricultural universities. The first agricultural university, Govind Ballabh Pant University of Agriculture and Technology, modelled after the Land Grant Colleges of USA was set up in 1960 at Pantnagar in Uttar Pradesh. This was followed by the establishment of State Agricultural Universities (SAUs) in other States.

At present, there are 29 agricultural universities located in 18 States of which three are specialized in nature–Dr Yashwant Singh Parmar University of Horticulture and Forestry, Tamil Nadu Veterinary and Animal Sciences University, and West Bengal University of Animal and Fishery Sciences. Besides, there are six deemed University of Animal and Fishery Sciences. Besides, there are six deemed universities *viz.*, Allahabad Agricultural Institute, Indian Agricultural Research Institute (New Delhi), Indian Veterinary Research Institute (Izatnagar, UP), National Dairy Research Institute (Karnal, Haryana), Central Institute of Fisheries Education (Mumbai), and Forest Research Institute (Dehra Dun, UP). Except the Allahabad Agricultural Institute and the Indian Agricultural Research Institute, all deal with specialized areas.

All the agricultural colleges and colleges in specialized areas like, fisheries, forestry, animal sciences, horticulture, dairy science and technology and home science earlier affiliated to general universities had been transferred to agricultural universities as their constituent colleges. Nine general universities also have agricultural faculties, *viz.*, Allahabad University, Annamalai University, Banaras Hindu University, Bundelkhand University, Chaudhari Charan Singh University, Meerut, Dr Bhim Rao Ambedkar University, Agra, Maharshi Dayanand Saraswati University, Ajmer, Mahatma Gandhi Chitrakoot Gramodaya Vishwavidyalaya, Nagland University, and Visva–Bharati.

EDUCATIONAL OPPORTUNITIES

Education is offered by agricultural universities at graduation, post graduation and doctoral levels in eleven fields:

- Agriculture,
- Veterinary Science and Animal Husbandry (Animal Science),
- Agricultural Engineering,
- Home Science,
- Fisheries Science,

- Dairy science and Technology,
- Agricultural Management (including Marketing, Banking and Cooperation),
- Forestry,
- Horticulture,
- Sericulture, and
- Food Science and Technology.

Of the six deemed universities, four *viz.*, Indian Agricultural Research Institute, Indian Veterinary Research Institute and the Central Institute of Fisheries Education and Indian Forest Research Institute offer only postgraduate and doctoral courses. The other two, *viz.*, the National Dairy Research Institute and the Allahabad Agricultural Institute have courses at all the three levels and also at the diploma level. A few general universities offer postgraduate courses in biological sciences which have a bearing on agricultural and animal sciences, such as, agricultural botany, agricultural zoology, agricultural biochemistry, forestry, fisheries, sericulture, food sciences.

Each state has its own system of admission to the first degree programmes *e.g.*, in Andhra Pradesh there is a common entrance test EAMCET for the selection of candidates for engineering, agriculture and medical courses. The Indian Council of Agricultural Research (ICAR) conducts an All–India Entrance Examination for filling up 15% of the total number of seats in all branches except Veterinary Science in State Agricultural Universities (SAUs), and the Central Agricultural University, Imphal (Manipur) and all seats in National Dairy Research Institute, Karnal (Haryana). From 2000 AD the system of direct nomination of candidates by the Council had been abandoned.

To encourage students to opt for pursuing courses in any State other than their home State, National Talent Scholarship of ₹.800.00 per month is awarded on the basis of the results of the Entrance Examination. The IARI also conducts a Combined Examination for the award of Junior Research Fellowships and admission to Master's Degree programmes in SAUs, Central Agricultural University (CAU), Imphal (Manipur) and the four deemed universities *viz.*, the Indian Research Institute. Twenty five% of the seats in SAUs and the CAU and all the seats in the four deemed universities are filled up on the basis of this examination. Students who opt to join Master's Degree programmes in universities and institutions other than from where they have obtained the Bachelor's degrees are awarded Junior Research Fellowships. The value of the fellowship is ₹.5,000.00 per month for graduates in Veterinary Science and ₹.3,600.00 per month for graduates in other disciplines. In addition, a Contingent Grant of ₹.6,000.00 per annum is also given. The Veterinary Council of India also conducts an All–India Common Entrance Examination for filling up 15% of total number of merit seats in veterinary colleges for the first degree programme. Till 1999, the examination used to be conducted by the ICAR.

The duration of the courses is four years except animal sciences and home science. In some universities Honours degree course in Agriculture needs six months of internship. The duration of animal science courses is five years including a compulsory internship of six months. Home Science course is of three–year duration. All the colleges follow either semester or trimester system. All universities follow grade point average (GPA) system for grading students qualifying in the examinations.

The entry requirement for all the first degree programmes, except dairy technology and agricultural engineering, is a pass in 10+2 examination with physical and biological sciences or vocational courses in agriculture, fisheries, veterinary science instead of either biological science or physical science. Mathematic and physical sciences are essential qualification requirements for dairy technology and agricultural engineering. Most universities insist on a minimum of 55% marks in the aggregate. Minimum age of entry is generally 17 years.

AGRICULTURAL SCIENCE

There are at present 66 colleges and university agricultural faculties within the agricultural university system. Besides, eight general universities also offer agricultural science courses. Most of the colleges and agricultural faculties provide first degree, postgraduate degree and doctoral degree progrmmes in agricultural sciences. The nomenclature of the first degrees awarded by most of the universities is either B.Sc (Agriculture) or B.Sc (Agriculture) (Honours). Only two universities, *viz.*, Chandra Sekhar Azad University of Agriculture and Technology and Govind Ballabh Pant University of Agriculture and Technology award B.Sc (Agriculture and Animal Husbandry), incorporating the Animal Husbandry component in the course.

At the Masters and Doctoral levels courses are available in a wide range of specialisations. M.Sc (Agriculture) course is of two–year duration. gives an illustrative list of subjects offered at the Master's degree level. Non–agricultural graduates are also admitted to the M.Sc (Agriculture) programmes in some universities (*e.g.*, Indira Gandhi Krishi Vishwavidyalaya, Jawaharlal Nehru Krishi Vishwavidyalaya and Indian Agriculture Research Institute) in some selected specialisations, such as, agricultural physics, agronomy, agro–meteorology, agricultural economics, biotechnology, plant pathology, plant breeding and genetics, agricultural botany, agricultural biochemistry, agricultural chemistry, entomology. They must, however, have studied the cognate branches of natural sciences, social sciences and technology. In some universities they are also required to take stipulated remedial courses in Agricultural disciplines for Master's degrees. Courses in M.Sc in Agricultural Biotechnology are now being introduced in several universities exclusively for agriculture graduates with the standard financial assistance of the Department of Biotechnology (DBT).

ANIMAL SCIENCES

The number of universities offering courses in animal sciences is 27 They include two universities exclusively devoted to animal sciences *viz.*, Tamil Nadu Veterinary and Animal Sciences University (Chennai) and West Bengal University of Animal and Fisheries Science (Calcutta), and the Indian Veterinary Research Institute (IVRI) (Izatngar, UP), IVRI offers only postgraduate and doctoral courses. Like agricultural sciences, most of the animal science colleges offer, besides first degree programme, Master's Degree programme is of two–year duration. The nomenclature of the first degree award is either Bachelor in Veterinary Science (BVSc) or Bachelor in Veterinary Science and Animal Husbandry (BVSc & AH).

Though the term Animal Husbandry does not occur in the nomenclature BVSc, the subject indeed is a part of the course. At the Master's and Doctoral degree levels a large number of specialisations are offered by most of the colleges. for an illustrative list). Several universities offer omnibus M.Sc degree courses in Animal Sciences, *e.g.*, Bharathiar University, Hyderabad University (Life Science–Animal Science), MJP Rohilkhand University (Plant and Animal Sciences). Although there are now separate colleges for dairy science and technology, traditionally, several Veterinary Science colleges have been offering MVSc courses in dairy related subjects. This has been discussed in (Dairy Science and Technology).

POULTRY SCIENCE

Poultry Science is one of the subjects of study in the BVSc & AH courses. It is also offered at the Master's level (MVSc & AH or M.Sc) in a number of universities, *e.g.*, Acharya N G Ranga Agricultural University, Hyderabad, Chandra Sekhar Azad University of Agriculture and Technology, GB Pant University of Agriculture and Technology, Indian Veterinary Research Institute, Jawaharlal Nehru Krishi Vishwavidyalaya, Kerala University, Konkan Krishi Vidyapeeth, Rajasthan Agricultural University, Tamil Nadu Veterinary and Animal Sciences University, and University of Agricultural Science, Bangalore. Dr BV Rao Institute of Poultry Management (Pune) is a specialized institution recognized by the Konkan Krishi Vidyapeeth.

AGRICULTURAL ENGINEERING

Agricultural engineers apply engineering principles to problems in agriculture. They design and develop agricultural equipment and machinery and also work on soil and water conservation, irrigation and drainage systems. Agriculture engineers contribute to making agricultural farming easier and more productive and profitable through the introduction of new farm machinery and through advancements in soil and water conservation. There are 19 universities which offer agricultural engineering courses at the first degree level. Of this

10 offer postgraduate degrees in the subject. The only institution outside the agricultural university system which has introduced the course is the Indian Institute of Technology (Kharagpur).

The nomenclature of the degree is either BE (Agriculture) or B.Tech (Agricultural Engineering) at the first degree level and ME/M.Tech at the postgraduate level. gives an illustrative list of subjects offered at the postgraduate level. Unlike Master's degree courses in other agricultural disciplines which are of one and a half–year duration, ME/M Technology courses in agricultural engineering (Nabi Bagh, Berasia Road, Bhopal–462038) under the ICAR conducts research in the subject.

FISHERIES SCIENCE

There are 12 agricultural universities which offer first degree course in Fisheries Science of four–year duration (BFSc of B.Sc Fisheries). Six universities have introduced Master's degree course of two–year duration (MFSc). Only two universities offer PhD course. The list of universities which offer fisheries courses at all the three levels is given in Outside the agricultural university system several institutions also offer Master's degree courses in fisheries–some specialized in nature. The most important one is the Central Institute of Fisheries Education and research in fisheries. Two other institutions–Central Marine Fisheries Research Institute (CMFRI) at Kochi and Inland Fisheries Training Centre (IFTC) at Barackpore (West Bengal) are associates of CIFE. All the three institutions offer only postgraduate programmes. CIFE offers MFSc courses in Fisheries Resources Management, and Inland Aquaculture while the CMFRI offers MFSc course in Mariculture. IFTC offers PG Certificate Course in Fisheries Development and Administration of one year duration.

Admission to all these programmes are made on the basis of an All–India Competitive Examination. Entry requirement is BFSc as well as B.Sc (Fisheries) degree with zoology, botany, chemistry and fisheries. CIFE earlier used to offer a two–year PG Diploma course in Fisheries Science which had been discontinued since 1998. Only three universities had introduced PhD programmes.

Universities outside the agricultural university system conducting fisheries science courses are:

- *Barkatullah Vishwavidyalaya (Bhopal)*–M.Sc (Fish Genetics), MFSc (at its Department of Applied Aquaculture), and
- *Cochin University of Science and Technology (Kochi*– M.Sc (Industrial Fisheries), M.Sc (Marineculture) (at its Faculty of Marine Sciences);
- *Andhra University (Vishakapatnam)*– M.Sc (Capture and Culture Fisheries), and M.Sc (Coastal Aquaculture and Marine Biotechnology), Kerala University–M.Sc (Aquatic Biology and Fisheries) and

- *Annamalai University (Annamalai Nagar)*–M.Sc (Coastal Aquaculture). In all thee course, students possessing B.Sc degrees with biological sciences are also admitted.

Other Courses in Fisheries Science: A subject which has a bearing on fisheries science is Limnology is the study of freshwater ecosystem (specially in lakes and ponds) including its chemical, physical and biological aspects. Although traditionally, Limnology is closely related to Hydrobiology, it has a great bearing on fishery. Barkatullah Vishwavidyalaya has set up a Department of Limnology.

The Department offers two M.Sc courses in Applied Limnology and Fishery Technology and Aquatic Environmental Science (Water Resource Management and Pollution Control). The other university which offers M.Sc (Limnology) course is the Rajasthan Agricultural University. Fisheries Science is also offered as one of the subjects in the vocational stream at the 10+2 and B.Sc degree levels. Central Institute of Fisheries Nautical and Engineering Training (CIFNET) at Kochi, Chennai and Visakhapatnam offers career training to candidates to become Master of Fishing Vessel and Engine Driver of Fishing Vessel. The course of 18 months duration leads to the award of Certificate of Competency.

FORESTRY

B.Sc (Forestry) degree course of four–year duration is offered by 12 agricultural universities. M.Sc (Forestry) course is available both in agricultural and non–agricultural universities. Master's degree course is of two–year duration. Forest Researchh Institute (FRI), (ICFRE, New Forest, Dehra Dun–248195), a deemed university offers six forest related courses:

- M.Sc Forestrry (Economics and Management),
- M.Sc (Wood Science and Technology),
- M.Sc (Environmental Management,
- PG Diploma in Plantation Technology (one–year duration),
- PG Diploma in Pulp and Paper Technology (one–year duration), and
- Postgraduate Diploma in Biodiversity Conservation.

Admission to all the courses is made on the basis of an entrance test conducted on an all–India basis.

The eligibility requirements are:

- *M.Sc Forestry (Economics and Management)*: Bachelor's degree in Science with at least one of t he subjects, *viz.*, Botany, Chemistry, Geology, Mathematics, Physics and Zoology or a Bachelor's degree in Agriculture or Forestry.
- *M.Sc in Wood Science and Technology*: Bachelor's degree with Physics, Mathematics and Chemistry or B.Sc degree in Forestry.
- *M.Sc in Environment Management*: Bachelor's degree in any branch

of basic or applied sciences or Bachelor's degree in Forestry or Agriculture or BE in Environment Science.

- *Postgraduate Diploma in Plantation Technology: (one–year duration)*: Postgraduate degree in Chemistry or Applied Chemistry or Industrial Chemistry and must have studied Botany at the graduate level or M.Sc in Agriculture.
- *Postgraduate Diploma in Pulp and Paper Technology*: (one–year duration)– Postgraduate degree in Chemistry or Applied Chemistry or Industrial Chemistry and must have studied Physics at the graduate level.
- *Postgraduate Diploma in Biodiversity Conservation*: (one–year duration)–M.Sc in any discipline.

Two universities, *viz.*, Birsa Agricultural University (Ranchi) and Gujarat University offer diploma level course in forestry. The two–year diploma course of the Birsa Agricultural University is open to candidates who have passed 10+2 examination. The qualification requirement for the one–year diploma course of the Gujarat University is a B.Sc degree. Forestry, as a subject is also available for study in the vocational streams both at 10+2 and B.Sc levels.

Forestry, Ecology and Environment

Wildlife Science and certain aspects of ecology and environment are closely related to forestry.–Environmental Science). Such courses are mostly offered by the universities outside the agricultural university system. The Wildlife Institute of India (Dehra Dun), affiliated to Saurashtra University (Rajkot) has introduced an M.Sc degree course in Wildlife Science.

The courses in this area are: PG Diploma in Social Forestry–School of Life Sciences, Dr B R Ambedkar University, M.Sc (Wildlife)–Aligarh Muslim University, M.Sc (Forestry, Wildlife and Ecodevelopment)–Guru Ghasidas University, MVSc (Wildlife Science)– Madras Veterinary College, Tamil Nadu Veterinary and Animal Science, Dr B R Ambedkar University, PG Diploma (Forestry Management)–Department of Environmental Biology, A P S University, (Rewa–480003), M.Sc (Agroforestry)–Bundelkhand University (Jhansi–284128), M.Sc (Forestry)–Pt Ravishankar Shukla University (Raipur–492010). As stated above, the FRI has two environment oriented forestry courses, *viz.*, M.Sc (Environment Management), and PG Diploma in Biodiversity Conservation.

Forestry Management: It may be mentioned here that besides the M.Sc Forestry (Economics and Management) offered by the FRI, the Indian Institute of Forest Management (IIFM), Bhopal, a specialized management institution set up by the Government of India has introduced a unique postgraduate diploma course of two–year duration. The award is equivalent to Master's degree in the subject.

FOOD SCIENCE AND TECHNOLOGY

As stated earlier, Food Science and Technology is considered as a subject allied to agriculture science. Courses in Post harvest Processing and Food Engineering is offered at the Master's Degree level in several agricultural engineering colleges.

This course is also offered as a branch of technology in several non-agricultural universities. Engineering and Technology). At the first degree level, the College of Agriculture Technology (Parbhani–431402) of the Marathwada Krishi Vidyapeeth offers B.Tech (Food Science). The College of Agriculture Engineering (Coimbatore–641003) of the Tamil Nadu Agricultural University offers B.Tech (Food Processing Engineering).

At the Master's degree level four courses are available in:

- *Allahabad Agricultural Institute*: M.Sc (Foods, Nutrition and Dietetics),
- *Kerala Agricultural University*: M.Sc (Food Science and Nutrition),
- *College of Agricultural Technology (Parbhani)*:M.Tech (Food Science),
- *Govind Ballabh Pant University of Agriculture and Technology*: M.Tech (Postharvest Process and Food Engineering).
- *Marathwada Krishi Vidyapeeth*: M.Tech (Food Science),
- Allahabad Agricultura Institute M.Sc (Food Science and Applied Nutrition),
- *Maharshi Dayanand Saraswati University*: M.Sc (Food and Nutrition),
- *Tamil Nadu Agricultural University*: M.Sc (Food Science and Nutrition), and
- *Bundelkhand University*: M.Sc (Food Science and Technology).

In a number of Home Science Colleges, Food and Nutrition is one of the specialisations in the Master of Home Science programmes.

HORTICULTURE

Dr Y S Parmar University of Horticulture and Forestry is the only University exclusively devoted to horticulture and forestry. Horticulture courses are offered both at first degree (B.Sc Forestry) levels. The duration of the courses are four years and two years respectively.

Dr Y S Parmar University of Horticulture which is open to candidates qualified in vocational courses in horticulture, and food preservation and processing. The gives a list of universities which offer the courses.

It includes two universities *viz.*, Chaudhary Charan Singh University, Meerut and Nagland University, outside the agricultural university system which offer M.Sc degree course in the subject. Horticultural Science (BHSc) course through distance learning mode.

The course is open to candidates who have passed the Class 10 examination. The course consists of three diploma courses in Fruit Production,

Vegetable Production, Floriculture and Landscape Gardening. The degree is awarded on successful completion of all the three diploma courses.

FLORICULTURE

This subject is included in the B.Sc (Horticulture) curriculum. Only a small number of agricultural universities offer the course at the Master's degree level, *e.g.* Dr Y S Parmar University of Horticulture and Forestry (also a PhD course), Punjab Agricultural University (Landscaping and Floriculture), University of Agricultural Science, Bangalore (Floriculture), Allahabad Agricultural Institute.

SERICULTURE

Course in Sericulture is available both at the agricultural and non-agricultural universities. Sri Padmavati Mahila Vishwavidyalayam (Tirupati) and the University of Agricultural Science, Bangalore offer B.Sc (Sericulture) course. M.Sc (Sericulture) courses are available at the Assam Agricultural University, Karnataka University, Central Sericulture Research and Training Institute (Mysore) affiliated to the Mysore University, Sri Padmavati Mahila Vishwavidyalam.

Sri Krishna Devaraya University, Tamil Nadu Agricultural University, and University of Agricultural Sciences, Bangalore (at its College of Sericulture). Diploma level courses are offered by Babasaheb Bhimrao Ambedkar University (Lucknow), and Tamil Nadu Agricultural University. Sericulture is also offered as a subject of study in vocational stream at 10+2 and B.Sc levels.

AGRICULTURAL MANAGEMENT

A new development in the field of agricultural education is the introduction of master's degree programmes in agricultural management which is known in USA as agribusiness management. Two universities– Universities of Agricultural Sciences (Bangalore and Dharwar), made a beginning by offering B.Sc courses in agricultural marketing and cooperation. Kerala Agricultural University introduced B.Sc and M.Sc courses in Cooperation and Banking. The Indian Institute of Management (Ahmedabad) was the first to introduce Postgraduate Diploma in Agribusiness Management (earlier known as Specialisation Package in Agriculture). A number of agricultural universities have now introduced management courses in agriculture and related subjects.

OTHER AGRICULTURAL COURSES

While ManyNnon: Agricultural universities offer postgraduate courses related to agriculture, a number of agricultural universities have introduced agricultural courses related to other disciplines. Some of the important ones are: agricultural Chemistry (oriented to soil science, agricultural economics, agricultural statistics, and agro meteorology.

CAREER OPPORTUNITIES

On obtaining a graduate or a postgraduate degree in a discipline of agriculture and allied sciences, there are a wide range of options and opportunities of a career in teaching, research and transfer of technology areas in SAUs, State Departments of Agriculture and Animal Husbandry, NGOs and in industry.

Even banks which advance credit and loans for agro–based projects employ agricultural specialists. The Union Public Service Commission conducts an annual competitive examination for recruitment in the Indian Forest Service. The employment opportunities are really multifaceted for competent persons.

The Indian Council of Agricultural Research (ICAR) (Krishi Anusandhan Bhavan, Pusa, New Delhi–110012), an autonomous body under the Department of Agricultural Research and Education (DARE) is one of the largest employers of scientific manpower in the country.

The research set–up includes 45 Central Institutes, four National Bureaux, 10 Project Directorates, 30 National Research Centres and 80 All–India Coordinated Research Projects. For effective communication of research findings among farmers, the ICAR maintains a network of 261 Krishi Vigyan Kendras, along with eight Zonal Coordinating Units. More than 6,500 research scientists work directly in ICAR's research establishments and about 5,000 work in SAUs, and projects funded directly by the ICAR.

Recruitment to these positions constituting the Agricultural Research Service (ARS) are made by the Agricultural Scientist Recruitment Board (ASRB) in 61 disciplines through a nation–wide competitive examination followed by a personal interview. These 61 disciplines apart, agricultural, animal and allied sciences include basic and fundamental sciences, home science and engineering.

This is, however, a combined competitive examination not only for recruitment in ARS but also used as National Eligibility Test (NET) for appointment of Assistant Professors and Lecturers in SAUs and for awarding Senior Research Fellowships. Generally, the competitive examination is held in October every year for which notification is made latest by April. The National Academy off Agricultural Research Management (NAARM) at Hyderabad imparts foundation training to new entrants in the ARS.

Scientific placements in ICAR are classified into Scientists, Scientists (Selection Grade). Senior Scientists and Principal Scientists. Promotion from Scientists to the level of Senior Scientists is through performance appraisal and the length of service in the previous grade. Lateral entry into these positions is open to scientists from other organisations and the SAUs. There is also ample opportunity for training and skill upgradation and active participation in research both within the country and abroad. Opportunities are also available for obtaining higher degrees for in–service candidates with study–leave benefits.

4

Cost Concepts and Production Function

COST CONCEPTS

The word 'cost' has different meanings in different situations. The accounting cost concept or the historical cost concept is not useful as such for business decision-making. The accounting records end up with the balance sheet and income statements which are meant for legal, financial and tax needs of the enterprise. The financial recordings reveal what has been happening. It is a historical recording which is not of very much help to the managerial economist in his business decision-making. The actual cost is not the relevant cost concept for business decision-making because it only reveals what has been happening.

The decision-making concepts of cost aim at projecting what will happen in the alternative courses of action. Business decisions involve plans for the future and require choices among different plans. These decisions necessitate profitability calculations for which a comparison of future revenues and future expenses of each alternative plan is needed.

VARIOUS CONCEPTS OF COSTS

A managerial economist must have a proper understanding of the different cost concepts which are essential for clear business thinking. The several alternative bases of classifying cost and the relevance of each for different kinds of problems are to be studied.

Total, Average and Marginal Cost

Total cost is the total cash payment made for the input needed for production. It may be explicit or implicit is the sum total of the fixed and variable costs. Average cost is the cost per unit of output. It is obtained by dividing the total cost (TC) by the total quantity produced (Q)

$$\text{Average cost} = \frac{TC}{Q}$$

Marginal cost is the additional cost incurred to produce an additional unit of output. Or it is the cost of the marginal unit produced.

Example

A company produces 1000 typewriters per annum. Total fixed cost is ₹1,00,000 per annum. Direct material cost per typewriter is ₹200 and direct labour cost ₹100.

Variable cost per typewriter = direct material + direct labour

= 200 + 100 = ₹ 300

Total variable cost (1000×300) = ₹300000

Fixed Cost = ₹100000

Total cost = ₹400000

TC = ₹ 400000

Average Cost $= \frac{TC}{Q} = \frac{400000}{1000}$ = Rs. 400

If output is increased by one typewriter, the cost will appear as follows:

Total variable cost (1001×300) = 300300

Fixed cost = 100000

Total = 400300

Here the additional cost incurred to produce the 1001th typewriter is ₹.300 (400300 - 400000). Therefore, the marginal cost per typewriter is ₹.300.

Fixed and Variable Costs

This classification is made on the basis of the degree to which they vary with the changes in volume. Fixed cost is that cost which remains constant up to a certain level of output. It is not affected by the changes in the volume of production. Then fixed cost per unit aries with output rate. When the production increases, fixed cost per unit decreases. Fixed cost includes salary paid to administrative staff, depreciation of fixed assets, rent of factory etc. These costs are fixed in the sense that they do not change in short-run. Variable cost varies directly with the variation in output. An increase in total output results in an increase in total variable costs and decrease in total output results in a proportionate decline in the total variable costs. The variable cost per unit will be constant. Variable costs include the costs of all inputs that vary with output like raw materials, running costs of fixed assets such as fuel, ordinary repairs, routine maintenance expenditure, direct labour charges etc. The distinction of cost is important in forecasting the effect of short-run changes in volume upon costs and profits.

Short-Run and Long-Run Costs

This cost distinction is based on the time element. Short-Run is a period during which the physical capacity of the firm remains fixed. Any increase in output during this period is possible only by using the existing physical capacity more intensively. Long- Run is a period during which it is possible to change the firm's physical capacity.

All the inputs become variable in the long-term. Short-Run cost is that which varies with output when the physical I capacity remains constant. Long-Run costs are those which vary with output when all the inputs are variable. Short-Run costs are otherwise called variable costs. A firm wishing to change output quickly can do it only by increasing the variable factors. Short- Run cost concept helps the manager to take decision when a firm has to decide whether or not to produce more or less with a given plant. Long-Run cost analysis helps to take investment decisions. Long-Run increase in output may necessitate installation of more capital equipment.

Opportunity Costs and Outlay Costs

This distinction is made on the basis of the nature of the sacrifice made. Outlay costs are those expenses which are actually incurred by the firm. These are the actual payments made for labour, material, plant, building, machinery, traveling, transporting etc. These are the expense items that appear in the books of accounts. Outlay cost is an accounting cost concept. It is also called absolute cost or actual cost. Whenever the inputs are to be bought for cash the outlay concept is to be applied. A businessman chooses and investment proposal from different investment opportunities.

Before taking the decision he has to compare all the opportunities and choose the best. When he chooses the best he sacrifices the possibility of making profit from other investment opportunities. The cost of his choice is the return that he could have earned from other investment opportunities he has given up or sacrificed. A businessman decides to use his own money to buy a machine for the business. The cost of that money is the probable return on the money from the next most acceptable alternative investment.

If he invested the money at 12 per cent interest, the opportunity cost of investing in his own business would be the 12 per cent interest he has forgone. The outlay concept is applied when the inputs are to be bought from the market. When a firm decides to make the inputs rather than buying it from the market the opportunity cost concept is to be applied. For example, in a cloth mill, instead' of buying the yarn from the market they spin it themselves.

The cost of this yam is really the price at which the yarn could be sold if it were not used by them for weaving cloth. The opportunity cost concept is made use of for long-run decisions. For example, the cost of higher education of a student should not only be the tuition fees and book costs but it also includes the earnings foregone by not working.

This concept is very important in capital expenditure budgeting. The cost of acquiring a petrol pump in Trivandrum City by spending ₹6 lakhs is not usually the interest for that borrowed money but it is the profit that would have been made if that 6 lakhs had been invested in an offset printing press, which is the next best investment opportunity. Opportunity cost concept is useful for taking short-rum decisions also. In boom periods the scarce lathe capacity used for making a product involves the opportunity cost of not using it to make some other product that can also produce profit. Opportunity cost is the cost concept to use when the supply of inputs is strictly limited.

Estimates of cost of capital are essentially founded on an opportunity cost concept of investment return. Investment decision involves opportunity costs measurable in terms of sacrificed income from alternative investments.

The opportunity cost of any action is therefore measured by the value of the most favorable alternative course which has to be foregone if that action is taken. Opportunity cost arises only when there is an alternative. If there is no alternative, opportunity cost is the estimated earnings of the next best use. Thus it represents only the sacrificed alternative. Hence it does not appear in financial accounts. But this concept is of very great use in managerial decision-making.

Out-of-pocket and Book Costs

Out-of-pocket costs are those costs that involve current cash payment. Wages, rent, interest etc., are examples of this. The out-of-pocket costs are also called explicit costs. Book costs do not require current cash expenditure. Unpaid salary of the owner manager, depreciation, and unpaid interest cost of owner's own fund are examples of book costs.

Book costs may be called implicit costs. But the book costs are taken into account in determining the legal dividend payable during a period. Both book costs and out-of-pocket costs are considered for all decisions. Book cost is the cost of self owned factors of production. The book cost can be converted into out-of-pocket cost. If a selfowned machinery is sold out and the service of the same is hired, the hiring charges form the out-of-pocket cost The distinction is very helpful in taking liquidity decisions.

Incremental and Sunk costs

Incremental cost is the additional cost due to a change in the level or nature of business activity. The change may be caused by adding a new product, adding new machinery, replacing machinery by a better one etc. Incremental or differential cost is not marginal cost. Marginal cost is the cost of an added (marginal) unit of output. Sunk costs are those which are not altered by any change. They are the costs incurred in the past.

This cost is the result of past decision, and cannot be changed by future decisions. Once an asset has been bought or an investment made, the funds locked up represent sunk costs. As these costs do not alter when any change in activity is made they are sunk and are irrelevant to a decision being taken now. Investments in fixed assets are examples of sunk costs. As soon as fixed assets have been installed, their cost is sunk.

The amount of cost cannot be changed. Incremental cost helps management to evaluate the alternatives. Incremental cost will be different in the case of different alternatives. Sunk cost, on the other hand, will remain the same irrespective of the alternative selected. Cost estimates of an incremental nature only influence business decisions.

Explicit and Implicit or Imputed Costs

Explicit costs are those expenses that involve cash payments. These are the actual or business costs that appear in the books of accounts. Explicit cost is the payment made by the employer for those factors of production hired by him from outside. These costs include wages and salaries paid payments for raw materials, interest on borrowed capital funds, rent on hired land, taxes paid to the government etc. Implicit costs are the costs of the factor units that are owned by the employer himself. It does not involve dash payment and hence does not appear in the books of accounts.

These costs did not actually incur but would have incurred in the absence of employment of self-owned factors of production. The two normal implicit costs are depreciation and return on capital contributed by shareholders. In small scale business unit the entrepreneur himself acts as the manager of the business. If he were employed in another firm he would be given salary. The salary he has thus forgone is the opportunity cost of his services utilised in his own firm. This is an implicit cost of his business. Thus implicit wages, implicit rent and implicit interest are the highest interest, rent and wages which self-owned capital, building and labour respectively can earn from their next best use. Implicit costs are not considered for finding out the loss or gains of the business, but help a lot in business decisions.

Replacement and Historical Costs

These are the two methods of valuing assets for balance sheet purpose and to find out the cost figures from which profit can be arrived at; Historical cost is the original cost of an asset.

Historical cost valuation shows the cost of an asset as the original price paid for the asset acquired in the past. Historical valuation is the basis for financial accounts. Replacement cost is the price that would have to be paid currently to replace the same asset. For example, the price of a machine at the time of purchase was ₹17,000 and the present price of the machine is ₹20,000. The original price ₹17,000 is the historical cost while ₹20,000 is the replacement cost. During periods of substantial change in the price level, historical valuation gives a poor projection of the future cost intended for managerial decision.

Replacement cost is a relevant cost concept when financial statements have to be adjusted for inflation.

Controllable and Non-controllable costs

Controllable costs are the ones which can be regulated by the executive who is in charge of it. The concept of controllability of cost varies with levels of management. If a cost is uncontrollable at one level of management it may be controllable at some other level. Similarly the controllability of certain costs may be shared by two or more executives. For example, material cost, the price of which comes under the responsibility of the purchase executive whereas its usage comes under the responsibility of the production executive.

Direct expenses like material, labour etc. are controllable costs. Some costs are not directly identifiable with a process or product. They are apportioned to various processes or products in some proportion. This cost varies with the variation in the basis of allocation and is independent of the actions of the executive of that department. These apportioned costs are called uncontrollable costs.

Business and Full Costs

A firm's business cost is the total money expenses recorded in the books of accounts. This includes the depreciation provided on plant and equipment. It is similar to the actual or real cost. Full cost of a firm includes not only the business costs but also opportunity costs of the firm and normal profits. The firm's opportunity cost includes interest on self-owned capital, the salary forgone by the entrepreneur if he were, working in his firm. Normal profit is the minimum returns which induces the entrepreneur to produce the same product.

Economic and Accounting Cost

Accounting costs are recorded with the intention of preparing the balance sheet and profit and loss statements which are intended for the legal, financial and tax purposes of the company. The accounting concept is a historical concept. It records what has happened. The past cost data revealed by the books of accounts does not help very much in decision-making.

Decision-making needs future costs. Economic concept considers future costs and future revenues which help future planning and choice. When the accountant describes what has happened, the economist aims at projecting what will happen. Accounting data ignores implicit. or imputed cost. The economist considers decision-making costs.

For this, different cost classifications relevant to different kinds of problems are considered. The cost distinctions such as opportunity and outlay cost, shortrun and long-run cost and replacement and historical cost are made from the economic viewpoint.

COST-OUTPUT RELATIONS

The cost-output relationship plays an important role in determining the optimum level of production. Knowledge of the cost-output relation helps the manager in cost control, profit prediction, pricing, promotion etc. The relation between cost and output is technically described as the cost function.

TC = f(Q)

Where,

TC = Total

Q = Quantity produced

F = Function

The production function combined with the prices of inputs determines the cost function of the firm.

Considering the period the cost function can be classified as:

- Short-run cost function and
- Long run-cost function.

In economic theory, the short-run is defined as that period during which the physical capacity of the firm is fixed, and during which output can be increased only by using the existing capacity more intensively. The long-run is a period during which it is possible to increase the firm's capacity or to reduce it in size, if trade is very bad.

SHORT-RUN COST-OUTPUT RELATION

The cost concepts made use of in the cost behaviour are total cost, average cost and marginal cost. Total cost if the actual money spent to produce a particular quantity of output. It is the summation of fixed and variable costs.

$$TC = TFC + TVC$$

Upto a certain level of production total fixed cost, *i.e.* the cost of plant, building, equipment etc. remains fixed. But the total variable costs *i.e.*, the cost of labour, raw materials etc. vary with the variation in output

$$AC = \frac{TC}{Q}$$

Or it is the total of average fixed cost (TFC/ Q) and average variable cost (TVC/Q) Marginal cost is the addition to the total cost due to the production of an additional unit of product. Or it is the cost of the marginal unit produced. It can be arrived at by dividing the change in total cost by the change in total output.

$$MC = \frac{TC}{Q}$$

In the short-run there will not be any change in total fixed cost. Hence change in total cost implies change in total variable cost only. Table represents the cost-output relation. The table is prepared on the basis of the Law of Diminishing Marginal Returns. The fixed cost ₹60 may include rent of factory building, interest on capital, salaries of permanently employed staff, insurance etc. These fixed costs are independent of output, whose amount cannot be altered in the shortrun. But the average fixed cost, *i.e.* the fixed cost per unit, falls continuously as the out put increase.

Table. Short-run Cost-Output Relations

Units of output Q	Total TFC Fixed cost	Total variable cost	Total cost TC (2+3)	Average variable cost AVC 3/1	Average fixed cost AFC 2/1	Average cost (5+6) AC	Marginal cost MC		
1	2	3	4	5	6	7	8	0	60
–	60	–	–	–	–	1	60	20	80
20	60	80	20						
2	60	36	96	18	30	48	16		
3	60	48	108	16	20	36	12		
4	60	64	124	16	15	31	16		
5	60	90	150	18	12	30	26		
6	60	132	192	22	10	32	42		

The greater the out put, lower the fixed cost per unit. The total variable cost (TVC) increases but not at the same rate. If more and more units are produced with a given physical capacity AVC will fall initially. AVC declines upto 3rd unit, it is constant upto 4th unit and then rises. This is because the efficiency first increases and then decreases. The variable factors seem to produce somewhat more efficiently near a firm's optimum capacity output level than at very low levels of output. But once the optimum capacity is reached, any further increase in output will increase AVC.

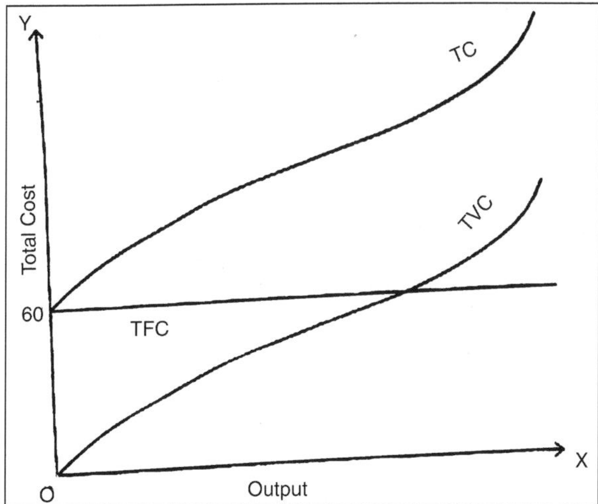

The average total cost (AC) declines first and then rises. The rise in AC is felt only after the AVC starts rising. In the table AVC starts rising from the 5th unit onwards whereas the AC starts rising from the 6th unit only. AFC continues to fall with increase in output. But AVC initially declines and then rises.

Thus there will be a stage where the AVC may have started rising, yet AC is still declining because the rise in AVC is less than the drop in AFC, the net effect being a decline in AC. Thus the table shows an increasing returns or diminishing cost in the first instance and eventually diminishing returns or increasing cost. The short-run cost-output relationship can be shown graphically also.

Fig shows the relationship between output and total fixed cost, total variable cost and total cost. TFC curve is a horizontal straight line representing ₹.60, whatever be the output TVC curve slopes upward starting from zero, first gradually but later at a fast rate.

TC = TFC+TVC. As TFC remains constant, increase in TC means increase in TVC only. As TFC remains constant the gap between TVC and TC will always be the same. Hence TC curve has the same pattern of behaviour as TVC curve.

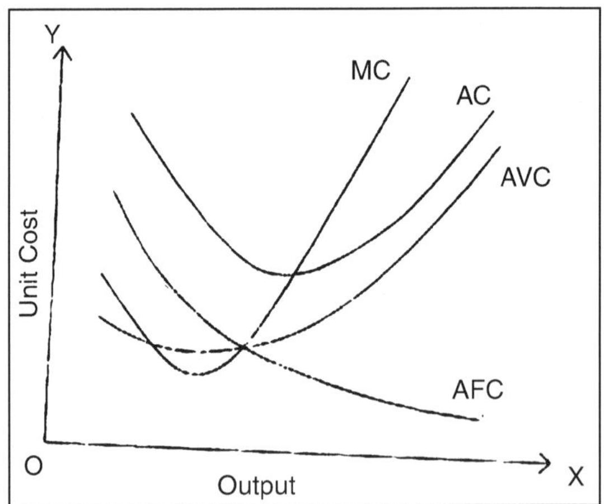

Fig shows the law of production more clearly. AFC curve continues to fall as output rises from lower levels to higher levels. This is because the total fixed cost is spread over more and more units as output increases. TVC increases with the increase in production since more raw materials, labour, power etc. would be required for increasing output. But AVC curve (i.e.variable cost per unit) first falls and then rises. This is due to the operation of the law of variable proportions.

The behaviour of AC curve depends upon the behaviour of AVC curve and AFC curve. In the initial stage of production both AFC and AVC are declining. Hence AC also declines. AFC continues to fall with an increase in output while AVC first declines and then rises. So long as AFC and AVC decline AC will also decline. But after a certain point AVC starts rising. If the rise in AVC is less than the decline in AFC, AC will still continue to decline. When the rise in

AVC is more than the drop in AFC, AC begins to rise. We can see that when the production is increased to 5 units AVC increases but AC still declines. Here the increase in AVC is less than the decline in AFC, the net effect being a decline in AC. AC curve, thus declines first and then rises. At first AC is high due to large fixed cost. As output increases the total fixed cost is shared by more and more units and hence AC falls. After a certain point, owing to the operation of the law of diminishing marginal returns, the variable cost and, therefore, AC starts increasing. The lower end of AC curve thus turns up. and gives it a U-shape. That is why AC curves are U-shaped. The least-cost combination of inputs is indicated by the lowest point in Ac curve *i.e.* where where the total average cost is the minimum.

It is the short-run stage of optimum output. It may not be the maximum output level. It is the point where the per unit cost of production will be at its lowest. A downward trend in MC curve shows increasing marginal productivity (i.e.decreasing marginal cost) of the variable input. Similarly, an upward trend in MC curve shows the rate of increase in TVC, on the one hand and the decreasing marginal productivity (*i.e.* increasing marginal cost) of the variable input on the other. MC curve intersects both AVC and AC curves at their lowest points.

The relationship between AVC, ATC and AFC can be summed up as follows:

- If both AFC and AVC fall, AC will also fall because AC=AFC+AVC
- When AFC falls and AVC rises
  - AC will fall where the drop in AFC is more than the rise in AVC
  - AC remains constant if the drop in AFC=rise in AVC
  - AC will rise where the drop in AFC is less than the rise in AVC.

LONG-RUN COST-OUTPUT RELATIONS

Long-run is a period long enough to make all inputs variable. In the long-run a firm can increase or decrease its output just as to its demand, by having more or less of all the factors of production. The firms are able to expand the scale of their operation in the long-run by purchasing larger quantities of all the inputs. Thus in the long-run all factors become variable. The long-run cost-output relations therefore imply the relationship between total costs and total output. As the change in production in the longrun is possible by changing the scale of production, the long-run cost-output relationship is influenced by the law of returns to scale. In the long-run a firm has a number of alternatives in regard to the scale of operations. For each scale of production or plant size, the firm has a separate short-run average cost curve. Hence the long-run average cost curve is composed of a series of short-run average cost curves.

A short-run average cost (SAC) curve applies to only one plant whereas the longrun average cost (LAC) curve takes into consideration many plants. At any one time the firm has only one size of plant. That plant remains fixed during that period. Any increase in production in that period is possible only with that plant capacity. That plant has a corresponding average cost (SAC) curve. But in a long period the firm can move from one plant size to another. Each plant has its corresponding SAC curve.

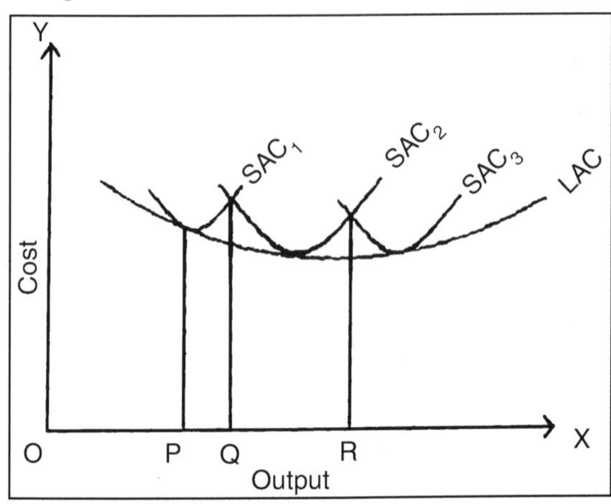

The long-run cost-output relationship is shown graphically by the LAC curve. To draw an LAC curve we have to start with a number of SAC curves. In the fig we have assumed that there are only three sizes of plants-small, medium and large, S ACj refers to the average cost curve for the small plant, S AC, for the medium size plant and SAC3 for the large size plant. If the firm wants to produce OP units or less, it will choose the small plant. For an output beyond OQ the firm will opt for medium size plant. Even if an increased production is possible with small plant production beyond OQ will increase cost of production per unit.For an output OR the firm will choose the large plant. Thus in the long-run the firm has a series of SAC curves. The LAC curve drawn will be tangential to the three SAC curves *i.e.* the LAC curve touches each SAC curve at one point. The LAC curve is also known as Envelope Curve as it envelopes all the SAC curves.

No point on any of the LAC curve can ever be below the LAC curve. It is also known as Planning Curve as it serves as a guide to the entrepreneur In his planning the size of plant for future expansion.The plant which yields the lowest average cost of production will be selected. LAC can, therefore, be defined as the lowest possible average cost of producing any output, when the management has adequate I time to make all desirable changes and adjustments. In the long-run the demand curve of the firm depends on the law of returns to scale. The law of returns to scale states that if a firm increases the quantity of all inputs simultaneously and proportionately, the total output initially increases more than proportionately but eventually increases less than proportionately. It implies that when production increases, per unit cost first' decreases but ultimately increases. This means LAC curve falls initially and rises subsequently.

Like SAC curve LAC curve also is Ushaped, but it will be always flatter then SAC curves. The U-shape implies lower and lower average cost in the beginning until the optimum scale of the firm is reached and successively higher average cost thereafter.The increasing return is experienced on account of the economies of scale or advantages of large-scale production Increase in scale makes possible increased division and _pecialization of labour and more efficient use of machines. After a certain point increase in production makes management more difficult and less efficient resulting in less than proportionate increase in output

Long-run Marginal Cost Curve

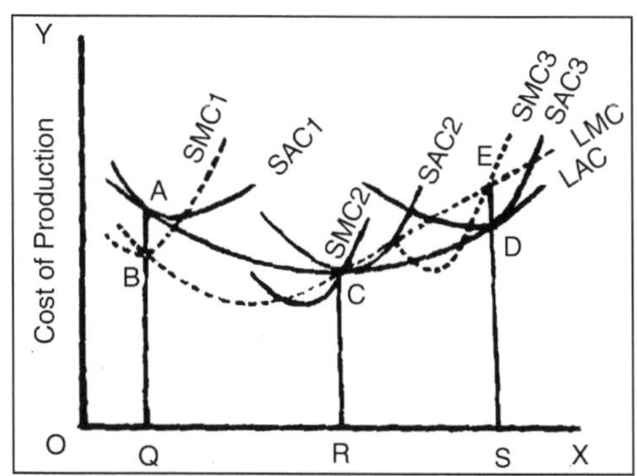

The long-run marginal cost curve represents the cost of an additional unit of output when all the inputs vary. The long-run marginal cost curve (LMC) is derived from the short-run marginal cost (SMC) curves. LMC curve intersects LAC curve at its minimum point C. There is only one plant size whose minimum SAC coincides with the minimum LAC and LMC.

$$SAC_2 = SMC_2 = LAC = LMC$$

The point C indicates also the optimum scale of production of the firm in the long-run or optimum output. Optimum output level is the level of production at which the cost of production per unit, *i.e.* AC, is the lowest. The optimum level is not the maximum profit level. The optimum point is where AC=MC. Here C is the optimum point.

PRODUCTION ANALYSIS

Production is an important economic activity. It directly or indirectly satisfies the wants and needs of the people. Satisfaction of human wants is the objective of production. In this session a general discussion of the concept of production and its functions are carried out.

MEANING OF PRODUCTION

Production is the conversion of input into output. The factors of production and all other things which the producer buys to carry out production are called input. The goods and services produced are known as output. Thus production is the activity that creates or adds utility and value. In the words of Fraser, "If consuming means extracting utility from matter, producing means creating utility into matter". Edwood Buffa, *"Production is a process by which goods and services are created"*.

FACTORS OF PRODUCTION

As already stated, production is a process of transformation of factors of production (input) into goods and services (output). The factors of production may be defined as resources which help the firms to produce goods or services. In other words, the resources required to produce a given product are called factors of production. Production is done by combining the various factors of production. Land, labour, capital and organisation (or entrepreneurship) are the factors of production. We can use the word CELL to help us remember the four factors of production: C. capital; Entrepreneurship; L land: and L labour.

CHARACTERISTICS OF FACTORS OF PRODUCTION

- The ownership of the factors of production is vested in the households.
- There is a basic distinction between factors of production and factor services. It is these factor services, which are combined in the process of production.
- The different units of a factor of production are not homogeneous. For example, different plots of land have different level of fertility. Similarly labourers differ in efficiency.
- Factors of production are complementary. This means their co-operation or combination is necessary for production.
- There is some degree of substitutability between factors of production. For example, labour can be substituted for capital to a certain extent.

BASIC CONCEPTS IN PRODUCTION THEORY

Transformation of inputs or resources into outputs of goods and services. For example: IBM hires workers to use machinery, parts and raw materials in factories to produce personal computers. The output of a firm can either be a final commodity (such as personal computer) or an intermediate product such as semiconductors (which are used in the production of computers and other goods). The output can also be a service rather than a good. Examples of services are education, medicine, banking, communication, transportation and many others.

To be noted is, that production refers to all of the activities involved in the production of goods and services, from borrowing to set up or expand production facilities, to hiring workers, purchasing ra"w materials, running quality control, cost accounting and so on, rather than referring merely to the physical transformation of inputs into outputs of goods and services. Inputs are the resources used in the production of goods and services.

As a convenient way to organise the discussion, inputs are classified into labour. (Including entrepreneurial talent), capital and land or natural resources. Each of these broad categories however includes a great variety of the basic input. For example, labour includes bus drivers, assembly line workers, accountants, lawyers, doctors scientists and many others. Inputs are also classified as fixed or variable. Fixed inputs are those that can not be readily changed during the time period under consideration, except at very great expense. Examples of fixed inputs are the firm's plant and specialised equipment.

On the other land, variable inputs are those that can be varied easily and on the very short notice. Examples of variable inputs are most raw materials and unskilled labour. The time period during which at least one input is fixed is called the short run, while the time period when all inputs are variable is called the long run. The length of the long run depends on the industry. For some, such as the setting up or expansion of a dry cleaning business, the long run may be only few months or weeks. For others, much as the construction of new electricity, generating plant, it may be many years. In the short run, a firm can increase output only by using more of the variable inputs together with the fixed inputs. In the long run, the same increase in output could very likely be obtained more efficiently by also expanding the firm's production facilities. Thus we say that the firm operates in the short run and plans increases or reductions in its scale of operation in the long run. In the long run, technology usually improves, so that more output can be obtained from a given quantity of inputs or the same output from less input.

PRODUCTION FUNCTION

Production is the process by which inputs are transformed in to outputs. Thus there is relation between input and output. The functional relationship between input and output is known as production function. The production function states the maximum quantity of output which can be produced from any selected combination of inputs. In other words, it states the minimum quantities of input that are necessary to produce a given quantity of output.

The production function is largely determined by the level of technology. The production function varies with the changes in technology. Whenever technology improves, a new production function comes into existence.

Therefore, in the modern times the output depends not only on traditional factors of production but also on the level of technology. The production function can be expressed in an equation in which the output is the dependent variable and inputs are the independent variables. The equation is expressed as follows:

Q=f (L,K,T..................n)

Where, Q = output
L = labour
K = capital
T = level of technology
n = other inputs employed in production

There are two types of production function - short run production function and long run production function.

In the short run production function the quantity of only one input varies while all other inputs remain constant. In the long run production function all inputs are variable.

Assumptions of Production Function

The production function is based on the following assumptions:

- The level of technology remains constant.
- The firm uses its inputs at maximum level of efficiency.
- It relates to a particular unit of time.
- A change in any of the variable factors produces a corresponding change in the output.
- The inputs are divisible into most viable units.

Managerial Use of Production Function

The production function is of great help to a manager or business economist.

The managerial uses of production function are outlined as below:

- It helps to determine least cost factor combination: The production function is a guide to the entrepreneur to determine the least cost factor combination. Profit can be maximized only by minimizing the cost of production. In order to minimize the cost of production, inputs are to be substituted. The production function helps in substituting the inputs.
- It helps to determine optimum level of output: The production function helps to determine the optimum level of output from a given quantity of input. In other words, it helps to arrive at the producer's equilibrium.
- It enables to plan the production: The production function helps the entrepreneur (or management) to plan the production.
- It helps in decision-making:Production function is very useful to the management to take decisions regarding cost and output. It also helps in cost control and cost reduction. In short, production function helps both in the short run and long run decision-making process.

COBB DOUGLAS PRODUCTION FUNCTION

Paul H. Douglas and C.W Cobb of the U.S.A have studied the production of the American manufacturing industries and they formulated a statistical production function.

It is popularly known as Cobb-Douglas Production Function. It is stated as follows.

Q = KLaC,,a) where, Q = output

L = quantity of labour

C = quantity of capital

K and a = positive constants

In this production function the output (Q) is a function of two inputs L and C. Cobb Douglas production function, about 3/4 of the increase in output is due to labour and the remaining 1/4 is due to capital. On this basis, Cobb Douglas production function can be expressed as under:

$$Q = KL^{3/4}C^{1/4}$$

$$L + C = \frac{3}{4} + \frac{1}{4} = 1$$

An important point in Cobb Douglas production function is that it indicates constant returns to scale. This means that if each input factor is increased by one per cent, output will exactly increase by one per cent. In other words, there will be no economies or diseconomies of scale. Although the Cobb Douglas production function is nonlinear, it can be transformed into a linear function by converting all variables into logarithms. That is why this function is known as a log linear function. In 1937, David Duerentt suggested that it will be better to present Cobb-Douglas production function in the form of following equation:

$$Q = KL^{a}C^{j}$$

In the equation, 'a' and 'j' stand for elasticity of production of labour and capital respectively.

Importance of Cobb-Douglas Production Function

Cobb-Douglas production function is most commonly used function in the field of economics. It graduates data on output and input well. Many economists used it independently. Hence, there are a number of varieties of the Cobb-Douglas form which yield variable elasticity's of production and substitution.It is useful in international or inter- industry comparisons. Cobb-Dougla's research has been a test of the marginal productivity theory of wages (or theory of distribution) as well as descriptions of production technology.

LAWS OF PRODUCTION

Production function shows the relationship between input and output. The law of production shows the relationship between additional input and additional output.

The laws of production consists of:

- Law of Diminishing Returns (to analyse production in the short period), and
- Laws of Returns to Scale (to analyse production in the long period).

LAW OF DIMINISHING RETURNS OR LAW OF VARIABLE PROPORTION

The law of variable proportion is the modern approach to the 'Law of Diminishing Returns (or The Laws of Returns). This law was first explained by Sir. Edward West (French economist). Adam Smith, Ricardo and Malthus (Classical economists) associated this law with agriculture. This law was the foundation of Recardian Theory of Rent and Malthusian theory of population.

The law of variable proportion shows the production function with one input factor variable while keeping the other input factors constant. The law of variable proportion states that, if one factor is used more and more (variable), keeping the other factors constant, the total output will increase at an increasing rate in the beginning and then at a diminishing rate and eventually decreases absolutely.

K. E. Boulding, *"As we increase the quantity of any one input which is combined with a fixed quantity of the other inputs, the marginal physical productivity of the variable input must eventually decline"*. In this law we study the effect of variations in factor proportion on output.

When one factor varies, the others fixed, the proportion between the fixed factor and the variable factor will vary, (*e.g.*, land and capital will be fixed in the short run, while labour will be variable).That is why the law is called the law of variable proportion. The law of variable proportion is also known as the law of proportionality, the law of diminishing returns, law of non-proportional outputs etc.

Table. Illustrates the operations of Law of Variable Proportion.

No. Of workers (Variable Input	Total Product (TP)	Average Product (AP)	Marginal Product (MP)	factor)
1	10	10	10	
2	24	12	14	
3	39	13	15	
4	56	14	17	
5	70	14	14	
6	78	13	8	
7	84	12	6	
8	84	10.58	0	
9	81	9	–3	

In the table we can see that both the average and marginal products increase at first and then decline. Average product is the product for one unit of labour. It is calculated by dividing the total product by the number of workers. Marginal product is the additional product resulting from additional labour. The total product increases at an increasing rate till the employment of the 4th worker. Beyond the 4th worker, the marginal product is diminishing.

The marginal product declines faster than the average product. When 7 workers are employed, the total product is maximum. For 8 workers marginal product is zero and the marginal product of 9 workers is negative. Thus when more and more units labour are combined with other fixed factors, the total product increases first at an increasing rate, then at a diminishing rate and finally it becomes negative. The idea can be more clearly illustrated with the help of a diagram.

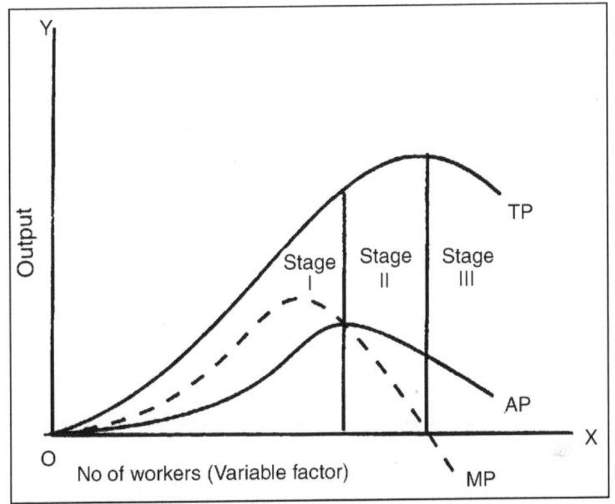

When one input is variable and others are held constant, the relations between the input and the output are divided into three stages.

The law of variable proportion may be explained under the following three stages as shown in the graph:

- *Stage 1*: Total product increases at an increasing rate and this continues till the end of this stage. Average product also increases and reaches its highest point at the end of this stage. Marginal product increases at an increasing rate. Thus TP, AP and MP - all are increasing. Hence this stage is known as stage of increasing return.
- *Stage II*: Total product continues to increase at a diminishing rate until it reaches its maximum point at the end of this stage. Both AP and MP diminish, but are positive. At the end of the second stage, MP becomes zero. MP is zero when the TP is at the maximum. AP shows a steady decline throughout this stage. As both AP and MP decline, this stage is known as stage of diminishing return.
- *Stage III*: In this stage the TP declines. AP shows a steady decline, but never becomes zero. MP becomes negative. It goes below the X axis. Hence the 3rd stage is known as stage of negative return.

Classical economists there were three laws of returns:

1. Law of increasing returns,
2. Law of constant returns, and
3. Law of diminishing returns.

But the modern economists do not accept this. According to them there are not three laws of production but there is only one law of production *i.e.* law of variable proportion. It has three stages.

It is necessary to understand the following terms:

- *Total Product or Total Physical Product (TPP)*: This is the quantity of output a firm obtains in total from a given quantity of input.
- *Average Product or Average Physical Product (APP)*: This is the total physical product (TPP) divided by the quantity of input.
- *Marginal Product or Marginal Physical Product (MPP)*: It is the increase in total output that results from a one unit increase in the input, keeping all other inputs constant.

Assumptions of the Law

The law of variable proportion is valid when the following conditions are fulfilled:

- The technology remains constant. If there is an improvement in the technology, due to inventions, the average and marginal product will increase instead of decreasing.
- Only one input factor is variable and other factor are kept constant.
- All the units of the variable factors are identical. They are of the same size and quality.
- A particular product can be produced under varying proportions of the input combinations.
- The law operates in the short run.

WHY DOES THE LAW OF VARIABLE PROPORTIONS OPERATE

The law of variable proportion operates on account of the following reasons:

- *Imperfect substitutes*: There is a limit to the extent to which one factor can be substituted for another. In other words, two factors are not perfect substitutes. For example, in the construction of building, capital cannot substitute labour fully.
- *Scarcity of the factors of production*: Output can be increased only by increasing the variable factors. In the short run certain input factors like land and capital are scarce. This leads to diminishing marginal productivity of the variable factors.
- *Economies and diseconomies of scale*: The internal and external economies of large scale production are available as production is expanded. Therefore average cost goes on diminishing. But this

continues only up to a certain stage. When the production is expanded beyond a level the diseconomies will start entering into production. Hence the output will come down (or cost will go up).

- *Specialisation*: The stage of diminishing returns comes into operation when the limit to maximum degree of specialisation reaches. This stage emerges when the fixed factor becomes more and more scarce in relation to the variable factor thereby giving less and less support to the latter. As a result of this, the efficiency and productivity of the variable factor diminish.

IMPORTANCE OF THE LAW OF VARIABLE PROPORTION

The law of variable proportion is one of the most fundamental laws of Economics. The law of variable proportion is applicable not only to agriculture but also to other constructive industries like mining, fishing etc. It is applied to secondary or tertiary sectors too. This law helps the management in the process of decision making. The law is a law of life and can be applicable anywhere and everywhere. The applications of this law are as follows:

Basis of Malthusian Theory of Population

Malthus based his theory of population on the law of variable proportion:

- Basis of the Ricardian theory of rent: Ricardo's theory of rent is based on this law.
- Basis of the marginal productivity theory of distribution: The marginal productivity theory of distribution is also based on this law.
- Optimum production: This law can be used to estimate the optimum proportion of the factors for the producer.
- Price determination: This law is also important in the price determination.
- Explanation of disguised unemployment: Less developed countries like India have good deal of disguised unemployment. Many farm workers are in fact surplus. This is called disguised unemployment. The law helps us in explaining the presence of disguised unemployment.

LAWS OF RETURNS TO SCALE

The law of variable proportion analyses the behaviour of output when one input factor is variable and the other factors are held constant. Thus it is a short run analysis. But in the long run all factors are variable. When all factors are changed in same proportion, the behaviour of output is analysed with laws of returns to scale. Thus law of returns to scale is a long run analysis. In the long period, output can be increased by varying all the input Factors this law is concerned, not with the proportions between the factors of production, but with the scale of production. The scale of production of the firm is determined by those input factors which cannot be changed in the short period. The term return to scale means the changes in output as all factors change in the same proportion.The law of returns to scale seeks to analyse the effects of scale on the level of output. If the firm increases the units of both factors labour and capital, its scale of production increases. The return to scale may be increasing, constant or diminishing. We shall now examine these three kinds of returns to scale.

Increasing Returns to Scale

When inputs are increased in a given proportion and output increases in a greater proportion, the returns to scale are said to be increasing. In other words, proportionate increase in all factors of production results in a more than proportionate increase in output It is a case of increasing returns to scale. For example, if the inputs are increased by 40% and output increased by 50%, return to scale are increasing (= >1). It is the first stage of production. If the industry is enjoying increasing returns, then its marginal product increases. As the output expands, marginal costs come down. The price of the product also comes down.

Constant Return to Scale

When inputs are increased in a given proportion and output increases in the same proportion, constant return to scale is said to prevail. For example, if inputs are increased by 40% and output also increases by 40%, the return to scale are said to be constant (= 1). This may be called homogeneous production function of the first degree. In case of constant returns to scale the average output remains constant. Constant returns to scale operate when the economies of the large scale production balance with the diseconomies.

Decreasing Returns to Sale

Decreasing returns to scale is otherwise known as the law of diminishing returns. This is an important law of production. If the firm continues to expand beyond the stage of constant returns, the stage of diminishing returns to scale will start operate. A proportionate increase in all inputs results in less than proportionate increase in output, the returns to scale is said to be decreasing. For example, if inputs are increased by 40%, but output increases by only 30%, (= < 1), it is a case of decreasing return to scale. Decreasing return to scale implies increasing costs to scale.

PRODUCTION FUNCTION WITH TWO VARIABLE INPUTS

So far we have assumed that the firm is increasing output either by using more of one input (in laws of return) or more of all inputs (in laws of returns to scale). Let us now consider the case when the firm is expanding production by using more of two inputs (varying) that are substitutes for each other. A production function with two variable inputs can be represented by isoquants. Isoquant is a combination of two terms, namely, iso and quant. Iso means equal. Quant means quantity. Thus isoquant means equal quantity or equal product. Isoquants are the curves which represent the different combination of inputs producing a particular quantity of output. Any point on the isoquant represents or yields the same level of output. Thus isoquant shows all possible combinations of the two inputs (say labour and capital) capable of producing equal or a given level of output. Isoquants are also known as iso product curves or equal product curves or production indifferent curves. An isoquant may be explained with the following example:

Equal Product Combinations

Combination	Units of labour	Units of Capital	Total Output
A	20	1	1000
B	15	2	1000
C	11	3	1000
D	8	4	1000
E	6	5	1000

In the schedule, there are five possible combinations. All the five combinations yield the same level of output *i.e.* 1000 units. 20 units of labour and 1 unit of capital produce 1000 units. 15 units of labour and 2 units of capital also produce 1000 units and so on. All combination are equally likely because all of them produce the same level of output *i.e.* 1000 units. Now if plot these combination of labour and capital, we shall get a curve. This curve is known as an isoquant. In the below diagram units of capital are measured on horizontal axis and units of labour on vertical axis. The five combinations are known as A, B, C, D and E. After joining these points, we get the iso product curve IQ. Here we assume that the level of technology remains constant. We also assume that the input can be substituted for each other. If quantity of labour is reduced, the quantity of capital must be increased to produce the same output. Thus an isoquant shows various combinations of the two inputs in the existing state of technology which produce the same level of output.

Diminishing Marginal rate of Technical Substitution

As already stated, an important assumption in the isoquant diagram is that the inputs can be substituted for each other. If a unit of labour is reduced, the units of capital must be increased in order to produce the same output. Here we want to know the rate at which one factor is substituted for the other. The term marginal rate of technical substitution refers to the rate at which one factor of production is substituted in place of the other factor, the quantity of output remaining the same. It is the rate at which one input must be substituted for another, in order to keep the same level of output.Thus the marginal rate of technical substitution of capital for labour may be defined the units of labour which can be replaced by one unit of capital; keeping the same level of output. In other words, it is the ratio of small decrease in the amount of labour and a small increase in the amount of capital so as to

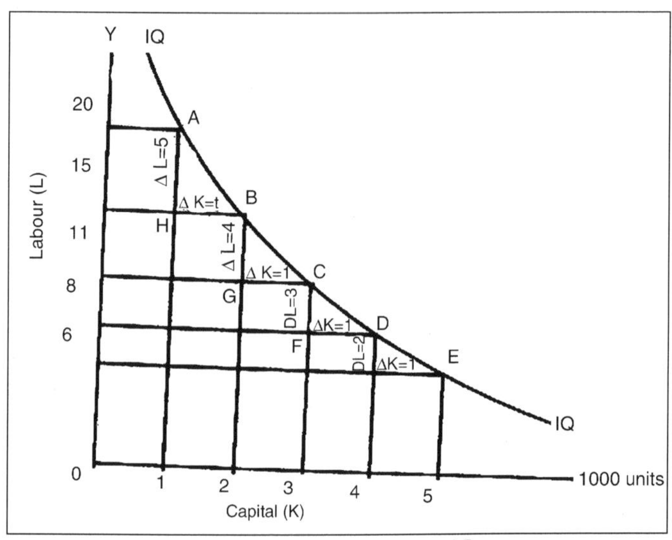

keep the same level of output. The ratio of $\frac{\Delta L}{\Delta K}$ is called the marginal rate of technical substituttion of capital for labour. L refers to changes in the units of labour and K refers to change in the units of capital. In Fig on the 1Q for 1000 units the MRTSKL over AB segment is,

$$\frac{AH}{HB} = \frac{\Delta L}{\Delta K} = \frac{5}{1}$$

Over the segment BC Is,

$$\frac{BG}{GC} = \frac{4}{1}$$

and so on.

In short, the marginal rate of technical substitution of $\frac{DL}{DK}$ measures the slope of the isoquant at a particular point. For example, the slope of the isoquant at point A is

$$\frac{\Delta L}{\Delta K} = \frac{5}{1}$$

where as at B,

$$\frac{\Delta L}{\Delta K} = \frac{4}{1}$$

it is Thus the slope of an isoquant at a point represents marginal rate of technical substitution. It is also important to note that the marginal rate of technical substitution is the ratio of marginal productivity of labour to marginal productivity of capital. As more and more units of capital are substituted to labour, each additional unit of capital contributes less and less output, while when labour is reduced each last unit of labour contributes more and more to output, because inefficient units of capital are coming to production while inefficient units of labour are going out of production.

Marginal productivity of capital will decrease and marginal productivity of labour will increase. Thus when we move from left to right on an isoquant (substituting more capital in place of labour)

$$\frac{MPK}{MPL}$$

diminish.

As more capital is used, marginal productivity of capital will get diminished. At the same time as the unit of labour is reduced, the marginal productivity of labour will increase. Hence the marginal rate of technical substitute of capital for labour diminishes so as to maintain the same quantity. It is shown as follows:

$$MRTS_{KL} = \frac{\Delta L}{\Delta K} = \frac{MPK}{MPL}$$

Isoquant Map or Equal Product Map

An isoquant map consists of a number of isoquants. An isoquant map gives a set of equal product curves which show different production levels. Each isoquant in the map indicates different levels of output. A higher isoquant represents a higher level of output. The distance of an isoquant from the origin shows the relative levels of output. The farther the isoquant from the origin the greater will be the level of output along it. But it should be noted that the distance between two equal product curves does not measure the absolute difference in the volume of output. Isoquant map is shown in the following diagram.

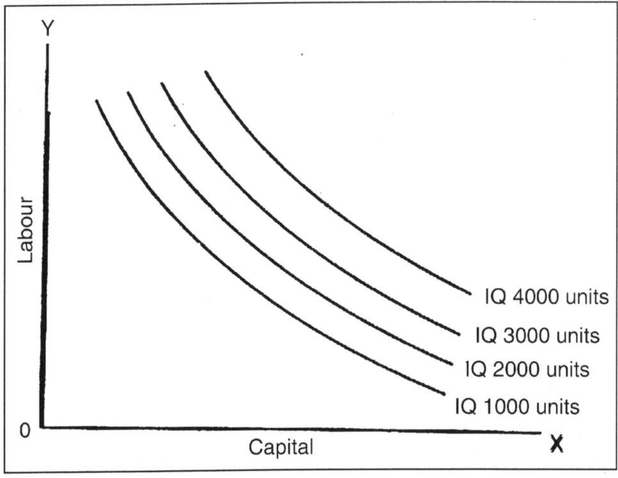

Properties or Features of Isoquant

The following are the important properties of isoquants:

- Isoquant is downward sloping to the right. This means that if more of one factor is used less of the other is needed for producing the same output.
- A higher isoquant represents larger output.
- No isoquants intersect or touch each other. If so it will mean that there will be a common point on the two curves. This further means that same amount of labour and capital can produce the two levels of output which is meaningless. The isoquant as shown in Fig will never exist.

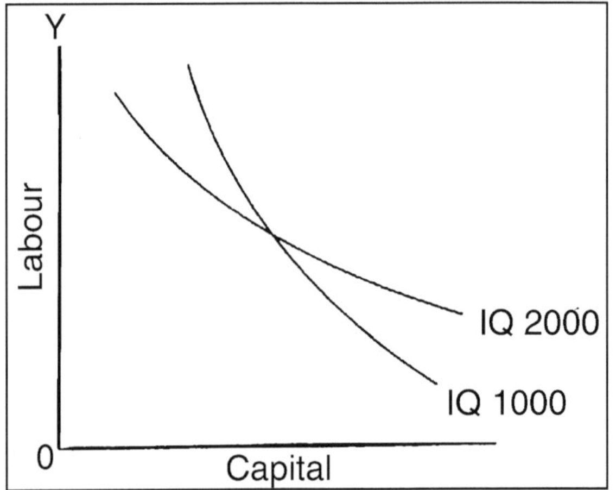

- Isoquants need not be parallel to each other. It so happens because the rate of substitution in different isoquant schedules need not necessarily be equal. Usually they are found different and therefore, isoquants may not be parallel.

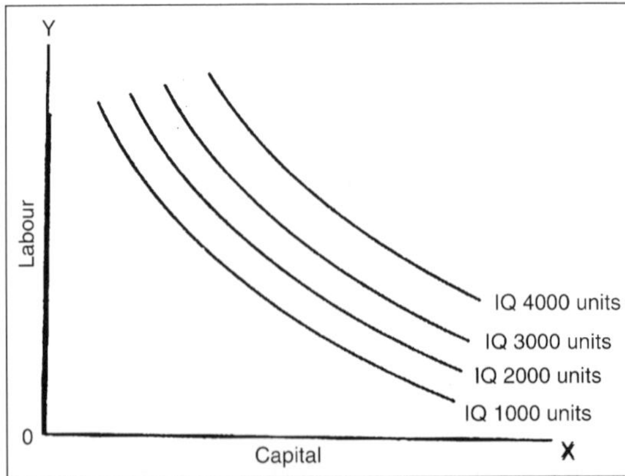

- Isoquant is convex to the origin. This implies that the slope of the isoquant diminishes from left to right along the curve. This is because of the operation of the principle of diminishing marginal rate of technical substitution.

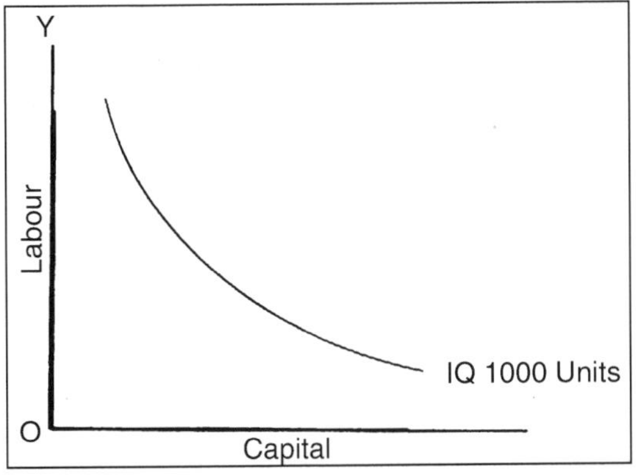

- No isoquant can touch either axis. If an isoquant touches X axis then it would mean that without using any labour the firm can produce output with the help of capital alone. But this is wrong because the firm can produce nothing with OK units of capital alone. If an isoquant touches Y axis, it would mean that without using any capital the firm can produce output with the help of labour alone. This is impossible.
- soquants have negative slope. This is so because when the quantity of one factor (labour) is increased the quantity of other factor (capital) must be reduced, so that total output remains the same. If the marginal productivity of the factor becomes zero the isoquant will bend back and it will have positive slope as shown below.

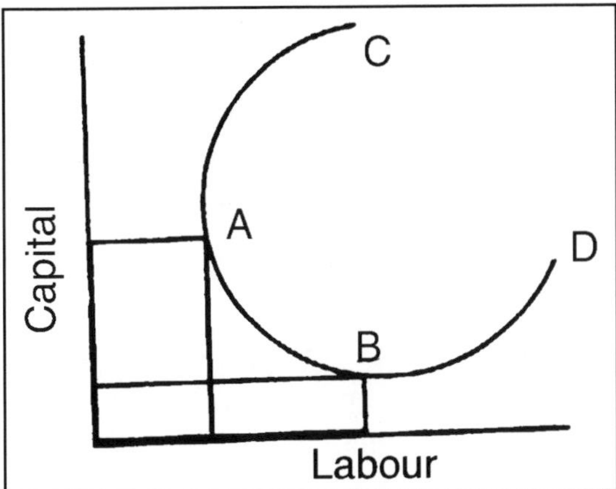

The portions AC and BD of the isoquant have positive slope. If the inputs are perfect substitutes, each isoquant will be a straight line (case a). If the inputs cannot be substituted at all, the isoquants will be right angles (case b). Typical isoquants lie between the extreme cases of straight lines and right angles (case c). Along a curved isoquant, the ability to substitute one input for another varies.

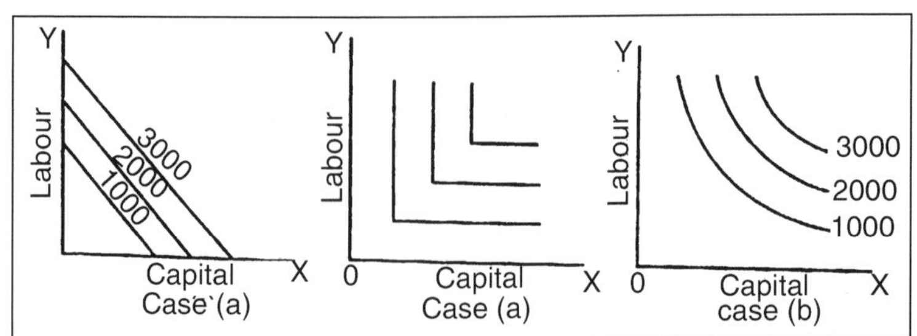

Optimum Input Combination (Least cost Combination or Producer's Equilibrium)

The isoquant shows different combinations of two factors producing the same level of output. However, the producer will not accept all combinations. He wants to maximise his profit. It is possible only by maximising the output at minimum cost. Therefore, he will select the optimum input combination which involves the least cost.

Optimum input combination or least cost combination is that combination which produces maximum output at the minimum cost. In other words, the optimum or least cost combination is that combination where the average cost of production is the minimum. This is the producer's equilibrium. This can be found out by combining the firm's production function and cost function. The production function is represented by isoquant and cost function is represented by iso-cost curve.

The principle of least cost combination is based on the following assumptions:

- Capital and labour are the two factors involved in production.
- All the units of both the factors are homogeneous.
- The prices of the input factors are given.
- The total money outlay is also given.
- There is perfect competition in the factor market.

In order to analyse producer's equilibrium the firm should combine its isoquant and iso-cost line.

Iso-cost Curve

In order to select the optimum quantity of two inputs, the firm has to consider their quantities and their prices. Factors of production are available at a price. Therefore their prices and amount of money which the firm wants to spend has to be taken into consideration. Isocost line represents these two things. An isocost line indicates the different combination of the two factors which the firm can buy at given prices with a given amount of money.

It shows all the combinations of labour and capital that the firm can purchase with a given outlay and at given prices. Thus isocost shows the prices of the two factors and the total amount of money to spend. To make it more clear, let us take an example. Suppose a firm deci to spend ₹5000 on 2 factors - capital and labour. If the weekly wage of a worker is ₹50, the firm can employ 100 workers. Similarly if one unit of capital costs ₹20, the firm buy 250 units of capital. Thus the firm can spend the whole amount of ₹5000 either on labour (100 workers) or on capital (250 units) or partly on labour and partly on capital. The isocost line is shown in the Fig

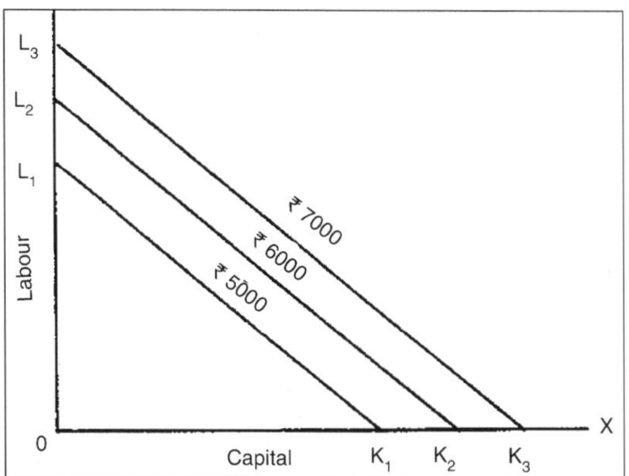

The isocost line L, K, indicates on outlay of ₹5000. With ₹5000 the firm can buy either OL, units of labour or OK., units of capital or any combination of labour and capital between the extremes L(K.. Similarly the isocost line L2 K... shows an outlay of ₹6000 which means that either 120 workers may be employed or 300 units of capital may be bought or some units of both capital and labour. Thus isocost line shows all those combinations of capital and labour which the firm can use with the given amount of money. An isocost curve represents the same cost for all the different combination of input. Isocost line is always a straight line (because the firm has no control over market prices of factors). The slope of the isocost line is determined by the firm's outlay and the price of two factors. It represents the ratio of the price of capital to the price of labour

$$= \frac{\text{Price of capital}}{\text{Price of labour}}$$

If the price of any one of the factors changes, there would be a corresponding change in the slope of the isocost line. If the firm wants to spend more amounts there will be a parallel upward shift in the isocost line. If it wants to spend less, there will be a parallel downward shift in the isocost line.

Selection of the Optimum or Least Cost Combination

The optimum or least cost combination (producer's equilibrium) can be found out with the help of isoquants and isocost lines. A firm's equilibrium will be attained at a point where the isoquant touches the isocost line. This may be explained with the help of the following diagram.

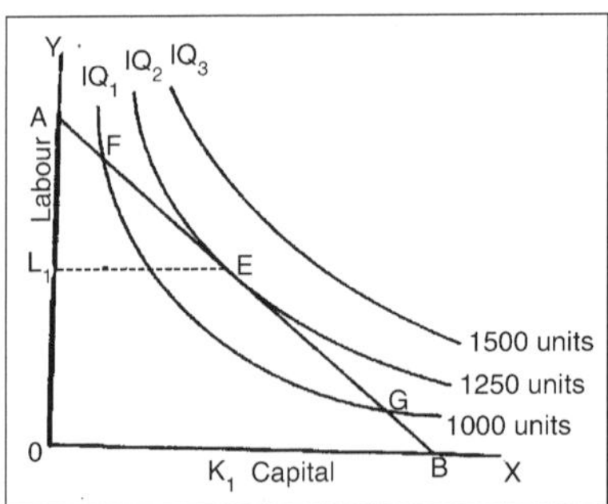

Equal product curves (IQ1,IQ2, and IQ3), represent output of 1000 units, 1250 units and 1500 units respectively. AB is the isocost line representing the outlay of ₹ 5000. At point E the isocost line AB is tangent to isoquant IQ2, representing 1250 units. The Isocost curve and Isoquant curve are equal at this point. Therefore combination of L1, labour K1, capital is the least cost combination to produce the output of 1250 units. F and G are not least cost combination because they lie on the lower isoquant curve indicating lesser output of 1000 units. Cost will be minimum at point E because it is at this point the Isocost line AB is tangent to Isoquant IQ2.

The firm is in equilibrium at point E. At E the average cost is ₹4 (5000/1250). At an output of 1000 units the average cost would be ₹5 (5000/1000). He cannot produce an output of 1500 units because he has only ₹5000 with him to spend. The combination at point E is thus the least cost combination. This combination will give maximum output at minimum cost. At the point E the slope of isoquant is equal to the slope of isocost line. The ratio between the prices of capital and labour and the MRTS are equal.

$$MRTS_{KL} = \frac{Price\ of\ capital}{Price\ of\ labour}$$

Capital is substituted for labour.

$$\text{Slope of isocost line} = \frac{Price\ of\ capital}{Price\ of\ labour}$$

This is the point of optimum input combination

$$MRTS_{KL} = \text{Slope of the isocost line} = \frac{Price\ of\ capital}{Price\ of\ labour}$$

The equality between the MRTS between price of capital and labour to the price ratio gives maximum output at minimum cost.

ECONOMIES OF SCALE

In the long run when scale of production is increased firm gets economies of scale up to a point. The term “economies” refers to cost advantage.

Economies of scale refer to advantages of large scale production. Marshall has classified economies of scale into two-internal economies and external economies. Diseconomies are the disadvantages which a faces when the scale of production is expanded beyond a certain level diseconomies may be of two types- internal and external diseconomies.

INTERNAL ECONOMIES AND DISECONOMIES

We saw that returns to scale increase in the initial stages and after remaining constant for a while, they decrease. The question arises as to why we get increasing returns to scale due to which cost falls and why after a certain point we get decreasing returns to scale due to which cost rises. The answer is that initially a firm enjoys internal economies of scale and beyond a certain limit it suffers from internal diseconomies of scale. Internal economies and diseconomies are of following main kinds:

Technical Economies and Diseconomies

Large-scale production is associated with technical economies. As the firm increases its scale of operations, it becomes possible to use more specialised and efficient form of all factors, specially capital equipment and machinery. For producing higher levels of output, there is generally available a more efficient machinery which when employed to produce a large output yields a lower cost per unit of output. Secondly, when the scale of production is increased and the amount of labour and other factors become larger, introduction of a greater degree of division of labour or specialisation becomes possible and as a result cost per unit declines.

However, beyond a certain point a firm experiences net diseconomies of scale. This happens because when the firm has reached a size large enough to allow utilisation of almost all the possibilities of division of labour and the employment of more efficient machinery, further increase in the size of the plant will bring high long-run cost because of difficulties of management. When the scale of operations becomes too large, it becomes difficult for the management to exercise control and to bring about proper coordination.

Managerial Economies and Diseconomies

Managerial economies refer to reduction in managerial cost. When output increases, division of labour can be applied to management. The production manager can look after production, sales manager can look after sales, finance manager can look after finance department. If scale of production increases further, each department can be further sub-divided for *e.g.* sales can be split into parts for advertising exports and customer service. Since individual activities come under the supervision of specialists, management's efficiency and productivity greatly improve.

Decentralisation of decision making authority also becomes possible in such a firm which enhances further the efficiency and productivity of managers. Thus specialisation of management enables large firms to achieve reduction in managerial costs. However, as scale of production increases beyond a certain limit, managerial diseconomies set in. Management finds it difficult to exercise control and bring coordination among various departments. The managerial structure becomes more complex and is affected by more bureaucracy, more red tape, lengthening of communication lines and so on. All these affect the efficiency and productivity of management and the firm itself.

Commercial Economies and Diseconomies

Production of big volumes of goods requires large amount of material and components. This enables the firm to place a bulk order for materials and components and enjoy lower prices for them. Economies can also be achieved in selling the product. If the sales staff is not being worked to capacity, additional output can be sold at little extra cost. Moreover, large firms can benefit from economies of advertising. As scale of production increases, advertising costs per unit of output fall. In addition, a large firm may also be able to sell its by-products-something which might be unprofitable for a small firm. These economies become diseconomies after an optimum scale. For example, advertisement expenditure and other marketing overheads will increase more than proportionately after the optimum scale.

Financial Economies and Diseconomies

In raising finance for expansion large firm is in favorable position. It can, for instance, offer better security to bankers and, because it is well-known, raise money at lower cost, since investors have confidence in it and prefer shares which can be readily sold on the stock exchange. However, these financial costs will rise more proportionately after the optimum scale of production. This may happen because of relatively more dependence on external finances.

Risk Bearing Economies and Diseconomies

It is said that a large business with diverse and multi-production capability is in a better position to withstand economic ups and downs, and therefore, enjoys economies of risk bearing. However, risk may increase if diversification instead of giving a cover to economic disturbances increases these.

EXTERNAL ECONOMIES AND DISECONOMIES

The use of greater degree of division of labour and specialised machinery at higher levels of output are termed as internal economies. They are internal in the sense that they accrue to the firm due to its own efforts. Besides internal economies, there are external economies which are very important for a firm.

External economies and diseconomies are those economies and diseconomies which accrue to firms as a result of expansion in the output of whole industry and they are not dependent on the output level of individual firms. They are external in the sense they accrue to firms not out of their internal situation but from outside *i.e.* expansion of the industry. These are available to one or more of the firms in the form of:

Cheaper raw Materials and Capital Equipment

The expansion of an industry may result in exploration of new and cheaper sources of raw material, machinery and other types of capital equipment. Expansion of an industry results in greater demand for the various kinds of materials and capital equipment required by it. This makes it possible to purchase on a large scale from other industries. This reduces their cost of production and hence their prices. Thus, firms using these materials and capital equipment will be able to get them at a lower price.

Technological External Economies

When the whole industry expands, it may result in the discovery of new technical knowledge and in accordance with that the use of improved and better machinery than before. This will change the technical co-efficient of production and will enhance productivity of firms in the industry and reduce their cost of production.

Development of Skilled Labour

When an industry expands in an area the labour in that area is well accustomed to do the various productive processes and learns a good deal from the experience. As a result, with the growth of an industry in an area a pool of trained labour is developed which has a favorable effect on the level of productivity and cost of the firms in that industry.

Growth of Ancillary Industries

With the growth of an industry, a number of ancillary industries may specialise in production of raw materials, tools and machinery etc. They can provide them at a lower price to the main industry. Likewise, some firms may get developed processing the waste products of the industry and making out some useful product out of it. This will tend to reduce the cost of production in general.

Better Transportation and Marketing Facilities

The expansion of an industry resulting from entry of new firms may make possible the development of transportation and marketing network to a great extent which will greatly reduce cost of production of the firms. Similarly, communication system may get modernised resulting in better and speedy information. However, external economies may also cease if there are certain disadvantages which may neutralise the advantages of the expansion of an industry. We call them external diseconomies.

DETERMINANTS OF AGRICULTURAL PRODUCTION

Climate is one of the main determinants of agricultural production Through out the world there is significant concern about the effects of climate change and its variability on agricultural production. Researchers and administrators are concerned with the potential damages and benefits that may arise in future from climate change impacts on agriculture, since these will affect domestic and international policies, trading pattern, resource use, and food security. The researchers are of the opinion that while crops would respond favourably to elevated CO2 in the absence of climate change, the associated impacts of high temperatures, changed pattern of precipitation and possibly increased frequency of extreme events such as drought and floods, would possibly combine to reduce yields and increase risks in agricultural production in several parts of the globe. In India agricultural production is often determined by the whims of nature. The climate Marginal and Small Farms change is expected to result in higher temperatures and rainfall. The higher expected temperature might lower the yields. However, at the same time, higher rainfall could enhance growing period of crops. Also the higher concentration of CO2 in the atmosphere under changed climatic conditions might act as aerial fertilizer and enhance crop yields.

All these factors have to be taken in to consideration while examining the climate change impact on agriculture. During the 1990s, researchers repeatedly claimed that global warming would have dire consequences for key crops. Professor Richer Adams, an agricultural economist says, "If you just take an agronomic model and make conditions hotter and drier, then, yes, crop yields go down." " But if you are a farmer, you see your crops aren't doing so well and plant a more resistant type. In India, climate change is expected to make an impact in agriculture, resulting in lower yields of crops. The objectives of this chapter are to examine the effect of fertilizer and labour inputs on crop productivity and to investigate the impact of climatic variables such as rainfall and temperature on crop production.Climate response functions have been estimated, using regression model by incorporating weather variables, in order to examine the impact of climate change on productivity of two crops. The impact of weather variables has been examined and the study is confined to two states.

METHODOLOGY

In a study Kaufmann R. K. and Seth E Snell (1997) had specified yield as a linear function of purchased inputs. For the purpose of analysis seed, fertilizer and labour inputs were considered in the regression model as explanatory variables and yield as the dependent variable. However, crop yield is affected not only by these purchased inputs but also by climatic variables and social factors. This integration allows complementing the earlier methodologies, which concentrate only on the purchased inputs and thereby, allows to better evaluating the adaptation strategy to climate change. The results show that climatic variables account for 19% of the yield change while the social variables account for 74% of the yield change.

Kavi Kumar and Parikh (2001) has also established a functional relationship between farm level net revenue and climatic variables, with a view to estimate the climate sensitivity of crop production in Indian agriculture. To assess the impact of climate related variables and agricultural production in India, the present study has been undertaken. For this purpose, two crops *viz.* Rice and Jowar have been selected. These two crops are predominantly grown in monsoon season and any change in climate, particularly rainfall and temperature would effect the productivity of these crops significantly. In the present chapter an econometric bio-model of crop production has been attempted. Agricultural production depends on not only climate related variables, but also on use of several factors like fertilizer, labour and other resources. For the purpose of present study, the following model has been used:

Y= f (F, HL, AR, NR, DFNR, MAXTEMP, MINTEMP)

Where,

Y= Crop yield on per hectare basis

F = Fertilizer used/ha.

HL = Human labour in hours/ha.

AR = Actual Rainfall (mm)

NR = Normal Rainfall (mm)

DFNR = Deviation from normal rainfall (mm. or %)

MAXTEMP = Mean maximum temperature during crop season (0C)

MINTEMP = Mean minimum temperature during crop season (0C)

The model was estimated for Rice and Jowar crops. The analysis was undertaken for the country as a whole, using state wise data for both these crops. The study was also undertaken using district wise data as well. For Rice crop, the state of Orissa has been selected, because this is the main crop of the state. For Jowar, the state of Karnataka has been selected, because of it's significance in the region. Data on different variables for various states has been collected from the publications of Directorate of Economics and Statistics, Ministry of Agriculture, as well as from the Economics and Statistics Directorates of various states.

Similarly district-wise data has been primarily collected from the publications of these two state govts. Least square technique has been used to estimate different regression equations for the country as a whole as well as for both the states. Several forms of equations were analysed and results were computed. The analysis was done under usual assumptions. It has been hypothesized that productivity of the selected crops is positively influenced by the application of chemical fertilizers and human labour. These two are the main purchased inputs in the production of these crops. Climate, in the present model, has been approximated by rainfall – actual, normal as well as deviation from the normal. Other variables representing the climatic factors are mean maximum and mean minimum temperature in crop growing period. This has been further hypothesized that extreme variations in these variables such as excessive rain or scanty rain and very high or low temperature would adversely affect the crop productivity in the selected states and districts for the selected crops.

Results and Discussion

In order to study the impact of climate change on productivity, regression equations were estimated using the model and data stipulated in the methodology. As already mentioned, earlier various forms of functions were estimated and out of these, linear form provided the best fit and therefore, only linear regression equations have been presented for Rice and Jowar crops for the country as well as both the selected states. For rice productivity and climate, using state-wise data for the country as a whole. Variable pertaining to fertilizer use, human labour, actual rainfall and temperature pertains to year 2000-01, whereas normal temperature consists of observations from a period of 30 years. Variation in the productivity of Rice. This implies that productivity of Rice on per hectare basis is influenced by these variables. Moreover, the fertilizer use variable had a highly significant coefficient, suggesting a significant impact of fertilizer use on productivity.

Surprisingly, the variables pertaining to actual rainfall and maximum temperature, during the growing period of the crop, had negative coefficient, implying that these two variables had negative impact on productivity. The mean minimum temperature had a statistically significant and positive coefficient, implying that this variable would effect the productivity of Rice positively.

Estimated regression equations for Rice crop and climate related variables, using data from various districts of Orissa state. Similar to the earlier analysis, results pertaining to the linear regression have been presented.

The results indicate that the variable of fertilizer use, normal rainfall, minimum and maximum temperature could explain 28% of variation in Rice yield. When actual rainfall variable was replaced by the deviation in the rainfall from the normal, the value of R2 dropped down to 7 percent, implying that the actual rainfall had better explanatory power, than that of deviation in rainfall from normal. Results also indicated that mean maximum and minimum temperature could explain a larger part of variation in the Rice yield. Maximum temperature had a negative coefficient. It has implication that the increasing temperature would effect the productivity of Rice negatively, in the state.

The results indicated that the use of fertilizer variable has a negative impact on Jowar productivity, which is not correct on theoretical grounds. However, the human labour variable has a positive and statistically significant impact on Jowar productivity. The deviation from normal rainfall had negative impact on productivity. This implies that rainfall contributes significantly in raising productivity of Jowar, which is normally a rainfed crop. The mean maximum temperature, during the growing season of the crop had a negative implication for the crop, while the minimum temperature, during the same period, would effect the crop productivity positively. The R2 in all five selected equations are good and it's value ranges between 40% to 52%.

The rainfall during the crop growth period has also negative coefficient. Whereas mean maximum temperature will effect the crop positively. The results indicate that the effect of climate related variables have mixed effects on productivity of Jowar, as rainfall shows negative impact, while maximum temperature has a positive effect. However, for understanding the real effect of these variables on productivity of Jowar crop, a detailed study is required.

Climate plays an important role in shaping agricultural production in India. Lack of irrigation makes agriculture a gamble with nature. The effects of climatic variability is quite visible in case of majority of farmers who are marginal and small and lack resources required for adjustment for climatic variations. The present study covers rice and jowar crops for the country as a whole as well as for the states of Orissa and Karnataka.

The study reveals that excessive rains and extreme variation in temperature would affect the productivity of these crops adversely thereby affecting the incomes of farming families in a negative manner. Thus suitable strategies pertaining to resource use, planting flood and drought resistant varieties of crops, better irrigation networks, and crop mix are to be adopted for mitigating the harmful effects of climatic changes.

CLUSTER VILLAGE PLANTATION: EMERGENCE OF SMALL-SCALE TEA CULTIVATION

With the emergence of small-scale tea cultivation, the nature of technological requirement has changed tremendously. The demand for efficient plant type, improved crop management practices and post-harvest technology would grow substantially in due course of time. This would require concerted effort in terms of private-public interface on R&D including the promotion of delivery system. The prestigious corporate bodies should invest more on effective demand-driven R&D on these crops. The limitation of the plantation crops is that processing is time-demanding and urgent. The harvest must be processed into marketable forms within a specified time to preserve the quality.

Thus growth of plantation sector must be tagged with the establishment of processing facilities including marketing network and infrastructure. These units have to be centrally located around the large number of small plantation units and managed by the stakeholder groups.

Since the processing units are capital as well as skill intensive, it is inaccessible to the small farmers. The cluster village approach and the farmers' cooperative management system could be a viable proposition. Studies show that only 2.5 per cent small farmers received institutional financial support, which needs to be enhanced for the betterment of the sector. This requires appropriate intervention and public sector support.

Marketing is the most critical deficiency in the region particularly for the consumer products like tea. The existing private participation in marketing is exploitative and public interventions weak. As the access to processing facilities is limited within the producer's proximity, the small producers have to transport the green leaves at least 6-8 hours by road, which causes quality deterioration. The public sector marketing infrastructure is almost nonexistent in case of coffee encouraging the middlemen to snatch the lion's share of the produce. In case of rubber, the Rubber Board is now trying to establish the market network. The long gestation period of the plantation crops locks up the initial investment till the commencement of the economic yield. Shorter gestation varieties are required to help quick recovery of returns to investment and attract more producers. In addition, the scarcity of plantation material even for the existing technology is also severe. The adequate supply of suitable planting material for the diverse agro-climatic is a major challenge. Transportation facility is a hurdle to plantation crops in the region. Perhaps properly, managed transport subsidy for these products could be planned.

The strategy of Build, Operate and Transfer (BOT) of the processing facility and other infrastructure for plantation crops is needed in the public sector particularly to help the small-scale sector. Hilly areas need special consideration in the regard.

Research Needs

The identification of proper cropping system for plantation crops requires more research initiatives. The companion crops along with plantation crops as base crop, must have varying morphological frame and rooting habit for minimum competition for space, light, moisture and nutrients. Further, the selection of host crops is crucial or else it attracts pests and diseases. The promotional activity in the sector should take cognizance of local needs, knowledge network, agroclimatic condition and market facilities in a multipronged manner. Plantation crops are highly income generating if managed properly. The cultivation of these crops was traditionally limited to corporate sector. The corporate revenue however, did not percolate down to the benefit of the society. Although, the region occupies a strategic position as the highest producer of tea in the country, the social gains due to the corporate agriculture is negligible. The changes are taking place in the recent years, resulting in the emergence of small-scale cultivation of tea.

Fig. Small scaleTea Farm

The implication of this development on the farm income has been significant. There are, of course, several inherent problems of small-scale cultivation of plantation crops like capital lock up due to long gestation period, capital intensive nature of production system, processing and marketing problems. The solution to these multidimensional problems requires effective state intervention. The farmers also face the problems such as quality deterioration of green leaves due to delay in processing and locational disadvantage of tea processing units. The capital infrastructure facilities such as processing units need to be located in the site around the cluster of smaller plantations and the production management by the cooperatives of the user groups. A cluster of village model may be encouraged to grow particular type of plantation crops, viz, tea, coffee or rubber so that processing can be done in the central processing units. The location of the central unit should accompanied by the infrastructure facilities like electricity, water, road and marketing network. The ancillary infrastructure such as regular supply of raw materials, inputs, agro-chemicals and other requirements must be available. In view of existence of customary laws and property ownership rights prevailing in the tribal societies, such a socially acceptable arrangement could substantially benefit the hill states.

PLANTATION CROPS IN NORTH EASTERN INDIA: CONSTRAINTS AND STRATEGIES

Plantation crops are high-value crops of great economic importance and provide huge employment opportunity, specially to the women throughout the year. The subcortical climate of Northeastern India is extremely favourable to the cultivation of many plantation crops. Among the three important crops viz, tea, coffee and rubber, tea was introduced in Assam and Tripura as an industrial crop during the middle of nineteenth century, which has spread to other non-traditional states in the region in recent years. Suitable land and climatic conditions provide favourable environment for tea, coffee and rubber plantation in Arunachal Pradesh, Manipur, Meghalaya, Mizoram and Nagaland, but it is not fully exploited. At present 3.33 lakh ha area are under these crops in the region, which is a major source of revenue to the economy of the states. The data reveal that out of 14.6 per cent total geographical area under cultivation in the region, the plantation crops cover only 8.97 per cent, of which tea alone covers 7.5 per cent (2.79 lakh ha), rubber 1.20 per cent (4419 ha) and coffee only 0.27 per cent (10.1 thousand ha). The share of tea is the largest, covering 85 per cent of area under plantation crops. Historically, the cultivation of tea being a corporate activity, the involvement of common farmers was totally absent in the past, but in the changing environment, a marginal presence is seen with a total area of 40.0 thousand ha in the small-scale sector. The development of this emerging phenomenon of small-scale tea cultivation in Assam attracted the non-traditional states to introduce it as cash crop among the small farmers.

Assam is the largest producer of tea in India (about 53 per cent of total production). Its share in the region is about 96.8 per cent of area and 98 per cent of production. The productivity of tea is about 1850 kilograms per ha. Coffee was introduced in NE states during 1960s. The implementation of the scheme of expansion of subsidy of Coffee Board Of India in 1979-80 has helped in increasing its area. The Assam Plantation Crops Development Corporation took initiatives to establish coffee and rubber plantation in the North Cachar and Karbi Anglong districts. Presently, the NE states have a modest coverage of about 10.1 thousand ha of coffee plantation and 44.7 thousand ha of rubber plantation. The cultivation of coffee and rubber helps checking soil degradation in the hill slopes.

Rubber occupies 44.72 thousand ha in NE India, which is about 8 per cent of the total area at the all India level and produces 2.28 per cent of total rubber production in the country. Though the entry of this crop started on experimental basis during 1950s, but gained momentum only after 1985 through the project "Accelerated Development of Rubber Plantation". Presently Tripura alone grows 25.38 thousand ha of rubber, which is 56.7 per cent of the total rubber area in the region.

Plantation Crop Based Farming System

The monoculture in small holdings is a nightmare during the year of slump and epidemic of pest and diseases. Raising more than one crops alongwith a particular plantation crop not only reduce the gestation period but also ensure steady and higher farm income even in the period of slump. Seasonal crops like vegetables in the formative years of the plantation crops and permanent crops like orange, arecanut, agar, tree beans, black pepper, gooseberry etc. could be grown in the matured plantation to augment productivity and profitability. Intercropping also stands as insurance against crop failure and price slump.

Premium Organic Farming

The organically, grown products have been gaining popularity worldwide and fetching premium price both at the domestic as well as international market. Since the virgin soil in the hill areas is favourable for tea cultivation, the natural production condition in the NE India could be highly gainful in the production of user-friendly tea. On account of high amount of organic matter and other plant nutrients in these soils, the plantation crops can be grown organically with minimum of agro-chemicals. The strategy to produce organic tea and popularize among the consumers would pay high dividend. Such innovation in value-addition of tea is potentially economically remunerative and helps conserve the precious soil and water resource.

Constraints

The cultivation of these plantation crops in the region has been traditionally a corporate activity. The production system is also highly knowledge intensive and scale biased. Therefore, the expansion of small-scale tea in the recent period confronts number of constraints including lack of information and extension services, timely supply of processing facilities and lack of required knowledge of agronomic practices. Inadequate training infrastructure to prepare the required skills among the farmers is also a reason for slow growth. Thus, the early stage of transition in the plantation economy requires effective planning strategies.

The post-harvest management in plantation crops is very crucial. The green leaves require quick processing facility and then necessary market facilities must follow, or else there could be total loss of production due to quality deterioration. Perfect knowledge is essential in every stage of the production of tea; viz, production, harvesting, processing and marketing. Hence information technology becomes crucial. Capital requirement is particularly very high in the initial period.

The common farmers find it difficult to invest the high amount without adequate institutional financial assistance, which is essential for the promotion of small-scale tea cultivation. In recent years, Tea, Coffee and Rubber Boards have introduced a number of schemes to promote the crops under small sector. NABARD also assists the tea growers. But indepth studies on the subject is severely lacking. It makes the information system on the knowledge on financial requirement, availability of credit and other constraints extremely scarce.

There is vast scope for expansion of tea, coffee and rubber in the region. Adequate policy support is needed to intensify small-scale cultivation of these crops in suitable areas. The production of tea could be enhanced if certain management practices are improved. The commodity boards such as Tea, Coffee and Rubber Boards have already taken various schemes to popularize respective crops in the region. More promotional schemes are essential as majority of the existing large tea gardens in Assam have crossed the economic age and some are over 70-80 years old. As a result, this has caused steep shortfall in production of tea. Thus scheme of replacing the older trees and replanting or expansion planting should be implemented. If the system is modernized and adequate technological changes are brought about, the sector could enhance the export earnings substantially.

COST OF CULTIVATION OF PRINCIPAL CROPS

In order to pursue its price support policy, the Government of India announces from time to time, the minimum support prices of principal crops. This necessitates the availability of relevant data on the cost of production of the crops concerned. To meet this requirement, a comprehensive survey of the Cost of Cultivation of Principal Crops was initiated in 1970-71. The survey is in operation in 16 States and covers 29 crops, the number and choice of crops in each State depending upon their importance to the State.

The Directorate of Economics and Statistics, Ministry of Agriculture (DESMOA) has the overall charge of implementing the survey programme through the Agricultural Universities in 13 States and general universities in three States by providing them cent per cent financial assistance. The survey design followed is that of three-stage stratified random sampling with the *tehsil or taluka* as the first stage unit, a cluster of villages as the second stage unit and an operational holding as the third and ultimate stage unit. The fieldwork consists of collecting from each sample household through the cost accounting method, data on all aspects of cultivation (inputs, outputs, prices paid and received) by keeping a detailed record on a day-to-day basis. The universities engage full time field men for this purpose. Training to the field staff is imparted by the universities and whenever necessary, supplemented by the DESMOA. The Cost of Cultivation Studies are primarily intended for use by the Commission for Agricultural Costs and Prices (CACP). In addition, these data are used by the Central Statistical Organisation, Planning Commission, other Economic Ministries of Government of India as well as research organisations.

Deficiencies

It is reported that the data collected and processed under the scheme do not suffer from any serious deficiencies, and the only problem is shortage of manpower in the Central Analytical Unit of DESMOA, which results in delay in the availability of final results. This is, however, far from true. The CACP does not obtain timely and sufficient inputs from these studies, which are required in the fixing of the minimum prices. The requirements of the National Accounts Division of CSO are also not met adequately. Implementation of the scheme by the Agricultural Universities is reported to be unsatisfactory. The data entry and processing still make use of a DOS-based computer package called FARMAP provided by Food and Agricultural Organisation (FAO) and no updating of the package has been undertaken. There has been no report on the results of the scheme until recently. (The DESMOA has now brought out a consolidated report.)

Cost of cultivation studies should continue in view of their importance in price administration of agricultural commodities and several studies relating to farm economy. Irrespective of the agency that is assigned this work, there should be a more focused attention to proper organisation and management of the studies. It is necessary to have an early review of the number of centres, methodology, sample size, the existing schedule and questionnaire, etc.

The universities should be encouraged to tabulate and analyse the data for which they should be provided the necessary support. The DESMOA should endeavour to release the survey results with least possible delay, and any strengthening needed for improving the performance of the scheme should be immediately provided.

The Commission recommends that:

- In view of the importance of the Cost of Cultivation Studies in the price administration of agricultural commodities and several studies relating to farm economy, the present programme should continue.
- Focused attention should be paid to the proper organisation and management of the Cost of Cultivation Studies.
- A review of the number of centres, methodology, sample size, the existing schedule and questionnaire, etc. of the Cost of Cultivation Studies should be undertaken.
- The Directorate of Economics and Statistics, Ministry of Agriculture (DESMOA) should minimise the delay in bringing out the results of the Cost of Cultivation Studies.

PRODUCTION OF HORTICULTURAL CROPS

There are two main sources that generate statistics of production of horticultural crops. The first is the Directorate of Economics and Statistics, Ministry of Agriculture (DESMOA), which operates a Centrally sponsored scheme "Crop Estimation Survey on Fruits and Vegetables" in 11 States covering 7 fruit and 7 vegetable and spice crops for estimating area and production. The fruit crops covered are mango, banana, apple, citrus, grapes, pineapple and guava. The vegetable and spice crops are potato, onion, tomato, cabbage, cauliflower, ginger and turmeric. The survey, which is still in a "pilot" stage follows a stratified three-stage random sampling design in the case of fruit crops, with village, orchard and fruit bearing tree as the sampling units at the successive stages. The sample size is usually 150 tó 200 sample villages in each major fruit-growing district, five orchards per sample village and four fruit bearing trees per orchard. The number and weight of fruits gathered from the sampled trees is observed and recorded, which form the basis for yield estimation. The survey approach in the case of vegetable crops is somewhat more complex due to special features of cultivation of these crops especially the short duration of the crop and the number of pickings required to record the harvested produce.

Fig. Horticulture Produce and Health

The second source of horticultural statistics is the National Horticultural Board (NHB), which compiles and publishes estimates of area, production and prices of all important fruit and vegetable crops based on reports furnished by the State Directorates of Horticulture and Agriculture. The methodology followed by NHB for estimating area and production has not been clearly spelt out. These estimates are apparently based on the informed assessment of local level officials dealing with horticulture and the reports of market arrivals in major wholesale fruit and vegetable markets.

The production estimates of fruits and vegetables available from the DESMOA pilot survey are based on sound technical methodology. However, the survey procedures are complex, time consuming and rather difficult to implement in practice. Further, the survey is limited to 11 States and its extension to the remaining States will take a long time due to the fact that many of them do not possess the necessary staff resources to carry out the fieldwork. Adoption of this methodology on a nationwide scale is a remote possibility. The estimates furnished by the NHB relate to the entire country but they are of doubtful reliability being essentially based on subjective reports received from the ground-level staff. There is, in fact, considerable divergence between the NHB and the DESMOA estimates for the States and the crops covered. Neither NHB nor DESMOA provide estimates of production of crops such as mushroom, herbs and floriculture that are of emerging commercial importance.

The methodology used in the DESMOA survey for estimation of production is complex, time consuming and not cost-effective. It is observed that the field staff does not always follow the procedures laid down for collection of data. It is obvious that an alternative and more feasible methodology needs to be developed for estimating production of horticultural crops. Such an approach may consider the possibility of using the flow of data from sources concerned with horticultural crops such as wholesale markets, growers associations, fruit and vegetable processing plants, export trade, etc. in order to develop a suitable model for estimation. Special studies need to be carried out in this connection, which may be entrusted to a team comprising representatives of the Indian Agricultural Statistics Research Institute (IASRI), DESMOA, NSSO (FOD) and one or two major States growing horticultural crops.

The Commission recommends that:

- The methodology adopted in the pilot scheme of "Crop Estimation Survey on Fruits and Vegetables" should be reviewed and an alternative methodology for estimating the production of horticultural crops should be developed taking into account information flowing from all sources including market arrivals, exports and growers associations. Special studies required to establish the feasibility of such a methodology should be taken up by a team comprising representatives from Indian Agricultural Statistics Research Institute (IASRI), Directorate of Economics and Statistics, Ministry of Agriculture (DESMOA), Field Operations Division of National Sample Survey Organisation (NSSO (FOD)) and from one or two major States growing horticultural crops. The alternative methodology should be tried out on a pilot basis before actually implementing it on a large scale.
- A suitable methodology for estimating the production of crops such as mushroom, herbs and floriculture needs to be developed and this should be entrusted to the expert team comprising representatives from Indian Agricultural Statistics Research Institute (IASRI), Directorate of Economics and Statistics, Ministry of Agriculture (DESMOA), Field Operations Division of National Sample Survey Organisation (NSSO (FOD)) and from one or two major States growing these crops.

Official vs. Trade Estimates of Production

Apart from the estimates of production compiled and published by the DESMOA, a separate series is also available for some major commercially important crops prepared by the trade organisations especially for cotton and oilseed crops. The estimates of cotton production are published by the Cotton Advisory Board (CAB) and those for the oilseeds by the Central Organisation for Oil Industry and Trade (COOIT).

The DESMOA and Trade series differ widely from each other causing confusion among users and debate over the veracity of either series. The Commission examined in some detail the divergence between the two series and its findings are as follows:

Cotton

The DESMOA compiles the production estimates on the basis of reports received from State Governments. These are obtained as the product of area sown under the crop through complete enumeration and the yield rate from crop cutting experiments. The CAB estimates are based on inputs from the Cotton Corporation of India, East India Cotton Association, Indian Cotton Mills Federation, etc. and these, in turn, depend on data on market arrivals, volume of cotton ginned and pressed in all ginning mills irrespective of the area sown or condition of the crop.

The two series of estimates differ from each other within a range of 13 to 45 per cent over the years, the DESMOA estimates being consistently less than the CAB estimates. The main reasons for divergence are seen to be:

- Shortcomings of the *girdawari* on which the official estimate of area is based and the inadequacy of the GCES to give due representation and weight in its sample to different factors such as irrigated and un-irrigated, hybrid and local varieties of crop. Cotton is harvested through several pickings spread over time and it is possible that the primary agency is not careful to follow the prescribed procedure of the crop cutting experiments;
- The CAB estimates on the other hand, are of a subjective nature being compiled on the basis of reports from several agencies without proper attention to full coverage and standard procedures.

The DESMOA has been making consistent efforts to reduce the divergence between the two estimates by holding discussions with the concerned agencies. The following measures are suggested in this connection:

- The sample of crop cutting experiments may be suitably increased and made representative of various types of cotton cultivation;
- The primary agencies responsible for area enumeration and crop cutting experiments should be trained thoroughly;
- The methodology followed by CAB should be improved by a careful review of the data from sources like market arrivals, ginning factories, Annual Survey of Industries (ASI), unorganised

manufacturing units, etc. in respect of cotton and the use of appropriate models.

Oilseeds

The situation in the production statistics of oilseeds is not very different from that of cotton. The magnitude of divergence between the two series in this case is of the order of 14 per cent in respect of 9 important oilseeds. The DESMOA estimates are based on the *girdawari* for area and crop cutting experiments under the GCES for yield, whereas the estimates of COOIT mainly depend on the feedback received from important markets about arrivals, trend of crop and the additional information provided by members of the industry. The main reasons for divergence, in this case too, are differences in methodology, post-harvest losses, incomplete market arrivals and the inclination of the oilseeds industry to underestimate production in order to lobby for larger imports. It is understood that the DESMOA constituted two regional committees in consultation with COOIT in Andhra Pradesh and Madhya Pradesh, respectively to look into the discrepancies and reduce them to the extent possible. The DESMOA should have the work of the regional committees completed expeditiously and in the light of their findings, undertake a special study of the major oilseed markets to devise more objective procedures of estimation to be followed by the trade agencies.

ECONOMIC THOUGHTS WITH CROP ROTATIONS

The job of the farm manager is to combine the resources of land, labour, management, and capital to provide the most farm profit. Since these resources are scarce, maximizing returns to each resource is important. Each crop grown in North Dakota has risk and uncertainty in terms of yield and/or price. Farmers differ in their ability to bear risk and in their attitude towards accepting risk, and these differences will have a direct bearing on the selection of a cropping programme. Federal farm programmes no longer provide stability to income from crops such as wheat. Other crops, such as dry bean, may offer a chance for more profit per acre but at some increase in risk. Federal Crop Insurance, which covers most crops, may be purchased to protect against yield and income risk. In deciding which crops to grow once the agronomic factors have been considered, the farm manager should gather information concerning costs of production and economic outlook and then budget the potential costs and returns from each enterprise. Computer assisted decision models available from the NDSU Extension Service will help analyze alternatives, both short and long term.

INCOME STABILITY

Crop rotations provide income diversification. If something happens to reduce profitability of one crop, income is not as likely to be adversely affected as if the total farm was planted to this crop; provided a profit potential exists for each crop in a rotation. This is especially important to the farmer with limited capital or a heavy debt. Price and yield variability won't necessarily always be reduced by diversification. Weather that affects barley will affect wheat and oats in the same way. Prices and yields for oilseeds (sunflower and soybean) are correlated with each other in the same manner. Therefore a crop rotation with cereals and row crops will likely lead to greater income stability, because crop price movements and yield variability due to weather will be less than diversification with only row crops or only cereal crops.

Time Management

Many crops are competitive where labour is concerned, particularly at seeding and harvest. It is possible to spread these operations over a longer period of time with a crop rotation. Spring seeded cereal grains generally compete with each other for labour, while row crops may be planted and harvested later than cereals. (Winter wheat fits well into a rotation with other cereals because of fall seeding and earlier harvest while equipment needs remain essentially the same.) This tends to even out labour requirements. The addition of forage and feed crops, combined with a livestock enterprise, can further utilize labour, spreading it into the winter months.

It may be helpful to calendarize the operations required to plant and harvest each crop, with special attention to the labour needed for each operation. The labour needed can be compared to the labour available (combined with a particular complement of machinery) to determine if the farm operations can be done in a timely manner.

Machinery Efficiency

Efficiency in machinery use comes from either getting the job done in a more timely manner at a low marginal cost or from spreading fixed costs over more hours or acres. The efficacy of a rotation may be limited by available machinery. The ability of the additional crop(s) in the rotation to pay the additional cost must be determined when implementing a new rotation requires the purchase of new equipment.

Weather and Pest Damage

Too little or too much precipitation is the most common weather problem in North Dakota. Within limitations, crop rotations can be used to adjust to rainfall limitations and moisture needs. Crops seeded or harvested at different times of the year will not be affected in the same manner by freezes, drought, or hail, lending stability to income.

Rotations provide control and limit the spread of insects and diseases. This is possible because most diseases and insects affect only one or a few crops.

Rotations help reduce disease buildup when host plants are confined to one or two seasons of cropping. Some insects may be controlled similarly, and infestations that do appear may be later and of little economic importance when compared to fields with a continuous single crop. Rotations, therefore, can reduce the need for pesticides, but they will not eliminate the need for pesticides entirely, nor will rotations be effective against all insects and diseases.

Climatic Thoughts

Climate is the greatest factor limiting the choice of crops for rotations in North Dakota. The freeze-free growing season varies from year to year but averages from about 110 days in the north central area along the Canadian border to over 130 days in the southeast corner of the state. The climate permits warm season crops such as corn, soybean and sunflower as well as cool season crops such as small grains and flax to be grown in some regions. In the cooler regions of the state, fewer growing degree days and a shorter season limit the choices to legumes, canola, small grains, flax, sunflower, and several specialty crops such as mustard, millet, buckwheat, safflower and canaryseed. Early corn hybrids can be grown but grain will not always mature. Variations in temperature from year to year can cause detrimental effects in all crops. Years with below normal mean temperatures tend to favour higher yields of the cool season crops, especially if there are few hot days. Maximum temperatures greater than 90°F during flowering and grain filling can cause substantial yield reductions in the cool season crops. Warmer season mean temperatures favour higher yields of the warm season crops.

Foliar disease problems are highly dependent on weather conditions. Many are favored by high humidity and warm temperatures. These conditions are more apt to occur in eastern North Dakota than in the western regions. Annual precipitation declines from southeast to northwest. It ranges from less than 14 inches in the northwest areas of the state to more than 20 inches in the extreme southeast. In regions west of the 18-inch rainfall zone, dryland production of such crops as soybeans, sugarbeets, and potatoes has not been economically feasible. Fortunately nearly half of the annual precipitation occurs during the growing season months of June, July and August.

Accumulated growing degree days (GDDs) can be calculated for various crops from daily temperature records. Accumulated growing degree days can be useful in many ways, including crop maturity predictions and crop growth stages. The same formula is used for all crops except that the base temperature and maximum temperatures may be different.

Reduced Risk

Crop rotations add diversity to farm operations and can help reduce risk, provide income stability, spread labour requirements, help control pests, and may add to efficient machinery use. Maintaining some flexibility within rotations to take advantage of price changes can help increase returns with little change in risk.

CROP ROTATIONS FOR INCREASED PRODUCTIVITY

Crop rotation is a planned order of specific crops planted on the same field. Crop rotation also means that succeeding crops are of a different genus, species, subspecies, or variety than the previous crop. Examples would be barley after wheat, row crops after small grains, grain crops after legumes, etc. The planned rotation sequence may be for a two-or three-year or longer period. Some of the general purposes of rotations are to improve or maintain soil fertility, reduce erosion, reduce the build-up of pests, spread the workload, reduce risk of weather damage, reduce reliance on agricultural chemicals, and increase net profits. Crop rotations have fallen somewhat into disfavour because they require additional planning and management skills, increasing the complexity of farming. A shift away from livestock programmes in most parts of North Dakota has also reduced the need for pasture and hay crops and eliminated some rotational crops such as alfalfa from many farms. Solid-seeded crops such as small grains and flax have predominated in the past, but row crops such as sunflower, pinto bean, corn and soybean provide additional planting options and more reasons for crop rotations.

GENERAL EFFECTS OF ROTATIONS

One immediate economic benefit of crop rotations is improved yields. For example, sunflower yields over eight years at Crookston, Minnesota (24) were often significantly greater in rotation with other crops than when continuous sunflower was grown. Wheat yields were also greater with rotation than continuous wheat in an eight-year study (22) conducted with different crops at Fargo. A study at the Agriculture Research Service at Mandan has shown that increased hard red spring wheat yields can be expected when an alternative crop is included in the rotation (27). Rotating to a different crop such as wheat on barley ground usually results in higher grain yields when compared to continuous cropping of wheat. Even greater benefits are usually obtained by rotating two distinctly unrelated crops, such as a small grain seeded into land where the previous crop was a legume or other herbaceous dicot such as flax or sunflower. Many of the reasons for the beneficial effects of rotations are not completely understood. Some of the more important beneficial effects that can be obtained from a well planned crop rotation are:

- Reduced insect and disease problems
- Beneficial residual herbicide carryover
- Improved soil fertility
- Improvements in soil tilth and aggregate stability

- Soil water management
- Reduction of soil erosion
- Reduction of allelopathic or phytotoxic effects.

Pest control is often an important reason for crop rotation. Rotations can be used to prevent or partially control several pests and reduce the reliance on chemical and mechanical control. A combination of crop rotation and pesticides is often more effective in reducing pest populations to economic levels than pesticides alone. Pesticides that provide economical control are not available for pests such as white mold in potato, dry bean, and sunflower, and crop rotations are the only feasible control method for reducing the impact of sclerotinia.

Disease Control

Crop rotation has tremendous potential for reducing and often preventing the transmission of disease. Disease pressures change with changing environmental conditions. Crop rotation, in combination with cultural practices plus necessary fungicides, is the most desirable method of disease control.

Soil Nitrogen

Legumes in the rotation can be used to increase the available soil nitrogen. Symbiotic nitrogen-fixing bacteria called rhizobia form nodules on the roots of legume plants and convert or fix atmospheric nitrogen to organic nitrogen. The amount of nitrogen fixed varies with species, available soil nitrogen, and many other factors. Fixed nitrogen not removed from the land by harvest becomes available to succeeding crops as the legume tissues undergo microbial decomposition. When the legume crop is seeded, rhizobia inoculum should always be applied to the seed to ensure the most productive commercial strains are available to form nodules and that inoculating bacteria are always present. Even though indigenous bacteria may be present in the soil, research shows improved commercial strains of rhizobia have more capacity to fix nitrogen. Legumes have the capacity to fix large amounts of nitrogen. Research in Minnesota (16) indicated that alfalfa fixed an average of 172 pounds of nitrogen annually during the first two years of production. However, only a portion of the nitrogen fixed is available to the next crop because much is removed in the harvested alfalfa.

Insect Control

Insects which can be controlled entirely or in part by rotations. In addition, insect populations may become greater within a region where only one or two crops are continuously grown in contrast to a region where several crops are grown in rotation. Insects such as corn borer, sunflower seed and stem weevil, and many others readily migrate to nearby or distant fields. Therefore, only partial control can be obtained by rotation. Increasing field isolation from fields seeded to the same crop the previous year will often increase the effectiveness of crop rotation as an insect control method.

Weed Control

Rotations can be used to cause shifts in weed populations. Populations of certain weed species can be suppressed by competition from the crop raised or by the selective use of herbicides. Wild mustard populations can be reduced by selective treatment of small grain grown in rotation with row crops. Grass weed populations, often a problem in small grains, can be reduced by the use of the appropriate herbicide in the previous row crop. Herbicides can have both beneficial and harmful residual effects on the next crop. Therefore, planning the correct sequence of herbicide use together with crop selection has become a necessary part of rotation management.

Soil Tilth and Structure

Many farmers who rotate crops comment on the improvement in tilth or friability of soil following soybean or other row crops. In a Colorado study (25) involving corn, sugarbeet, and barley planted on succeeding years, soil aggregate stability was increased from 67 to 76 percent when three years of alfalfa were added to the rotation. Increased aggregate stability reduces the tendency of the soil to puddle or crust, increases rate of water infiltration under certain conditions, and may also reduce wind erosion.

Soil Moisture

Crop rotation can lead to greater overall efficiency in soil water utilization. Spring seeded small grains usually deplete soil water 3 to 4 feet deep. In contrast, sunflower, safflower, corn and sugarbeet are deep-rooted crops which can deplete soil water to depths of 5 to 6 feet. Therefore, deep-rooted crops such as sunflower following small grains can take advantage of the extra reserve of deep moisture and also any nitrogen which was positionally unavailable to a shallow-rooted crop. Alfalfa and sweetclover, also deep-rooted crops, can be used to dry up saline seeps and other wet areas. Depletion of soil water in saline areas prevents the accumulation of salts on the surface, permits movement of the salts downward by leaching, and allows recropping to a cash crop such as wheat. Alfalfa or sweetclover should be seeded on the upslope recharge area to use and remove soil water as deeply as possible from the soil profile, reducing lateral flow of water and salts into the saline seep discharge area.

Reduction of Soil Erosion

Crop rotations combined with recommended tillage practices can play an important role in reducing wind and water erosion. Solid seeded crops such as small grains provide more protection against water erosion than row crops. Permanent crops such as hay or pasture provide even more protection against erosion. Management of crops to provide sufficient residue throughout the year is essential for satisfactory control of both wind and water erosion. No-till or minimum till farming is highly desirable as a conservation practice, but crop rotation must be used to reduce the buildup of insect, disease and weed pests. Common pest problems associated with continuous no-till wheat have been *Fusarium* head blight (scab), wheat streak mosaic, root rots, tan spot, wheat stem sawfly, increases in winter annual grass species, and serious infestation of perennial noxious weeds such as quackgrass and Canada thistle. Other crops grown continuously have had similar types of problems.

The effect of various crop rotations (29) on soil erosion is vividly. The addition of barley and hay or pasture to the rotation was estimated to reduced the degree of soil erosion by more than 50 percent when compared to continuous corn. The expected reduction in soil erosion would be even greater on steeper slopes.

Allelopathy-phytotoxicity

The reasons for improved yields due to crop rotations are not completely understood. Research has attempted to reveal some of the unknown factors. Terms such as phytotoxicity, allelopathy and autotoxicity are coming into common usage. Phytotoxicity, a general term, is defined as chemical that is toxic to plant growth whether it is derived from plant products or synthetic (herbicide or other pesticide residues). Allelopathy refers to plant material or chemicals derived from these materials which inhibit the germination, growth or growth of another species. Autotoxicity refers to plant material which inhibits the germination, growth and growth of the same species.

Legumes such as alfalfa, while often beneficial to non-related species, exhibit autotoxic effects to alfalfa seedlings. Research in Illinois indicated older stands caused greater inhibition of new seedlings. This study (21) indicated that one year out of alfalfa was sufficient to nullify the detrimental effects of the alfalfa.

Rotational Benefits to Corn and Sorghum

Corn yields following alfalfa and soybean, even with 300 pounds of applied nitrogen per acre, were greater than with continuous corn. The beneficial effects of alfalfa on corn yields during the second and third years following alfalfa. Even with 75 to 150 pounds of added nitrogen, the residual benefits of alfalfa are still evident. First-year corn yields were the same after either soybean or alfalfa.

Sugarbeet Rotations

Yields and quality are usually highest when sugarbeet follows barley or wheat in the crop rotation. Yields are usually high when sugarbeet follows corn, potatoes or summer fallow in rotation, but higher than desirable soil nitrogen levels may reduce crop quality. Three years research in Minnesota indicates sugarbeet yielded significantly less when following soybean versus barley in rotation. One year of research indicates sugarbeet yields were reduced following dry edible beans in rotation. Several possible explanations for reduced yields when sugarbeet follows soybean include: (1) herbicide carryover; (2) lack of available soil water; (3) increased rhizoctonia root rot; or (4) alleopathic effects.

Typical Red River Valley sugarbeet rotations include: Sugarbeet — soybean or dry edible bean — small grain-small grain or, if using a three year rotation, only one year of small grain. In areas where corn is more common, a desirable rotation is sugarbeet — soybean — corn. Soybean following sugarbeet is desirable because the soybean may adjust to periods of moisture stress better than small grains following sugarbeet. Planting small grains prior to sugarbeet reduces root rot potential in the sugarbeet. Early harvested small grains also allow time for sugarbeet growers to soil sample, apply fertilizer, and prepare seedbeds for the subsequent sugarbeet crop.

Sugarbeet Rotation Guidelines

- Three year rotations are the absolute minimum length of an acceptable rotation.
- Four year or longer rotations are desirable to minimize root disease, Cercospora leaf spot and herbicide carryover.
- Avoid canola in crop rotations with sugarbeet if at all possible, because it is an alternate host for sugarbeet cyst nematode.
- Avoid herbicide carryover that may damage sugarbeet or rotational crops.
- Manage fertilizer nitrogen use throughout the rotation.
- American Crystal Sugar Company data shows a trend towards more sugar production per acre in rotations of five years or more.

MONSOON CRISIS AND CROP PRODUCTION ESTIMATES

While it is a fact that late monsoons, drought, and floods had an impact on food production in the country, its influence on prices for commodities like rice had been nominal (as compared to other commodities). This is primarily due to excellent food grain production last year that immensely aided in boosting government stocks. In the current crop season, however, crop estimates point to a gloomy picture.

India's overall food grain production in Kharif 2009 is estimated to come down by 16 percent with significant downfalls in Rice and Coarse Cereals respectively. Moreover, in the case of Pulses, estimates are down by 7.5 percent, mainly due to low rainfall in central, western and northern India. Seasonality issues also came to the fore in the case of fruits & vegetables, notably Potato.

Large tracts of Potato were destroyed in West Bengal & Bihar (two main potato growing regions) due to late blight infestation. As a result, strains on food reserves in the country inevitably become evident, and hence the inflationary tendencies. Such a scenario, besides stoking inflationary fear, is also instilling a fear that the country would be unable to manage satisfactory growth in agriculture GDP.

An optimistic counterview is being put forth repeatedly which suggests that Rabi harvest would satisfactorily suffice for the shortage of food articles and would also cover-up for the losses sustained so far. Estimates however, do not support this proposition. Experts point out that it is the third quarter, when Kharif harvest takes place and the fourth quarter (for Rabi) that are extremely important for the Agriculture GDP of the country. These two quarters alone account for nearly 60 percent of the agriculture GDP, with Kharif accounting for nearly one-third and Rabi, a little over than a quarter. As Kharif estimates points to a sharp decline, such a scenario puts forth immense pressure on Rabi season to match up. However, this is an onerous task; the country would require substantial growth figures in fourth quarter. To elucidate, Widely consumed pulses varieties such as Moong, Tur are mainly kharif crops and their production has already declined; wheat production already has reached a record level of 81 Million tonnes last year and to make up for the loss this year, wheat production has to reach 93 Million tonnes, which is nearly impossible. Besides, oilseeds will have to grow by 26 percent to maintain overall oilseeds production at last year's level. Consequently, the substitution effect that Rabi harvest can have will be limited; it is highly unlikely that improvement in Rabi food grains would cover-up losses in kharif. Shortages in the availability of many commodities seems imminent this season and food inflation is going to have a longer horizon than expected. Here, it is equally important to present an interesting view, which states that we cannot confidently attribute the price increases beign witnessed currently to commodity shortages.

Can we fully attribute this prices increase to shortage of food-grains and vegetables? It is pertinent to mention that we have been having two consequently good agriculture seasons prior to 2009; our stockpiles, especially of food-grains is at more than optimum levels. A closer look at half yearly GDP data yields another interesting observation and brings in an element of doubt on attribution of inflation singly to poor production estimates & figures. An interesting point of view has come up, which states that in real terms agriculture GDP as a percentage of private consumption expenditure at nearly 24 percent, is constant for first half of both 2008-09 and 2009-10. Essentially, this means that agricultural supply as a share of demand in real terms is constant. It is not the price for a single commodity that is rising but all agricultural prices covering food grains and fruits and vegetables. These prices are rising when the share of output to demand in real terms is constant, it is not falling. Accordingly it is premature to state that inflation is stemming from supply constraints. On the other hand, the focus of policy makers is to attribute price rise to kharif grains, but this might be fallacious as the share of grains in both price and in the output indices is pretty low, in fact around a sixteenth. We cannot confidently say that there is supply crisis in food products, and that inflation is a result thereof.

INTERNET BASED DATA EXCHANGE SYSTEMS

Modern agriculture aims for the production of high quality food and raw materials in sufficient quantity for a wide range of customers. Further objectives consist of preservation of resources and protection of the environment. Means to achieve these goals are machines, equipment, and processes with high efficiency and effectiveness. These modern machines and processes are rather complex and consist of various cooperating subsystems. Moreover, agricultural production takes place in an open system which has various relations to its surrounding. This means that state conditions of the surrounding systems as well as the interactions between the agricultural production process and its environment have to be taken into account. Mass or energy flows must therefore be accompanied by information flows. This has led to the introduction of an information-based agriculture, the so-called "precision agriculture".

This kind of agricultural production serves for aiming at the following targets: on one hand one strives for a production process which is in accordance with the demands of plants or animals and realizes this in a site-specific or even single-plant-specific or single-animal-specific way. This results in the necessity to supply data about reference values and controlled variables in great variety, amount, and with short delay time, to transmit these data and process them.

On the other hand, new knowledge, improvements and enhancements should be included in a simple and compatible way into technical equipment and production processes. Furthermore, maintenance and service of modern machines and process equipment should be handled according to their real operation times and circumstances. This also requires the sampling, transmission, and processing of data in a compatible way, since the data may be generated, transmitted, and processed in different units. In summary, the compatible data transmission is a necessary condition for achievement of all the aims formulated above. Communication technology thus serves as the backbone of precision agriculture. This chapter considers the information flows in different areas of agricultural production as well as their physical and logical realization.

CROP FORECASTS

Final estimates of crop production based on area through complete enumeration and yield rate through crop-cutting experiments become available much after the crop is harvested. However, the Government needs advance estimates of production for various decisions relating to pricing, distribution, export and import, etc. The Directorate of Economics & Statistics, Ministry of Agriculture (DESMOA) releases advance estimates of crop area and production through periodical forecasts in respect of principal food and non-food crops (food grains, oil seeds, sugarcane, fibres, etc.), which account for nearly 87 per cent of agricultural output. Four forecasts are issued, the first in the middle of September, the second in January, the third towards the end of March and the fourth by the end of May.

The first forecast relating to the *kharif* crops is mostly based on reports prepared by the States mainly guided by the visual observation of field officials. The second forecast covering both the *kharif* and *rabi* crops takes into account additional information obtained from various sources including agricultural inputs, incidence of pests and diseases, and weekly reports of State departments of agriculture regarding area coverage, conditions of standing crops, etc. Results of Remote Sensing data are also considered at this stage. In the third forecast, the earlier advance estimates of both the *kharif* and *rabi* seasons are firmed up, again taking into account information received from sources such as Market Intelligence Units, Meteorological Department and the Crop Weather Watch Group (CWWG). The fourth forecast is based on firm figures supplied by State Agricultural Statistics Authorities (SASAs) who are by then in a position to obtain fairly dependable estimates of yield rates through GCES. In addition to the four forecasts, the DESMOA issues the "Final Estimates" of crop area and production in December. As a few States continue to revise their data on delayed receipt of information, the all-India crop statistics are brought out as "Fully Revised" in the next crop year in the following December.

Recently, the Ministry of Agriculture has set up a National Crop Forecasting Centre (NCFC) with the object of examining the existing mechanism of building forecasts of principal crops and developing more objective techniques. The NCFC takes into account information on weather conditions, supply of agricultural inputs, pests, diseases and related aspects including the proceedings of CWWG in the formulation of scientific and objective forecasting methods to replace the present system. The work of the NCFC is still at a preliminary stage and it needs more statistical support to be able to develop appropriate models of forecasting.

DEFICIENCIES

The present system of crop forecasts being based mostly on subjective appraisal at various levels does not reflect the ground situation correctly. This is specially the case with regard to the preliminary forecasts, which have to be fairly reliable for taking several policy decisions. There is need for more objective forecasting based on timely and detailed information on crop condition, meteorological parameters, water availability, crop damage, etc. The NCFC is still not in a position to develop a scientific procedure of forecasting using multi-dimensional models and assimilating the information received from various sources. The DESMOA is handicapped due to non-receipt of timely information from the States and it often has to prepare such forecasts based on incomplete data. Frequent changes in the production figures especially of food grains between one forecast and another, and the "final" and "fully revised" estimates cause confusion and doubt among the users. While releasing these figures, the DESMOA may indicate the reasons for the change.

The system of forecasting crop production in the country by the Ministry of Agriculture needs to be replaced as soon as possible by an objective method using appropriate statistical techniques. The recent establishment of the NCFC, which has been assigned the responsibility of streamlining and improving the quality of forecasting, should go a long way in accomplishing this objective. However, it needs additional professional support, comprising statisticians and multi-disciplinary team of experts to devise scientific techniques of crop forecasting.

Remote Sensing technology can also provide a satisfactory means of developing reliable estimates of crop area and condition of the crop at various stages of growth for forecast purposes. The Space Application Centre (SAC) is already at an advanced stage of experimenting with the approach of Remote Sensing to estimate the area under principal crops through the scheme known as "Forecasting Agricultural output using Space, Agro-meteorology and Land based observations" (FASAL).

Incidentally, this will form an important input in the forecasting methodology to be developed by NCFC. The land-based observations should be used to measure quantitative changes in crop growth besides discriminating one crop from another.

The Commission, therefore, recommends that:

- The Ministry of Agriculture and the National Crop Forecasting Centre (NCFC) should soon put in place an objective method of forecasting the production of crops.
- The National Crop Forecasting Centre (NCFC) should be adequately strengthened with professional statisticians and experts in other related fields.
- The programme of Forecasting Agricultural output using Space, Agro-meteorology and Land based observations (FASAL), which is experimenting the approach of Remote Sensing to estimate the area under principal crops should be actively pursued.
- The States should be assisted by the Centre in adopting the objective techniques to be developed by the National Crop Forecasting Centre (NCFC).

AGRICULTURAL PRODUCTION IN WORLD MARKET

The continuous interaction of the development of production and the world market had already come out in the early stages of the rise of the capitalist social formation, and the determinant place in this interaction, moreover, was taken by capitalist industry. As a result of his thorough investigation of extensive historical data, Marx came to the conclusion that when in the 16th, and partially still in the 17th century the sudden expansion of commerce and emergence of a new world market overwhelmingly contributed to the fall of the old mode of production and the rise of capitalist production, this was accomplished conversely on the basis of the already existing capitalist mode of production. The world market itself forms the basis for this mode of production. On the other hand, the immanent necessity of this mode of production to produce on an ever-enlarged scale tends to extend the world market continually, so that it is not commerce in this case which revolutionises industry, but industry which constantly revolutionises commerce.

Marxist political economy consequently looks upon the rise and development of the world capitalist market as a constituent of a broader process, *i.e.* the gradual conversion of capitalism into a universal socio-economic system. This methodological approach has enabled it to disclose the unequal character of the division of labour between countries that is inherent in this system, and the exploiter nature of commodity exchange and of capitalist international economic relations in general on the world market, based as they are on private property in the instruments and means of production.

The struggle for foreign markets has always been an urgent economic need for capitalism, since a striving to extend its sphere of influence without limit is inherently characteristic of it, in contrast to previously dominant modes of production. Because of the operation of objective economic laws, capitalist enterprise inevitably outgrows the boundaries of the community, region, or country, the economic exclusiveness and isolation of countries being broken down by commodity circulation itself.

As a result, capitalist production becomes inconceivable without foreign trade and world economic relations at a certain stage of its development, which in turn reflects growth of the social division of labour on an international scale. Marx stressed that capitalist production rests on the *value* or the transformation of the labour embodied in the product into social labour. But (his is only [possible] on the basis of foreign trade and of the world market. This is at, once the precondition and the result of capitalist production. He expressed the same idea even more succinctly in the formula 'capitalist production does not exist at all without foreign commerce'.

All that in no way signifies, of course, that any capitalist enterprise indispensably works for an external market and sends what it produces beyond the local or national economy. At the same time it constantly experiences the effect of the already existing system of international business relations and is drawn into their orbit, if not directly, then indirectly. The capitalist, even the one who is wholly oriented on the home market, is forced to compare his own costs of production with world prices as well as with the market prices in his country. An influence of the same order has to be allowed for when an all-round appraisal is being made of the position of labour power in capitalist countries, including the spheres where its value depends wholly or predominantly on domestic factors of production.

Capitalism's international economic interconnections arose later, historically, than its domestic ones, the latter being original and basic. Their level and trend depended to a decisive degree on how far each nation developed its own 21 productive forces, division of labour, and internal dealings. That, however, does not eliminate the undoubted fact that extension of both the home and foreign market under capitalism represents different aspects of a single process; the boundaries between them are very mobile and arbitrary. As the world market develops the problem of the limits of the home market of each country taken separately proves to lie very tightly bound up with that of extension of its external economic relations. Hence one of the essential principles of Marxian research into the development of capitalism in scope and depth is that, when analysing international relations of production (including the capitalist class's colonial policy), it is not important where the boundary between the home and foreign market is drawn; what is important is that capitalism cannot exist and develop without constantly expanding the sphere of its domination, without colonising new countries and drawing old non-capitalist countries into the whirlpool of world economy.

The rise of capitalism's international exploiter relations is inextricably linked with the forming of a system of world economy appropriate to them. The watershed on this point between Marxian and capitalist science is clear and distinct. Although the creation of this system was completed on the whole under imperialism, it by no means follows that its present-day history can be separated from the preceding history of the development of the capitalist mode of production and that imperialist exploitation of some countries by others begins only with capitalism's transition from free enterprise to the domination of monopolies. Many of the features of the international division of labour typical of the monopoly stage had already arisen and begun to take on a stable, long-term character during the transition of capitalist society to the machine stage of production. They were not brought about by chance, transitional factors but wore caused by deep-seated changes in both the home and external conditions of capitalist reproduction.

The analysis of international economic inter-relationships made in their day by the founders of Marxist political economy indicated that it was large-scale machine industry that prepared the ground for the subsequent formation of a world economy. Machine production, as Marx and Engels pithily put it, produced world history for the first time, insofar as it made all civilised nations and every individual member of them dependent for the satisfaction of their wants on the whole world, thus destroying the former natural exclusiveness of separate nations.

It is through the international division of labour on the world market that the tendency to bring countries together economically, constitutionally inherent in capitalism, is manifested. The kernel of this pattern, however, discovered by Marx, is that this tendency, while progressive in itself, led at the same time, because of capitalist methods and the forms of economic association of the different countries, to consolidation of the division of the world into industrially developed countries, and economically backward agrarian and primary commodity producing countries exploited by them. The antagonism between these two main groups of countries, which are opposite poles of the world capitalist economy, has become one of its main contradictions.

This contradiction has become specially acute in the stage of imperialism, and a very important factor in subsequent origin and development of the crisis of the colonial structure of the capitalist economy, a crisis that is irreversible for the monopoly capitalist class. The break-up of the colonial system after World War II, and the marked deepening of the internal contradictions of world capitalism, which are undermining the historically formed foundations of its system of unequal international economic relations, have put on today's agenda, with all urgency, the issue of eliminating the exploiter system of division of labour that completely dominated the world economy in the past.

It would be wrong to treat this task (which corresponds to the vital interests of all nations without exception) as the need to liquidate the progress already made in the internationalisation of social production. The anti-imperialist struggle for genuine national independence, just like the transition of countries to a higher socio-economic system, does not eliminate the objective need to develop the social (including the international) division of labour, and leads to a change in and perfecting of the forms in which this essentially progressive process is manifested. It is self-evident, Marx wrote to Ludvig Kugelman on 11 July 1868, that this necessity of the distribution of social labour in definite proportions cannot possibly be done away with by a *particular juring* of social production but can only change the mode of *its appearance.*

The underlying principles of a Marxist-Leninist analysis of the ways and causes of capital's internationalisation of social production have not lost their theoretical value over the years. The topicality of many of them, moreover, is growing, especially in today's situation of the coexistence and opposition of two world social systems and of the natural extension of economic and technical co-operation on the basis of mutual advantage and equal international division of labour.

In this situation capitalist ideologists are trying in every way to prove the 'erroneousness', in particular, or at least 'obsoleteness' of the Marxist-Leninist political economy's analysis. Above all they endeavour to refute its conclusions about the irreversibility of tendencies towards a steady deepening of capitalism's internal contradictions. But the whole long history of capitalist economics, and of its mistakes, its constant wavering between one conception and another, its fallacies and failures, shows that theories that consider the international market relations of capitalism to be legitimate and that are abstracted from a socio-economic analysis of the production sphere, at best contain superficial analogues of the real trends of development. In the main they bring out the consequences but not the causal connections of this development. At the same time it would clearly he an oversimplification of things to consider that the theoretical findings of capitalist political economy in the sphere of the world economy's market relations are in general isolated from real analysis of the reproduction processes. In a number of cases they more or less adequately reflect important features of the backlash of these relations in the production sphere. And this effect determines many of the essential features of the capitalist economy at the various stages of its development.

In the last instance (Engols wrote to Conrad Schmidt on 27 October 1890) production is the decisive factor. But as soon as trade in products becomes independent of production proper, it has a movement of its own, which, although by and large governed by that of production, nevertheless in particulars and within this general dependence again follows laws of its own inherent in the nature of this new' factor; this movement has phases of its own and in its turn reacts on the movement of production.

All this calls for close attention to research both into the ways and determinant tendencies in the genesis of the world market and into its place in the process of extended capitalist reproduction. Not only is such research of educational value historically; it is also very necessary for an analysis of current changes in the structure of the world capitalist economy. A systems analysis of its inner and external interconnections in today's international situation cannot be made sufficiently full without detailed allowance for the general patterns and long-term trends of development of these interconnections.

Lenin more than once stressed the need to study broad socio-economic phenomena in historical retrospect, since the most important thing if one is to approach this question scientifically is not to forget the underlying historical connection, to examine every question from the standpoint of how the given phenomenon arose in history and what were the principal stages in its development, and, from the standpoint of its development to examine what it has become today.

There were relatively broad trade and financial relations between separate countries and peoples, of course, in the socio-economic formations that preceded capitalism, but it was capitalism that first formed a world market which played a progressive, revolutionary role in the subsequent increase of mankind's productive forces and growth of its social production. Marx, attributing paramount importance to that, wrote that 'the specific task of bourgeois society is the establishment of a world market'. It was with the formation of a world market that the level of development of capitalism began to be marked by the degree of growth both of domestic and of international market relations.

There was a qualitatively new leap in the shaping of these relations associated with the vast increase in trade and colonial expansion of the young European capitalist class. This expansion became a decisive factor in the primitive accumulation of capital. The world market thus created important material preconditions for victory of the capitalist mode of production over the feudal. At that time the merchant capital of European powers undoubtedly prevailed in international economic relations, but its dominance on the world market began to decline as the capitalist mode of production was consolidated in the countries that were the basis of its existence. The subordinating of merchant capital to industrial, natural to the new mode of production, was also manifested then in the realm of international trade. As a result the material conditions were laid for an ever increasing intensification of the action of the mechanism of the economic exploitation of all the countries of the world by a handful of 'advanced' countries. And the wider the gap in levels of labour productivity becomes between this handful of advanced countries and the economically backward ones, the greater is the exploitation suffered by the latter on the world market. This pattern was expressed with maximum clarity in the following formula of Marx:

The favoured country recovers more labour in exchange for less labour, although this difference, this excess is pocketed, as in any exchange between labour and capital, by a certain class. In that way, in particular, the main antagonistic contradiction of the capitalist mode of production, *i.e.* that between its constantly increasing social character and the private capitalist forms of appropriating the results of social labour, thus found expression within the world market.

The putting of capitalism onto the rails of large-scale machine industry during the industrial revolution, which was completed in the second half of the nineteenth century, meant the beginning of a new, higher stage in the development of world economic relations. Large-scale industry in fact shaped the world market of the epoch of mature capitalism. And its dependence on external economic links and the international division of labour in turn also grew immensely. As Karl Marx said in his day: Large-scale industry, detached from the national soil, depends entirely on the world market, on international exchange, on an international division of labour. In this situation the antagonistic contradictions of the world market stemming from the basic economic contradiction of capitalist society, have become an ever more serious obstacle to a further rise of social production. One of the most convincing bits of evidence of that were the world economic crises that were converted into a constitutionally inalienable feature of the whole economic system of capitalism. Years of comparatively rapid industrial boom began to alternate with regular consistency with periods of stagnation and direct destruction of already created productive forces. This cyclicity, determined by the objective laws of capitalist production, was intensified in turn by industry's mounting dependence on the foreign market. It was their comprehensive study both of the internal, home factors of the cyclic development of capitalist business and of the international ones that enabled the authors of classical Marxist political economy to draw the conclusion, confirmed by the whole subsequent course of social development, that economic crises would remain, while capitalism existed, one of the incurable ills determining its historically transient character.

For more than a century and a half now, since 1825, capitalism has periodically suffered from cyclic crises. All the attempts of capitalist economists to work up prescriptions to cure this illness without eliminating its basis, namely its exploiter relations of production, have unfailingly proved unsound and bankrupt. The capitalists as a class have demonstrated more and more clearly with the course of time their incapacity to control the productive forces of society rationally not only within the context of the separate national economies but also and especially on the scale of the world economy.

The world cyclic crisis of 1974–75, the greatest since the war, which developed under an unprecedented sharpening of several of modern capitalism's most important world problems, *viz.* the monetary, energy, raw material, and food crises, was convincing evidence of that indisputable fact in our day. It swept almost all the main centres of capitalism simultaneously and in turn interrupted their economic development. During the crisis the monopoly capitalists as usual exerted immense efforts to shift its most serious consequences onto the working masses of their own countries and the peoples of the agrarian and primary producer periphery.

As capital internationalises society's productive powers the connection between the reproductive processes of the individual countries (including those that are the epicentres of world crises under the impact of the economy's cyclic movement) is becoming closer and closer. Therefore, when we are determining the objective patterns of capitalism's development, the question of the interaction of the national cycles within the context of a single world cycle (study of which was begun by Karl Marx) is posed in all its acuteness. We shall dwell in detail on the features of the cyclic development of today's world capitalist economy later, here it is necessary to stress the following from the standpoint of the matter we are examining. Despite the fact that the cyclic synchronousness of the movement of capitalist production and of the world market already has a history of 150 years, a line of refusing to recognise the general patterns of this movement still clearly dominates capitalist economics. When, however, the course of the world cycle is studied, its development is mainly considered as a kind of arithmetical sum total of the results of cyclic fluctuations within the national economies taken separately. As a result it comes about that the specific features of national development are, as it were, the sole decisive factor in the shaping of each world cycle. In that case the role of the system of international socio-economic connections and of the internationalisation of social production, which in essence convert these countries into links in a single economic chain, is patently underestimated.

Since the beginning of the 70s, it is true, because of the steady exacerbation of modern capitalism's international economic problems, an increasingly negative attitude towards such a 'narrowly nationalist' approach to analysis of the main world crisis processes (including its cyclic development) has been traceable in capitalist economic literature. Sometimes, while justly noting the close connection between these processes, and in particular between national overproduction crises, within the context of the capitalist economy, most capitalist economists as usual, however, prefer to identify their prime causes with the processes taking place at any definite moment in the sphere of the international market and political relations. They thus willy-nilly leave aside objective study of the system of international exploiter relations of production that underlies the deep internal contradictions of the world capitalist economy, which are inexorably undermining its main foundations.

The political dependence of most of the countries of the world on the main centres of capitalism has played an extremely important sole in the long history of the building up of this system. The structure of its unequal, exploiter relations was also moulded by that dependence in the imperialist stage, the crisis of which developed with particular force in the second half of this century as a consequence of most colonial countries' winning of national independence.

THE AGRARIAN AND RAW MATERIAL PRODUCING COUNTRIES

The winning of political independence by the bulk of the countries of the colonial world in the postwar period opened up fundamentally new opportunities for them to fight to step up their national development, and for socio-economic progress and equality in international relations against imperialist diktat and exploitation by expatriate monopoly capital. As Leonid Brezhnev said at the 25th Congress of the CPSU: Glancing at the picture of the modern world one cannot help noticing the important fact that the influence of states that had only recently been colonies or semi-colonies has grown consider ably.

It may definitely be said about the majority of them that they are defending their political and economic i ights in a struggle against imperialism with mounting energy, striving to consolidate their independence and to raise the social, economic and cultural level of their peoples. In these conditions important changes are occurring or coming into life in the structure and distribution of the developing world's social production, which are putting their stamp on the processes that govern the peculiarities of the former colonies' and semi-colonies' position in the present international division of labour, including their mounting struggle to lay the foundations of their economies. In the 50s through the 70s the physical volume of their industrial production as a whole rose by more than 450 per cent, so that now, in contrast, to the earlier stages of their economic history, industrial goods, especially manufactures, are beginning to predominate in the material production of most of them. At the end of our period somewhat more was produced by manufacturing industry in value terms (in 1970 prices) than in agriculture, and roughly four times as much as in mining. As the general economic capability, and especially the industrial potential, of these countries grew there was an inevitable consolidation of the demarcation of class forces, a deepening of the heterogeneity of their social development, and a growth of class struggle. For the immense majority, at the same time, that were to one degree or another within the orbit of the laws of the world capitalist economy, it remains characteristic that the tasks of the anti-feudal revolution have not been completed and the socio-economic survivals of the colonial period are very burdensome. Many of the new sovereign states had begun to carry through radical reforms during the liberation struggle that were both antifeudal and anti-capitalist. In thatsituation the differentiation of their paths and levels of economic development greatly broadened.

In spite of essential differences of that kind, however, all the emancipated countries are part of the agrarian and raw material periphery of the industrial centres of capitalism. Even the most economically advanced of them are still mainly exporters of raw materials arid importers of machinery, equipment, and other industrial goods. They 158 continue to he in an unequal position within the capitalist world system and subjected to exploitation by expatriate monopoly capital, which is why they are being urgently faced with a number of common internal and external economic problems.

The most important trends in the changing postwar structure of the periphery's social production have been analysed above. How, however, was this production distributed among the developing countries in the first postwar decades?

As will be clear from the graphs the growth rates of aggregate production were very fast in Latin America, where most of the countries had achieved national independence and taken the road of independent capitalist development long before break-up of the colonial system began. As a result the postwar years have been marked by a gradual raising of the role of Latin America in the aggregate product of the developing world, from 40 to 44.5 per cent, so that it is now greater than that of the Asian region although the latter had nearly four times its population at the end of the period surveyed. This growth did not come about through the contribution of all Latin American countries, but occurred on a background of a marked imbalance of their economic development and was mainly determined by a few leading countries, primarily Brazil and Mexico, for which much higher growth rates were typical. At the end of the 70s more than 60 per cent of the aggregate product of the region was produced in these two countries alone, whereas they produced around 40 per cent of it at the beginning of the 50s. At the same time certain countries (Haiti, Honduras, Barbados, etc.), still caught up in heavy chains of dependence on expatriate commodity monopolies, remained among the most economically 159 backward appendages of the world capitalist economy, with the usual low growth rates typical of semi-colonial countries. A steady deepening of the unevenness of Hie intor-regional. and especially of the intraregional, distribution of production has become typical of the various groups of commodity producing countries in the other continents. In Africa, where colonialism succeeded in retaining key positions in many areas for a number of years in the postwar period, the course of economic development has proved to be relatively slow, so that the weight of the continent in the aggregate social product of developing countries has had a clear tendency to fall, despite the fact that the total GDP of African countries has risen substantially.

As national independence has been consolidated and African countries have thrown off the yoke of colonial exploitation, however, their growth rates, it must be noted, as in other areas of the developing world, have gradually risen. They have been highest, as a rule, in the Arab countries in North Africa, where the positive consequences of the breakup of the colonial system made themselves felt much earlier than in Tropical Africa. The rapid increase in income from exploiting their oil wealth, moreover, provided some of them with favourable material conditions for their struggle for quicker economic development.

There has been an ever wider difference in levels and rates of development in Asian countries, where around two-thirds of the developing‘ world's population lives. Most of them, which were in forced dependence on a handful of European powers during nearly the whole history of the forming of the world capitalist economy, were able to win national independence at the start of the postwar period. In the 50s they had already begun an active fight for accelerated growth of their previously stagnating productive forces. The mean annual growth rates of the GDP of all the developing countries of Asia reached 4.5 per cent in that decade, 5.1 per cent in the 60s, and around 6 per cent in the 70s. This accelerated growth was due to no small degree in recent times, however, to the 'oil boom' in the Near and Middle East. The real volume of the GDP (in value terms) increased more than sixfold in that region in the 50s through the 70s, and was more than one-third of the GDP of all the developing countries of

Asia, although its population at the end of the period was only 7 per cent of the continent's total. At the same time the GDP of all the other developing countries in South and South-East Asia, which have immense human resources, rose less than threefold.

If we examine these processes through the prism of the data on population growth, the generalisations made above, stemming from a comparative description of the regional dynamics of production, obviously need to be made more precise, and corrected. The successive changes in the indicators of per capita GDP for the separate regions and countries enable the scale of the shifts in the geographical distribution of their productive forces to be brought out more clearly.

In almost all the groups of countries in the table, there is a quite marked tendency, albeit extremely varied in dynamics and significance, towards a differentiation of population growth rates, in addition to a sharpening of the differences in dynamics of production. This trend characterised one of the inevitable consequences of the break-up of the colonial system, and could not help having an essential influence on the ratio of economic potentials, and consequently on the mutually interlocked processes of economic development.

In the Asian region a particularly wide gap has been formed in the dynamics of per capita production of the aggregate social product between the oil-producing countries of the Near and Middle East and the overwhelming majority of the countries of South and South-East Asia.

Similar processes have been occurring in Africa, for all its special features. The growing uncvenness of development has been deepened there, even more than in Asia, by considerable differences in rates of population growth. In some cases these differences, it is true, have encouraged a convergence of the dynamics of per capita production in the separate groups of countries. That is confirmed, in particular, by comparison of the lines of postwar development of North and Tropical Africa. Population has grown faster in the former, which has led to a certain levelling out of the aggregate indicators of per capita growth of production used in the table. At the same time there have been quite different trends within each of these regions.

In the biggest North African country, Egypt, for example, there was an obvious slowing of the growth rates both of production and of population in the 60s and 70s. The annual rates of per capita growth of GDP in those years were 1.5 per cent in Egypt and only 0.2 per cent in Sudan. In other words, they were lower than in many of the countries of Tropical Africa whose economies on the whole still suffer maximally from the burden of harmful survivals of the colonial period compared with other developing countries. Although some of the new states south of the Saharajiave achieved a relatively high growth of production (Kenya, Gabon, Ivory Coast, Nigeria, Malawi, etc.), most of them still have extremely slow and very unstable rates of development. In quite a few countries, moreover, the main indices of the dynamics of GDP growth have been lower in recent decades than the growth of population (Burundi, Chad, the Central African Empire, Uganda, Upper Volta).

The long-term trends in the distribution of production in the former colonial regions are primarily governed by the resultant tendencies of the development of a few of the biggest countries (as regards area, population, and natural 164 resources). The ratio of their economic capabilities is therefore important in a generalised description of intraregional processes, including the contradictory consequences of the 'demographic explosion' in the Third World.

In Latin America, for example, GO per cent of the inhabitants and nearly two-thirds of the aggregate GDP of the whole region were concentrated in Brazil, Mexico, and Argentina. Among the 'Big Three' production developed at the lowest rates in Argentina in the postwar years, but the comparatively slow dynamics of its population growth led to its per capita production, for example, exceeding Brazil's in the 60s and Mexico's in the early 70s. It is typical that the economies of several small countries (Uruguay, El Salvador, Paraguay, Haiti, Honduras, and others) wore below the average of the developing countries of South and Southeast Asia as regards the same indicators in those years, not to mention of bulk of the emancipated countries of Africa. The examples given, whose number could be greatly extended, very clearly confirm that there has been a steady sharpening of the unevenness of economic development of the former colonies and semi-colonies in recent decades. This irresistibly intensifying process, however, in no way refutes the need (in addition to the study of the features of the economic growth of each country) for a comprehensive systems approach to analysis of the summary trends of their interconnected development within the whole developing world. Such an approach helps, on the one hand, to bring out the objectively operating trends in which the extremely contradictory and isolated processes and phenomena characterising the shifts in the distribution of the productive forces of the separate countries and their regional groups are ultimately reduced, and on the other hand, gives the possibility of better understanding and appreciating the specific features of their development.

In this connection comparative analysis of the long-term changes in the industrial structure of the social production of countries in Asia, Africa, and Latin America is becoming of paramount importance.

As these countries are industrialised this process will undoubtedly hectare more and more pronounced. Its effect gives grounds for supposing that even before the end of this century the share of agriculture in the GDP of most of the developing countries of Asia and Africa may fall by 50 to 50 per cent and reach the level attained in Latin America al the beginning of the 80s. At the same time the proportion of agriculture in the GDP of the Latin American region as a whole will also probably diminish, gradually approaching the present average level of the industrial capitalist countries (around 4 per cent). An inevitable consequence of that will be the pushing of increasing numbers of the rural population into the cities.

Another very important trend determining bottle the current structure of changes in the production of the developing countries and their probable future structure has become the general though not uniform rise-in the role of industry in their GPP. The scale of its growth, moreover, has been quite regularly higher in the economically more backward countries. Thus the proportion of industrial output in the aggregate product for the period considered in the graphs increased in the African region by 120 per cent (from 12 to 26 per cent), in the Asian region by almost 100 per cent (from 14 to 27 per cent), and in the Latin American region by almost a third (from 24 to 31 per cent).

As a result of the increasing imbalance of this growth, a trend towards a certain convergence of the significance and place of industry in the general structure of these regions' production has been noted in the postwar period. The proportion of industry in the GDP of countries in South and South-East Asia and in Africa was 50 per cent less than in Latin America at the beginning of the 50s; at the beginning of the 80s the gap had noticeably closed and was estimated now at 1:1.3 for the former and 1:1.2 for the latter.

This trend will intensify, in all probability, in the future, and characterise one of the tendencies of developing countries' uneven economic growth. It can be expected that the weight of industry in the GDP of most Asian and African] countries will come close to the present level in the leading Latin American countries in the next two or three decades, while the latter will reach the average level of the present-day industrial centres of capitalism.

These very general estimates provide the data needed, but only the initial data, for studying the significance and place of industry in the regional economies. They naturally smooth over the vast differences in structure and sectoral dynamics of the industrial production of the separate regions and countries.

A more and more concrete analysis of the separate industries is a central task of the part that follows, but here we must bear in mind that these processes of industrial development in agrarian and raw material producing countries are largely linked with rapid growth of mining, whose output is mainly sold on the world capitalist market, and in fact is still really controlled to one degree or another by expatriate monopoly capital. The rapid growth of the mining of minerals, and in particular of fuel, has played no small role in the regions being considered in the postwar rise in the proportion of industry in the gross product.

It would not be legitimate, however, to conclude from this that the steady raising of the role of industry in the gross product of developing countries is more or less wholly 168 linked with the working of minerals. The rapid development of their manufacturing industries in recent decades has had an ever increasing effect, especially the development of heavy industry, the volume of whose production rose on the whole by almost 150 per cent in 1968–80. At the beginning of the 80s the heavy industries of all developing countries were producing 30 per cent more output in value terms (in added value in 1975 prices) than the light industries. There is little doubt that their basic industries will also grow al faster rates in the next few decades, which will further a gradual raising of their role in industrial production.

For a comparative estimate of the long-term trends bringing out both the general and the particular in the production sphere of the main developing regions of capitalism, it is essential to compare the mean annual growth rates of their main industries (including per capita rates) over some considerable period. Because of the inadequacies of the economic statistics of developing countries it is very difficult to bring out these growth rates in summary form (in contrast to developed countries). The comparison can only be attempted on the basis of very approximate calculations, which allow us to characterise the most general trends of the sectoral shifts with a certain degree of accuracy. At the same time they can be used as a starling point of sorts for studying the specific features of the development of production in the separate countries and groupings in each of the regions.

In agriculture, which is still in a slate of deep, protracted depression in the developing world as a whole, Latin America and most of the countries of the Near and Middle East have displayed relatively faster growth, so that a line towards an increase in their share in developing countries' total production of farm produce has begun to show., with a corresponding drop in the role of South and South-East Asia and Africa.

As a result they have become further differentiated as regards per capita farm production. By the beginning of the 80s the Latin American countries on the whole considerably surpassed the countries of Asia and Africa in this respect. It is unlikely that there will be any closing of this gap in the near future.

The fight to eliminate the extreme backwardness of agriculture will undoubtedly remain one of the most pressing socio-economic problems of most of the countries of the former colonial world in the coming decades. It is the slow development of their agriculture, compared with population growth, that is the decisive cause of the consistent tendency manifested since the war towards a widening of the gap in GDP per capita between the developing and developed countries of the capitalist world.

In the 60s and 70s, however, this trend began to be more and more actively countered by processes developing in most of the other sectors of the economies of the former colonial periphery of capitalism, and primarily in industry. The international statistics clearly indicate that the per capita growth rates of industrial production in economically most backward regions of capitalism's periphery have noticeably exceeded the industrial centres in per capita growth rates of industrial production. In the developing countries of Asia per capita industrial production increased by a factor of 4.3 from 1950 to 1978, in Africa by 3.5, and in the developed capitalist countries taken together by 2.6. The countries of Latin America also showed a rather faster growth in this respect, on an average, than the main economic regions of capitalism.

In present conditions there has begun to be a tendency towards a certain closing of the gigantic, gap in per capita industrial production formed under colonialism, together with 171 a gradual increase in the weight of the agrarian and raw material producing countries in the industrial production of the non-socialist world. In Hie very early 50s this gap was estimated at 1:35 for Asian countries, 1:32 for Africa, and 1:5.5 for Latin America. By the end of the 70s it had been clearly reduced and was expressed by the following approximate ratios: Asia 1:24, Africa 1:27, and Latin America 1:5.3. In the middle of 70s the substantial slowing of industrial growth rates in the developed countries connected with the greatest postwar cyclic crisis of the capitalist world economy fostered a consolidation of this trend.

The general course of this process leads to the conclusion that it is acquiring a quite stable, irreversible character in the present situation. Being a natural consequence of the break-up of the colonial system, it has already begun to have (and in all probability will continue to have) a growing impact on the steady deepening of the crisis of the unequal system of international capitalist division of labour built up on a colonial basis.

At the same time the facts adduced confirm the extreme complexity and difficulty of the problem of overcoming the age-old industrial backwardness of the former colonies and semi-colonies, especially with their constant exploitation by expalriate monopoly capital. The solution of such a major and objectively inevitable historical task will obviously require several decades and will continue for a long time to be one of the urgent problems of the light of the peoples of the liberated countries for final liquidation of the heavy legacy of the colonial period and imperialist domination of their economies.

To reduce their backwardness by even two-thirds from the present mean per capita industrial production of the developed countries, for instance, it would take the countries of South and South-East Asia around a quarter of a century at the rates of real industrial growth of the 60s and 70s, Africa more than a quarter of a century, and Latin America around 30 years. Then, however, per capita output of industrial goods in each of these regions would the respectively one-eighth, a ninth, and about a third below the level already reached by the advanced capitalist countries at the end of the 70s. If that level remains unchanged in the future, then in that hypothetical case the way out for most developing countries would have to be a 15-fold or 16-fold expansion of the volume of industrial production within the present-day world capitalist economy. These figures cannot, of course, serve as a generalised criterion of a quantitative, let alone a qualitative, estimate of the future parameters and goals of the industrial development of all the developing countries of Asia, Africa, and Latin America. In fact, however, they help determine only the scale of the industrial backwardness of developing countries. It inevitably follows from them that the struggle for a cardinal solution of the problem in the present transitional epoch will give rise to an urgent need to develop a long-term strategy and-strictly scientific approach to the global outlook for industrialisation of the former colonies and semi–colonies on quite other principles of social and world economic relations compared with those historically built up by capitalism.

The postwar processes in the agrarian and industrial spheres have consequently had a different effect on the resultant ratio of per capita GDP in the groups of countries under consideration. In the agrarian sphere they have fostered a widening of the economic gap, and in the industrial sphere a narrowing.

But since the role of the agrarian sector in the GDP of developing countries is more significant than in the centres of capitalism, and the industrial sector less significant, the gap between them in per capita output of the main sectors (agriculture, industry, and building) has also continued to widen in recent decades, and for Asian and African countries was more than 10:1 at the beginning of the 80s against 8:1 in the first postwar years. In other words, at the turn of the decade to the 80s, per capita production in value terms (in comparable prices) was much lower in developing countries compared with capitalist ones, than at the turn of the 40s and 50s.

As for industry, its growth in developing countries has still not led to any real qualitative shifts in the liquidation of age-old industrial backwardness. The struggle to lay an industrial foundation for their national economies is still more or less, as a rule, in the initial stage. In spite of a narrowing of the gap in per capita industrial output, they now produce dozens of times less product than the average for capitalist countries. The most powerful, technically advanced branches of production, moreover, that can more efficiently exploit the fruits of the present scientific and technical revolution are concentrated in the latter. That is affecting the dynamics of productivity in the industry of both groups of countries. In the 60s and 70s its annual growth rates in the economic centres of capitalism were double that in the developing countries.

There has been a quite stable tendency towards a gradual, tough slow, rise in the proportion of circulation and services in the GDP of the developing world, which rose perceptibly in 1900–80. As a result of the rapid expansion of this sphere its weight in the GDP of the Asian and African regions rose by a quarter and nearly a third respectively in the 50s through the 70s. It rose a little as well in Latin America on the whole and constituted more than half of that region's GDP at the end of the 70s. In other words, there was a certain convergence of structural proportions in the sectors of non-material production of the main developing regions, but the historical underdevelopment of these sectors still remains a distinguishing sign of the economic backwardness of the vast majority of the former colonies and dependent countries of these regions.

The proportion of developing countries in the aggregate production of the services and circulation sphere of the world capitalist economy is beginning to grow. At the start of the 80s it was 10 per cent against 11 per cent in the early 50s. The per capita gap between them and the developed countries, it is true, not only did not in fact diminish but even widened a bit on the whole, and was estimated at 15.5:1 in the late 70s, *i.e.* was considerably wider than in the sectors of material production. For the main sectors of the circulation and services sphere this gap has not built up in the same way; in practice it has always been narrower in trade. But it is in that sector, as in agriculture, that the capitalist countries continued steadily to outpace the developing countries in per capita indices of growth, so that, although the proportion of the latter in the total value of the home trade of the capitalist world has risen since the war (from one-seventh to one-sixth), there has been another trend in per capita terms While the value of per capita trade (in constant 1975 prices) in the GDP of capitalist countries was 12 times as much as in developing countries at the beginning of the 60s, it was 16 times as much at the start of the 70s. This trend above all determined the effect in the circulation and services sphere of the tendency towards a further widening of the general economic gap in per capita GDP between the two groups of countries.

The intensification of this trend also to no small extent was promoted by processes taking place in the sectors producing so-called services. Developing countries' backwardness in this respect has long been deeper than in the other sectors of the sphere of social production we are considering. At the turn of the 50s and 60s it corresponded approximately to the level of their industrial backwardness. At that time less than one-tenth of the value of the services created in all capitalist countries was produced in developing countries, and the gap per capita was nearly 20:1. In recent years there have been changes in various directions in these ratios. The rapidly increasing dynamics of the growth of services in developing countries has led to their share rising in absolute terms to one-seventh at the end of the 70s. But in per capita terms the gap continued to widen for a long time, and in the early 70s could be expressed as 19.5:1, which was mainly due to the backwardness in this 175 area of the economically less developed and more densely populated countries of the African and Asian regions.

In the second half of the 70s alone, especially during the world cyclic crisis of 1974–75, a long-term consequence of which was a marked slowing of the growth rales of services in the centres of capitalism, did this gap begin to narrow a bit; at the beginning of the 80s it was expressed by a ratio of 17.5:1 (in 1975 prices). In other words, it has remained wider than in industry. The extreme backwardness of the services sphere governs several of the paramount aims of the long-term socio-economic strategy being developed by developing countries today in their striving to attain the maximum possible speeding up of the rates of social progress in present-day conditions and to raise the standard of living of their populations.

The only major group of services and circulation sectors in which developing countries managed to get a relatively stable increase in the dynamics of per capita production over that of the developed countries in the postwar decades was transport and communications; the grand total of per capita production in them increased by a factor of 3.4 against 2.4 in the developed countries. There was a corresponding rise (from 11 to 16 per cent) in developing countries' weight in the aggregate value of the product of transport and communications in the world capitalist economy. In per capita terms their mean annual rates of development have been higher of late than those of the industrial regions, so that in the area of the infrastructure, and in industry, there has begun to be a relatively new and apparently promising trend towards a certain narrowing of the gap in per capita indices, though it still remains extremely wide.

If the present dynamics of the growth of production and population is maintained the gap should be halved at least on an average in the coming two or three decades in each of the main regions of the developing world, but its ultimate closing will undoubtedly still remain an urgent task for a long time.

At the same time there was a clearly increasing unevenness in the development of transport and communications in the developing countries, which, as the figures given above show, 176 was organically characteristic of all the other sectors of the circulation and services sphere. Its dynamics will also undoubtedly be a close function of the degree and scale of development of material product ion and of the population growth rates in the various regions and countries of the developing world. On the whole, however, one can say with confidence that as the productive forces rise the weight of this sphere in the social production of these countries will gradually increase although it will still lag greatly behind the corresponding average indicator for the industrialised countries for several decades.

The wide gap between the developing countries and the centres of capitalism in all the decisive areas of economic activity consequently remains one of the objective realities of our time. Formed long ago, during the building of the world capitalist economy on a colonial basis, it now characterises many of the most important features of that economy, and of the whole system of its postwar international relations.

The developing countries of Asia, Africa, and Latin America, given the existing differences in their levels of sociopolitical and economic development, arc inevitably coming up against a need to deal with several common problems, vitally important for all developing countries, on both an international and a national scale. They include the very intricate set of each country's national problems, but ultimately the struggle to cope with all of them, taken together is objectively directed to eliminating the pernicious survivals of the colonial period from the affairs of human society" and to emancipating the developing countries from neocolonialism and continuing capitalist exploitation.

At the same time, as will be clear from the facts adduced above, the gap in levels of economic development remains extremely wide, in spite of considerable progress by the developing countries in coping with these problems, and moreover retains a tendency to widen in several determinant indicators, above all in gross product per capita. The relations of inequality and rapacious exploitation of the natural and human resources of the developing countries by expatriate monopoly capital prevailing in the world capitalist economy are furthering maintenance of this trend, even since the break-up of imperialism's colonial system.

The capitalist social system itself not only bears responsibility for the socio-economic backwardness of the peoples of the former 177 colonial world, but the exploiter system of international division of labour created by it largely continues today to fetter their productive forces. The basic patterns of the world capitalist economy still operate in the direction detrimental to the developing countries.

The striving of the developing countries to spread the liquidating of colonialism to the economic sphere, to put an end to their exploitation by the industrial powers of the West, and to achieve creation of the necessary external and internal conditions for attaining a level of development in the foreseeable future corresponding to the needs of today, is quite justified. At the same time all the nations of the earth without exception have an interest in the speediest attainment of these aims.

The struggle for a steady acceleration of socio-economic and cultural progress in the former colonies and semi-colonies is therefore becoming an inseparable part of the fight of all progressive mankind for detente and the consolidating of lasting peace, for further development of the scientific and technical revolution for peaceful purposes, and for a favourable solution of the other global problems of today on which the whole subsequent course of world development to an enormous extent depends.

In his day Karl Marx concluded that mankind thus inevitably sets itself only such tasks as it is able to solve, since closer examination will always show that the problem itself arises only when the material conditions for its solution are already present or at least in the course of formation. In the present historical situation more favourable objective conditions are being created than ever before for the countries of Asia, Africa, and Latin America that have liberated themselves from the imperialist yoke, or are in the course of doing so, for a successful struggle to overcome the backwardness inherited by them from the past in all sectors of 178 the economy and oilier areas of social affairs.

But every kind of obstacle is still being put in the way of this bard, long, stubborn light with the world capitalist economy by the former colonialists and expatriate monopoly capital. In these conditions the developing countries are uniting their efforts more and more firmly in the anti-imperialist movement to establish a new international economic order.

The Soviet Union and other socialist countries are supporting these efforts in every way possible and demonstrating their solidarity with the progressive aims of the struggle of the peoples of the developing world for a better future. As the Central Committee's Report to the 26'th Congress of the CPSU stressed: the CPSU will consistently continue the policy of promoting cooperation between the USSR and the newly-freo countries, and consolidating the alliance of world socialism and the national liberation movement.

The long-term trends reviewed in this chapter thus not only help us better to understand some of the general results of the changes that have already taken place in the structure of the distribution of the productive forces of the two groups of countries of the postwar capitalist world, but also to distinguish several objective premises for analysing the probable outlook for subsequent structural shifts leading to aggravation of the internal contradictions and crisis phenomena in the capitalist economy.

Study of these trends obviously calls for a need to allow in every way for the effect on them of the spontaneously operating laws of the cyclic development of the capitalist mode of production.

5

Status in Employment in the Agricultural Sector

INTRODUCTION

This patterns and trends based on Census '96 and the annual commercial agricultural surveys for specific variables related to full–time, part–time, casual or seasonal employment. Household members in the rural survey were not required to answer an equivalent question regarding employment status.

STATUS OF EMPLOYMENT BY POPULATION GROUP AND PROVINCE

Census '96 suggests that among people employed in the agriculture and hunting sub–sector, 90% were full–time and the remainder (10%) worked on a part–time basis. Figure shows the variation in full– and part–time employment by population group and gender. As illustrated in Figure full–time employment in the agricultural and hunting sub–sector was highest among white men and lowest among African and coloured women. According to Census '96, among white men employed in the agriculture and hunting sub–sector, 97% had full–time jobs compared with 83% among African women and 75% among coloured women.

Census '96 results also indicate large provincial differences in the patterns of full– and part–time employment in the agriculture and hunting sub–sector. Figure shows that there is a notable gender bias in terms of part–time employment. The difference in the proportion of men to women employed part–time is smallest in Gauteng and largest in Free State and Northern Cape.

Figure shows that, according to Census '96, the proportion of women employed on a part–time basis (19%) was three times higher than men (6%) employed on this basis. Part–time employment among women was highest in Northern Cape (39%) and lowest in Gauteng (10%). By comparison, among men employed part–time in the agriculture and hunting sub–sector, differences ranged between 10% in Northern Cape and only 4% in Mpumalanga.

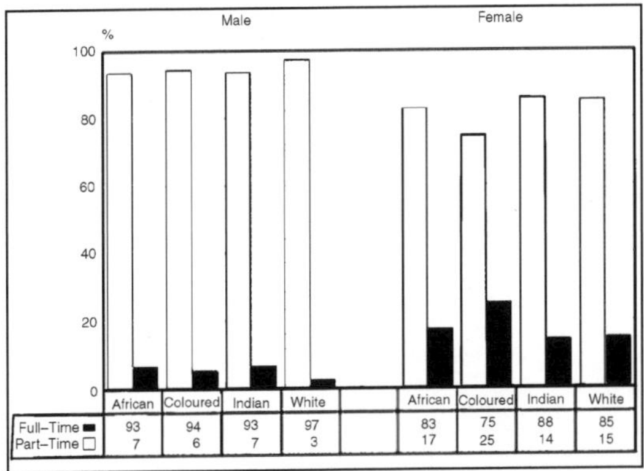

Fig. Full–Time and Part–Time Employment of People in the Agriculture and Hunting Sub–Sector by Population Group and Gender, October 1996

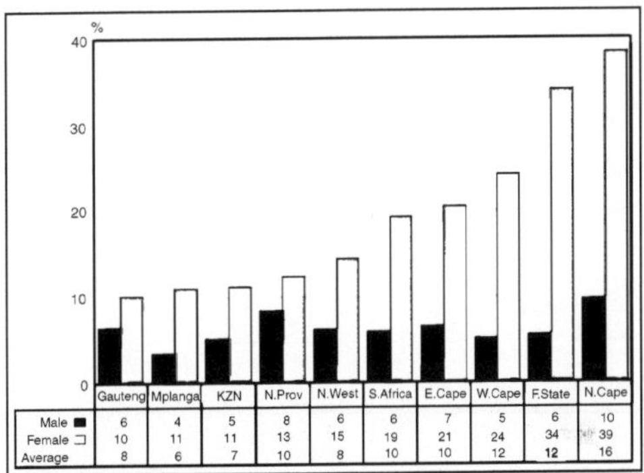

Fig. Part–Time Employment in the Agriculture and Hunting Sub–Sector by Province and Gender,

REGULAR AND CASUAL WORK

The casual and regular employment categories discussed below in relation to commercial farming activities are not directly comparable to the full–time and part–time categories reviewed earlier, because they refer to different concepts and are used in separate datasets. To be a casual or seasonal worker, a person can be in full–time employment for a limited time period, or else one could be in part–time employment for a limited period. However, they do provide an indication of the security of employment in the commercial farming sector.

Figure shows that, on the basis of the annual commercial agricultural surveys, the number of employees engaged in regular work on commercial farms declined from 724 000 in 1988 to 610 000 in 1996, a decline of 15,7% over the period as a whole.

As discussed earlier, since total employment fell by a larger percentage, the proportion of people engaged in regular employment was substantially higher in 1996 (67%) than in 1988 (59%). Nonetheless, in actual numbers, there were fewer regular employees in 1996 (610 000) than in 1988 (724 000) (On this, see also the NDA case study, pp. 34–38).

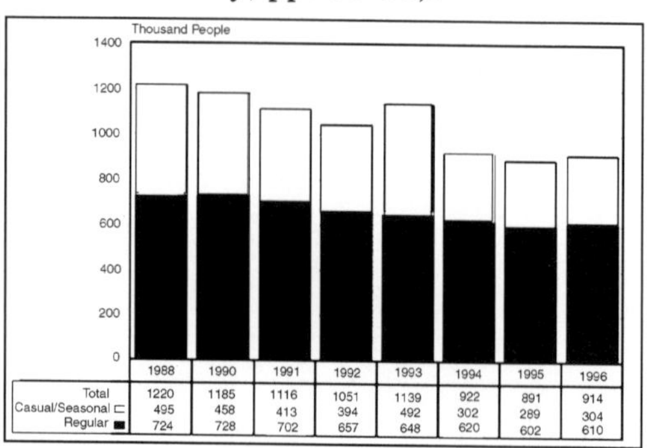

Fig. Regular and Casual Work in the Commercial Farming Sector,

On the basis of the annual commercial agricultural surveys, Figure shows large provincial differences in regular and casual/seasonal employment in the commercial farming sector. Of the total 914 000 employees on commercial farms during 1996, 67% were employed on a regular basis, while 33% were engaged as casual/seasonal workers. However, in terms of the provinces, regular employment in the commercial farming sector ranged from 86% of the workforce in Gauteng, to 42% in Northern Cape.

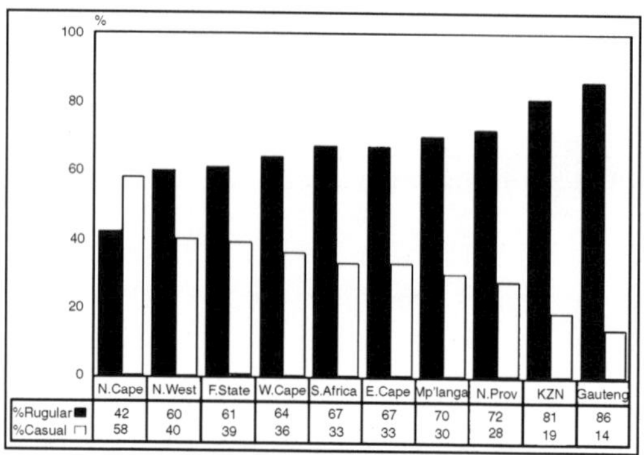

Fig. Regular and Casual Employment on Commercial Farms by Province,

Part–time work cannot be equated with seasonal and casual work. In addition, large seasonal variations in employment are a characteristic feature of the agriculture sector. This makes comparisons between Census '96 and the annual commercial agricultural surveys difficult since the census data relate to October 1996, while the employment data from the annual commercial agricultural surveys are annual averages. However, definition and timing issues aside suggests that the security of employment in terms of those who have regular jobs in the commercial farming sector or full–time jobs in the agriculture and hunting sub–sector varies enormously by province.

CASE STUDY

Recent trends in employment in the agricultural sector by the National Department of Agriculture The Presidential Job Summit, held in October 1998, resolved that each economic sector should hold its own job summit. Because of difficulties in accurately tracking all employment trends in agriculture from the available surveys, the National Department of Agriculture (NDA) undertook a case study based on a mail survey to some commercial farmers to provide up–to–date information regarding the employment situation in agriculture. The case study aimed to provide data which could inform the discussion at the Minister's Indala on job creation, held in October 1999. The questions asked in the mail survey were also designed to identify trends in various categories of employment within agriculture from 1994/95 through to 1998/99.

The Questionnaire

The questionnaire included five questions:

- Which of these categories represents the largest portion of the gross income from your farming operations?
  - Field crops (summer and winter crops, sugar cane, tobacco, lucerne and other field crops);
  - Horticultural products (viticulture, fruits, vegetables, potatoes, tea and flowers);
  - Livestock products (wool, mohair, ostriches, livestock, poultry and dairy);
  - Mixed farming (field crops and livestock products or horticultural products and livestock products).
- How many farm workers were employed during the financial years 1994/95, 1996/97, 1998/99?
  - Regular farm workers (defined as a worker employed permanently during the year);
  - Seasonal farm workers (defined as a shearer, reaper, fruit picker etc.,);
  - Family farm workers (defined as a paid or unpaid worker but not included under regular or seasonal farm workers).
- From those regular farm workers that you employed, how many were?
  - Skilled (defined as a worker with experience and/or training);
  - Unskilled (defined as a worker without experience and/or training).
- Did you hire contract workers (employed on contract but not seasonal) during these years?
- What sources did you use in order to determine the above information?
  - Memory

- Records
- Both

Issues Covered by the Case Study

- The level and trend in employment of regular, seasonal and family farm workers by commercial farmers.
- The level and trend in employment of skilled and unskilled regular farm workers.
- The level and trend in employment of contract workers.

The level and trend in employment in agriculture with respect to field crops, horticulture, animal production and mixed farming activities.

METHODOLOGY

In the absence of an adequate sampling frame, the NDA constructed a list frame based on two sources of information: details of commercial farmers available within the NDA itself (11 114 names and addresses); and a list obtained from Agri SA of 6 518 names and addresses of farmers in the commercial farming sector. After eliminating duplication in the lists, the sample size was set at 10 000 commercial farmers of which 5 000 were randomly selected from each of the two address lists available to the NDA.

Completed questionnaires were received from 4 149 commercial farmers. Since it was a mail survey, it was easy to implement and provided an up–to–date picture of employment in the agriculture sector in critical respects. However, the list frame from which the sample was drawn was not complete and only covered some farmers in the commercial sector. As a consequence, the results cannot be generalised to the overall population since the sample was not representative. The results of the case study are therefore only broadly indicative.

Results

In spite of the weaknesses of the survey methodology, the results of the case study by the NDA provide important insights about recent developments in the pattern of employment in the agriculture sector. Figure A shows that, among both regular workers and those employed by their family, employment continued a downward trend since 1994/95. Even though seasonal employment has been on upward trend in the past four years, the rate of increase slowed between 1996/97 and 1998/99.

- For example, in 1998/99 the number of regular workers in employment had fallen by a cumulative 7,6% since 1994/95. However, the decline of 2,9% in 1996/97 was less steep than occurred in the subsequent two–year period when employment fell by 4,8%.

The decline in employment of family workers on commercial farms was minimal in 1996/97 (down 0,8% since 1994/95). However, by 1998/99 employment of these workers fell by as much as 4,5%. As a result, the decline in employment of family workers was down 5,3% between 1994/95 and 1998/99.

- Employment of seasonal workers rose by 2,2% in the two years to 1996/97 and by an additional 1,2% in the two years to 1998/99 such that over the period 1994/95 to 1998/99 the number of seasonal workers had increased by 3,4%.
- Figure B shows the percentage change in employment on farms by type of major activity of the commercial farmers included in the NDA case study. The important trends highlighted in the case are as follows:
- Over the period 1994/95 to 1998/99, the percentage decline in employment of seasonal workers (down 9,3%) was highest among farmers whose main source of gross income from farming operations was animal production. By contrast, while over the same time period seasonal workers in mixed farming operations was also down 4,2%, horticultural farmers increased the employment of seasonal workers by 17,3%. Farmers who derived the most income from the sale of field crops also increased their employment of seasonal workers (up 6,3%) over an equivalent period.

The results of the NDA case study suggest that, over the period 1994/95 to 1998/99, commercial farmers engaged in almost all types of farming activities reduced their employment of regular workers.

But for horticulture (up 1,2%), employment of regular workers fell in every other major type of farming operation covered by the case study. For example, among commercial farmers whose main source of income was field crops, employment of regular workers declined by 6,1%. Among those whose main source of income was either mixed farming or animal production, the decline was even steeper–11,9% and 14,4% respectively

In terms of the employment of family members, the greatest decline over the period 1994/95 to 1998/99 was among those commercial farmers whose main source of income was animal production (down 27,6%). Among commercial farmers whose main source of income was field crops, the number of family members employed fell by 5,3%. The decline in employment of family members by farmers whose principal source of income was mixed farming was minimal (down 1,1%).

Notably, horticultural farmers increased the number of family members they employed by 9,5% over the period 1994/95 to 1998/99. In terms of contract workers, commercial farmers included in the NDA case study reported that, they accounted for an increasing proportion of the agricultural labour force, rising from 18,8% in 1994/95 to 21,6% in 1996/97 and 24,2% in 1998/99. Figure C highlights the upward trend in employment of skilled workers among commercial farmers included in the NDA case study. In 1994/95, 60% of workers employed by commercial farmers were skilled, rising to 63% in 1996/97 and 65% by 1998/99. This upward trend is reflected in the commensurate decline in the proportion of unskilled workers over the same period, from 40% in 1994/95 to 35% in 1998/99.

The results of the NDA case study conducted in 1999 among some commercial farmers suggest that employment of regular workers declined by 7,6% during the period 1994/95 to 1998/99, equivalent to an annual fall of 1,8% over the period. The growth of employment of seasonal workers was strongest among farmers engaged in horticulture (up 17,3% from 1994/95 to 1998/99) and field crops (up 6,3%) over an equivalent period. The number of seasonal workers employed by farmers whose main source of income was from animal production and mixed farming declined by 9,3% and 4,2% respectively over the period 1994/95 to 1998/99. At the same time, the number of family workers decreased for field crop farmers and animal producers, but increased substantially (up 9,5%) for producers of horticulture. Notably, among the commercial farmers included in the NDA case study, contract workers hired by these farmers accounted for an increasing share of those in employment over the period under review.

TYPE OF EMPLOYMENT IN AGRICULTURE

INTRODUCTION

This noteworthy patterns in the type of employment (whether self–employed, an employer, an employee or working in a family business) reported in the agriculture and hunting sub–sector during Census '96, and in the rural areas of the former homelands according to the rural survey of 1997.

TYPE OF EMPLOYMENT BY POPULATION GROUP AND PROVINCE

On the basis of Census '96, Figure shows that the distribution of Indians and whites in the agriculture and hunting sub–sector by employment type is markedly different from that of Africans and coloureds. Figure shows relatively small provincial differences. For example, among Indians employed in the agriculture and hunting sub–sector, 14% were self–employed and an additional 11% were employers.

Among whites, 13% were self–employed and 39% were employers. By contrast, among Africans and coloureds employed in the sub–sector, only 2% were either self–employed or employers, the vast majority (95%) worked as employees. Provincial differences in the type of employment available in the agriculture and hunting sub–sector are illustrated in Figure. Census '96 indicates that 90% of people employed in agriculture and hunting were employees, an additional 5% were employers and 3% reported that they were self–employed. However, 92% of the employed labour force in Western Cape and Free State were employees compared with 86% in Northern Cape where 9% of the agricultural labour force were employers.

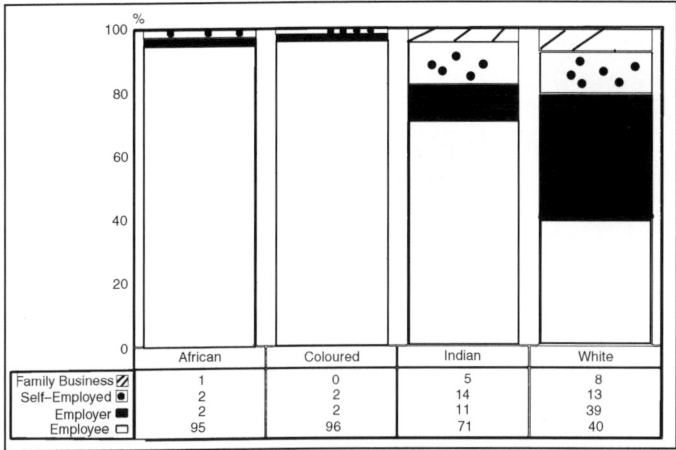

Fig. Type of Employment in the Agriculture and Hunting Sub–Sector by Population Group,

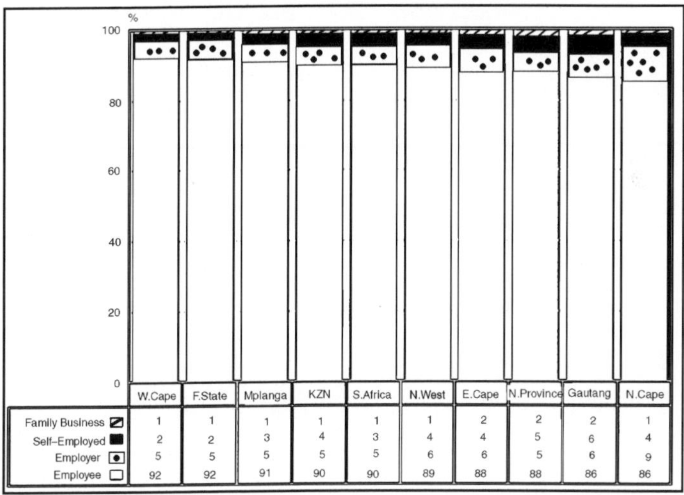

Fig. Type of Employment in the Agriculture and Hunting Sub–Sector by Province,

TYPE OF EMPLOYMENT IN THE FORMER HOMELANDS

Those who reported in the ru ral survey in the former homelands that they were employed on the farm or the land, whether for a wage or as part of the household farming activities are regarded as a good proxy for employment in small–scale or subsistence farms. In the discussion that follows, this group is compared with those who reported that they worked in the formal and informal sectors of the labour market (mostly non–agricultural work).

Figure shows that more than half of all employed people on small–scale and subsistence farms (54%) in the former homeland areas worked in a family business, an additional 25% were self–employed, 19% were employees and a relatively small proportion (2%) were employers. This pattern of employment reflects the subsistence nature of much of the agriculture that occurs in the former homeland areas. As expected, most employed people in the informal sector were self–employed (67%) although 21% worked as employees. In the formal sector, 92% of all employed people were employees.

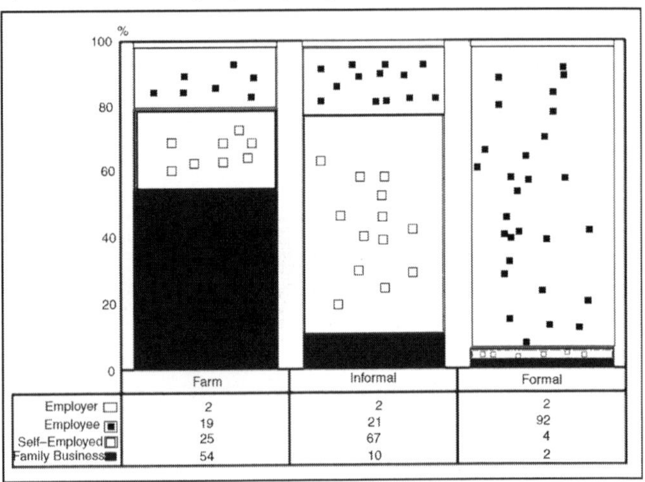

Fig. Type of Employment in the Former Homelands by Broad Employment Category,

When looking at the provinces according to where former homelands were situated, Figure shows large provincial differences in the type of employment among people engaged in farm work in the former homelands according to the rural survey. In the former homeland areas of Eastern Cape, 72% of people working on farms did so as part of the family business, compared with 12% in the former homeland areas in Free State.

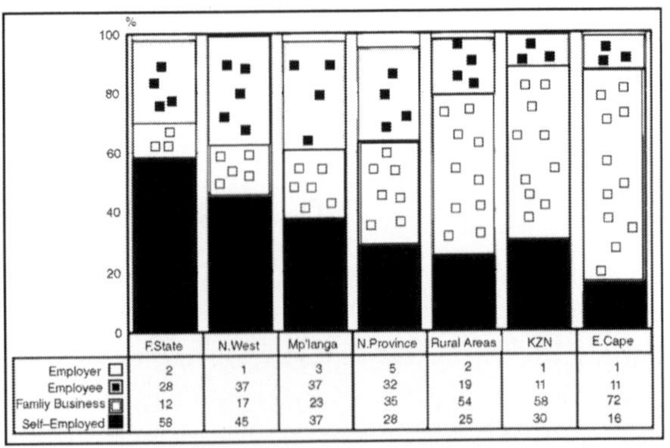

Fig. Type of Employment Among Farm Workers in the Former Homelands by Frovince,

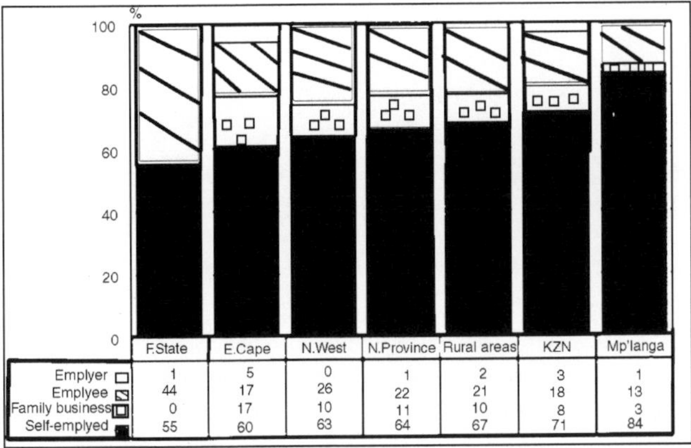

	F.State	E.Cape	N.West	N.Province	Rural areas	KZN	Mp'langa
Emplyer	1	5	0	1	2	3	1
Emplyee	44	17	26	22	21	18	13
Family business	0	17	10	11	10	8	3
Self-emplyed	55	60	63	64	67	71	84

Fig. Type of Employment Among Informal Sector Workers in the Former Homelands by Province,

Figure shows that, among informal sector workers in the former homelands, in every province, self–employment ranks highest. Over half of all informal sector workers in the former homelands in each province were reported as being self–employed. In contrast to the type of employment among either people working on farms or in the informal sector, Figure shows that formal sector workers living in the former homeland areas were predominantly employees. In every province except Eastern Cape, more than 90% of people working in the formal sector were employees.

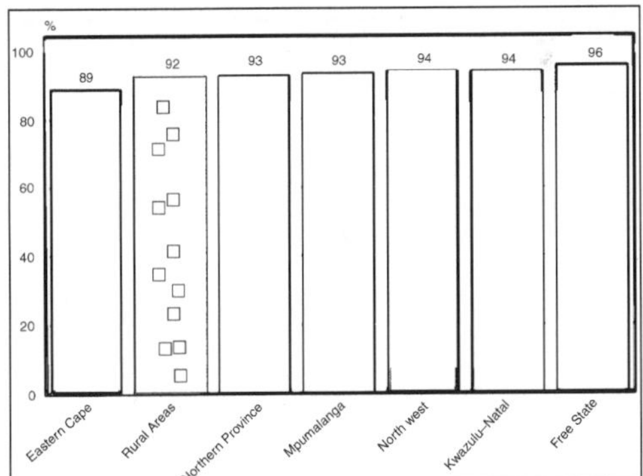

Fig. Type of Employment Among Formal Sector Workers in the Former Homelands by Province,

The analysis suggests that, using Census '96 data, most employed people in the commercial agricultural labour force are employees. In terms of the four major population groups, Census '96 also indicates that, in the agriculture and hunting sub–sector, the distribution of jobs by employment type is more even among Indians and whites than among Africans or coloureds. Nine in every ten Africans or coloureds are engaged as employees. By comparison, one in every four Indians are either self–employed or employers. Notably, nearly two in every five whites are employers. However, on the basis of the specialised rural survey conducted in the former homelands, there are notable differences in the type of employment among the three broad employment categories identified in this survey (*i.e.* farm, formal and informal). Whereas formal sector workers in the former homelands tend to be predominantly employees, people engaged in small–scale and subsistence farm work tend to work mainly in family businesses, while the largest proportion of informal sector workers are self–employed.

OCCUPATION OF PEOPLE IN AGRICULTURE

INTRODUCTION

The occupation status of labour force participants is related to their age–sex structure and level of education attainment This highlights occupational patterns among those employed in the agriculture and hunting sub–sector, on the basis of Census '96 results, and then discusses the occupations of people employed in the former homeland areas, on the basis of the results of the rural survey.

OCCUPATIONS IN AGRICULTURE AND HUNTING

As shown in Figure, the results of Census '96 suggest that whites and Indians are higher in the occupation hierarchy than Africans or coloureds. According to Census '96, among the relatively few coloured people employed in agriculture, 82% were found in elementary jobs such as fruitpicking and weeding. Among the preponderant group of Africans employed in the agriculture and hunting sub–sector, 58% were in jobs classified as elementary compared with 22% among Indians and only 12% among whites. At the higher end of the occupation hierarchy, 15% of Indians and an equivalent proportion of whites (15%) were employed as managers, professionals or technicians compared with only 1% of either Africans or coloureds.

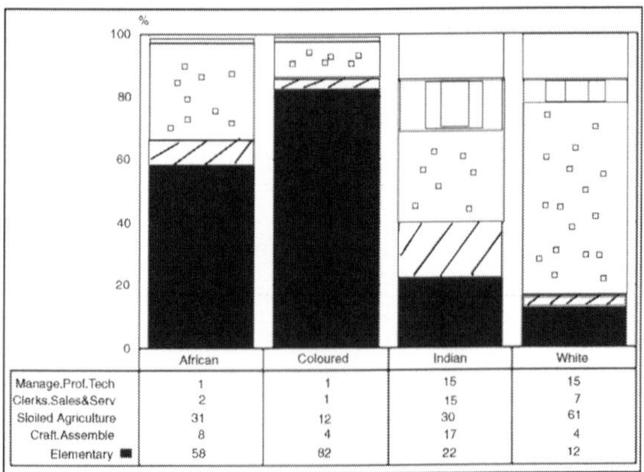

	African	Coloured	Indian	White
Manage.Prof.Tech	1	1	15	15
Clerks.Sales&Serv	2	1	15	7
Skilled Agriculture	31	12	30	61
Craft.Assemble	8	4	17	4
Elementary ■	58	82	22	12

Fig. Occupations in the Agriculture and Hunting Sub–Sector by Population Group,

Reflecting the dominance of Africans in the agricultural labour force and the low levels of education they have attained, Figure shows the distribution of men and women in the agriculture and hunting sub–sector by occupation status on the basis of Census '96. More than two in every three women (70%) in the agriculture and hunting sub–sector did jobs classified as elementary, while 55% of men fell into this occupation category. The second largest occupation category among both men and women was skilled agricultural work accounting for 32% of jobs among men and 22% among women.

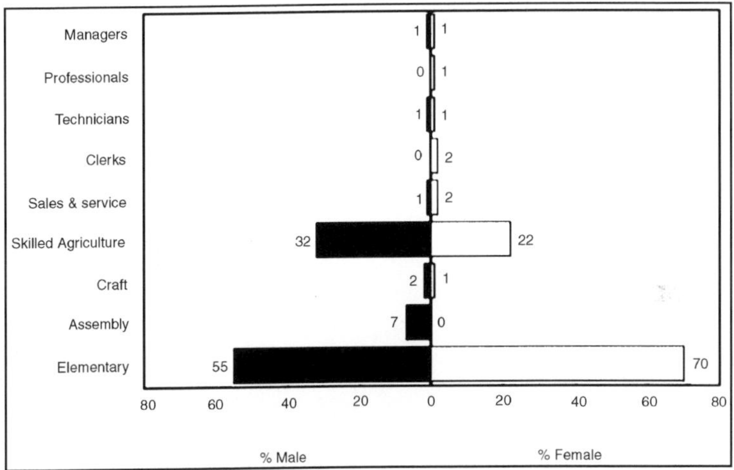

Fig. Occupations in the Agriculture and Hunting Sub–Sector by Gender,

OCCUPATIONS IN THE FORMER HOMELANDS

Figures illustrate the differences in occupational status among the three broad employment categories discussed earlier *i.e.* farm, informal and formal sector employment, on the basis of the rural survey of 1997. As noted earlier, in the absence of a specific question regarding the economic sector in which people worked, people who stated that they worked on farms–whether for a wage or as part of the household's farming activities–are regarded as a good proxy for the agriculture sector. The vast majority of these people working on farms were in subsistence or small–scale agriculture. On the basis of the rural survey, this section compares the occupation status of those who were working on farms with people who reported that they were either employed in the formal or informal sector in the former homelands.

Reflecting the importance of subsistence farming in the former homelands, Figure shows that among people engaged in farm work, the single largest occupation category among both men and women was skilled agriculture.

- Four out of every five (80%) people working on farms in the former homelands were engaged in 'skilled agriculture'. But, as shown in Figure, more than four out of every five (83%) women had such jobs compared with 74% of men.
- The second largest occupation category among both men and women

employed on farms in the former homelands was elementary work, accounting for 12% of employment opportunities among women and 10% among men.

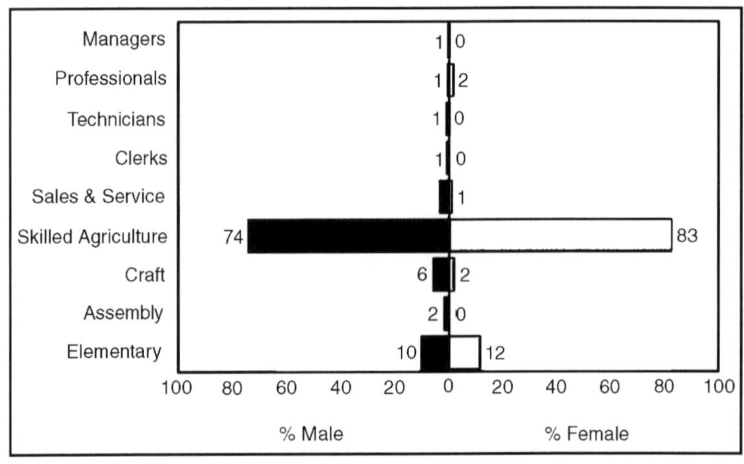

Fig. Occupation Status of People Doing Farm Work in the former homelands,

Figure, based on the rural survey, shows that elementary work requiring low levels of education and skill is the single largest occupation category among both women and men who are informal sector workers in the former homelands. Overall, the rural survey indicates that, in the former homelands, one in every two workers in the informal sector (50%) was engaged in routine work classified as 'elementary'. But, as shown in Figure nearly two in every three (63%) women had such jobs compared with 35% of men. The second largest occupation category among both men and women in the informal sector was craft and related work, accounting for 14% of jobs among women and 30% among men.

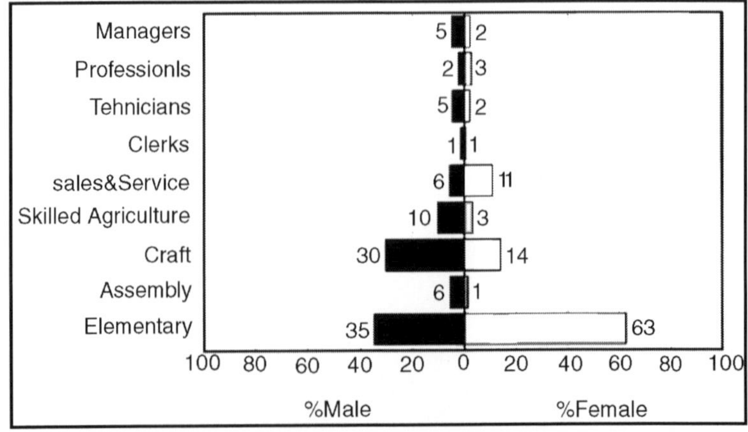

Fig. Occupation Status of Informal Sector Workers in the Former Homelands,

Figure, based on the results of the rural survey, shows that among formal sector workers in the former homelands, elementary work was also the single largest occupation category among both men and women. As illustrated in Figure, one in every three (33%) formal sector workers in the former homelands had the occupation status 'elementary'. This type of routine work accounted for 46% of jobs among women and 25% among men. Craft and related work was the second largest occupation category among men (22%), while one in every five women (20%) was employed as a professional (which includes teachers).

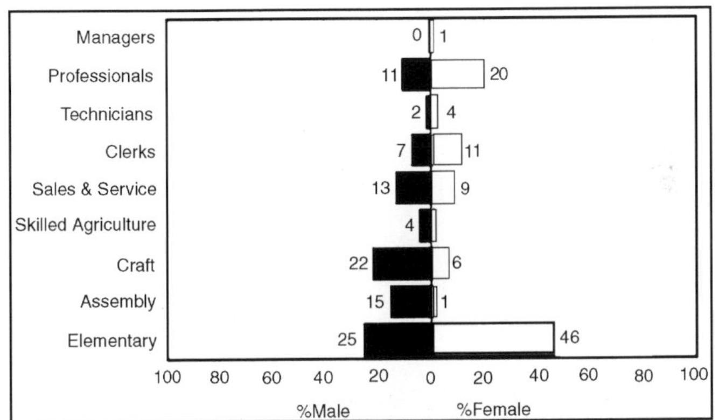

Fig. Occupation Status of Formal Sector Workers in the Former Homelands,

Overall, Figures shows that the distribution of jobs by occupation in the former homelands was more even among formal sector workers than either those engaged on farms or people employed in the informal sector. For example, whereas 14% of workers in the formal sector were professionals, only 3% of informal sector workers and 1% of people engaged in farm work fell in this occupation category.

DOMESTIC WORKERS

In the rural survey, 126 000 people living in the former homelands reported that they were domestic workers. This is 6% of the 2,2 million people who were employed. The vast majority of domestic workers (81%) were classified in the formal sector, 15% worked on farms and 4% worked in the informal sector. Other notable features of domestic workers included the following:

Ninety per cent of all domestic workers were women of whom 15% were between the ages of 50–59 years.

- *Twenty: N*ine per cent of domestic workers had no schooling and an additional 68% had achieved 'less than matric'.
- *Ninety*: Five per cent of domestic workers were employees.

Census '96 suggests that 11% of employed people were engaged in private households as domestic workers. The large differences in the level of educational attainment by population group were discussed. Reflecting this, the analysis on the basis of Census '96 results, that the distribution of jobs by occupation is overwhelmingly of a routine or 'elementary' nature in the agriculture and hunting sub–sector. In the former homelands, the rural survey suggests that whereas people employed on farms are in skilled agriculture, the single largest occupation category among informal sector workers is routine or elementary work. Although occupations in the formal sector of the former homelands tend to be more evenly distributed, in all three sectors women tend to feature more predominantly at the lower ends of the occupational hierarchy.

INCOME AND REMUNERATION IN AGRICULTURE

The remuneration received by employed people–whether as cash wages and salaries or as payment in kind–is related to their age, level of education and occupation status. This patterns and trends in remuneration in the agricultural sector on the basis of the data from Census '96, as well as with respect to the annual commercial agricultural surveys, relating to the commercial farming sector.

Individual incomes of employed people in the rural survey were not measured since the principal focus of this survey was the household, and the incomes of employed people within households are not reported separately. Nonetheless, the scope of the discussion has been broadened by grouping people into households in which employed people live and those in which no household members are employed. This enables an assessment of the level and source of incomes of households in which employed people live in the former homeland areas.

INDIVIDUAL INCOMES BY POPULATION GROUP AND PROVINCE

Figure illustrates the distribution of monthly incomes by population group among employed people in the agriculture and hunting sub–sector, as reported in Census '96. The census question was phrased in terms of all types of income: as a result, the income bands reported include remittances, payments in kind and all types of grants. However, the value of home produce, for example growing maize or other products for home consumption, is not taken into account. Among Africans employed in the sub–sector, according to Census '96, the vast majority (79%) had monthly incomes of R500 or less, falling to 67% among coloureds and 18% and 10% among Indians and whites respectively. By comparison, whereas 46% of whites received monthly incomes in the highest income bracket (R3 501 and more), only 1% of Africans and 18% of Indians had incomes in this range.

However, there are even larger inequities in the distribution of income by gender. Census '96 indicates that, in the agriculture and hunting sub–sector, as many as 83% of all women fell into the lowest income bracket (R0–R500) compared with 65% of men who had incomes in this range. Differences also emerge sharply in relation to the income distribution by population group. For example, among African men in the agriculture and hunting sub–sector, 76% had monthly incomes in the lowest income bracket compared with 88% of African women. But relatively few white men (9%) or women (17%) fell into this income bracket. Instead, among white men, more than half (52%) had incomes in the highest income bracket (R3 501 and more).

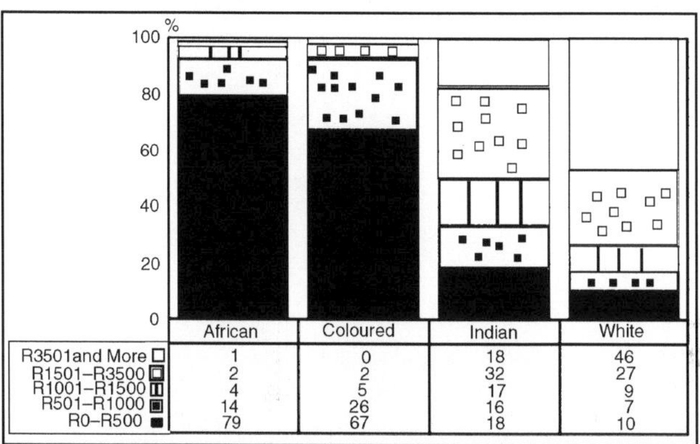

	African	Coloured	Indian	White
R3501and More	1	0	18	46
R1501–R3500	2	2	32	27
R1001–R1500	4	5	17	9
R501–R1000	14	26	16	7
R0–R500	79	67	18	10

Fig. Monthly Income of People Employed in the Agriculture and Hunting Sub–Sector by Population Group,

According to Census '96, the provincial distribution of monthly incomes of people employed in the agriculture and hunting sub–sector also showed a marked variation. In the wealthier provinces of Gauteng and Western Cape, a smaller proportion of people were in the lowest income band (R0–R500). For example, among the relatively few people employed in the sub–sector in Gauteng, 53% had monthly incomes of R500 or lower, and in Western Cape 56% had incomes in this range. By comparison, more than four out of every five people employed in the sub–sector in Free State (81%) and Northern Province (81%) were in this income category (R500 or less).

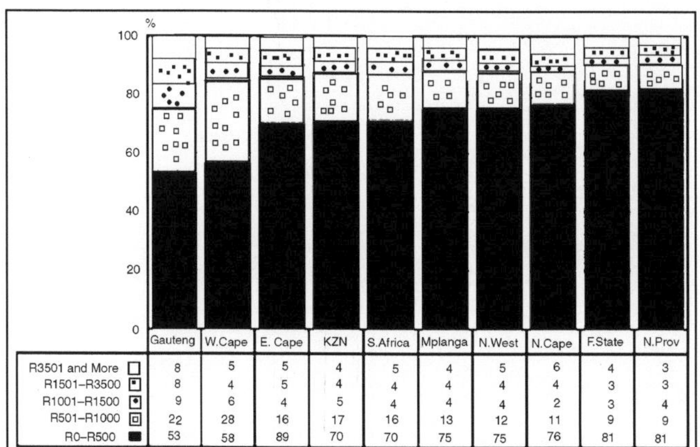

	Gauteng	W.Cape	E. Cape	KZN	S.Africa	Mplanga	N.West	N.Cape	F.State	N.Prov
R3501 and More	8	5	5	4	5	4	5	6	4	3
R1501–R3500	8	4	5	4	4	4	4	4	3	3
R1001–R1500	9	6	4	5	4	4	4	2	3	4
R501–R1000	22	28	16	17	16	13	12	11	9	9
R0–R500	53	58	89	70	70	75	75	76	81	81

Fig. Monthly Income of People Engaged in the Agriculture and Hunting Sub–Sector by Province,

REMUNERATION IN THE COMMERCIAL FARMING SECTOR

This section discusses patterns and trends, derived from the annual commercial agricultural surveys, in remuneration in the commercial farming sector. Although gender distinctions are not made in these surveys, differences in remuneration by population group and between regular and casual/seasonal employees are indicated. This is because the number of employees is an average for the relevant year while remuneration relates to the last day of February each year. On the basis of the annual commercial agricultural surveys, Figure illustrates the trend in average remuneration since 1988 and also the trends in remuneration of both casual and regular employees in the commercial farming sector. As illustrated in Figure, the average monthly remuneration of employees in the commercial farming sector more than tripled over the period 1988–1996, from R142 in 1988 to R524 in 1996. This trend does not take inflation into account. Although the trend for both casual and regular employees has also been upward, remuneration levels among casual workers in 1996 were still substantially lower than among regular workers. By 1996, the remuneration received by casual workers in the commercial farming sector was only around a quarter (26%) of that received by regular employees (up from 19% in 1990).

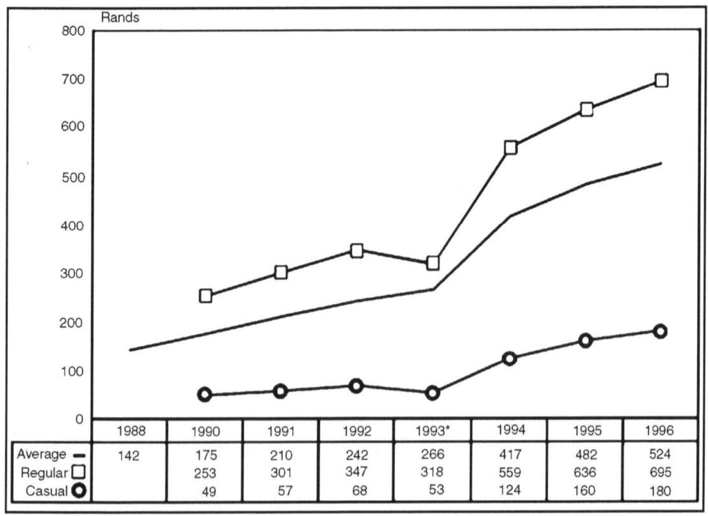

	1988	1990	1991	1992	1993*	1994	1995	1996
Average ▬	142	175	210	242	266	417	482	524
Regular ☐		253	301	347	318	559	636	695
Casual ○		49	57	68	53	124	160	180

Fig. Average Monthly Remuneration of Employees in the Commercial Farming Sector,

Figure shows that, in the commercial farming sector, there are large differences in average remuneration levels and trends by population group. The results of the annual commercial agricultural surveys indicate that, in the commercial farming sector, the average remuneration for all employees is closer to that for Africans and coloureds and markedly different from that of either Indians or whites. This reflects the dominance of Africans among employees in the commercial farming sector, and the low level of wages they receive. Figure shows that, apart from Indian employees, monthly remuneration increased in both 1995 and 1996 for Africans, coloureds and whites. The increase in remuneration among African employees over the period 1994–1996 was 28,9% compared with 14,9% among white employees during the same period. However, in 1996, the level of remuneration among Africans was barely 12% that of whites.

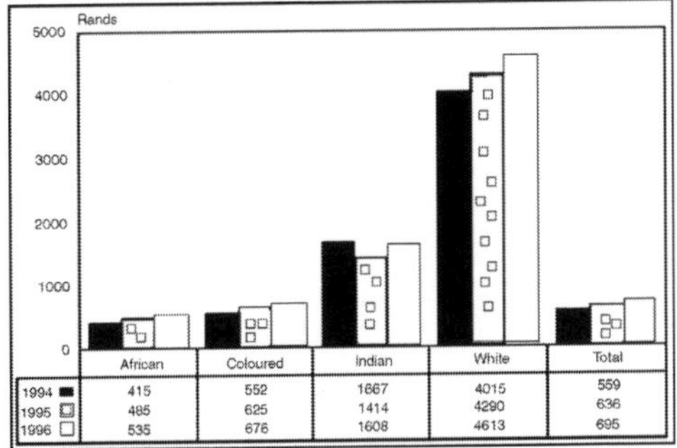

Fig. Average Monthly Remuneration of Regular Employees in the Commercial Farming Sector, 1994–1996

Figure shows that, according to the annual commercial agricultural surveys, 'in–kind' payments (such as free housing, rations and clothing) constituted a larger proportion of the remuneration paid to Africans than any other population group. For example, in 1996, 'in–kind' payments accounted for one quarter (25%) of the remuneration paid to Africans employed on a regular basis in the commercial farming sector. This type of payment fell to 21% among coloureds and 11% among whites.

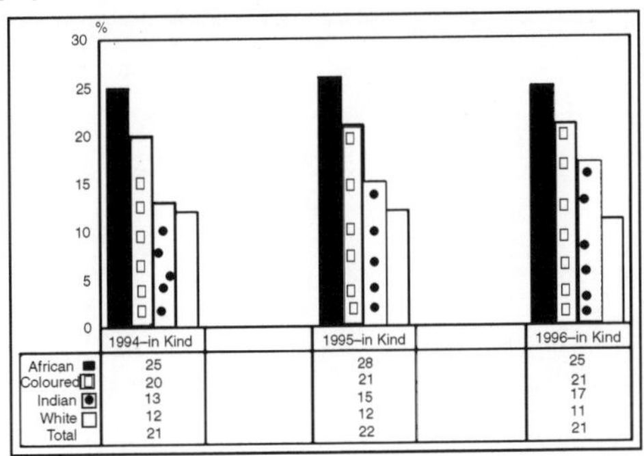

Fig. Payment in Kind to Regular Employees,

The annual commercial agricultural surveys also indicate that, in the commercial farming sector, the distribution of average monthly remuneration varies substantially across the nine provinces. For example, in 1996, the monthly remuneration (including 'in–kind' payments) among employees in Gauteng (R820) was nearly two–and–a–half times higher than in Northern Cape (R341).Figure shows that, in the commercial farming sector, the proportion of 'in–kind' payments tended to be generally lower in the provinces where average remuneration was highest. For example, in 1996, employees on commercial farms in Gauteng received the highest monthly remuneration of R820 of which only 14% was payment in kind. By comparison, in 1996 the average remuneration of employees in Free State (R388) and Northern

Cape (R341) was the lowest of the nine provinces, yet 'in–kind' payments accounted for 27% and 24% respectively of total remuneration in these provinces.

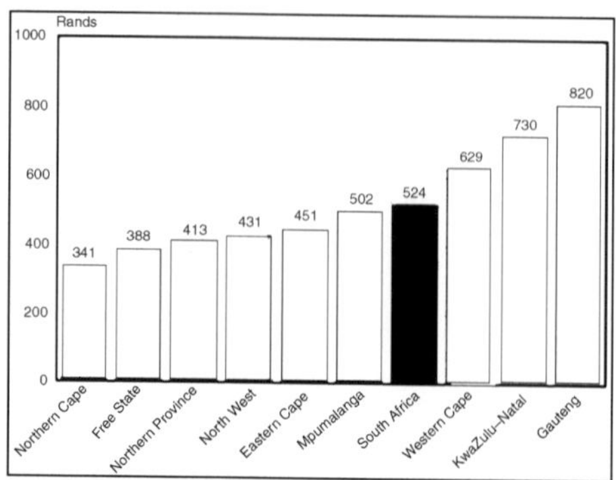

Fig. Average Monthly Remuneration to Employees in the Commercial Farming Sector by Province, 1996

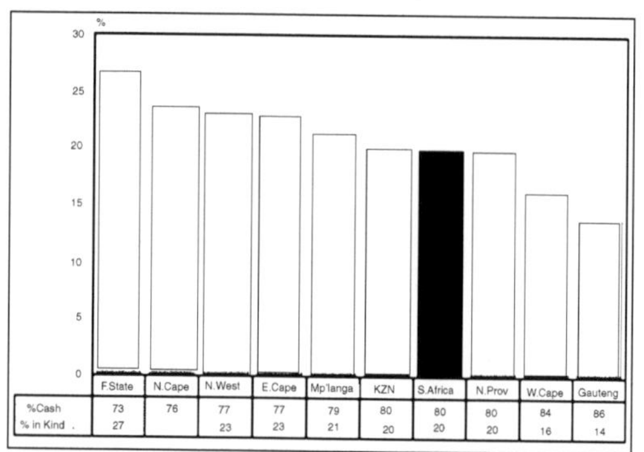

	F.State	N.Cape	N.West	E.Cape	Mp'langa	KZN	S.Africa	N.Prov	W.Cape	Gauteng
%Cash	73	76	77	77	79	80	80	80	84	86
% in Kind	27		23	23	21	20	20	20	16	14

Fig. Payments in Kind to Employees in the Commercial Farming Sector,

HOUSEHOLD INCOMES IN THE FORMER HOMELANDS

As noted earlier, the rural survey reported only on household incomes in the former homelands. Of the 2,4 million households covered in the former homelands, 1,6million had members that were engaged in farming activities.

This section reviews the income distribution of households engaged in farming activities divided into two broad labour market categories: households with at least one employed person, and households in which no member is employed. However, the conclusions drawn must be interpreted with caution because the household incomes reported do not include a valuation of 'own–consumption'.

Even in the rural survey, there are some households engaged in subsistence farming activities where respondents reported that they were unemployed. In the first instance, the discussion focuses on the main source of income that was reported by these two types of households in the rural survey of 1997.

This is followed by a discussion of the distribution of income of the two broad categories of households identified above. Among households engaged in farming activities in the former homelands, the rural survey indicates that 71% (1,2 million) had at least one employed household member. In the remaining 29% (475 000 households), no–one was employed although some of these people could have been engaged in subsistence activities.

Figure shows large differences in the dependence on various sources of income by each of these two broad categories of households.

- As expected, the rural survey indicates that, in the former homelands, salaries and wages were the most important source of income for those households in which at least one member was employed. Two out of every five (43%) of such households depended on a salary/ wage.
- Even in households in which at least one member was employed, more than a quarter of such households (26%) depended on pensions as the principal source of income while an additional 19% depended on remittances.
- Among households in which no household member was employed, pensions were the most important source of income. More than half (53%) of such households relied on pensions as the principal source of income and an additional 28% depended on remittances.
- The rural survey results indicate that, in the former homelands, farming activities were not the principal source of income for either type of household. For example, in households with employed people, only 4% depended on income from farming activities as the main source of income, and in households without employed people 3% depended on such activities as the main source of income.

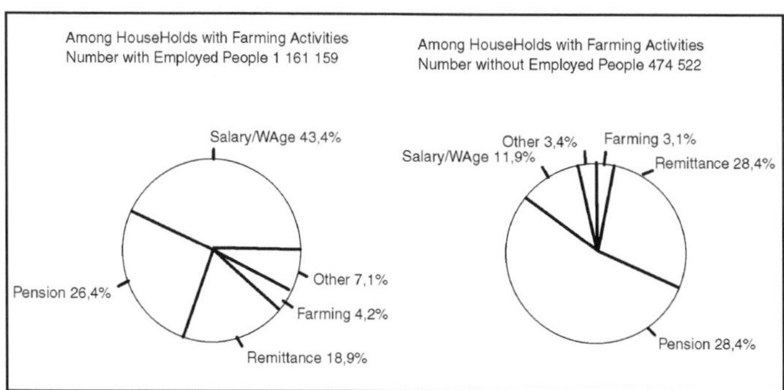

Fig. Principal Source of Income of Households Engaged in Farming Activities by Broad Labour Market Status, June 1997

Figure shows that, in the former homelands, among the 253 000 households which depended on pensions as the main source of income, 55% had household members that were employed. In the remaining households (45%), no household member was employed, but this figure could have included some form of subsistence farming. Among the 63 000 households which depended on farming activities as the main source of income, 77% had household members who were employed.

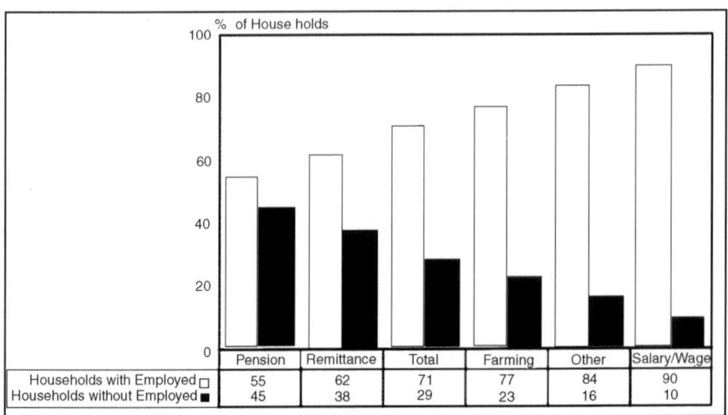

Fig. Principal Source of Income of Households Engaged in Farming Activities,

Figure shows that, among those households in the former homelands that were engaged in farming activities, a larger proportion of households in which no member was employed fell into the lowest income brackets compared with households in which at least one person was employed.

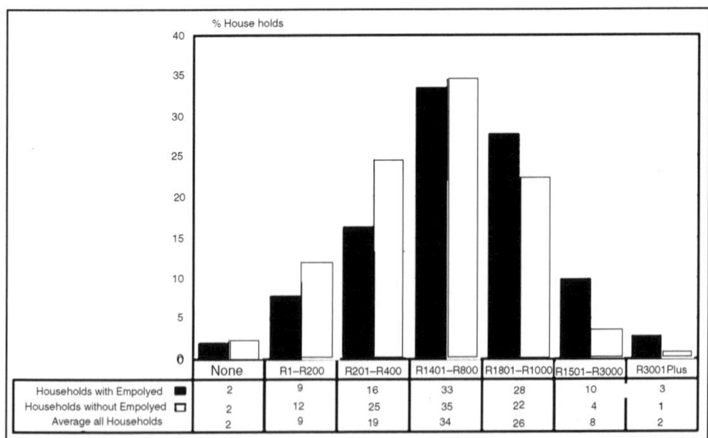

Fig. Income Distribution of Households Engaged in Farming Activities,

- Among the 1,6 million households in the former homelands that reported that they were engaged in farming activities during the rural survey, 475 000 reported that no household member was employed. Nearly two out of every five of these households (39%) survived on monthly incomes of R400 or less–equivalent to R4 800 or less on an annual basis.

- By comparison, among those households in which at least one person was employed, 26% reported monthly incomes of R400 or less.
- Reflecting the importance of pensions as the main source of household income in the former homelands, for both types of households similar proportions (33% and 35%) were in the R401–R800 monthly income category.

On the basis of Census '96 results, suggests that, among people employed in the agriculture and hunting sub–sector, the income distribution of Africans (and to a lesser extent, coloureds) is markedly different from that of Indians or whites. According to Census '96, almost one in every four Africans received monthly incomes of R500 or less, while almost half (46%) of all whites employed in the sub–sector received monthly incomes in excess of R3 500. These incomes exclude remuneration in kind. Provincial differences in the distribution of income are also marked. These patterns (indicated by Census '96 results) are similar to the average remuneration of employees in the commercial farming sector on the basis of the annual commercial agricultural surveys. Although average monthly remuneration in the commercial farming sector rose steadily in the three years to 1996, the remuneration of Africans was only 12% of that paid to whites in 1996. In terms of the former homelands, the rural survey conducted in 1997 suggests that more than one–quarter of all households (26%) in which at least one member was employed survived on a monthly household income of R400 or less.

6

Agriculture and Macroeconomy

MACROECONOMIC PROJECTIONS

INTRODUCTION

Projecting the future course of economic development is a risky business; it is particularly risky to project the medium–term prospects for Guyana beyond the year 2000 given the range of uncertainties it faces. Perhaps the most significant influence on the course of future economic developments will be the speedy and effective implementation of the macro and sectoral policies that have been described in this Strategy in order to overcome key constraints and to unlock the door for renewed economic expansion and opportunities for every Guyanese. Assuming that these policies will be implemented, and recent experience would argue in favour of such an assumption, another important influence would be the Government's commitment to address some of the more troublesome structural, regulatory and legal deficiencies.

As already outlined above, this will mean the creation of an economic policy framework conducive to creating and maintaining international competitiveness, sustaining the high GDP growth rates in recent years, and reversing the rate of environmental degradation. This suggests a range of possible future development scenarios, but only two will be outlined here. The first and best case scenario of future growth prospects is based on the assumption that the Government will implement the Development Strategy along the lines described in the document and will create an enabling environment for expanded growth at a sustainable level and the international economic environment will not turn unfavourable. The second and less optimistic scenario is based on the assumption that the Government fails to take the full range of measures necessary to revitalise the Guyanese economy and that the international economy is less propitious for Guyana's development.

In quantitative terms, the two scenarios bracket an aggregate economic growth rate of 6 per cent per year. To illustrative the importance and cumulative impact of achieving such growth on a sustained basis, it can be observed that 6 per cent annual growth over twenty years leads to more than a tripling of incomes per capita. To be precise, after twenty years of such growth, incomes would be 320 per cent of their current level. This is mere arithmetic, but it shows why several East Asian countries have been able to rise to prosperity within the time span of a generation or slightly more. Compounding is a powerful effect if sustained. This kind of growth is not out of Guyana's reach, provided that decisive, growth–oriented policies measures are implemented in a consistent manner, at both macroeconomic and sectoral levels.

THE EXTERNAL ENVIRONMENT

Growth prospects for Guyana are dependent in part on growth performance in its major external markets. Present projections for the OECD countries suggests continuing growth of their output with a slight improvement in the rate, from 2.6 per cent in 1995 to 2.7 per cent in 1997–2001. These growth rates, if attained, will stimulate increased demand for Guyana's exports. In other words, any constraints to export expansion would be found on the side of domestic policies and production. Similarly, for the remainder of the 1990s, inflation in US dollars is projected to average about 2.1 per cent, while the US dollar is expected to depreciate slightly against major currencies. Given that a large proportion of Guyana's imports come from the U.S., such an outcome would be beneficial because it would make such imports cheaper relative to imports from the rest of the world. However, as discussed in threatening clouds hover over the future of the preferential prices that Guyana receives for its primary exports, *viz.*, sugar and rice, and therefore the policy reforms for those sectors suggested are urgently required. Diversification of Guyana's export base also is essential in order to realise the country's growth aspirations.

FUTURE GROWTH SCENARIOS

The High Growth Scenario

The first scenario, which takes an optimistic but not unrealistic view of future developments, is predicated on the assumption that the Government will take early action to introduce trade reforms and investment and land development policies and also begin to correct the existing structural, legal and regulatory deficiencies as described throughout this Strategy.

Specifically, it is assumed that Government will:

- Hold the line on the local component of public sector capital expenditures and raise revenues to bring the overall balance to about 2.9 per cent of GDP by 2004;
- Rapidly increase nominal wage rates in the public sector so as to reduce the differential between private and public sector wages to about 15 per cent;

- Carry out the needed reforms in education and training, giving greater emphasis to primary education and involving the private sector in decisions on labour force training;
- Continue to work towards achieving a more competitive real exchange rate;
- Privatise GEC and carry out the prescribed improvements in harbours, roads and air transport facilities;
- *Implement Far*: Reaching trade policy reforms so as to reduce the anti–export bias of the current incentive structure;
- Promote increased savings through financial sector reforms and measures for public expenditure reduction;
- Move quickly to clarify and codify investment incentives;
- Simplify and make more uniform the tax regime;
- Simplify the registration procedures for small businesses;
- In the natural resource sectors, put into place new measures for introducing greater security of land tenure, flexibility in land markets, longer forestry concessions and better management of fisheries stocks.
- Undertake measures needed to maintain a balance between the environment and production.

The successful implementation of these measures would, in the short term, go far towards maintaining the existing growth rates. Moreover, the shift in relative prices favouring tradeable goods, brought about by an exchange rate policy that is more propitious for growth, should lead to increased utilisation of resources towards finding a niche in the world market in the context of efficient export–oriented growth. On balance, in this more favourable scenario, the economy is projected to grow at an average annual rate of 7.3 per cent during 1996–1999, and 6.8 per cent thereafter.Prospects for Guyana maintaining its sugar and rice quota, given projections of recovery in the European Union are favourable.

Nevertheless, the outcome also depends, in the case of rice, on the continuity of the current arrangements of rice exports to the EU through the OCT. There are some concerns that this loophole may be closed. Even so, the assumption is that there will be positive resolution of this issue, thereby generating the same outcome of rice exports. Beyond 2000, however, the projections assume that there will be no preferential market arrangements for rice.

Thus, the growth in rice production is predicated on the industry taking early actions in reducing cost of production, improving yields, and processing rice into cereals and other rice based products for markets in the Caribbean. For sugar, the assumption is that some protocol with the EU would exist after 2002, but that the real price will continue to slip.

Table. Medium–Term Prospects, High Growth Scenario

	Preliminary 1995	Projections 1996–99	2000–2004
	Annual Percentage Growth Rates (1994 constant prices)		
Gross Domestic Product	5.1	7.3	6.8
Agriculture	7.2	6.4	5.4
Industry	0.9	11.8	9.8
Services	3.0	3.0	3.0
Exports (GNFS)	9.4	5.4	5.1
Imports (GNFS)	5.8	6.9	5.7
Total Expenditure	1.4	8.1	6.8
Consumption	–3.5	8.8	8.1
Investment	17.5	6.0	2.2
Gross Domestic Income	9.8	7.8	6.4
Gross Domestic Savings	63.1	0.6	0.3
Memorandum Items			
Per capita GDP	4.8	7.0	6.5
Per capita GNP	–4.0	9.4	6.6
Per capita total consumption	–3.8	8.5	7.8
Per capita private consumption	–7.6	6.0	9.9

In addition, capitalisation of the sugar industry, and cost reductions and efficiency gains at the farm and factory level, are expected to improve Guyana's competitiveness at least in the Caribbean. Thus, rationalisation of the industry in the next few years will be critical in attaining the medium–term objectives for the entire economy.

Based on these factors, the volume of sugar production is expected to decline by a third in 2000 and thereafter grow at an annual rate of 2.5 per cent over the medium term.The mining sector output is projected to grow at 9 per cent over the medium term on account of conclusion of investment agreements between the Government and investors from Canada and Australia.The formulation of a clear mining policy in addition to recent reforms in sale and gold exports are expected to generate more domestic interest in gold exploration and mining. Between 1996 and 1999, the manufacturing sector's output is projected to remain fairly constant as the sector undergoes restructuring.

From 2000 onwards, as incentives shift towards export oriented activities, manufacturing output is projected to expand at an average annual rate of 8.3 per annum. Services, in particular banking, are expected to respond positively to the projected increases in manufacturing and mining output. Beyond 2000, diversification and industrial value–added could contribute to continuing expansions of domestic output. The expenditure policies discussed above are projected to reduce real growth of the local component of the capital programme below that of GDP and, jointly with financial sector reforms, enable domestic savings to increase from 30.2 per cent in 1995 to about 35.5 per cent of GDP in 1998 and to 31.1 per cent by 2004.

Public savings are projected to average about 7.9 per cent of GDP throughout the projection. Apart from high wage increases, the restrained growth of local investment programmes envisioned in the medium term will be necessary to establish and maintain viable macroeconomic balances.Over the medium term, it is anticipated that the implementation of the policies proposed will stimulate private sector investment in the core productive sectors as well as new investments to improve physical infrastructure.

Thus, gross investment is projected to reach 44.2 per cent of GDP by 1999 and thereafter decline steadily to 37.8 per cent of GDP by 2004. The incremental capital– output ratio will decline from its high level of 9 in 1995 to about 6.9 in 2004.

Balance of Payments and Financing Requirements

Another important element of the medium–term economic outlook is the viability of the balance of payments. The terms of trade are not projected to improve over the medium term, based on the World Bank's current long–term price projections and current preferential trade agreements.

If implemented in a timely basis, the impact of macroeconomic and trade policies on sectoral outputs would offset the negative effects of the deteriorating terms of trade. Under the high–growth scenario, real exports of goods and non–factor services are projected to grow at 5.1 per year between 1996 and 1999 and 3.5 per cent per annum thereafter.

Real imports, on the other hand, are projected to grow at 5.2 per cent per year between 1996 and 1999 and 3.8 per cent per year thereafter. The current account deficit of the balance of payments is projected to decline from 12.4 per cent of GDP in 1995 to 7.6 per cent of GDP in 2004. Guyana's past debt strategy has led to increased foreign indebtedness and high debt service ratios.

As a result, the country has become vulnerable to debt servicing problems especially if access to external finance were to become unduly restricted. However, it is assumed that with viable macroeconomic balances, access to concessional financing from the IFIs and bilateral agencies will be enhanced.

The projected fairly steady medium– and long–term disbursements have been assumed to consist mainly of concessional financing from the IFIs. Predicated on the timely adoption of the above measures, debt servicing is not projected to create undue strain to the economy.

The debt service–to–export ratio is projected to decline from 39.0 per cent in 1995 to 15.9 per cent in 1999 and to average 16.5 per cent per year thereafter. The interest burden ratio is projected to decline sharply from 19 per cent in 1995 to about 7.0 per cent in 2004. The ratio of debt service to government revenue is a useful measure of the burden of debt, since the only way in the long run that a government can honour its debt is through payment out of its revenues.

A long–run ratio of debt service to government revenue more than 20 per cent would impose significant pressure on public sector finances and limit capacity to undertake needed public sector reforms. On average, debt service to revenue is projected at 33 per cent implying less flexibility than is desirable for Government in the use of its revenues. It also implies that efforts will have to be redoubled to improve revenue administration and collection.

Table. Balance of Payments under the High Growth Scenario

	Preliminary 1995 US$ millions	Projections 1996–1999	2000–2004	
Resource balance	17.8	–26.5	–58.6	
Exports of GNFS	423.6	516.9	713.3	
Imports of GNFS	441.3	543.4	771.9	
Net factor payments	–93.2	–63.2	–88.2	
of which interest on public debt	–86.0	–48.9	–55.2	
Net transfers	23.7	27.8	31.1	
Current account balance	–77.7	–50.9	–102.4	
Long–term capital inflows				
Direct foreign investment	27.0	27.6	57.1	
Net long–term loans	11.0	62.2	51.9	
Disbursements	44.0	81.6	91.7	
Repayments	61.0	30.3	45.9	
Other long–term inflows	28.0	10.8	6.1	(net)
Changes in reserves (– = increase)	64.8	–29.0	–23.1	
	Ratios			
Memorandum items				
External debt indicators				
Debt/GDP	326.8	193.1	114.3	
Debt service/XGS	39.0	19.8	16.7	

The Low Growth Scenario

In contrast to the scenario described above, the low growth scenario envisages an economy operating at a reduced scale, generating lower rates of output, employment and income growth. This scenario will also require as a minimum, policy measures to improve Guyana's competitiveness, except that some of the more structural constraints would not be addressed. The scenario envisages a fiscal effort of lesser magnitude, in particular with revenue generation which keeps the overall deficit at about 5.8 per cent of GDP throughout the projection period. In this low growth scenario, no major rationalisation and realignment will take place at Guysuco, and issues with the power generation and distribution system will take longer to resolve. Investment is assumed to grow modestly at about 39 per cent of GDP over the projection period.

Furthermore, the efficiency of investment is expected to fall as a result of continued distortions in the incentive framework.

Table. Medium–Term Prospects, Low Growth Scenario

	Preliminary 1995	Projections 1996–99	2000–2004
	Annual Percentage Growth Rates (1994 constant prices)		
Gross Domestic Product	5.1	6.1	4.9
Agriculture	7.2	6.4	5.4
Industry	0.9	11.8	9.8
Services	3.0	–2.8	–14.8
Exports (GNFS)	9.2	5.1	3.5
Imports (GNFS)	5.2	5.2	3.8
Total Expenditure	1.4	6.1	5.2
Consumption	–3.5	6.2	6.3
Investment	17.5	6.0	2.2
Gross Domestic Income	9.8	6.6	4.5
Gross Domestic Savings	63.1	5.7	0.06
Memorandum Items			
Per capita GDP	4.8	5.8	4.6
Per capita GNP	–4.0	8.2	4.8
Per capita total consumption	–3.8	5.8	6.0
Per capita private consumption	–7.6	2.8	8.0

Since this scenario does not assume a full measure of cost reduction policies in Guyana's export products nor a significant reduction in the anti–export bias of the system of tariffs and the exchange rate, the export and overall economic potential of the economy would be limited. Exports of GNFS will grow at an average annual rate of 5.5 per cent throughout the projection period and imports of GNFS by 4.3 per cent.

As a result of slowed growth of exports, the current account of the balance of payments is projected to improve between 1996–1999 and thereafter deteriorate averaging 6.2 per cent of GDP between 2000–2004. The larger financing requirements that this scenario would require would make it difficult to implement some of critical public sector reforms that are essential for implementation of policies and programmes.

Table. Balance of Payments Under the Low Growth Scenario

	Preliminary 1995 U.S.$ million	Projections 1996–1999	2000–2004
Resource balance	–17.8	–19.1	–36.8
Exports of GNFS	423.6	514.6	670.9
Imports of GNFS	441.3	533.7	707.7
Net factor payments	–93.2	–62.7	–78.3
of which interest on public debt	–86.0	–48.8	–34.4
Net transfers	23.7	27.2	28.1
Current account balance	–77.7	–46.9	–73.9
Long–term capital inflows			
Direct foreign investment	27.0	17.4	19.7
Net long–term loans	11.0	52.4	19.2
Disbursements	44.0	71.9	59.0
Repayments	61.0	30.3	45.9
Other long–term inflows (net)	28.0	10.8	6.1
Changes in reserves (– = increase)	–64.8	–29.1	–22.7

CONCLUDING REMARKS

Guyana requires rapid and sustainable economic growth, and the projections developed demonstrate that it is feasible. For it to take place, a shift has to occur from the policy preoccupation with short–term issues of crisis management and stabilisation to fundamental issues regarding the ways to encourage durable and rapid growth which benefits all segments of the population. Policy decisions require a longer–term orientation and need to be based on a clear analytic framework such as that developed in this Strategy.

On the side of international markets, the long–term outlook for Guyana's major export commodities viz, sugar and rice is unclear. To overcome this obstacle and other constraints, the effort required will have to be massive and well–coordinated, and must fit into a well–defined, well–comprehended, overall Strategy.

In this regard, the quest to achieve macroeconomic stability should not be viewed as an end in itself but a means to spur and support economic growth. It has to be recognised that, however, genuine and well–intentioned the restructuring effort may be, nothing will survive on a sustainable basis, unless there is macroeconomic order. This complementarity can best be achieved through a properly sequenced and phased macroeconomic programme. However, no programme of macroeconomic stabilisation can succeed unless appropriate structural changes are introduced. The link is a critical one and has to be preserved in order to prevent reversals and failures. The recommendations made in this Strategy take cognisance of all the above. To ensure a continuation of sound policy formulation, there must be a mechanism for regular monitoring and critical evaluation of the policy measures adopted and procedures to utilise this feedback for developing further rounds of policy reforms as they are required.

THE MACROECONOMY: UNEMPLOYMENT AND INFLATION

- How is the unemployment rate defined and measured?
- What is the cost of unemployed resources?
- What is inflation? Why is it a problem?
- What is frictional unemployment? And why is it not harmful?

Unemployment is the number of adults (16 and over) who are willing able to work and actively seeking jobs though they could not find one. The population is divided into three groups: those under age 16 or institutionalized those not in the labour force, which includes the sum of the employed and the unemployed. Labour force = all U.S. residents –residents under 16 years of age–institutionalized adults–adults not looking for work. You are in the labour force if you are working or actively seeking work but did not find one. Therefore, labour force is the sum of the employed and the unemployed.

- In 1997 total population 267,90,000
- Less under 16 and/or institutionalized –64,767,000
- Less not in labour force –66,837,000
- Equals labour force 136,297,000
- Employed 129,558,000
- Unemployed 6,739,000
- Unemployment rate = (6,739,000) (136,297,000)* 100=4.9%.

Full time students, homemakers and retiree are excluded from the labour force. Therefore, unemployed rate is the percentage of the labour force that is not working. Take look at the historical prospective of unemployment rates from 1890 to the present time on p.143 of your textbook. Unemployment rate was very low less than 2% during WWI and WWII, but higher than 25% during great depression. Unemployed criteria: A job looser is a person who was involuntarily laid off (40–60)% of the unemployed. A job leafier is a person who voluntarily ended employment (10–15)% Duration of unemployment: the duration of unemployment is inversely related to the overall level of economic activity. That is as economic activity contracts, cyclical unemployment increases and as growth occurs cyclical unemployment decreases. The U.S. Bureau of labour statistics (BLS) determines who is employed and who is not by a nationwide random survey.

Discouraged workers (hidden unemployment) are individuals who have stop seeking for jobs because they believe that they can not get jobs. The number of discouraged workers is large during recession than prosperity. By not counting discouraged workers as unemployed it understates the unemployment rate. Official data include that all part–time workers as fully employed. However, some economist argue that people who work part time, but are willing to work full time should be considered as semi–hidden unemployed. Therefore, the BLS data understates the unemployment rate. Labour participation rate is the proportion of working age persons who are in the labour force. Labour force participation rose from around 60% in 1950 to about 70% today.

TYPES OF UNEMPLOYMENT

- Frictional unemployment: those searching for jobs or waiting to take jobs soon. The problem is that individuals do not have information about job vacancies that can fit their qualifications (*e.g.* after your graduation you are looking around to what offer you will take).
- Structural unemployment is due to changes in the structure of the economy or demand for labour. For example, the changes may be due to technological change when certain skills become obsolete (unneeded). The change may be also due to geographic distribution of jobs.
- Seasonal unemployment is the unemployment that fluctuates with the seasons of the year.
- Cyclical unemployment is caused by the recession phase of the business cycle (deficit demand unemployment).

Full employment is the level of frictional and structural unemployment. Full employment does not mean zero unemployment. The full employment of unemployment rate is also referred to as the natural rate of unemployment. The natural rate of unemployment is the unemployment that would exist in the absences of cyclical unemployment. The natural rate of unemployment is achieved when labour markets are in balance. That is the number of job seekers equals the number of job vacancies. At this point the economy's potential output is being achieved. The natural rate of unemployment is not fixed but depends on the demographic make up of the labour force and the laws and customs of the nations. Wait unemployment is unemployment that is caused by wage rigidities (minimum wage laws and negotiated wages by labour unions). What is the value of the natural rate of unemployment in the U.S.?

In the 1950s and 1960s the council of economic advisors agreed on 4%, whereas 1970s that rate went up to 5%. The rate again changed to 6–7% in the early 1980s and 5% by the late 1980s. Particularly 1986, the council agreed on 6.5% and today it is less than 5%. Therefore, the natural rate of unemployment varies over time within a range from 4–7%. The recent drop in the natural rate of 6.5% to less than 5% was de to the aging of the work force and increased competition in product and labour markets. It will also vary across countries, as labour markets and macroeconomic policies differ.

WHAT IS THE COST OF UNEMPLOYED RESOURCES

The cost of being unemployed is more than the loss of income and status suffered by the person who is out of work. If resources are unemployed, the economy will operate inside its production possibility curve rather than on the curve. This loss of output can be measured in terms of the Gross Domestic Product (GDP) gap. GDP gap = potential real GDP–actual GDP. Potential GDP is the level of output produced (non–labour resources are fully utilized) at the natural rate of unemployment (= unemployment rate). Potential GDP measures our capability of producing at the natural rate of unemployment. Therefore, the cost of unemployment equals GDP gap. The gap widens in times of economic contractions (recessions) and narrows in times of economic expansions. This economic measurement is known as the Okura's law. He described the relationship between unemployment and GDP: forever 1% of unemployment above the natural rate, a 2% GDP gap occurs.

Non economic costs include loss of self–respect and social pressure:

- Unequal burdens of unemployment it terms of occupation, age, race, gender, education, duration may happen.
- *International comparisons*: In 1987–97, unemployment rates in 5 industrial nations (U.S., U.K., France, Japan, and Germany) were compared. U.S. unemployment rate was below the rates in France, Germany and U.K. in the last 10 years.

Inflation: Is the sustained rise in the overage level of prices. That is when the average of all prices of goods and services is rising. Inflation is measured by the percentage change in prices level. Prices of some goods rise faster than others, which means that relative prices are changing at the same time that absolute prices are rising. The measured inflation rate records the average change in absolute prices. To measure inflation, subtract last year's price index from this year's price index and divide by last year's indexes, then multiply by 100 to express as a percentage.

Purchasing power of money is the amount of goods and services it can buy or the dollar value in terms of buying goods and services. Therefore, during inflation the purchasing power of a dollar falls, and vice versa for deflation. Deflation is a situation where the average of all prices of goods and services is falling. International comparison of inflation rates for five industrial nations. Although in the late 1970d, U.S. inflation rates increased to double–digit inflation (13–13%), inflation rate came back to 2–4% over the last 10 years. In this period, inflation rates of U.S. were neither high nor low relative to other industrial nations. In 1996, some nations experienced double–digit and even triple–digit inflation: annual inflation rate in Venzuela, 120%; in Bulgaria, 123%; in Turkmaistan, 992%; and Angola 4145%. In 1993 annual inflation rate in all industrial nations, 2.8%; all developing nations, 52.9; in Brazil, 2,148%; and in Zair, 1,987%%; in U.S., 3%; and Japan, 1.3%. Inflation can also be measured by computing a price index. Price index = cost of market basket in current year divided by cost of market basket in base year. That is the cost of a market basket today expressed as a percentage of the cost of that market basket in the base year.

Types of price indexes:

- Consumer Price Index (CPI) is a weighted average of prices of a specified set of goods and services (650 items) purchased by urban consumers (the cost of living index).
- Producer Price Index (PPI) is a weighted average of prices of commodities that firms buy from other firms.
- GDP Deflator measures the changes in prices of final goods and services produced by the economy. It is a broader measure of price change.

CAUSES OF INFLATION

- *Demand*: Pulls inflation (inflation as a result from demand side). That is spending increases faster than production, will cause the average level of prices to rise. For example in resources are fully employed (*i.e.* the economy is producing at maximum capacity), in the short run it may not be possible to increase output to meet the increased demand. The rest will be that rising prices ration the goods and services.
- *Cost: Pushes Inflation Supply Side*: Firms raise prices to avoid losses because of rise in per– unit production costs.
- *Suppliers Who Want to Increase Their Profit Margins Faster Than Their Cost Increase Create Profit*: Push pressures by rising prices. That is supply shocks may happen as a result of unexpected increases in the price of raw material.
- *Wage*: Push pressures as a result of labour unions and workers who are able to increase their wages faster than their productivity.

Anticipated vs Unanticipated Inflation

If the rate of inflation that most of the people expect matches the actual inflation rate, then inflation is fully anticipated. If the actual rate of inflation is greater than the expected one, then inflation is not anticipated (you have unanticipated inflation). Individuals can protect themselves from inflation if it is anticipated. The problem is that both anticipated and unanticipated can not be calculated.

Inflation and Interest Rate

Nominal interest rate is the market interest rate expressed in today's dollars. Real interest rate: the nominal interest rate minus the anticipated rate of inflation. The real rate of interest can be positive, negative or zero. *Redistribute effects of inflation:* If nominal income rises faster than prices, then your real income will increase (real wage = W/P).

- *Fixed*: Income groups will be hurt because their nominal income does not rise in inflationary times, for example, private pension, families living on fixed welfare.
- Savers(or lenders, creditors) will be hurt by unanticipated inflation, because interest rate my not cover the cost of inflation. Note that the U.S. has indexed social security benefits, which means that these payments increase when consumer price index increases.

However, borrowers (debtors) can be helped by unanticipated inflation, because their interest rate payments may be less than the inflation rate. Therefore, they borrowed dear money and are paying back cheap dollars that have less purchasing power. Protecting against inflation can be done when inflation is anticipated because lenders start increasing nominal interest rates by the amount of expected inflation. Similarly, workers demand cost of living adjustments (COLAs). That is an increase in wages to cover the price level increases. What is business cycle (fluctuations): Business cycle is pattern of rising real GDP followed by falling real GDP(the ups and downs of the economic activity). The business cycle contains 4 phases:

The expansion (boom) is when real GDP is increasing; the peak, which marks the end of an expansion and the beginning of a contractions. The contraction (recession) is when real GDP is falling; and the trough, which marks the end of a contraction and the beginning of an expansion. A depression is a prolonged period of severe economic contractions(more than one year). Leading indicators: a variable that changes before real output changes. For example of new orders for industries, have new building permit signal new construction, the prices of stocks, and so on. External shocks (Factors that can increase or decrease in the level of economic activity)

- *Wars*: Stimulates demand for goods and services and leads to an economic expansion
- *Weather conditions*: A bad weather (or hurricanes) can influence agricultural output and hence can lead to a recession.
- *Oil Shocks*: In the 1970–75 and 1979–80, OPEC countries increased international price of oil, which led to recession.

7

Price

PRICE LEADERSHIP

Price leadership is a feature of oligopolistic situation. One firm assumes the role of a leader and fixes the price of a product or the entire industry. Price leadership can be seen when most or all of the firms in an industry decide to sell their product at a price fixed by one among them. The other firms in the industry follow this price. These price followers simply accept the price fixed by the price leader and adjust their output to this price. The price leader may be the biggest firm in the industry or it may be a firm with the lowest cost of production. Its leadership may be established as a result of price-war in which it emerges as the winner. Independent pricing by each firm in the industry is rarely seen in the oligopolistic situation. Instead there will be some agreement among the various firms with regard to the price that is to be charged. The agreement among these rival firms may be formal or informal. There may be a formal agreement among the various firms to follow the price fixed by a leader chosen from among them. Or there may be only an informal understanding among themselves.

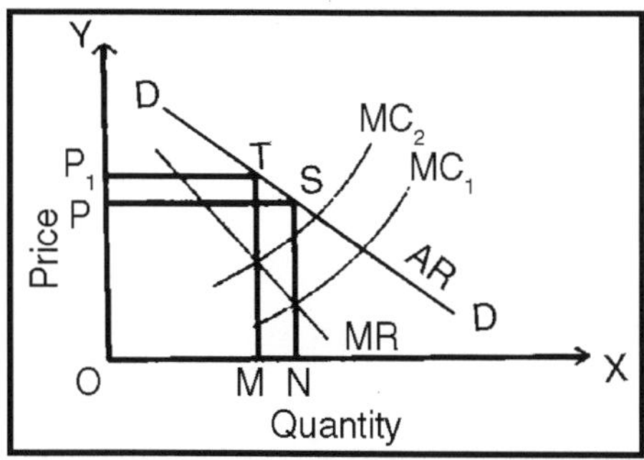

The price and output decisions are illustrated in the figure. Here it is assumed that there are only two firms A and B and firm A has a lower cost of production than B. These two firms are producing homogeneous products and are having equal share in the market. Thus these firms face the same demand curve which will be half of the total market demand curve. DD is the demand curve facing each firm which is half of the total demand curve for the product. MR is the marginal revenue curve of each firm. MC, is the marginal cost curve of firm A and MC2 is the marginal cost curve of the firm B. As the firm A has a lower cost of production than the firm B, MC, is drawn below MC2. If the price is fixed independently each firm will fix a price at which MC=MR. Then price of A would have been OP and B would have been OP. But in the oligopolistic market the firm B cannot make maximum profit by fixing the price as OP, The firm B is to fix its price as OP, the price the low cost firm A has fixed. Firm B can sell its product only if it accepts its price as OP, the lower price. While A makes maximum profit, B is to be satisfied with a lower profit. Thus firm A is price leader and firm B has to follow it.

TYPES OF PRICE LEADERSHIP

The following are the important types of price leadership:

- *Price Leadership of the Dominant Firm*: One firm controls a major portion of the total market supply and hence dominates the entire market. The supply of other firms in the market is individually insignificant. The dominant firm fixes the price and the other firms simply accept this price. The other firms in the industry fix their output to the price fixed by the leading firm. The leader fixes a price that will give it maximum profit.
- *Barometric Price Leadership*: In the barometric price leadership an old experienced firm, not necessarily dominant one, assumes the role of a leader and fixes a price acceptable to all the firms in the industry. In order to fix the price this experienced firm takes into consideration the demand for the product, cost of production, competition from the rival producers etc. The leader, while fixing the price, does not look after its own interest rather it considers the interest of all the firms in the industry. As the leader protects the interests of all the firms in the industry, all the firms happily follow the price leader.
- *Aggressive Price Leadership*: When the dominant firm wants to eliminate its rivals in the market it may turn to aggressive price leadership. For this it may use both legal and illegal methods. The other firms unwillingly accept the leader and the price fixed by it.

FEATURES OF A PRICE LEADERSHIP FIRM

- The firm has a considerable share in the total market supply.
- The firm is reputed one for fixing a suitable price.
- The firm has initiative in taking timely action after considering the various factors.
- The firm has a relative cost advantage which gives it a supremacy among the various firms in the industry.

MERITS AND PROBLEMS OF PRICE LEADERSHIP

Merits:

- Price war leading to unhealthy competition among the various firms can be avoided.
- This ensures the survival of both large and small firms.
- Helps to reduce uncertainty in the oligopoly market situation.
- The price fixed by the leader, considering the possibilities of entry of new firms, helps to restrict the entry of new firms.
- It helps to avoid government interference or any public criticism.
- Frequent price changes, especially those of a retaliatory nature, can be avoided.

Problems:

- If the leader is not able to make a correct estimation of the reactions of his followers he may lose his leadership.
- The rival follower may charge lower prices. This price cutting may be in the form of discounts and rebates, credit facilities, after-sales services, 'money back' guarantee, easy installment facilities etc. The price leader who charges high price now loses part of his market.
- Even when the rival firms follow the price fixed by the leader they may indulge in 'non-price competition' to increase their sales. This avoids a direct confrontation with the leader but helps to reduce the share of the leader in the market. This non-price competition may be possible with the concessions. Advertising and other sales promotion methods like product quality improvement etc. help this
- As the high price results in super profitability it may attract new entrants into to the industry who may not accept the leader.

PRICING POLICY

Pricing assumes a significant role in a competitive economy. Price is the main factor which affects the sales o f a organisation. A good price policy is of great importance to the producers, wholesalers, retailers and the consumers. Marketers try to achieve their long-run pricing objectives through both price policies and price strategies. If the prices are high, few buyers purchase and if the prices are low, many buyers purchase. Thus market may be reduced or increased. That is, the price increases in relation to the sales revenue. Thus pricing is a critical situation.

Therefore, a sound pricing policy must be adopted to have maximum sales revenue. In the early stages of men, prices were set by buyers and sellers negotiating with each other. The seller may demand a higher price than expected and the buyer may offer a price less than the expected one. Ultimately they arrive at an agreeable price through bargaining. Now in the competitive economy, development of large business aims to have one price policy. In certain cases, the buyer looks at the price as an indicator of product quality. If the price is higher, the buyer believes the products to be of high quality. In case the quality is not up to the mark he expects, he feels that the price is high. Hence, one cannot say that the price is high or low, without considering the quality of the product to be purchased. The price is greatly affected or influenced for future production and marketing. Prices play an important role in the economy. The time within which the product is sold varies. The goods, which are of a perishable nature and frequent changes of style, may not be stocked for long time. In the case of durable goods, they can be stocked for longer time, in the hope of getting favorable price rise. Holding the stock depends upon the financial resources of farmer, middleman, wholesaler etc., and the perish ability of the goods.

PRICE

Price may be defined as the exchange of goods or services in terms of money. Without price there is no marketing in the society. If money is not there, exchange of goods can be undertaken, but without price; *i.e.*, there is no exchange value of a product or service agreed upon in a market transaction, is the key factor which affects the sales operations. What you pay is the price for what you get. Price is the exchange value of goods or services in terms of money. Price of a product or service is what the seller feels it worth, in terms of money, to the buyer.

IMPORTANCE OF PRICE POLICY

A well formed price policy has special importance if price rise is a continuous process in planned economy. It has not only the influenced the living standard of people but due to increase in the expenditure of full planning, the prescribed aims and objectives of the planning are shattered. As a result, there is obstruction of economic development. But in underdeveloped countries, with economic development, price rise is quite natural. Till the increase in monetary income of the public is more than price rise, there is no comprehension. But when there is more price rise than investment and national income, there is a need to protect from the defects of monetary fluctuations. It requires price regulation.

In short, in developing countries, the significance of price policy can be known from the following facts:

- *To Maintain Appropriate Living Standard*: Price rise lets living standard of people fall and economic development of the country is obstructed. To maintain the proper living standard, price control is essential.
- To Maintain Planning. As price rises, the work of planning increases which results in obstruction in the prescribed aims and objectives of the planning. To maintain the planning process in a fine manner, prices should be controlled at all costs.

- *Protection from Monetary Fluctuations*: When price increase is more than investment and national income increases, monetary fluctuation defects are created. To remove them appropriate price control is required.
- *Establishment of Balance in Demand and Supply*: In a developing economy, due to changing circumstances, balance of demand and supply disrupts by which consumer, producer and investor have to take hardships. This shows that there is need to balance the demand and supply in a proper way.
- *For Well Adjusted Distribution Management*: With the view point of consumers for quick supply of goods on less prices distribution management should be well adjusted. For this, it is necessary to control the consumer price.
- *Multifaced Development of National Resources*: The major objective of economic planning is multifaced development of national resources. Thus, price policy should be quite independent as price regulation can adjust this motto.

PRICING OBJECTIVES

To perform the marketing job efficiently, the management has to set goals first pricing is no exception. Before determining the price itself, the management must decide the objectives of pricing. These objectives are logically related to the company's overall goal or objectives The main goals in pricing may be classified as follows.

- *Pricing for Target Return (on investment) (ROI)*: Business needs capital, investment in the shape of various types of assets and working capital. When a businessman invests capital in a business, he calculates the probable return on his investment. A certain rate of return on investment is aimed. Then, the price is fixed accordingly. The price-includes the predetermined average return. This is seller-oriented policy. Many well-established firms adopt the objective of pricing in terms of "return on investment." Firms want to secure a certain percentage of return on their investment or on sales. The target of a firm is fixed in terms of investment For instance a company may set a target at 10 or 15% return on investment. Further this target may be for a long term or short term. Wholesalers and retailers may follow the short term, usually a year they charge certain percentage over and above the price, they purchased, which is enough to meet operational costs and a desired profit. This target chosen, can revised from time to time. This objective of pricing is also known as pricing for profit. Certain firms adopt this method as a satisfactory objective, in the sense they are satisfied with a certain rate of return.
- *Market Share*: The target share of the market and the expected

volume of sales are the most important consideration in pricing the products. Some companies adopt the main pricing objective so as to maintain or to improve the market share towards the product. A good market share is a better indication of progress. For this, the firm may lower the price, in comparison to the rival products with a view to capture the market. By reducing the price, customers are not exploited rather benefited. The management can compare the present market share with the past market share and can know well whether the market share is increasing or decreasing When the market shares decreasing, low pricing policy can be adopted by large scale manufacturers who produce goods needed daily by the consumers. So margin of profit comes down because of low price, but the competitors are discouraged from entering the market. By low pricing policy, no doubt, market share can be increased, besides attracting new users.

- *To Meet or Prevent Competition*: The pricing objective may be to meet or prevent competition. While fixing the price, the price of similar products, produced by other firms, will have to be considered. Generally, producers are not in a haste to fix a price at which the goods can be sold out one has to look to the prices of rival products and the existing competition and chalk out proper price policy so as to enable to face the market competition. At the time of introduction of products to the market, a low price policy is likely to attract customers, and can establish a good market share. The low price policy discourages the competitors.
- *Profit Maximisation*: Business of all kinds is run with an idea of earning profit at the maximum. Profit maximisation can be enjoyed where monopolistic situation exists. The goal should be to maximise profits on total output, rather than on every item- The scarcity conditions offer chances for profit maximisation by high pricing policy. The profit maximisation will develop an unhealthy image. When a short-run policy is adopted for maximising the profit, it will exploit the customers. The customers have a feeling of monopoly and high price. But along run policy to maximis the profit has no drawbacks. A short-run policy will attract competitors, who produce similar goods at low cost. As a result, price control and government regulations will be introduced.
- *Stabilize Price*: It is a long-time objective and aims at preventing frequent and violent fluctuations in price. It also prevents price war amongst the competitors. When the price often changes, there arises no confidence on the product. The prices are designed in such away that during the period of depression, the prices are not allowed to

fall below a certain level and in the boom period, the prices are not allowed to rise beyond a certain level. The goal is to give and let live. Thus firms forego maximum profits during periods of short supply of products.

- *Customer Ability to Pay*: The prices that are charged differ from person to person, just as to his capacity to pay. For instance, doctors charge fees for their services awarding to the capacity of the patient.
- *Resource Mobilization*: This is a pricing objective, the products are priced it such a way that sufficient sources are made available for the firms' expansion, developmental investment etc. Marketers are interested in getting back the amount invested as speedily as possible. The management may fix a higher price and this trend will invite competitors with low priced similar products.
- *Survival and growth*: An important objective of pricing is survival and achieving the expected rate of growth. Profits are less important than survival. P. Drucker, avoidance of loss and ensuring survival are more important than maximisation of profit.
- *Prestige and goodwill*: Pricing also aims at maintaining the prestige and enhancing the goodwill of the firm.

FACTORS AFFECTING PRICING POLICY

Price policy is government by external factors and internal factors. External factors are-elasticity of demand and supply competition goodwill of firm, trend of the market, and management policy. Keeping in view above facts, certain general considerations which must be kept in view while formulating a suitable price policy:

Internal Factors

Organisational Factors

Pricing decisions occur on two levels in the organisation. Over-all price strategy is dealt with by top executives. They determine the basic ranges that the product falls into in terms of market segments. The actual mechanics of pricing are dealt with at lower levels in the firm and focus on individual product strategies. Usually, some combination of production and marketing specialists are involved in choosing the price.

Marketing Mix

Marketing experts view price as only one of the many important elements of the marketing mix. A shift in any one of the elements has an immediate effect on the other three-Production, Promotion and Distribution. In some industries, a firm may use price reduction as a marketing technique. Other firms may raise prices as a deliberate strategy to build a high-prestige product line. In either case, the effort will not succeed unless the price change is combined with a total marketing strategy that supports it. A firm that raises its prices may add a more impressive-looking package and may begin a new advertising campaign.

Product Differentiation

The price of the product also depends upon the characteristics of the product. In order to attract the customers, different characteristics are added to the product, such as quality, size, colour, attractive package, alternative uses etc. Generally, customers pay more price for the product which is of the new style, fashion, better package etc.

Cost of the Product

Cost and price of a product are closely related. The most important factor is the cost of production. In deciding to market a product, a firm may try to decide what prices are realistic, considering current demand and competition in the market. The product ultimately goes to the public and their capacity to pay will fix the cost; otherwise product would be flapped in the market.

Objectives of the Firm

A firm may have various objectives and pricing contributes its share in achieving such goals. Firms may pursue a variety of value-oriented objectives, such as maximising sales revenue, maximising market share, maximising customer volume, minimising customer volume, maintaining an image, maintaining stable price etc. Pricing policy should be established only after proper considerations of the objectives of the firm.

External Factors

External factors are those factors which are beyond the control of an organisation.

The following external factors would effect the pricing decisions:

- *Demand*: The nature and condition of demand should be considered when fixing the price. Composition of the market, the nature of buyers, their psychology, their purchasing power, standard of living, taste, preferences and customs have large influence on the demand. Therefore the management has to weigh these factors thoroughly. If the demand for a product is inelastic, it is better to fix a higher price for it. On the other hand, if demand is elastic, lower price may be fixed.
- *Competition*: In modern marketing, a manufacturer cannot fix his own price without considering the competition. A number of substitutes

enter the market these days. Hence the influence of substitutes has also to be considered when fixing a price. A firm must be vigilant about the prices charged by competitors for the similar products. If prices are fixed higher than the prices charged by competitors, the customers are likely to switch over to the products of competitors. On the other hand, if the prices charged are much lower than the prices of the rivals, the customers may become suspicious about the quality and hence lower price may not lead to higher sales. To avoid competitive pricing, a firm may resort to product differentiation. Sometimes a higher price may itself differentiate the product. In view of these, the management must be very careful in determining the prices.

- *Distribution channels*: Distribution channels also sometimes affect the price. The consumer knows only the retail price. But there is a middleman working in the channel of distribution. He charges his profit. Thus when the articles reach the hands of consumers, the price becomes higher. It sometimes happens that the consumers reject it.
- *General Economic conditions*: Price is affected by the general economic conditions such as inflation, deflation, trade cycle etc. In the inflationary period the management is forced to fix higher price. In recession period, the prices are reduced to maintain the level of turnover. In boom period, prices are increased to cover the increasing cost of production and distribution.
- *Govt. Policy*: Pricing also depends on price control by the Govt, through enactment of legislation. While fixing the price, a firm has to take into consideration the taxation and trade policies of govt.
- *Reactions of consumers*: An important factor affecting pricing decisions is the attitude of consumers. If a firm fixes the price of its product unreasonably high, the consumers may boycott the product.

METHODS OF PRICING

There are four basic pricing policies:

- Cost-based pricing policies.
- Demand - based pricing policies.
- Competition - based pricing policies.
- Value-based pricing policies.

Cost-based Pricing Policy

The policy of setting price essentially on the basis of the total cost per unit is known as cost-oriented pricing policy. In about 68% of consumer goods companies and about 89% of industrial products manufacturing companies take their pricing decision based on cost of production. The following are the four methods of pricing which fall under cost-oriented pricing policy.

Cost Plus Pricing

The theory of full cost pricing has been developed by Hall and Mitch. Business firms under the conditions of oligopoly and monopolistic competitive markets do not determine price and output with the help of the principle of MC = MR. They determine price on the basis of full average cost of production AVC + AFC margin of normal profit.

This is the most common method used for pricing. Under the method, the price is fixed to cover all costs and a predetermined percentage of profit. In other words, the price is computed by adding a certain percentage to the cost of the product per unit.

Under this method, cost includes production cost (both variable and fixed) and administrative and selling and distribution cost (both variable and fixed). This method is also known as margin pricing or average cost pricing or full cost pricing or mark-up pricing. This method is very popular in wholesale trade and retail trade.

Advantages of Cost Plus Pricing

- This method is appropriate when it is difficult to forecast the future demand.
- This method guarantees recovery of cost. Hence it is the safest method.
- It helps to set the price easily.
- Both single product and multi product firms can apply this method for pricing.
- It ensures stability in pricing.
- If this method is adopted by all firms within the industry, the problem of price war can be avoided.
- It is economical for decision making.

Disadvantages of Cost Plus Pricing

- This method ignores the effect of demand.
- It does not consider the forces of market and competition.
- This method uses average costs, ignoring marginal or incremental costs.
- This method gives too much importance for the precision of allocation of costs.

Target Pricing

This is a variant of full cost pricing. Under this method, the cost is added with a predetermined target rate of return on capital invested. In this case, the company estimates future rates, future cost and calculates a targeted rate of return on investment after tax. This method is also known as rate of return pricing.

Advantages of Target or Rate of Return Pricing:

- This method guarantees a certain rate of return on investment.
- This method can be used for pricing new products.
- Prevention is better than cure' principle is applied in this method.
- This is a long term price policy.

Disadvantages of Target Pricing:

- His method is not practical when there is a tough competition in a market.
- This method ignores the demand of the product.
- It is difficult to predetermine the cost of products.

Marginal Cost Pricing

Under both full cost pricing and rate of return pricing, the prices are set on the basis of total cost (variable cost + fixed cost). Under the marginal cost pricing, the price is determined on the basis of marginal or variable cost. In this method, fixed costs are totally excluded.

Advantages of Marginal Cost pricing:

- This method is very useful in a competitive market.
- This method helps in optimum allocation of resources. It is particularly useful when the products have low demand.
- This method is suitable to pricing over the life cycle of the product.
- It is the most suitable.method of short run pricing.
- The method is useful at the time of introducing a new product.

Disadvantages of Marginal cost pricing:

- Firms may not be able to cover up costs and earn a fair return on capital employed.
- It requires a better understanding of marginal costing technique.
- When costs are decreasing this method is not suitable because it will result losses.
- This method is not suitable for long run.

Break Even Pricing

This is a form of target return pricing. In fact, it is a refinement to cost-oriented pricing. Under break even pricing, break even analysis is used for point. Even pricing, break even analysis is used for pricing. The firm first determines the break even point.

It is the point at which the total sales are equal to total cost no profit no loss point at which the total sales are equal to the average total cost of product. Thus, both variable cost and fixed cost are covered under this methods but it does not include any profit.

Importance of Break Even Pricing

This method of pricing helps in understanding the relationship between revenue and cost of the company in relation to its volume of sales. it helps in determining that volume at which the company's cost and revenue are equal. This method of pricing is very important in profit planning. It shows the effects on profit of changing the amount invested in advertisement of changing the sales compensation methods of adding a new product or of changing a marketing in focusing channel this methods of pricing helps the marketer in a calculating output or sales to earn a desired profit calculating margin of safety changes in price making decisions, and changes in cost and price etc.

Demand - based Pricing Policy

Under this pricing policy, demand is the basic factor. Price is fixed simply adjusting it to the market conditions. In short, the price is fixed just as to the demand for a product. Where the demand is heavy, a higher price is charged. When the demand is low, a low price is charged.

The following are the methods of pricing which fall under this policy:

- *Differential pricing*: Under this method the same product is sold at different prices to different customers, in different places and at different periods. For instance, a cinema house charges different rates for different categories of seats. Telephone authorities charge less for trunk calls at night than during day. This method is also called discriminatory pricing or price discrimination.
- *Modified Break-even analysis*: This is a combination of cost based and demand based pricing techniques. This method reveals price-quantity mix that maximizes total profit. In other words, under this method, prices are fixed to achieve highest profit over the BEP in consideration of the amount demanded at alternative prices.
- *Premium Pricing*: It is a phenomenon of the 1990s. It is based on the principle that the product or brand should be positioned at the top of the market and must offer greater v a l u e i n qualitative terms than similar brands in other price segments. In short, it is called high pricing. The BPL, group followed this when they invaded the refrigerator market with a ₹37,000 brand (a four - door, 350 liter, frost - free refrigerator). The other companies which follow premium pricing include Titan, Sony TV, Arial and Dove Conditioner.
- *Neutral Pricing*: It means offering extra value or benefits with the brand cost or price remaining competitive. Cadbury is offering 30 per cent more chocolate in its 5 Star bar at same price.
- *Competition-based Pricing Policy*: It is the policy of fixing the prices mainly on the basis of prices fixed by competitors. This policy does not necessarily mean setting of same price. With a competition

oriented pricing policy, the firm may keep its price higher or lower than that of competitors. Actually this policy implies that the firms 'pricing decisions is not based on cost or demand, prices are changed or maintained in line with the competitor's prices. The following methods fall under this policy.

- *Going rate pricing*: Under this method, prices are maintained at par with the average level of prices in the industry. The firm adjusts its own prices to suit the general price structure in the industry. In other words, it is the method of charging prices just as to what competitors are charging. This method is usually adopted by firms selling a homogeneous product in a highly competitive market. Under this method a firm accepts the price prevailing in the industry to avoid a price war. This method is also called acceptance pricing or market equated pricing or parity pricing. LML Vespa was following this method for a number of years with market leader Bajaj. This method is particularly useful where cost ascertainment is difficult. This technique is adopted in the situation of price leadership.

Advantages of going rate pricing:

- It helps in avoiding cut-throat competition among the firm.
- This method is found more suitable when costs are difficult to measure.
- This method is less expensive because calculation of cost and demand is not necessary.
  It is suitable to avoid price war in oligopoly.
- This can be used for pricing new products.

Disadvantages of going rate pricing:

- This method is not suitable for long run pricing.
- Cost of the product and other marketing factors are not considered at all under this policy.

Customary Pricing

- In case of some commodities the prices get fixed because they have prevailed over a long period of time. For example, the price of a cup of tea or coffee is customarily fixed. In short, these prices are fixed by custom. The price will change only when the cost changes significantly. Before changing the customary prices, it is essential to study the prices of competitors. Customer prices may be maintained even when products are changed. For example, the new model of a radio may be parked at the same level as the discontinued model. Thus, under this method, the existing price is maintained as long as possible.
- Sealed bid pricing: In all business lines when the firms bid far jobs, competition based pricing is followed. Costs and demand are not

considered at all. The firm fixes its prices on how the competitors price their products. It means that if the firm is to win a contract or job, it should quote less than the competitors.

Value Based Pricing

Under this policy the price is based on value to the customer.

The following are the pricing methods based on customer value:

- *Perceived - value pricing*: Another method is judging demand on the basis of value perceived by the consumers in the product. Thus perceived value pricing is concerned with setting the price on the basis of value perceived by he buyer of the product rather than the seller's cost. When a company develops a news product. it anticipates a particular position for it in the market in respect of price, quality and service, 'Then it estimates the quality it can sell at this price. The company then judges whether at this level of production and sale, it will have a satisfactory return investment. If it appears to be so, the company goes ahead with translating the perception into practice, otherwise it drops the proposal. Jerome Rowitch, owner of the Sculpture Gardens Restart in Venice. California invited a selected group of affluent residents to dine at his restaurant and told them pay what they felt their meals were worth. Did it work?. The 100 plus diners who Rowitch up on the deal paid in average ₹.50, about 30% higher than the prices he would have normally charged. A firm can try this pricing approach of Jerome Rowitch.
- *Value for money pricing:* This is now seen as more than a pricing method. Under this method price is based on the value which the consumers get from the product they buy. It is used as a complete marketing strategy. Videocon did it when they launched their 63 cm flat screen Bazooka when BPL's HR and Onida's KY Series models are dominating the flat sit-in TV segment. Bazooka perceived value was ₹25,000. But driven by value for money strategy, Videocon priced Bazooka at ₹21, 000 only.

PRICING OF NEW PRODUCTS

The introduction of a new product will pose a challenging problem for any firm. In the case of new products there is no past information for ascertaining trends and consumer reaction.

If the new product is with high distinctiveness among the existing products, then price should be fixed on the basis of such factors as demand, market - target and the promotional strategy. In the case of pioneer product, the estimation of its demand is very difficult.

The estimate of demand for such products should be made on the basis of the following factors:

- *Product acceptability*: The manufacturer should ascertain whether the new product will be accepted by the consumers or whether the consumers are willing to buy the product. The willingness to buy depends upon a factor like whether it would meet their requirements.
- *Range of prices*: It is very essential to assess the reactions of the consumers at different prices. For this, a market research will have to be undertaken. The core question that arises is at what prices different quantities of the product are demanded.
- *Expected volume of sales*: The next task is to determine the anticipated volume of sales at different prices. This depends upon demand elasticity and cross elasticity.
- *Reaction to price*: The assessment of the reaction of the consumers to the price is a very tricky task. The company which introduces a new product will have to monitor the activates of the rivals in order to find out the marketing strategies that they are going to adopt.

In short, the price of a new product should be fixed after taking into account the potential demand, objectives, degree of competition and strategy of competitors etc.

Methods or Strategies of Pricing of New Products

In pricing a new product, generally two type are followed:

Price Skimming

When a new product is introduced in the market, the firm fixes a price much higher than the cost of production. The consumers are ready to pay a high price to enjoy the pleasure of being the first users of the product. The high price charged helps to skim the cream off the market at a time when there is no competition this is possible because the newly introduced product reached the hands of the consumers after a long waiting and by the time it comes to the market a heavy demand for the same has accumulated. When fixing the price the producer takes this advantage of the market. This market situation will not continue for long. In the long run new firms will enter into the industry. In the long run the number of enthusiastic buyers who are ready to buy at a high price will decrease.

For example, when electronic goods like TV, tape recorders, calculators, VCR etc, were introduced their prices were very high. But gradually when more and more new producers imitated these products their price came down. The firm makes a huge profit by price skimming. The price skimming policy is followed as long as there is heavy demand without any competition from a rival. The principle behind price skimming is to make hay while sun shines. In the long run the possibility of making huge profit by price skimming disappears. The price, in fact, gets normalized around the cost of production.

Under the following situations the price skimming policy can be easily followed:

- The new product is a novel item which can attract customers and is having no competitors at present.
- The product is meant for the higher income group whose demand is inelastic. The firm can charge a high price which will help them to realise a good share of the heavy initial investment in the form of research and development expense.
- There are heavy initial promotion expenses and the firm wants to realise it from the customers before other competitive firms-enter in. The firm, after squeezing the enthusiastic buyers, goes on reducing the price step-by-step so that it can reach the various sections of consumers who are willing to buy it at lower prices.

Penetration Pricing

The price fixed is relatively a lower one. This pricing is resorted to when the new product faces a strong competition from the existing substitute product. When the new firm enters an existing market where there are a number of firms it has to penetrate the market and achieve an acceptance for its product. In order o attain this it will charge only a very low price initially, hoping to charge a normal price later when it is established in the market. For example, a firm may, when it introduce a new bath soap in the market give a 100 gms Piece free when consumers buy two 200 pieces at a time. Later when it picks up sales it takes out the initial discount. In a foreign market a new country may have to penetrate through a highly competitive price. The penetration price may be sometimes below the cost of production.

This can be justified in the following cases:

- The lead time in production is short.
- Increased production will result in reduced cost of production.
- The product is meant for mass consumption.
- The product is one where brand loyalty counts.
- The product cannot be protected by patent right.
- The fear of competition.

KINDS OF PRICING

Business firms nay opt various kinds of pricing for products.

A few, important of them are explained below:

- *Psychological Pricing*: Many consumers use the price as an indicator of quality. Costs and other factors are important in pricing. Yet, psychology of the price is also considered certain people prefer high priced products, considered to be of high quality. Costly items diamond, jewellery etc., reveal the status of the person who wears them. They demand highly priced items. For example, highly priced television sets carrying prestige prices are in demand. Then in the retail shops another pricing 'odd pricing' issued. The paces are set at odd amounts, such as ₹19.95 instead of ₹20; ₹299.90 instead of ₹300 Odd prices, by psychology brings more sales. An article priced at ₹9.90 will have more sales than when it is priced ₹10.

- *Customary Pricing*: Customers expect a particular price to be charged for certain products. The prices are fixed to suit local conditions. The customers are familiar with the market condition. Manufacturers cannot control the price. Such products are typically a standardized one. Certain business people reduce the size of the product, if the cost of manufacturing increases, Sometimes, the firm changes the price by adopting new package, size etc. For example confectionary items.
- *Skimming Pricing*: It involves a high introductory price in the initial stage to skim the cream of demand. The products, when introduced in the market have a limited period free from other manufacturers. During this period, it aims at profit Maximisation, just as to the favorable market condition. Generally, the price moves downwards are when competitors enter into the market field.
- *Penetration Pricing*: A low price is designed in the initial stage with a view to capture market share. That is if the pricing policy is to capture greater market share, then this is done only by adoption of low prices in the initial stage. Because of the low price, sales value increases, competition falls down.
- *Geographical Pricing*: The distance between the seller and the buyer is consided geographic pricing. In India, the cost of transportation is an important pricing factor because of vide geographical distance between the production centre and consuming centre. The majority producing centers are located in Bombay, Delhi, Calcutta and Madras and at the same time consuming centers are dispersed throughout India. There are three ways of charging transit.
  - F.O.B. Pricing: In FOB (original) pricing, the buyer will have to incur the cost of traansit and in FOB (destination) the price influences the cost of transit charges.
  - Zone Pricing: Under this, the company divides the market into zones and quotes uniform prices to all buyers who buy within a zone. The prices are not uniform all over India. The price in one zone varies from that of another one. The prices are uniform within a zone. The price is quoted by adding the transport cost.
  - *Base Point Pricing*: Base point policy is characterized by partial absorption of transport cost by the company. One or more cities

are selected as points from which all shipping charges are calculated

- *Administered Price*: Administered price is defined as the price resulting from managerial decision and not on the basis of cost, competition, demand etc. But this price is set by the management after considering all relevant factors. There are many similar products manifesting different firms and m ore or less the price tends to be uniform. Usually the administered price remains unaltered for a considerable period of time.
- *Dual Pricing*: under this dual pricing system, a producer is required compulsorily to sell a part of his production to the government or its authorized agency at a substantially low price. The rest of the product may be sold in the open market at a price fixed by the producer.
- *Mark up Pricing*: This method is also known as cost plus pricing. This method is generally adopted by wholesalers and retailers. When they set up the price initially, a certain percentage is added to the cost before marking the price. For example, the cost of an item ₹10and is sold at ₹13 the Mark up is ₹3 or 30%.
- *Price Lining*: This method of pricing is generally followed by the retailers than wholesalers this system consists of selecting a limited number of prices at which the store will sell its merchandise. Pricing decisions are made initially and remain constant for a long period. The firm should decide the number of lines and the level of each price line. Many prices are not desired and the prices should not be too close to each other or too far from each other. For example shoe firm have several types of shoes, priced at ₹120, 140, 170 etc., a pair.
- *Negotiated Pricing*: It is also known as variable pricing. The price is not fixed. The price is fixed upon bargaining. In certain cases, the product may be prepared on the basis of specification or design by the buyer. In such cases, the price has to be negotiated and then fixed.
- *Competitive Bidding*: Big firms or the government calls for competitive bids when they went to purchase certain products or specialized items. The probable expenditure is worked out then the after offer is made quoting the price, which is also known as contract price. The lowest bidder gets the work.
- *Monopoly Pricing*: Monopolistic conditions exist where a product is sold exclusively by one producer or a seller. When a new product moves to the market, its price is monopoly price there no problem is no competition or no substitute. Monopoly price will maximize the profits, as there is no pricing problem.

PROCEDURE FOR PRICE DETERMINATION

Formulating price policies and fixing the price are the most crucial aspects of managerial decision making, Price which is an important device for the firm to maximize its revenue and also to widen its market. In this connection it is needed to understand some guidelines and principles to be followed while determining the price.

GUIDELINES FOR PRICE DETERMINATION

There is no specific procedure applicable to all firms for price determination however following steps may be followed to determine the price.

- Determine demand for the product.
- Anticipate and analyse the competitive reaction.
- Establish expected share of the market.
- Select pricing strategy.
- Consider company's marketing policies.

Determining Demand for the Product

The marketer has to make out estimation for his product. Each price that the company might charges will lead to a different level of demand. There is a relation between the prices charged on the resulting demand. In the normal case, demand and price are inversely related, *i.e.*, higher the price, lower the demand. There are two practical steps in demand estimation they are, first, to determine whether there is a price which the market expects and second, to estimate the sales volume at different prices. Comparison of the prices of rival products is a good guide in pricing products. In certain cases, the marketer conducts regular survey of potential buyers, retailers, and wholesalers etc., to determine the expected price. When we know the expected price, we can compute sales volume at different price levels. If demand is elastic rather than inelastic, sellers will consider lowering their price, to produce more total revenue. That is a product with elastic market demand. It is usually priced lower than the product with an inelastic demand.

Anticipate and Analyse the Competitive Reaction

The competitors can influence the price. Competition may arise from:

- Similar products
- Close substitute and
- Unrelated products seeking the same consumer's disposable income.

When the marketing field is easy to enter, then the number of competitors is greater, and there is a room for more revenue. To anticipate the reactions of the competitors, it is necessary to collect information about their product, cost structure, market share etc.

Establish Expected Share of Market

A marketer must decide the share of the market at the expected price. Low priced products may capture larger share of the market, and a high priced product may capture a small share of the market. Large share of the market can also be captured by advertisements and non-priced competition. Share of the market is also decided by the factors, such as present production capacity, cost of plant, extension etc.

Select Pricing Strategy

A good and proper pricing policy may be employed to achieve a predetermined share of the market.

There are two methods:

- Skimming Pricing: This price strategy is characterized by high initial price of the product, at the time of introduction of the product in the market. Manufacturers aim at profit maximisation at the shortest period, where market conditions are also favorable. The price is brought down when competitors enter into the market field. Under this, the price is fixed high, because the product is characteristic for its distinctiveness and exclusiveness etc. Skimming is suitable for new products, because:
  - At the initial stage, competition is at minimum, and the distinctiveness of the product leads the market,
  - If the market is unfavorable the price can be brought down easily. And at the same time, if the price is too low, it is very difficult to raise the price,
  - High price creates a vision of superior product.
- *Penetrating Price*: Price skimming strategy adopts a high introductory price to skim the milk of the market, whereas penetration pricing strategy adopts a low introductory price to speed up or capture the widespread market acceptance, penetrating pricing strategy is characterized by low initial price of the product, when introduced a the market. The aim is to catch the major portion of the market.

The policy is satisfactory when:

  - The cost of production comes down because of large-scale operations,
  - There is fear of stiff competition,
  - The product's demand is highly price elastic,
  - The public accepts the new product as a part of its daily life.

Consider Company's Marketing Policies

The price of product is influenced by the nature of product's durabilityperishability or non-perishability. Perishable products have to be disposed of within a limited time *e.g.*, fruits, milk, vegetables etc. Durable products *e.g.*, car, radio, cloth, scooter etc., are concerned prices which need not be reduced. But when the fashion changes, the marketer may compel the stockist to sell out the stocks before they become obsolescent. Channels of distribution select the types of middlemen, and the gross marginal requirements of these middlemen will influence a manufacturer's price. Wholesalers as well as retailers may purchase from a producer, who often sets a different factory price for each of the above two. Larger the promotional methods used, larger will be the expenses and this will reflect in the manufacturer's price, as the set price has to cover the expenses.

PRINCIPLES OF PRICE POLICY

Dr. V.K.R.V. Rao has laid down the following basic principles of price policy:

- *Equality in Increase of Income and Production*: Price Policy should be such that national income and national production should have equal increase. This will not take possibility of price increase. As such, the government should try that the increase in income should not be less than of production increase in a developing country; otherwise it will lead to rise in prices.
- *Income Increase by Transfer*: In a developing economy, an increase in any class or sector necessarily should be by transfer of less income of other sector class otherwise increase in demand of a class and decrease in demand of another class will substitute and give birth to price rise *i.e.* inflationary impulse in the economy.
- *Balance in Savings and Investment*: It should balance in savings and investment as far as possible otherwise decrease in savings, monetary fluctuation will result. In other words, saving must be matched with increased investment.
- *Adequate Distribution Management*: If compulsory consumer goods supply is just as to demand, there will be price stability. But, this is not possible in short time. Under such conditions, price control, distribution control and price encouragement policy should be used in coordination. To keep balance in demand and supply of compulsory goods, proper rationing is must.
- *Control over the Prices of Goods of Compulsory Consumption*: In underdeveloped countries, inflation is caused by the increase in the prices of consumption goods and not by capitalized price increase. Hence, by price policy only compulsory consumer goods prices should be controlled. Further more, it gives birth to cost inflation and this type of rise in prices should be controlled immediately.
- *Formation of Buffer Stock*: In developing countries, buffer stock should be created for controlling price increase caused due to draught, heavy rain, famine, and flood like sudden seasonal or temporary causes. During crisis such stock can supply the goods required.

8

Impact on Vegetables Diseases: Agricultural Economic

THE IMPORTANCE OF ECONOMICS OF DISEASE INCURSION

An economic framework can be used to explain why a government response is typically needed for the prevention and control measures in a disease infected industry. Relying on control by private firms is usually ineffective because any incursion of a disease has an external effect on market activities. Costs are not borne solely by the source of the incursion, but spillover (intentionally or unintentionally) into other areas, without affected parties being able to exact a compensation for the damage incurred.

Therefore, many of the impacts of a disease outbreak are spillovers in the sense that the market mechanism is unable to transmit back the true cost of a plant disease outbreak to an infected source. For instance, neither commercial nor backyard scale citrus growers have adequate incentives for voluntary eradication. Citrus canker containment and eradication actions demonstrate many of the characteristics of a public good. Disease-free industry status has aspects of non-rivalry in consumption (that is, one orchard's ability to enjoy disease-free status does not deprive others) and nonexclusion in provision (that is, it is difficult to exclude growers from enjoying this status).

Growers often face powerful incentives not to report disease incursions to the authority responsible for monitoring and surveillance, because the removal of trees can impose major financial losses to orchards. The first infected farm in

Emerald sought an injunction from the court to stop trees being cut and destroyed after the original outbreak in June 2004. In Florida, a legal battle continued for some time to determine whether the regulatory authority should have the right to trespass the property to test for canker infestation and to remove diseased trees. However, failure to control the disease would result in negative external effects on other growers as citrus canker would spread to other residences and commercial orchards. Therefore, the costs to other growers are not usually internalised into private decisions, but are of concern to public regulatory agencies and other stakeholders. Furthermore, prevention of disease outbreaks requires extensive monitoring and surveillance both by the regulatory authority and individual grower. On the part of the growers, this imposes additional costs on them. While there may be market incentives to maintain a disease-free status, there will often be some incentives for free-riding at the individual grower level. This can occur if growers fail to monitor or eradicate in an effort to reduce costs. Therefore, there is potential for market failure at both the prevention and eradication stages and thus a role for government intervention at both levels.

When a disease outbreak occurs, a public policy framework in the form of a benefit-cost test is usually employed to justify control and eradication measures. This often involves a mixture of public and private costs being incurred to avoid more wide-spread private costs if disease became established. Governments have a range of policy mechanisms to use when addressing disease outbreaks. These include the use of public information and suasion methods to encourage appropriate action and voluntary compliance. Incentives for growers to voluntarily report, control and monitor outbreaks can also be enhanced with the use of financial instruments. Regulatory and control measures are an alternative or extensions to voluntary mechanisms, and have advantages in terms of response certainty and timelines. However, the use of regulatory approaches to control may generate offsetting flow-on effects if they reduce growers' incentives to report and monitor outbreaks. Therefore, there is a number of economic issues raised in disease control measures. From the perspective of society, it is important to determine whether the control and eradication measures are worth the cost of implementation. An economic analysis is considered appropriate for this purpose.

ECONOMIC ANALYSIS APPROACHES TO DISEASE OUTBREAKS

Broadly speaking, two approaches are used to estimate the economic cost of an incursion, namely impact modelling and economic surplus analysis. Impact modelling can take the form of an input-output (I-O) model or a computable general equilibrium (CGE) model. An I-O model captures the supply and demand of goods and services in an economy (within an industry, region and economywide) in a particular period, as well as the interdependencies among the industries and associated primary factors of production. By tracing these linkages between sectors, the model estimates the effect of an impact on the region's output, employment, income and imports, often expressed in the form of multipliers. An I-O model can be used to capture the direct effects (output, income and employment) of a change in demand or supply as well as the indirect or flow-on impacts on its ancillary sectors (suppliers of inputs and process industries). It can also be used to measure the demand substitution effects, that is, consumers' shift of consumption to substitute commodities. Computable general equilibrium (CGE) models are constructed on the same data as the input-output models. A CGE model can provide information about the magnitude and sources of economic losses and the appropriate design of mitigation strategy (for example, eradication vs containment).

Both I-O and CGE models are able to capture the economy-wide impacts and inter-industry linkages, however, a CGE model has greater flexibility in terms of underlying assumptions and generates less biased estimates compared to I-O model. Furthermore, CGE models have advantages over I-O models in that they can be used to estimate not only the economic impacts but also the distributional impacts. However, I-O models have advantages in that they help to understand the social and political impacts. Elliston, Hinde and Yainshet assessed the economic impacts of an incursion of karnal bunt in a hypothetical situation in South-eastern Queensland using an input-output model. This study, however, failed to capture the changes in economic surplus.

The I-O model estimated the changes in output and employment, not the economic welfare, making it difficult to assess the overall gains or losses to society. Wittwer, McKirdy and Wilson estimate both the micro and macroeconomic effects of a hypothetical incursion of karnal bunt in wheat in the wheat belt of Western Australia using a CGE model. The analysis showed that quarantine restrictions in foreign markets dominated economic losses of the incursion of exotic plant diseases or pests.

Using the MONASH Multiregional Forecasting Model (MMRF), a version of CGE model, Dent *et al* estimated the likely impact of a foot-and-mouth disease (FMD) outbreak in Queensland and other regional economies. The study estimated the direct impact on 'at risk' industries and associated products as well as the flow-on effects to other industries and the economy as a whole. The study found that an outbreak of FMD would impact not only the livestock farming and meat processing industries, but also other sectors in the economy (for example, tourism). The impact of the hypothetical FMD outbreak in Queensland (a major beef cattle state) was proportionately more severe than the national impact. In Queensland, the real GDP was projected to be $2,340 million below the base case, while employment was projected to be 33,900 jobs below the base case in Year 7 alone.

These losses are far greater than the projected Year 7 losses in the national livestock farming industry and the national livestock product (mainly meat processing) industry ($200 million and 5100 jobs). Although the estimated total control cost of FMD outbreak ($500 million) appears significant, however, it is considered to be minor when compared to the potential loss of the national economy. Economic surplus analysis is used to estimate the net gains and losses of different impacts to society, and is normally preferred to impact modelling as a more appropriate measure of welfare changes. Within this framework, a partial equilibrium approach can be used to estimate the net losses due to an incursion, and the distribution of such losses between producers and consumers, expressed as changes in producer and consumer surplus. The economic surplus approach can be performed at a case study level, where the net surplus can be estimated with the application of cost-benefit analysis (CBA).

With this method it is possible to demonstrate how a disease outbreak can reduce the welfare gains which might otherwise have been obtained from the industry in the absence of an incursion. The economic surplus method has been used to estimate the cost of weeds in annual winter cropping system in Australia, and to measure the benefits of the virus prevention programme in deciduous fruit trees in the US. Jones *et al* estimated the economic costs of weeds and their distribution in Australian annual winter cropping systems using the economic surplus model. The loss of economic surplus due to weed infestations and weed control expenditure was estimated at $1,133 million in 1999. The distribution of total economic surplus suggested that producers appropriate the bulk of the economic welfare gained from the control measures (about 95 per cent), while consumers gained to a small extent (about 5 per cent) from the reduced market prices resulting from increased production due to weed control. The economic surplus approach measured both direct and indirect costs, but non-monetary impacts were not considered.

Cembali *et al* estimated net economic benefits of a virus prevention programme for apples, sweet cherries and clingstone peaches in the United States at the nursery, grower and consumer levels as changes in consumer and producer surpluses. Empirical estimates of the expected yield losses at both nursery and grower levels were made using the method of avoided losses. Avoided costs were used to estimate programme benefits in three economic sectors: nurseries (avoided change in producer surplus), producers (avoided change in consumer and producer surpluses), and consumers (avoided change in consumer surplus). The empirical estimates suggested that the total benefits for all three sectors were approximately $227.4 million a year, or more than 420 times the cost of the programme.

Paarlberg, Lee and Seitzinger measured the welfare effects of an FMD outbreak in the United States using the economic surplus method. They decomposed the effect by groups, including livestock producers with animals quarantined and slaughtered and producers not quarantined, using lost sales and producer surplus measures respectively. Similarly, consumer surplus was decomposed for consumers with and without changes of consumption behaviour (that is, whether or not consuming beef considering potential human health effects from an outbreak).The researchers argued that decomposition of aggregate welfare (consumer or producer surpluses) for different groups could provide more accurate estimates of changes for the policy-decision, and help to design compensation provisions. Rabbits impose economic costs on wool producers, governments, communities and the environment. Vere, Jones and Saunders provided an economic analysis of rabbit control measures in the Australian temperate pastures through integrating estimates of the costs of rabbits in the pasture systems and the benefits of implementing control practices from the introduction of rabbit haemorrhagic disease (RHD). The approach taken was to:

- Determine the changes in livestock production at the farm level due to supply shifts;
- Simulate these changes within a livestock industry model (that is, quantities, prices and elasticities);
- calculate the resulting economic welfare changes (that is, net benefits) and the relative benefits and costs of improved rabbit control over time.

The study showed that controlling rabbits in temperate pastures by RHD had the potential to generate substantial long-term economic benefits — the benefit-cost ratios were between 2.9:1 and 16.2:1 for a 25 per cent rabbit reduction and for a 50 per cent reduction the ratios were between 5.9:1 and 32.4:1. Zansler, Spreen and Muraro employed cost-benefit analysis to determine whether the citrus canker eradication programme in Florida could be a useful policy tool in combating the economic ramifications associated with the outbreak using the predicted values of the benefits and the costs associated with the intervention.

The results of the benefit-cost analysis suggested that benefits of the programme outweighed the costs. This review of current literatures on plant or pest disease incursions demonstrates that both economic surplus and CBA cannot sufficiently capture the indirect or flow-on effects of an impact. On the other hand, I-O or CGE model cannot take into account non-market impacts or estimate net welfare change. Both approaches have their strengths and limitations. In this paper, the approaches of economic surplus and CBA are used to indicate the economic efficiency of citrus canker outbreak control and eradication strategies in Queensland.

CASE OF CITRUS CANKER OUTBREAK

The citrus industry in Australia makes a substantial contribution to the national economy and the generation of employment. Major citrus fruits in Australia include oranges (navel and valencia), mandarins, lemons, limes and grapefruit. In 2002-03, citrus production in Australia consisted of 81 per cent oranges (valencia 45 per cent and navel 36 per cent), 14 per cent mandarin, 4 per cent lemon and lime and 1 per cent grapefruit. The industry produces around 830 thousand tones of fruit per year with a gross value of production of $426m in 2002-03. Citrus is one of the major horticultural exports in Australia, generating around $160m of annual export income and contributing $250m directly to value-added products. Exports accounted for around 20.6 per cent of total production in 2002-03. There was a record export of citrus by value of $201m in 2002-03. The focus of both the production and export of citrus is on fresh fruits and processed juice products.

The citrus industry is Australia's largest fresh fruit exporting industry. Commercial citrus production in Queensland is localised in the Central Burnett and Central Highland regions; out of 3,000 growers (cultivating 32,000 hectares of land) in Australia, about 300 are located in these regions. Seventy five per cent of Queensland's citrus is produced in the Gayndah- Mundubbera (Central Burnett) region and the Emerald Shire (Central Highland region); the remainder is grown in Bundaberg, Capricorn Coast Region, Wide Bay, Mareeba (Far North), Sunshine Coast and some other small patches of land in the State.

The citrus industry generates about $80m annually to the Queensland economy and supports several thousand jobs, particularly for seasonal workers. The majority of fruit is transported to southern markets and some is exported. Citrus canker is a highly contagious disease that causes defoliation and dieback, severely blemished fruit, weakens trees and eventually reduces production, although it is not harmful to humans. The disease was first discovered in Queensland in early June 2004 on a 1,200 hectare (ha) orchard with 220,000 citrus trees (Evergreen Farm) near Emerald in Central Highlands region. Immediately after the detection of the incursion, a Pest Quarantine Area (PQA) was declared for the Shires of Bauhinia, Emerald and Peak Downs, surrounding the infested orchard. As well, an interstate ban on the movement of *Rutacae* (the plant family to which citrus belongs) fruits was imposed.

The trade ban was also imposed on the Gayndah/Mundubbera region due to its proximity to Emerald citrus growing region and the possibility that disease might spread through the movement of plant material and seasonal workers. Growers were restricted from trading fruit or plant material within Queensland or interstate. The interstate trade of citrus for fruits grown outside of the Central Highlands and the Gayndah/ Mundubbera region resumed on the 22 July, while for citrus growers in the Gayndah/Mundubbera region trade resumed on the 13 January 2005. Furthermore, all Australian citrus growers were required to undergo stricter quarantine checks before exporting fruit to New Zealand pending quarantine surveys to establish state, area or property freedom from citrus canker. While the European Union stopped importing citrus from Australia until a canker-free status was established for the whole country, export to other markets, particularly canker infected markets in Asia, did not face any restriction. Citrus canker was widespread on the first affected property. Under the National Citrus Industry Biosecurity Plan (NCIBC) introduced in April 2004, a 'cookie cutter' approach involving destruction of trees within 600 metres of an infected area is considered to be effective control. By late 2004, all the 220,000 trees on the first affected property were taken out with successive 'cookie cuts'.

A second incursion within the Emerald irrigation area was reported on October 5, 2004 on Queensland's largest citrus orchard, known as 2PH Farms, having 326,000 fruit trees. This orchard is only 7 km away from the first infested farm and subsequent DNA testing confirmed that this latter outbreak was linked to the first one. By July 2005, three orchards in Emerald were affected with six outbreaks and over half a million citrus trees had been destroyed.

Some of the revenue and expenditure impacts on the Emerald region can be estimated as follows:

- Annual loss of revenue to growers from tree removal as of July 2005 was $21. 3m/year (500,000 trees at $42. 6 estimated annual production/tree);
- Annual loss of revenue to growers if all citrus trees removed from Emerald would be $31. 95m/year (750,000 trees at $42.6/tree);
- Surveillance and control cost allocation by government was $13m (perhaps more than 50 per cent spent in the Emerald region);
- Several hundred full-time jobs and more than one thousand part-time jobs are anticipated to have been lost.

With disease outbreak in livestock, compensation is automatically paid. However, this was not the case with a citrus canker outbreak as no cost sharing deed for emergency pest management was in place during the Emerald incursion. The Queensland citrus industry has been affected by the loss (short to midterm) of some overseas markets and if domestic consumers reduce demands for citrus fruits. Such losses will flow the temporary ban on interstate trade. Losses may also extend to domestic markets, especially through to other parts of the economy, such as transport, wholesale and retail sectors. On the eradication side, the citrus canker outbreak has generated higher control costs for private industry, as well as considerable costs for eradication and control by the regulatory authorities. This raises questions as to the impact on Queensland's citrus industry and society as a whole, and whether public expenditure on control and eradication was an efficient use of funds.

THE PRESSLER AND THE NATIONAL CITRUS INDUSTRY BIOSECURITY PLANS

A debate has taken place about the most efficient way to perform control and eradication measures in the region. Under the NCIBP, all trees within 600 meters of an infection are removed, and then monitoring continues. After the first disease detection on the second farm, the owner, John Pressler, put forward a proposal to destroy all the citrus plants in Central Highlands region around Emerald.The core of this proposal, referred to in the media as the Pressler Plan, was for growers to destroy all remaining trees with financial support from the Government. This would involve funding for the growers of $16m ($50 payment for destruction per tree). This would reduce any chance of canker spreading and then allow the area to re-plant after two years. The rationale behind the Pressler Plan was that if the current eradication programme failed to eliminate the disease completely from the region, on-going outbreaks would lock growers out of markets for long periods of time. If implemented, the Pressler Plan would provide growers with certainty about their re-establishment and market access.

After the destruction, the growers will be required to fallow the land for the next two years, replant and wait for the new trees to bear their first crop. An orchard will return to its production in five to six years time. Considering Emerald's isolation from the other growing regions in the State and the high probability of returning to production, this proposal received support from the growers in the region. However, the government rejected the Pressler Plan, preferring to continue with the response strategy under the nationally approved response plan.

It was argued that the response plan would be effective and that the risk of continued outbreaks was very low. Subsequent to the rejection of the Pressler Plan, two further outbreaks were discovered at the 2PH farm, and another outbreak discovered at a third farm in the region. Finally, the National Management Group in June 2005 supported the removal of all citrus trees, including domestic and wild native trees in the Emerald PQA, but without any provision of compensation or voluntary agreement with growers. The effectiveness of the NCIBP in eradicating the disease is a key issue. Citrus canker is still endemic in Florida (USA) despite applying the 'cookie cutter' approach for more than a decade in response to citrus canker outbreaks. Grower and industry concern at Emerald was that under the 'cookie cutter' approach all citrus trees in the region might eventually face destruction as further infections were detected.

BROAD BEAN

Fig. Broad Bean Collection

CHOCOLATE SPOT

Chocolate spot is one of the commonest diseases of broad beans and field beans. Dark brown spots appear on the leaves and stems. They may be small, more or less circular, and scattered, in which case little harm is done, or they may spread rapidly, cover the whole leaf surface and cause decay of the stems and death of the plants. In severe outbreaks very few pods mature. Brown spots occur on the pods as well and may penetrate to the ripening seed. Typical chocolate spot may be caused by the ubiquitous mould Botrytis cinerea, but there is also a specialized species, B. fabae, peculiar to broad beans, which causes a similar disease. Chocolate spot is favoured by moisture, ill-drained soil, shade and crowded planting. Hence it is a much more disastrous disease of field beans than of isolated rows of beans in gardens. It is also encouraged by potassium deficiency or by malnutrition of any kind.

MINOR LEAF SPOTS

Cercospora fabae Fautrey causes small chocolate-coloured spots or so across on broad-bean leaves. Under favourable conditions they become larger with a sunken grey centre and a raised dark-brown margin. In wet weather both sides of the spot may bear a silver-grey layer of conidia. Similar spots may be caused by the pycnidial fungus Ascochyta fabae Speg. This fungus may also cause light sunken spots with a broad dark-brown margin on the pods and is known to be seed-borne. Both Cercospora fabae and Ascochyta fabae are widespread but neither is usually considered important enough to warrant control measures.

SCLEROTINIA DISEASE

Broad beans, and especially field beans, are susceptible to a stem rot similar to that caused in other plants by Sclerotinia sclerotiorum. In the case of these beans, however, the cause of the trouble is usually a distinct fungus, 5. trifoliorum var. fabae, very closely related to the fungus of the well-known red clover rot. Although the race commonly found on broad beans has been distinguished from S. trifoliorum by small technical differences it can also cause rotting of red clover, and the typical S. trifoliorum can cause rotting of broad beans. Both fungi also attack common vetch, garden pea, sainfoin, lettuce, and possibly other plants.

BEANS—DWARF AND RUNNER

Anthracnose

Except in the warmest and driest parts of the earth dwarf and runner beans are liable to surfer severely from attack by the anthracnose fungus, the conidial stage of which is only too well known. It has become fairly common especially in cool wet summers, but the ascospore stage has only been found. All kinds of dwarf and runner beans may be attacked. The disease is seed-borne and the seedlings may show brown stripes on their stems. In damp weather new spots readily arise, extending lengthwise into sunken brown stripes.

On the leaves the spots generally start on the under-side of the veins, though the surrounding leaf tissue may also be killed. The most conspicuous symptoms are those on the pods, which are circular or elliptical sunken brown spots with a darker edge. From these the fungus grows into the seed, in which it remains alive until germination, and then attacks the seedling. On dark-coloured seeds it is difficult to see the spots resulting from infection. On white-seeded varieties the larger spots are pale brown but small ones may escape notice. The fungus overwinters in the soil, especially on dead pods and other plant fragments. Plants attacked in the seedling stage or soon after may be killed outright; at later stages the damage is mainly to the pods.

The fungus fructifies as minute pinkish pustules of slimy spores on the surface of the spots and these are scattered, especially by splashes of rain and by handling when the pods are being picked. Enclosed localities where the air is apt to be moist and still favour the disease. Manuring with potash and superphosphate may make the plants a little less sensitive; sulphate of ammonia should only be used on a table crop, not in seed production. Bean varieties differ greatly in susceptibility so that considerable success has been attained in developing resistant types. Resistance may be dependent on one or more inherited factors but so far these have always been dominant in hybrids. It soon became evident, however, that the fungus, too, exists in numerous races different in infective capacity.

Hence a bean variety may be resistant to several races of the fungus but not to others. Hence new varieties have to be exposed to infection by all known races of the anthracnose fungus before they can be described as resistant, and preferably this property should be combined with resistance to other diseases like halo blight, rust and mosaic. So successfully has this been done that some bean varieties now contain three hereditary factors for resistance and are resistant to 34 races of the anthracnose fungus. Actually they all become infected but in resistant varieties the fungus only penetrates the skin and then dies.

Fusarium Wilt

The chief symptom is a rolling inwards of the leaf edges, followed by wilting of part or the whole of the plant. The fungus occurs only in the vascular strands which are stained dark brown as in Vertidllium wilt, especially at the base of the plant. It is apparently not seed-borne and infection presumably comes from the soil, through wounds made by soil insects or by the mechanical splitting of the stem base by secondary roots. The optimum temperature for its growth is 79-82° F.

Foot Rot

Foot rot is caused by a soil-borne fungus prevalent in the Evesham district of Worcestershire. It attacks the roots and stem bases of dwarf beans, turning them reddish brown. The leaves turn yellow and only the first-formed pods swell properly. Foot rot causes most loss in dry seasons, when it may reduce the yield by one half. Strong-growing varieties like Flageolet are somewhat resistant as they put out fresh roots from the lower part of the stem to replace the diseased ones. The same fungus has been found to cause a similar disease in French beans grown under glass. In this case sowing in sterilized soil or peat is recommended, followed by protecting the stem base with the rim of a bottomless pot when the seedlings are planted out in the house.

Rust

This is found on dwarf and runner beans all over the world. The cluster cup stage of this rust is white. This is usually followed by cinnamon-coloured pustules of uredospores on both sides of the leaf and finally by blackish-brown pustules of teleutospores. Bean rust is only occasionally reported. Sprays and dusts give no control of rust and if it breaks out the diseased plants should be burnt or composted and replaced by a resistant variety.

Red Nose

When beans are germinated in the seed-testing laboratory a slight pink discolouration is sometimes noticed at the micropyle or germ pore. This has been called " red nose " and is due to infection with the common fungus Pleospora herbarum. This fungus cannot cause disease of the growing crop but the infected seeds often decay or give sickly seedlings that die early. If they survive this stage they grow into normal healthy plants.

Treatment with one of the proprietary organomercury seed dressings often gives improved germination. Beans harvested under unfavourable conditions, or otherwise of poor quality, may be attacked during germination by bacteria and moulds like Penicillium, which reduce the percentage germination. Treatment with an organo-mercury seed dressing or with red copper oxide may give a definite improvement in germination. Some beans germinate and develop their cotyledons (seed leaves) normally but the terminal bud or plumule is seen to be lacking. An axillary bud of one of the cotyledons may grow out to replace it but only gives a poor plant. The cause may be bacterial infection or damage at threshing, which has cracked the embryo just above the attachment of the cotyledons. Microscopic examination will decide which cause is involved. Finally, beans may germinate badly (and cook badly) after a very hot, dry autumn or after storing in a dry warm place which hardens the skin of the seed. Storage in a damp warm place also brings about certain enzyme reactions within the bean and leads to formation of a " hard kernel," which also reduces germination and cooking quality.

Halo Blight

A number of bacterial diseases are known to affect dwarf and runner beans but their symptoms are usually somewhat similar so that they can only be distinguished by bacteriological investigations. The disease is usually attributed to Pseudomonas phaseolicola. This is seed-borne, and infected seed gives rise to stunted, spotted or yellow deformed plants which usually soon die. From them the bacteria are spread, probably largely by rain splashes, to healthy adjacent plants. On the leaves small, irregular, watersoaked spots appear, that are at first pale, but later turn brown with a transparent halo-like margin.

Similar spots may appear on stems and petioles and from them small drops of bacterial slime may ooze out. When the pods appear they too become spotted and sometimes deformed, or even killed. Seeds from infected pods are likely also to be infected with the bacteria. Sometimes they are spotted, wrinkled, or shrivelled, but they may bear no obvious mark of infection and yet give rise to an infected seedling. It too is seed-borne and infected seedlings may be killed by it as they emerge above ground. On older plants it forms minute watersoaked spots or pale-green wilted areas which enlarge, dry out and turn brown. They usually have a yellow border. Reddish streaks appear on the stems, or reddish lesions may girdle the stem at the level of the cotyledons, or one of the lower nodes. The stem easily breaks at these points. On the pods there are dark-green, watersoaked spots that become dry, brick red and sunken.

RED PEPPER

Fig. Red Pepper

LEAF SPOT

The spots are at first watersoaked but soon dry out and are then white with a dark-brown margin. When many spots occur on one leaf it turns yellow and drops. Spots may sometimes occur also on the leaf-stalks and fruit stalks. The fungus cannot penetrate the skin of the fruit but may grow into it through the stalk and then sets up a " stalk rot." It is likely to appear sooner or later where the plant is only grown on a small scale as a glasshouse crop. Spots appear on the fruit, starting as small translucent or dark-red depressions, which quickly grow larger and gradually become lighter in colour. The pustules of the fungus form a dark coating on the diseased tissue and exude pinkish masses of conidia, which are spread by rain splashes or on clothes or tools of workers.

Sap Warts

When pepper is kept wet, especially if the atmosphere is nearly saturated or when great changes in humidity occur, it easily develops oedema. This takes the form of a large number of very small grey-brown warts on the underside of the leaf. One should try to avoid excessive humidity or much change in the moisture supply to the plant.

Grey Mould

We are not sure whether Botrytis is the primary cause of the damage or net. Quite likely the fruit suffered first from blossom-end rot and the grey mould followed and increased the damage. Leaves and stalks may also be attacked. The plants must not be kept too dry or the fruit will develop blossom-end rot, or too damp or Botrytis will be encouraged. Indeed the art of growing this, like other greenhouse crops, consists in supplying the plants with enough water in a damp enough atmosphere without letting them become moister than is necessary.

Blossom-end Rot

Capsicum fruits may develop blossom-end rot like tomatoes. The first sign of the disease is a more or less sunken area at the tip, or close to it, on the half-grown fruit. The spot is usually a little paler than the surrounding healthy tissue but it may be dark-green and translucent.

Gradually the spot grows larger but it does not cover the whole of the blossom half of the fruit as may happen in tomato. The spots may, however, become infected by fungi or bacteria, which set up a rot that may involve the whole fruit. The spots are not primarily due to a parasite, however, but to a physiological disturbance.

Higgins has studied the problem closely in Georgia, both with controlled watering and under natural conditions out of doors. In all cases it was shown that drought caused the appearance of the spots. In the open air they become infected by bacteria or fungi in the course of a few days. In fairly young spots neither fungi nor bacteria were found.

Only as the spots increased in size did these organisms invade them and thrive on the already damaged tissue of the fruit. The spots start by collapse of the large, thin-walled cells round the ends of the vascular bundles. Red-pepper plants should not be exposed to drought, especially when the fruit is half-grown and has been growing vigourously.

POTATO

Fig. Potato

POTATO BLIGHT

The attack on potato leaves starts as a rule at the edge or tip of a leaflet as a light-green spot, which quickly becomes brown and limp, and later blackish-brown and dry. Under damp conditions the brown spots have a marginal zone of fine white mould, composed of conidiophores and conidia of the fungus, which burst through the skin of the leaf 2-3 days after infection. There are at first a few scattered spots, usually on the lower leaves; but others quickly follow and the whole potato haulm may be destroyed in about a week.

The diseased leaves have a characteristic sickly sweet smell which can often be detected at some distance from a diseased crop. Brown streaks develop too on the stems and even the flowers and berries may be attacked. Potato blight on under-side of the leaf. Tubers attacked by potato blight show leaden or dull purplish-grey, slightly sunken spots or irregular blotches in the skin. When they are cut through, rusty-brown streaks are seen growing from the skin into the flesh. In time the whole tissue becomes destroyed by a rather dry brown rot.

Commonly, however, P. infestans is quickly followed by secondary fungi, especially species of Fusarium and bacteria, which obscure the symptoms of blight and may cause an evil-smelling soft wet rot to supervene. In all its stages the blight fungus needs oxygen and it cannot penetrate rapidly into the flesh by itself. The secondary invaders feed on the starch grains that the blight fungus has only superficially attacked. P. infestans conidia may be formed on diseased tubers. The most important source of infection every summer is certainly slightly infected seed tubers. These may give rise to:

- Quite a normal sprout,
- Infected sprouts which soon die or
- Infected sprouts which come above ground, bear conidia and thus infect the lower leaves of the crop.

The potato blight fungus can also grow out from diseased tubers and small dead shoots into the soil where it lives for a time, and may produce conidia which are splashed on to the leaves by rain. The appearance of the fungus in a crop from diseased seed tubers has been doubted but was seen by de Bary. Severely attacked tubers are readily destroyed by bacteria and millipedes, and sprout feebly or not at all. It is only those tubers which are slightly infected which are able, when planted, to produce shoots that come above ground. In June and July spread of infection from these diseased sprouts to lower leaves of the crop proceeds unnoticed.

These centres of infection form starting points for the incredibly rapid blazing up of the disease which occurs when conditions become favourable to it in July and August. It may be supposed that it will break out at many places at the same time if the conidia are carried a short distance by the wind. It may be of importance whether the early potatoes lie on the windward or leeward side of the late varieties. Sometimes one may notice that a hedge has afforded a certain amount of shelter and that blight has started opposite a gateway or other gap in the hedge. Small potato patches in town gardens become attacked at the same time as fields in the country.

In experiments with cultures in sterilized soil or manure, where the blight fungus encounters no competition from other organisms, it has survived the winter out of doors. The possibility of it overwintering in ordinary field or garden soil is very small but it must be remembered that there are always some groundkeeper tubers not killed by frost and the fungus may naturally survive the winter in some of those.Heaps of chats discarded when the crop was graded or left on the site of an old pit are another possible source of infection. If the potato tops are killed early by blight and the tubers are left to ripen in the soil a very small crop is obtained but the tubers do not become infected, provided they were covered by a good thick layer of soil.

If blight attack comes late, retarded by weather conditions or by spraying, so that the tops are still green and bear fresh blight spots when the crop is lifted, there is great danger of the tubers becoming infected, especially in wet weather. Liability of the tubers to become infected depends partly on the variety, partly on the soil. Haulm and soil remain infectious for 10, possibly 20, days after the haulm has died. Haulm cut down by frost is at once freed from infection.

ALTERNARIA BLIGHT

This leaf spot disease is known and feared under the name " early blight " because it tends to appear earlier than true potato blight, called there " late blight." It is due to the mould Alternaria solani, formerly called Macrosporium solani Ell. & Mart., which causes leaf spotting also on tomato and egg plant. More or less circular brown or blackish spots appear on the potato leaves from July onwards. They are limited by the leaf veins though in severe outbreaks several spots may become united. Under a lens the spots are seen to be marked with darker, irregularly concentric lines, hence the name " target spot" sometimes applied to them.

In damp weather a fine olive-brown mould may appear on the surface. Some varieties show considerable resistance to the disease and only very small brown spots develop on their leaves. This is the form of Alternaria blight usually seen in Britain, where, indeed, the disease is regarded as of no economic importance and where conidia are seldom to be found on the spots. It seems clear, in fact, that not all the " target spot " on potato leaves in this country is attributable to Alternaria infection. Very early spraying with Bordeaux mixture prevents an outbreak of Alternaria blight; according to one investigator Burgundy mixture is even more effective. Where the disease has been prevalent care should be taken that the tubers do not become infected by spores from the haulm at lifting, and to store them in a dry cool place. The optimum temperature for Alternaria rot of the tubers is 60° F. and its growth ceases at 41° F. Alpha, Bravo, King Edward, Majestic, Kerr's Pink, Edzell Blue and Up-to-Date are all susceptible; Juli is fairly resistant and Golden Wonder more so. This fungus causes a minor leaf spot disease which in some parts of Europe causes premature withering of potato haulm in severe seasons. The leaf spots appear from July onwards; they are at first yellow, then brown on the upper surface, and are tinged greyish-purple with the conidia on the under-side of the leaf. The routine sprays against potato blight control this disease as well.

POTATO WART DISEASE

Wart disease increases rapidly on land where potatoes are frequently grown, as in gardens md allotments, and in a space of 2-3 years it may attain such proportions as to ruin the crop. Direct losses of crop from the disease on an agricultural scale have been small but stringent quarantine regulations against it hamper export of produce from infected districts and discourage the cultivation of susceptible varieties. Hence the regulations which aim at excluding wart disease from countries in which it does not yet occur cannot be held to be unreasonable.

On several occasions the disease has been brought in with small consignments of potatoes among immigrants' luggage or by small-scale commercial traffic across a frontier. Only plants of the nightshade family, Solanaceae can be attacked by this fungus. Tomatoes develop swellings on roots and stem, and under experimental conditions small warts on the leaves also. Henbane and a number of species of Solanum develop small swellings on the roots and eventually small galls on the stems. It has not proved possible to infect thorn apple (Datura stramonium], deadly nightshade (Atropa belladonna) or any kind of tobacco. In a wet season warts may be found on the stems and lowest leaves of potatoes, and even on the inflorescence, but as a rule the attack is confined to the tubers and is first noticed at digging.

The stolons may be affected but the roots are never attacked. As a rule growth of the haulm is normal and unchecked. The warts on the tubers start as tiny white granular swellings growing out from the eyes. They quickly enlarge into cauliflower-like structures which may be larger than the tuber itself. Above ground they are light green, below ground at first white, then brown. Old warts decay and turn black and even at the normal lifting time many will be partially rotten, or break off and decay in the soil, leaving only a small scar on the tuber.

Occasionally new small outgrowths may develop in the clamp around the scars, giving a disease picture like that of powdery scab. Powdery scab infection of the sprouts occasionally produces swellings simulating wart disease, as may also irregular second-growth, covered with scab. Sometimes microscopic examination is necessary to distinguish between these diseases. The swellings of crown gall also resemble those of wart disease but the former is known on potato only from artificial inoculations. The wart disease swellings contain a vast number of minute, brown, thick- walled resting sporangia which become liberated into the soil as the tissues decay. When they germinate a number of extremely minute, mobile swarm spores emerge and swim about until they meet a young potato tuber. They then penetrate the skin of an eye and settle down inside the potato cells. Here in a fortnight clusters of from 1 to 7 summer sporangia are formed which liberate hundreds more swarm spores.

These are partly responsible for multiplying the number of infected cells on and around the developing wart, partly for infecting other tubers. Second generations of summer sporangia form during the summer, and their development requires 10-20 days. They do not overwinter but are replaced in the mature wart by the thick-walled winter sporangia, formed after a kind of sexual process. These not only survive the winter but remain alive in the soil for very many years; they are not destroyed even when an infected potato is eaten and digested by an animal. The formation of warts is due to the potato cells being stimulated to abnormal growth and multiplication by the fungus cells which invade them. The wart disease organism is one of the most primitive of fungi and never develops any kind of mycelium.

METHODS OF SPREAD AND REQUIREMENTS FOR INFECTION

The most important and most dangerous means by which infection spreads is the transport of seed potatoes, not only diseased tubers but healthy potatoes from infected land, which may carry resting sporangia in the soil adhering to them. Potato peelings in kitchen waste added to compost heaps or manure and dung of animals fed on raw potatoes may also carry infection. The fungus may be carried from infected land in soil on carts, tools, boots, and the feet of domestic animals and poultry. Soil particles transported by storms, or floods, or by crows and other wild birds may also spread the disease. Resting sporangia can germinate over a wide temperature range (40 to 86° F.) but best at 66-68° F. Presence of oxygen and nitrates encourages germination. Invasion of the host cells by the swarm spores also occurs over a wide temperature range (45-86° F.), best at 60-68° F., and oxygen is needed for this process. Soil reaction seems to have little effect on infection. It occurs over the whole range between pH 3.9 and 7.5, even pH 5 is said to be quite favourable.

Soils more acid than these are seldom cultivated and one can feel no assurance that infection will not occur on soils more alkaline than 7.5. No essential difference has been found between infection on clay and sandy soils. Extreme drought may completely prevent outbreak of potato wart disease. On the other hand the warts become particularly large with a heavy fall of rain. Plants that mature early or form no tubers owing to virus disease, etc., may escape attack, as may very early varieties. Resting sporangia in the soil survive longest when the ground is under permanent grass or is left unbroken for other reasons.

After a severe outbreak infection has been proved to persist in the soil for 12-16 years. Wart disease is easily and completely controlled by growing immune varieties. No potatoes from an infected crop may be sold for planting and no tubers visibly affected with wart disease may be sold for any purpose. Only approved immune varieties of potato may be grown on land where wart disease has occurred at any time.

In a scheduled Protected Area the only potatoes allowed to be planted are tubers from a crop certified to conform to official standards of purity and health and to have been grown on land free from wart disease.It is also forbidden to remove rubbish or compost from such places or to dispose of manure. Export of tubers from boroughs where infected areas occur is also prohibited. There is no practicable method of destroying wart disease resting sporangia in a field soil. On a very small scale soil can be disinfected by steaming; baking the soil is not effective. Treatment of soil with 5 per cent formalin for 24 hours also kills the sporangia. Incorporation of sulphur in the soil also has some effect but only in large quantities which make the soil sour and are unreasonably expensive. Implements used on infected land may be disinfected by dipping in 2 per cent formalin solution, but disinfection of potato " seed " has not proved effective. Cooking of potatoes used as fodder helps to prevent contamination of manure and is, in any case, required by the Wart Disease Order as far as infected tubers are concerned.

COMMON SCAB

The disease called common scab of potato is caused by the ray fungus Actinomyces scabies, which also attacks beet, carrot, radish, swede and turnip. Care is needed to distinguish between it and powdery scab. The ray fungi are generally regarded as being somewhat intermediate in structure between bacteria and fungi. Several hundred species occur in soils, where they play a large part in the breakdown of decaying organic matter; others live in water and a few cause disease in animals. Potato scab appears as rough, scabby spots on the otherwise smooth skin of the tubers. The spots may grow together and the whole surface of the tuber may be covered by them.

If careful examination is made when the layer of cork begins to form in the skin the first signs of disease will be detected as small grey-brown spots under the lenticels where the fungus is stimulating the living cells to production of additional layers of cork. The outer cork is burst open and the new cork follows suit, producing the scabby outer surface of the lesion. The more prone the variety is to cork formation the scabbier it will be.

Roots and stolons of potato may be slightly attacked. Tubers that protrude above ground are not affected, nor do scabs increase in the clamp. Tubers are the most readily infected; if they have a long growing period, the period during which they become scabby is increased, hence, perhaps, the various reports that " spraying induces scab." A strong earthy smell due to the presence of the actinomycete is peculiar to common scab; powdery scabs have no such smell. The fungus may overwinter either in the soil or in the scabs on tubers. It can survive on cellulose and similar plant products in the soil for years at a time. Several instances have been reported in which disinfected tubers planted in freshly broken forest soil produced scabby crops.

On the other hand an interval of several years between potato crops has sometimes led to a striking reduction in the amount of scab. The fungus reproduces simply by its fine hyphae breaking up to form spores, easily disseminated in soil and water. Manure may be regarded as infected if it comes from farms where scabby potatoes are used raw as fodder. Infection may also be spread by compost and, of course, by planting infected tubers.

VIRUS DISEASES OF TOMATO

COMMON TOMATO MOSAIC

Symptoms vary from ill-defined, light-green spots, mainly between the veins of the leaflets, to quite a bright, clearly defined, light and dark-green mottle. The surface of the leaves may also be slightly uneven or even curled. Tomato variety, nutrition and the time of year all affect the expression of symptoms; thus, during the sunny warm days of summer the mottling is most obvious, and during spring and autumn the curling becomes apparent. At low temperatures the symptoms may be almost entirely lacking but the plants remain infected and infectious to others. Flowers of infected plants may be deformed, sterile and fall off.

There may be slight streaking of the stems and pale, slowly ripening spots on the fruit. Infection from tomato plants. The invisible infectious matter, or virus, occurs in the sap of almost all the cells of an infected tomato plant, including the cells of its numerous hairs.

These are easily broken and it is a familiar experience that one cannot handle a tomato plant without getting sap on one's hands, tools and clothes. If one touches an infected plant and then a healthy one a mere trace of sap transferred from one to the other is enough to transmit the infection. Hands, knives and other tools are the most important agents of spread. Aphides do not spread this disease. The incubation period is from 5 to 20 days or 28 days in our experiments out of doors. It persists for a very long time in dead plants and purified virus preparations can remain viable in the laboratory for 5 years. The virus is not killed until heated for 10 minutes at 194° F. or until treated for 24 hours with 60 per cent alcohol, but it is sensitive to soap. Probably tomato sap dried on clothes can remain infectious for a long time.

Fig. Virus Diseases of Tomato

Virus liberated from a plant into the soil can remain infectious for a long time if the soil is moist; freezing and drying the soil renders it non-infective. Infection from other plants and products. Common tomato mosaic is caused by the same virus as common tobacco mosaic, which is common in all tobacco-growing countries. Fermented, commercialj smoking or chewing tobacco may retain the virus in an infectious condition. Hence chewing tobacco is a common source of infection in commercial tobacco production. Besides species of Nicotiana this virus can infect most plants belonging to the family Solanaceae and also species in other families, notably asclepias, snapdragon, larkspur, zinnia, beans, spinach and possibly celery. Potato, black nightshade and woody nightshade (bittersweet) show no symptoms, but they are carriers of infection. From these hosts the virus can be returned to tomato.

The nightshades afford a means of carrying it over winter as also do susceptible greenhouse ornamentals like Petunia, Solanum and others. There seems little danger to the tomato crop from mosaic-infected potatoes though there is evidence of one such a transmission out of doors. It may be supposed that the virus multiplies more luxuriantly in vigourously growing plants. The statement that a crop can be " manured out of mosaic " only means that suitable manuring may overcome the consequences of infection; the virus in the plants is not destroyed. When nitrogen is very deficient the mottle becomes invisible; if nitrogen is then supplied it reappears. The influences of light and temperature have been mentioned above. Attacks are often found to start near doors and ventilators, which can scarcely be due to draughts but rather to infection from outside the house.

SPOTTED WILT

Then a large number of tiny bronze-coloured spots appear either in rings or scattered over the whole leaf surface. Growth stops for a time so that infected plants appear stunted. Young seedlings may be killed but more often the plant resumes growth after a time, but its leaves become distorted and have a rather conspicuous yellowish mosaic mottling. The fruit may be unaffected or it may bear pale-red, yellow or almost white markings, often in concentric rings. The virus is sap-transmissible but not to the same degree as tomato mosaic. It is not spread by aphides but only by thrips.

Curiously enough it is only in the larval stage that thrips can take up the virus from an infected plant, but once they have done so they remain infective throughout their life. Lycopersicum Virus 3 is not very resistant, it remains viable only a few hours in expressed tomato sap, is inactivated by drying, by oxidizing agents and by exposure for 10 minutes to a temperature of 108° F. It has a very wide host range and commonly infects many popular greenhouse perennials which then form reservoirs of infection for the next tomato crop. Most of these show little sign of infection or bear only a few rather inconspicuous ring marks on their leaves.

TOMATO YELLOW LEAF

It starts as a well-marked mosaic mottle on the youngest leaves. The older leaves turn yellow, except along the main veins which remain dark-green. As the plant grows the yellow spreads until only the topmost leaves remain green. The whole picture resembles nitrogen starvation. Some evidence of seed transmission has been obtained. In properties the virus closely resembles that of common tomato mosaic. The aster yellows virus can also infect tomato and causes a certain amount of yellowing and a bushy type of growth, as it stimulates development of leafy buds and shoots in the axils of the leaflets as well.

AUCUBA MOSAIC

This disease is caused by a strain of the common tomato mosaic virus and must not be confused with aucuba mosaic of potato, caused by quite a different virus. Bright yellow spots often appear on the leaves of tomato plants infected with common mosaic. If these are punched out and used for inoculation the aucuba mosaic disease is produced. It is also sometimes found by itself in commercial tomato houses. About 5 days after inoculation the youngest leaves curl down and their surface becomes rough, wrinkled or corrugated. By the seventh or eighth day yellow spots appear and become gradually larger, until in extreme cases the whole leaf surface is yellow, with a few raised islands of dark-green standing out on it like blisters. More often the yellow and green areas are of about equal extent and intimately intermingled. Plants are not killed by the virus but their growth is checked and the fruit may be mottled. Properties of the virus are the same as for common tomato mosaic. There is some evidence that seed-borne infection can take place in a very small number of seedlings, perhaps by virus dried on the seed coat.

TOMATO DISTORTING OR ENATION VIRUS

This is another strain of the common tomato mosaic differing in that, in addition to causing mottling of the leaves, it stimulates the plant to excessive and unnatural growth. The leaflets may be increased so that a fern-like effect is produced with very many small leaflets crowded together, gradually diminishing in size and ending in a corkscrew-like tendril. In some cases small outgrowths (enations) are formed on the under-side of the midribs. There is a tendency to excessive growth and production of giant plants crowded with foliage.

Bushy Stunt

This is a distinct and apparently rather uncommon virus which is easily transmitted by sap but has no known insect vector. In seedlings it causes yellow and purple colouration of the leaves, yellow spotting and death of the young leaves and often a sunken brown lesion at soil level, causing the seedlings to fall over. In older plants it causes cessation of growth by the terminal shoot and stimulation of the side shoots, hence the name " bushy stunt." The lower leaves turn yellow or purple and often there are concentric rings of bright yellow or purple, or purple lines along the veins of a yellow leaf. Ultimately the lower leaves shrivel and drop off. This virus is particularly interesting because it has been purified and obtained in the form of minute cubical crystals.

Misshapen Fruit

The tendency to production of ridged and misshapen fruit is an inherited one, as shown by Pape. It is also, however, influenced by conditions of cultivation. Thus, Kondine Red is a variety rather prone to bear ridged fruit but it only does so when the plants are set very far apart and richly manured. To avoid this disfigurement seed should be saved only from carefully selected plants with well-shaped fruit. The seed crop should be grown under conditions conducive to misshapen fruit so that any inherited tendency to do so becomes evident. In normal commercial fruit production spacing and manuring should be that found by experience to suit the variety grown.

Blossom-end Rot

The most striking symptom is a dark, more or less sunken, area at the blossom or style end of the fruit, *i.e.* farthest from the stalk. The trouble begins as a water-soaked spot at or near the base of the style, or the whole of that end of the fruit may look as though bruised. The affected part soon becomes leathery and usually turns black. As the rest of the fruit continues to swell the blossom end becomes slightly sunken or remains abnormally flattened. Various bacteria and fungi are commonly to be found in the affected tissues and have from time to time been described as the cause of blossom-end rot. They are, however, purely secondary invaders, living in tissue already damaged by a physiological disturbance. Especially if the surface of the fruit remains moist these secondary organisms may enter and set up an extensive rot. Tomato varieties in which the style remains attached for a long time seem particularly susceptible to blossom-end rot, perhaps because fungi and bacteria become established on the dead style and are hence ready to invade even a small spot of true physiological blossom-end rot.

The most important preventive measure is regular watering to avoid alternate drying out and soaking of the soil. It may be worth while to pick off the dead corolla and style on varieties that retain them long after the fruit has set. Otherwise fungi or bacteria established in the dead tissue may set up secondary rots following blossom-end rot. The variety Comet seems particularly susceptible to this trouble.

Hollow Fruit

Fruits divided by a single septum into two compartments are particularly prone to develop empty spaces between the septum and the fruit wall. Such fruit when shaken often makes a rustling or rattling sound. A larger or smaller part of the seed and flesh inside may be black and dead. This unfortunate phenomenon, which appears especially towards the end of the summer, is not due to attack by any parasite. It is due especially to a period of drought during the swelling of the fruit but other growing conditions may possibly cause it. In such circumstances when there is a heavy crop only part of it will contain normal contents.

Greenback

Greenback appears as a hard green or yellow area at the top of the fruit, surrounding the stalk. When ripening starts this part does not turn red like the rest but remains green and then slowly goes yellow or orange. It never becomes red and soft like the rest of the flesh. Greenback, like blotchy ripening, is due to a deficiency of potassium, especially in fruit exposed to strong sunlight. Tomatoes forced to ripen at a temperature exceeding 90° F. do not turn red but yellow. Lycopin, the red colouring matter, is not formed at such high temperatures. Greenback always occurs on the uppermost part of the fruit as it hangs on the truss, which is, of course, the part most exposed to the sun. When defoliating tomatoes one should be careful to leave enough leaves to shade the trusses during the hottest part of the day. If the foliage is scanty, side shoots should be allowed to grow out and produce a couple of leaves before being stopped. Glasshouses should be shaded during the hottest periods. Care should be also be taken to supply enough potassium and water. Kondine Red and Tuckwood are very prone to greenback, Selandia much less so.

Blotchy Ripening

In blotchy ripening larger or smaller parts of the fruit surface do not change colour with the rest as the tomato ripens. When it begins to turn red they remain green for a time but gradually turn yellow, develop a waxy appearance and a turnip-like flavour.

The vascular bundles in the blotches are often dark and show faintly through the skin as dark lines. The blotches may occur on any part of the fruit, a feature which distinguishes them from greenback which occurs only round the stalk. Blotchy ripening is seen mainly in June and July. Tomato varieties differ greatly in susceptibility to it; Kondine Red is one of the most susceptible. Blotchy ripening is due to cultural factors or to diseased roots. In manurial experiments at Cheshunt it has been demonstrated that the greatest number of fruits with blotchy ripening occurred on unmanured plots and on plots deficient in potassium and nitrogen.

If tomato roots are diseased, if they receive too much water or too little, they cannot absorb enough nutrients and this may lead to blotchy ripening. The dampness of the subsoil should therefore be taken into account. It may well happen that the top 6-9 inches of soil are fairly moist but that the deeper levels are too dry. Tomatoes seem to develop most blotchy ripening in heavily limed soil. In Danish nurseries blotchy ripening is often prevalent where there is a large amount of phosphoric acid in the soil. If a heavy dressing of manure is given the roots may be damaged and thus less able to absorb nutrients so that the plants may starve on over-manured soil. Blotchy ripening is usually worst in new houses where growth is unusually vigourous. In summers with plenty of sunshine less potassium and more nitrogen should be supplied than in dull, cloudy seasons.

Cracked Fruit

Cracking of tomato fruit occurs in two chief forms, single large cracks and many small ones; both types occur mostly on the top half of the fruit. The large cracks happen especially when a dry period is suddenly followed by a damp one. They are therefore usually found in the outdoor crop, where the grower has least control over the moisture relations of the plant. Cracking may also result from a sudden acceleration of growth for other reasons, as after manuring. The skin makes poorest growth under cool conditions and then has difficulty in keeping pace with rapid expansion of the flesh. The numerous small cracks on tomato fruit occur especially in greenhouses where there are great fluctuations in atmospheric humidity. Growers should therefore be careful not to stop night heating too early It is probably the increased root development that counteracts the effect of a fluctuating water supply. Potassium permanganate is usually used for watering, etc.

Rolling of the Leaves

Tomato leaflets sometimes roll up so much that the upper surface becomes completely overarched by the upcurled margins which may meet above the midrib of the leaflet. Such leaves feel very hard and stiff. Varieties and individual plants may differ somewhat in the degree of leaf rolling. Tomatoes, perhaps because they are more extensively stripped than the glasshouse crop. The rolling of tomato leaves has no connection with the leaf roll disease of potatoes, which is due to virus infection. Rolling up of the top leaves may occur on young, actively growing plants. It occurs mainly when the crop has been heavily manured so that there is a high concentration of nutrient elements. Such plants have dark-green foliage and the top may have a violet tint somewhat reminiscent of spotted wilt. It occurs mainly in spring, particularly on tomatoes but also on other greenhouse plants such as pelargoniums and early forced potatoes. The outer cells become gorged with water, swell and burst the skin.

The swellings then have a white powdery appearance but gradually turn brownish as the broken tissue falls away. Affected leaves have a tendency to roll. Edema occurs when the roots are absorbing more water than the leaves are able to transpire. A warm, moist soil increases the rate of water absorption but damp air, poor ventilation and shade check transpiration from the leaves. The condition may also become serious when, after a cool period with slow growth, the temperature rises and supply of water and nutrients to the foliage is suddenly increased. Such plants have relatively few leaves unable to cope with the large increased water supply resulting from the altered conditions. To check oedema the soil should be kept fairly dry and there should be thorough ventilation. This condition arises in plants that have became much more prevalent after the adoption received too much water or excessive nitrogen of petroleum oil sprays against red spider.

The or have experienced a sudden change in con-film of oil checks transpiration from the leaves, ditions when planted out. The grower often finds a few plants which times been noticed some time after severely early attract notice by remaining short because pot-bound plants have been planted out. Once the roots have grown out into the new than in normal plants. These should be rogued soil they are able to absorb more water than out before the crop is planted out as such can be dealt with by the rather stunted tops, plants are partially or completely unfruitful.

Some time after planting out the stems growth. As a rule there are only a few of these may become soft and flaccid; in bad cases the in each batch of seedlings. Like the short-plants fall over without any actual rot taking jointed plants they are practically sterile, place. When such a stem is cut open the pith These varieties seem to be due to inherited is found to be wholly or partly wanting. Plants defects. They occur scattered amongst normal that have fallen over in this way may remain plants and should be weeded out as early as green for a long time but make no growth. possible.

CARROT

VIOLET ROOT ROT

The fungus has a reddish-purple mycelium which grows in a network of fine threads over the underground parts of diseased plants, which gradually collapse as the tissue beneath the mycelium decays. It may grow through the soil to the next plant and attack it also. In dry weedy soil the fungus may persist in the same place for many years. Many different kinds of plants may be attacked. Potato, turnip, swede, sugar-beet, mangold, broad bean, red, white and Alsike clover, asparagus, carrot, celery, chicory, parsley, salsify, seakale, carnation, holly, and the weeds wild carrot, plantain and creeping buttercup. It is the most injurious root disease of sugar-beet and becomes a serious problem where carrot growing is practised intensively. Baudys and others consider that different races of the fungus exist and call that on carrot.

This view does not find general acceptance and it is wiser to consider the possibility of infection spreading from any of the above-mentioned crops to any other. The fungus persists in the soil for many years and little can be done to get rid of it once it has appeared in a field. Long rotations, avoiding root crops for a considerable number of years, offer the best hope of control. On a small scale it may possibly be killed by soaking the soil with corrosive sublimate solution at the rate of 2 oz. sublimate plus 18 oz. saltpetre to 22 gallons of water.

Carrot Fungus

The disease appears in late summer on one-year-old carrots as sunken grey spots on the upper part of the root, often forming a sunken ring round the rosette of leaves. Many blackish pimple-like pycnidia appear on the surface of the spots, from which there ooze out in damp weather red globules or tendrils, composed of innumerable conidia embedded in mucilage not sink in as much as in Rostrup's description. The spots became blackish-brown, covered with a short loose grey mycelium mingled with white mycelial tufts. Pycnidia were gradually formed in the grey patches. The fungus may spread freely during storage and may grow from infected roots into healthy ones and destroy a whole consignment.

Numerous other fungi (Stemphylium radicinum, Sclerotinia sderotiorumy Botrytis cinerea, Fusarium spp.), however, often cooperate in this decay. The fungus does most damage to the seed crop. When infected roots are planted out to seed, spots gradually appear on the stem and leaf stalks, especially at the axils of the leaves. Often the spots are situated one above another and run together to form a streak down the stem because the mycelium tends to spread along the furrows. Infection becomes widespread by means of the conidia during the summer. When flowering commences the disease has usually advanced so far that the root decays, the stem withers, the leaves hang down and the plant dies without setting seed. Seeds that do mature may also be infected and bear small black pycnidia. The disease was formerly much more important than at present. Commercial seed production is now usually from carrots that overwinter where they were sown and are less exposed to the disease than carrots taken up in autumn, stored over winter and replanted in spring.

Black Rot

Dry blackish spots appear on the leaves, leafstalk and stems of growing plants but the phase of the disease most often seen is a slow rather hard blackish rot on the stored root. It usually occurs on the neck but may also occur farther down the side of the carrot. Under dry conditions the rot is slow and dry but under damp conditions it becomes a wet rot covered with a blackish-grey mould Fusarium sp. and other secondary fungi often appear on the decaying spots. In carrots planted for seed the tops may wither. The disease is seed-borne and kills seedlings by rotting the roots and hypocotyledonary stem.

Downy Mildew

The upper surface of the leaf bears yellowish spots which later turn black and may cause the leaves to shrivel and fall. On the under-side of the spots is a loose white mould. This fungus is much more common on parsnip and races of it exist on many wild umbelliferous plants such as goutweed, hedge parsley and angelica. These should not be tolerated in and around gardens as, even if the race of mildew attacking them does not infect carrot, they may also harbour the carrot fly. An attack of downy mildew may be checked at the outset by spraying or dusting with a copper fungicide. Remains of infected plants should be burnt or otherwise destroyed in autumn.

Cracked Roots

Boron deficiency has not been reported in English carrot crops. In pot experiments with carrots on moorland peat, however, 0delien in Norway found the roots very much cracked. Manuring with small quantities of boron compounds prevented the cracking. On slightly acid peat soils in Canada longitudinal cracking of carrots has similarly been controlled by manuring with 20 Ib. borax per acre. Carrots grown in sand cultures without boron also developed wide cracks, and leaves which turned yellow round the edges. Longitudinal cracking may also be due, however, to a sudden acceleration of growth when rain follows a dry spell.

ROOT ROT OF CELERY AND SCAB OF CELERIAC

These diseases are of general occurrence but seldom attain any real importance. In celeriac, brown smooth spots appear on the skin of the crowns and gradually develop a cracked, warted skin. In early and severe attacks development of the crowns is checked and their upper surface becomes covered with a brown or yellowish-brown, scabby skin which may crack, and the crowns do not keep well. This condition, too, is sometimes called "rust" but it has no connection with true rust caused by Puccinia apii.

In the scabby patches tiny dark pycnidia are formed and these may also be found on seedlings at the base of the leaf stalk and occasionally on the seeds and leaves. In severe attacks seedlings still in the seed box may develop damping off symptoms, *i.e.* they rot at the soil level and die. Celery is attacked by P. apiicola mainly at the base of the leaf stalks and the rot spreads thence into the crown and the roots. The decayed leaf stalks are bluish-green or black and the rotting roots are brown. Celery roots may also sometimes be attacked by soil fungi such as species of Pythium, causing a reddish root rot, Thielaviopsis basicola, causing a black root rot, and the ubiquitous Corticium solani.

HEART ROT AND OTHER BACTERIAL DISEASES

Bacterial soft rot involving the heart leaves and spreading up the leaf stalks and down into the stock is not uncommon in celery. The cause is probably the common soft-rotting bacterium. Damage by the fly larvae may begin the trouble and it is likely to become prevalent when there is no proper rotation of crops.

Danish experiments indicate that excess lime and boron deficiency are another important cause of heart rot. A non-parasitic form of black heart is widespread in celery fields. It seems to follow periods of either drought or excessive soil moisture, especially if the crop is growing rapidly. A purely bacterial disease is that caused by Pseudomonas jaggeri (Jagger) Stapp. This organism causes small rusty-brown spots on the leaves. It can be controlled by dusting the seed beds weekly with copper lime dust and in the field crop by spraying with Bordeaux mixture.

ONION

SMUT

By careful examination smut can be detected on quite young seedlings. It appears as opaque dark spots or streaks under the skin of the first and subsequent leaves and sometimes in the bulb scales of young onions. The leaves first attacked are often abnormally thickened and twisted. Sooner or later the skin over the streaks splits irregularly, exposing the black spore powder. These spores contaminate the soil and many remain alive there for twenty years or more. Many of the infected seedlings are killed outright by the disease; others survive and grow, but are malformed, while still others grow almost normally but develop fresh smut lesions on their leaves and bulbs.

Individual plants may completely recover from the attack; diseased leaves and bulb scales are thrown off, and the bulbs ripen more or less normally, though they are always small. The smut fungus which causes this disease can grow and infect seedlings at temperatures between 50° and 85° F. High temperatures after sowing therefore favour the fungus. Infection takes place from the soil and can occur only in the seedling stage, from about the second day after germination until the first leaf is developed.

Older plants cannot be infected. The fungus enters that part of the seedling which is beneath the soil or just above its surface. It penetrates the epidermis and permeates the tissues as far as the growing point, after which the new leaves become infected as they develop. The incubation period is 5 days. Wherever possible onions should be sown in soil free from smut spores. When they are big enough to be transplanted they can safely be transferred to infected land. It can attack many species of Allium and no resistant varieties of onion or leek are known. Various methods of dry seed treatment have been tried to avoid the troublesome formalin treatment. Good results were obtained with Brassicol but the method should be tested in larger-scale experiments before being generally adopted. The onion seed was slightly damped and then mixed with half its weight of Brassicol.

Neck Rot

It may spread in storage. The diseased scales become somewhat brown and transparent, looking as though cooked, and in a moist atmosphere they develop a short hairy coating of grey mould. Bacteria often follow as secondary invaders and set up a rapid soft rot. In the later stages of decay small black sclerotia form on the diseased part or even over the whole bulb. They may sometimes form a continuous scab, especially at the neck of the bulb. The disease is usually controlled when the bulbs are dried thoroughly and quickly after lifting and are then stored in a cool, dry, well-ventilated place. If they remain damp for long, neckrot may be very destructive. It is advisable to bend over the tops before growth has ceased. Onions are best stored at 35° F. Onions that have made very luxuriant growth seem more susceptible than those grown at a normal rate. White-scaled varieties are more susceptible than those with coloured scales.

Downy Mildew

This disease does not usually break out until the bulb is about to form. Then a pale coating of the fungus appears on leaves and stalks. As the leaves wither the fungus turns brownish purple. In damp weather this coating may appear before there is any discolouration of the infected leaves, but they soon become pale and translucent and shrivel from the tip downwards. In mild attacks one may mistake this yellowing for normal ripening. Gradually the infected leaves wither to the base, often being replaced by new ones which are also usually attacked. The dead parts are often covered later by a nearly black layer of the mould Stemphylium botryosum. In severe attacks the bulbs remain small, shrivelled or unripe. The disease also attacks shallots and in them it appears first on those grown from infected bulbs.

The leaves are small and wither quickly, becoming pale, flaccid and covered by the greyish-purple layer of mildew. From these plants the disease spreads to the rest of the crop and causes symptoms like those described on onion. Both on onion and shallot the fungus grows down from the leaves into the bulb scales and persists there until the following year. Thus shallots and onion sets are a common source of infection. In severely infected bulbs the outer scales become brown, translucent and shrivelled. Some may die during the winter; others survive and sprout prematurely. Within the tissue of the infected leaves resting spores may be found, which can survive the winter and even remain alive for 5-6 years in the soil where onion tops have decayed.

Cause and Importance

Onion downy mildew is caused by the fungus Peronospora destructor, formerly often known as P. schleideni Unger. It can attack all varieties of onion and shallot, but is seldom seen on leek. When onion sets are used it is important to obtain them from a completely healthy crop. If that cannot be done the sets should be graded and only the large sound ones planted and these should be carefully polished. The fungus in the sets may be killed by keeping them for more than 8 hours, or up to 24 hours, at a temperature of 104 degree F.

In some experiments good results have been obtained by dipping sets in copper sulphate solution, or lime water, but there were no untreated controls for comparison. There is much to indicate that the fungus penetrates the bulb scales too deeply to be completely killed by such treatment. Seed should be harvested from sound plants. The soil should not have carried a diseased onion or shallot crop in the previous four years. Remains of a diseased onion crop should be burnt. When nearly all the onion tops in one onion-growing district were burnt for several years in succession, to control onion fly, the incidence of downy mildew was reduced at the same time. Onion beds should be well drained and exposed to sun and wind. Spraying and dusting are less effective than one might desire. It is difficult to get the liquid or powder to adhere to the onion leaves. If it is tried a spreading agent should be added.

White Rot

The disease usually appears about the end of May or beginning of June, especially in autumn-sown crops. The older leaves turn yellow and fall over and the plants can be easily pulled up because their roots are rotten. Round the base of the bulb there is a soft, flurry, white mycelium, hence the name " mouldy nose" sometimes applied to the disease. In later stages this mould becomes matted and innumerable tiny, round, black sclerotia, none bigger than a pin's head, develop in it. They are readily detached and left in the soil where they may remain alive for many years. All varieties of onion may be attacked, though some are more resistant than others.

The fungus also attacks shallot, leek, and garlic and may occur on the wild crow garlic so that land may be infected with it that has never carried an onion crop. The sclerotia may also be found in seed samples and spread in that way. Probably the most important means of spread, however, is by infected sets and transplants. After an outbreak of white rot, onions, shallots and leeks should not be grown on the same ground for at least 4 years, preferably not for 8 or 10 years. Infected plants should be burnt.

Shanking

This disease of onion and shallot closely resembles shanking of tulip. The outward symptoms are yellowing and shrivelling of the leaves and softening of the base of the plant. Some or all of the roots are soft and watersoaked. When-an affected bulb is cut longitudinally the bases of the youngest leaves and the tissues of the growing point are found to be discoloured, soft and often contracted.

The light-green or white healthy tissue contrasts sharply with the dull buff infected area. In some cases infection has been shown to occur from the soil in which the seedlings were raised prior to transplanting. This is not always the case, however, as the disease may occur hi onions drilled out of doors. Onion seed should not be sown in soil that has carried a tomato crop, as the Phytophthora spp. which cause foot rot and damping off of tomatoes are the same as cause shanking. Onions for transplanting should be raised in sterilized soil.

Root Rot and Foot Rot

Various species of Fusarium may attack onion, both seedlings and older plants. Roots of seedlings often become attacked by Fusarium from infected seeds, and they turn yellowish-pink and decay. The plants put out new roots which are often also attacked. The decay spreads upwards from the roots, and if the bulbs have formed the scales may rot at the base and the leaves turn yellow at the tip.

The decayed parts of the bulb become reddish-brown or grey-brown, dry, mealy and overgrown by a pink or white mould; finally they become dry, shrivelled mummies. Alternatively there may be secondary infection by bacteria, causing a-soft, wet, stinking rot. Slightly infected bulbs may be overlooked at lifting and decay in storage.

Mould Rot in Storage

During storage onions may be seen with soft or dry areas on which there is a sparse blue-green covering of mould, usually beneath the outer scales. This is a species of Penicillium. A similar trouble occurs on garlic. The powdery black mould Aspergillus niger van Tiegh may occur in a similar situation and in Southern Europe a mould with yellowish-brown spore clusters causes rotting of garlic and onion bulbs. These moulds attack bruised bulbs or those damaged by frost or sunscald and stored in ill-ventilated places.

Virus Diseases

These are common in shallot, much less so in onion, and are commonly referred to under the names yellow dwarf and mosaic, but the viruses causing them have not been extensively studied. Possibly some forms of the disease, however, may be caused by the common Cucumber Mosaic Virus, which has been shown to be transmitted by the shallot aphis, Myzus ascalonicus Doncaster.

Infected shallots are small with twisted, compressed, limp leaves, usually streaked with yellow. They make only small bulbs, which may be soft and not keep well. This condition is general where half a crop may be affected.

It is at least as common in English shallots and occurs to some extent in onions, especially in seed crops or in the vicinity of diseased shallots. Similar symptoms have been seen in the perennial Welsh onion, Allium cepa L. clon perutile Stearn. The shallot aphis occurs on stored bulbs as well as in the field, so possibly some transmission of the disease occurs in storage. Cucumber Mosaic Virus is also transmissible mechanically, as by bruising sets or transplants. Soil infection and seed-borne, infection have not been proved. Infections may not give rise to visible symptoms in the first year but the bulbs will yield diseased plants if replanted. Onion and shallot sets should only be taken from healthy crops.

If the health of a consignment is suspected a sample may be planted in a greenhouse during the winter, if infected bulbs are present they will give obviously diseased foliage. It was apparently this disease that Buchanan cured by keeping the bulbs at 84° F, for 112 hours.

CUCUMBER

ANTHRACNOSE

The seedlings may be attacked and fall over but this seldom happens. Leaf spots are the usual symptom at all stages of growth of the crop. They are pale green and transparent, later becoming dry, reddish brown, with a pale margin and tend to fall out. They enlarge more quickly than those of blotch and are more apt to fuse together into large withered areas, which may kill the whole leaf. Sunken dry patches, later becoming dry and floury, appear on leafstalks and stems. Sunken pale spots also appear on the fruit.

The diseased tissue commonly bears pinkish coni-dial pustules of the fungus, easily distinguishable under a magnifying glass. In greenhouses that have contained an infected crop the fungus occurs in the soil, on the glass, especially at joins, on decaying wood, old paper, etc.When the disease has occurred the houses should be thoroughly cleaned after the crop has been removed, sulphur should be burnt in them, all crop debris destroyed, the woodwork and glass should be sprayed with formalin 2:100 and the soil should either be renewed or thoroughly disinfected.

Gummosis

When the seed has been sown in infected soil the seedlings may be attacked. As a rule the first symptom is a water-soaked spot on the hypocotyl below the seed leaves and often a dark stripe extending as far as the latter, on which dark spots may also develop. If the attack is severe the stem cracks at the attacked places. Under favourable conditions the infected seedlings may survive but the fungus is easily spread further from these lesions. In older plants oblong spots with yellowish-brown margins may develop on the stems and leaf stalks. On the leaves the fungus causes yellow or greyish-yellow spots which burst open.

They are larger and more irregular than the small regular spots characteristic of blotch. The disease on the fruit is the most general, most characteristic and best-known phase. Depressions occur in the skin, but several such spots often fuse to form large irregular patches. The spots often exude a gummy liquid, which hardens into a yellow or brown bead, entirely or partially filling the depression. This characteristic gummy discharge gives the disease its common name " gummosis".

The conidia of the fungus form a grey or greenish-black layer over the depressions and on the edge of the spots. The disease is caused by the mould fungus Clados-poriurn cucumerinum. Races of this fungus isolated from many different places varied greatly in their capacity for infection. It can over-winter in the soil, on woodwork, glass, etc.

Cucumber seed extensively but was unable to demonstrate seedborne infection; its possibility is not, however, to be excluded. The fungus can grow at temperatures between 32° and 85° F. but thrives best about 70° F., whereas cucumber plants grow best about 80° F.

If the atmospheric humidity is kept below 85 per cent development of the fungus is greatly checked. The fruits may also be attacked. There the spots are at first small, dark and somewhat sunken, not marked off from the surrounding healthy tissue by a sharply defined border. They quickly increase in size and may sometimes cover half the upper side of the fruit or more. Often the diseased tissues sink in to form a constriction in the fruit. This usually happens at one end of the cucumber; if it is at the stalk end naturally the entire development of the fruit stops.

Mildew

Mildew may be very serious on outdoor cucumbers, it is of general occurrence but usually less serious on the hothouse crop. The disease begins as small white spots which may gradually coalesce to form a continuous powdery white coating over the shoot tips and leaves, particularly on the upper surfaces. When mildew is found in a greenhouse the ventilation should be improved and the old leaves removed as soon as possible. The remedies for mildew may also be tried usual.

Bacterial Leaf Spot

This disease first appears as round or irregular transparent spots on the shoots and later on as well-defined, watersoaked, brown leaf spots, which dry up and fall out, just as in blotch. In the morning one often sees on the under surface of the spots small, clear, bacteria-filled droplets which dry to leave a chalky deposit. Watersoaked spots yielding a slimy white discharge may also arise on stems and leaf stalks. On the fruit the spots are at first very small, round and watersoaked, but later turn chalky white at the centre as the tissues die and dry out.

The disease is spread at pruning, by water splashes, and perhaps by insects.

It can be transmitted on the seed, which may be disinfected by soaking for 5-10 minutes in corrosive sublimate solution, following by rinsing in clean water and drying. This disease is due to a bacterial infection of the vascular bundles and effects cucumbers, melons and gourds. The leaves develop pale green spots that quickly spread and are followed by a general withering of the leaves and shrivelling of the stems. When the latter are cut a sticky, whitish, bacterial slime exudes from the bundles. This is a serious disease of outdoor cucumbers where it is spread by the knife at cutting and by insects, especially by a leaf beetle.

Chlorine Poisoning

Cucumbers have often been injured by being given stable manure, or latrine contents, to which chloride of lime had been added as a disinfectant. The leaves suddenly develop yellow areas at the tips, along the edges, or between the main veins. The newly set fruits suddenly stop growing and are spoilt; often they shrivel from the tip. Generally the injury appears at irregular intervals, *i.e.* it appears suddenly, then an improvement occurs, followed by another bad period, and so on. When one realises that the damage is due to injury to the roots by chlorine from the chloride of lime one can understand that the first outbreak follows application of the manure. Then when the chloride has been partly washed out the plants recover until damage to the roots again takes place. One should make sure that chloride of lime is not added to the manure or latrine contents that are to be used. If one discovered that it has been added one should water the plants very heavily to try to wash it out as quickly as possible. A tendency to bitterness in cucumbers is unfortunately quite common, especially amongst those grown in hothouses, but it has also occurred in cucumbers grown out of doors for sweet pickles. The bitterest fruits are dark outside and yellow inside but in most cases one cannot see from the outside whether a cucumber is bitter or not. The bitterness begins at the stem end and spreads through the flesh from there. There may be a noticeable difference in taste between two slices cut close to one another. A cucumber which is not bitter when pickled may become so later. Bitter cucumbers are most frequently met with from June to August. On the whole the smooth types are far more liable to bitterness than the spiny-skinned kinds.

This is well known to many housewives and it is, therefore, easier to sell a spiny variety than a smooth one.Various factors encourage bitterness in cucumbers. There is some difference of opinion as to which is most important but it appears that sudden changes in growing conditions are of great importance. The phenomenon is often encountered when a period of sunshine follows a long period of cloudy weather, when the plants are too dry, or when they are very severely pruned. Other factors predisposing to bitterness are: damage to the roots by parasites, over-watering, and use of too strong manure or of fertilizers containing chlorine, wide variation in atmospheric or soil temperatures and, finally, setting of too many fruits. Individual plants may vary greatly in their tendency to bear bitter fruits. One should endeavour to maintain steady growth by supplying heat during cold nights, ventilating and shading in strong sunlight, watering and cutting at the appropriate times, and avoiding too strong manuring. Bitter cucumbers are stained deeply by potassium iodide solution which may be useful in detecting them.

Shrivelled Cucumbers

Frequently cucumbers on hothouse plants cease growing and shrivel when about 2-4 inches long, without any obvious cause. The phenomenon is most frequent at high temperatures, with a moist atmosphere and wet soil. It also seems to be worst on plants carrying many large fruit. Several other conditions may stop growth of the young fruits: damage to the roots by chlorine, too strong farmyard manure, too cold water, drought, draughts, big ranges in temperature, or heavy pruning, leaving too few leaves so that transpiration is reduced.

Stoppage in Root Growth

The roots may be damaged, so that they turn brown and no new roots are produced for a time, if too fresh manure or manure containing chlorine is used, or if the plants are watered with very cold water. This check to root development may cause injury to the fruits or of the leaves. A root rot of cucumbers, associated with species of Fusarium, the primary cause is believed to be bad cultural conditions, such as lack of drainage and poor aeration of the soil.

Blind Shoots

Cucumbers in houses sometimes develop "blind shoots", *i.e.* the shoots suddenly stop growing and the tip ultimately withers, when side shoots develop to replace it. Even if these succeed, there has been a check to growth and, moreover, some side shoots may be destroyed also, so that it is some time before the plant but usually these are not the cause of blind shoots. The trouble is not due to parasites but to unsatisfactory conditions of growth which cannot always be precisely identified. It may occur where there is a draught from a hole in the glass, or from the ventilator.

Good results have been obtained by putting cones over shoot tips exposed to draughts. The most frequent cause, however, seems to be that the plants were growing too vigourously, *i.e.* they had been given too strong manure, especially an excess of nitrogen and also too much warmth. Blind shoot tips are therefore most frequent on plants with large dark-green leaves. The larger the plants are when planted out the better. Large plants have a shorter time in which " the top can go " than small ones that take longer to attain their full height. The plants should not receive extra nitrogen until they have begun to set fruit. Temperatures during growth should not exceed 86° F.

Drooping Leaves

Cucumber leaves may develop transparent withered edges and in the course of a few hours the condition may spread over the whole leaf, which collapses as though scalded. The stalk remains normal. In some cases the leaves may have been noted beforehand to be pale yellowish-green between the veins; in other cases there was nothing peculiar about them. This phenomenon is almost confined to the spring months. No parasite has been found associated with it, and after a time it ceases to occur, though affected plants suffer some check in growth. In one instance the damage seemed to be associated with the use of too fresh cow dung in the beds. Circumstantial evidence indicates that the trouble is due to some cultural fault. Cucumbers are a forced crop, grown at a high temperature and richly supplied with both food and moisture. If, therefore, they are checked even for only a short period, by a sudden rise or fall in temperature, or if the roots are damaged by too warm or too cold water or by too fresh manure, they receive a shock which finds expression in some kind of malformation of growth.

BEET

RUST

Beet rust is one of those which has all its stages on the same host plant. The orange-coloured cluster cups (aecidia) appear in May on the under-surface of leaves of young plants, and occasionally on the leaf stalks. This stage is seldom seen on seedlings but more often on the young leaves produced by overwintered roots kept for seed production. Spores from the cluster cups spread to young beetroot plants, on which successive generations of uredospores appear as rust-coloured pustules all through the summer. Towards the close of summer they become replaced by pustules of the dark-brown teleutospores. Beet rust is most prevalent on mangolds and sugar-beet, but occurs also on garden beet, spinach beet and the wild sea beet (Beta maritimd). The most important control measure is to keep seed crops as far away as possible from fresh sowings. It may also be as well to inspect seed crops at regular and frequent intervals in spring as long as the cluster cups appear and remove the leaves that bear them.

They should at once be put in a pail of lime water or other disinfectant fluid to prevent spores from being spread about the crop. Mother roots for seed crops should, if possible, be chosen from plants free from rust and stripped of leaf stalks which mighl bear the fungus.

Leaf Spots

Ramularia beticola Fautr. & Lamb, and Cercospora beticola Sacc. cause very similar circular leaf spots with a whitish centre and dark-purple margin on beetroot. On spinach beet the spots are pale with brown edges. When necessary, spraying or dusting with a copper fungicide should be practised. A leaf spot of mangolds caused by Stemphylium botryosum Wallr.

Black-leg

The young seedlings turn brown at the soil level and shrivel up. Black-leg is worst on wet and sour soils which should be improved. Various fungi may play a part in the disease, including species of Pythium in the soil and Phoma betae Frank which is seed-borne. Hence treatment of the seed with the standard seed disinfectants may have a beneficial effect.

Beet Mosaic

Mosaic is very general in seed crops of mangold and sugar-beet, but seems less prevalent in garden beet, where it is only found in individual plants with conspicuously mottled leaves. In our infection experiments red beet proved not very susceptible and spinach beet even less so. Hence attacks are only to be feared when these crops are grown in the vicinity of sugar-beet or mangold seed crops. Beet mosaic will, however, attack spinach and hence overwintered spinach may be a source of infection from which the virus may be spread to beet by aphides. In our experiments the common goosefoot was not infected but wild sea beet did develop mosaic.

Heart Rot, Dry Rot and Canker

The innermost leaves turn black and die and gradually all the leaves on the plant may wither. Later new clusters of healthy leaves may appear on the crown outside the dead heart. On the root a slow, dry brown decay starts at the shoulder and gradually penetrates the tissues. In garden beet black spots may appear in the flesh. Heart rot and dry rot are much better known in sugar-beet and mangolds than in red beet. In the former they are known to be associated with limed soils and with dry years. Of late years excellent control has been obtained by manuring with borax at the rate of about 20 Ib. per acre. On soils where previous experience has shown that beet is liable to suffer from trouble of this kind borax should be applied in spring. Care must be taken not to exceed the recommended rate or the plants will be poisoned. Not more than 1 oz. to 12 square yards should be given. Watering with very dilute borax or boric acid solutions may check an outbreak that is just beginning.

Beet Yellows

Yellows is a common disease in sugar-beet and mangold crops where it affects all the plants in large patches or over whole fields. The virus may be spread by aphides to garden red beet, spinach beet and spinach and to goosefoot. Infected spinach beet develops stiff yellow leaves. Leaves of infected red beet are also stiff, but the yellow colouration tends to be masked by the red pigment in the leaves. Leaves of the diseased plants are gorged with starch, and are often prematurely attacked by the black mould (Alternaria) which normally only appears on the dying leaves in autumn. The disease is not carried by the seed and there is no infection from the soil. The virus overwinters in beet plants, especially in seed crops, and is spread from them by aphides. As far as garden beet and spinach are concerned it seems to be prevalent only in the vicinity of sugar-beet crops.

ALFALFA DISEASES

There are more than a dozen diseases of alfalfa. They can be grouped into two categories: those that affect the stems, crowns, or roots and those affecting the foliage. The stem and root-rot diseases are the most serious. Major losses of stand have been caused by Phytophthora root rot, anthracnose, and Sclerotinia crown rot. Verticillium wilt is a constant threat because some farmers are still growing old varieties that lack resistance to this disease. Phytophthora root rot has been responsible for loss of stand in the seedling year when rainfall is above average and/or surface and subsurface drainage is poor.

It is caused by a soilborne fungus that becomes active under wet soil conditions and may attack both seedlings and older plants. Dark brown, decayed areas on the tap root two to three inches below the soil surface are early indicators of Phytophthora root rot. Soil moisture is the key factor affecting disease development. Any improvement in surface and subsurface drainage will reduce losses from this disease as well as from other less common root rots. Varieties with good levels of resistance are now available. Phytophthora specific fungicide seed treatments are available to help prevent loss of stands due to seedling damping-off. Fungicides are labeled for use at planting either as a broadcast application or incorporated on fertilizer granules and applied in a band beneath the seed. Aphanomyces root rot may contribute to poor alfalfa establishment and reduced growth in wet soils. Seedlings may die (damping off) if infection occurs at an early stage of development. Older seedlings are yellowed and stunted. When Aphanomyces and Phytophthora occur together, they form a destructive disease complex.

Alfalfa varieties with moderate to good levels of resistance are available for control of Aphanomyces root rot. Anthracnose is a major cause of thinning of older alfalfa stands. Seedlings may be killed or crown and crown buds of older plants may be affected. Wilted and dead bleached stems are characteristic of the disease. Diamond-shaped lesions (cankers) with light-brown centres and dark margins develop on the lower stems. Anthracnose is a warm, wet-weather disease. Resistant varieties are available. Anthracnose has long been recognized as a destructive disease of red clover in the southern areas.

The use of resistant varieties of red clover controls this problem. Sclerotinia crown rot occurs almost exclusively on late-summer seedings, especially when minimum-tillage methods are used. Affected plants wilt and the cottony-white mold changes to hard black bodies on the crowns or lower stems. This disease is usually seen during the cooler periods of the year. Crop rotation, with two to three years away from alfalfa, aids in control. Verticillium wilt may be spread from field to field with infested seed and in manure from animals fed infested hay. This soilborne disease usually does not become a problem until the third production year. It can be recognized on scattered plants that become yellow and stunted, and then gradually die, leaving a thin, unproductive stand. Control is mainly through use of disease-free seed, resistant varieties, and crop rotation. There are several foliage diseases of alfalfa. Any of these may cause considerable loss of leaves during periods of prolonged wet or humid weather. Little can be done about these diseases in the year that they occur.

OAT DISEASES

In the past, oat diseases have resulted in considerable yield losses. Many of these diseases are no longer important since the development of resistant varieties. Diseases that have caused problems in recent years include loose smut, covered smut, and barley yellow dwarf virus. Several new resistant varieties are available for control of barley yellow dwarf virus. Only seed guaranteed to be free of the smut diseases or seed treated with a fungicide to control smut diseases should be planted.

CORN DISEASES

The major corn diseases can be grouped into four categories: leaf blights, stalk rots, ear rots, and viral diseases. Leaf Blights: A number of leaf-blight diseases occur on corn. The most common are gray leaf spot, Stewart's bacterial leaf blight, and northern corn leaf blight. These diseases can be found in almost any field, depending on the year and susceptibility of the hybrid planted. Some leaf-blight diseases are most often found associated with continuous corn, especially in reduced-tillage, continuous corn fields. These are anthracnose, gray leaf spot, eyespot, and northern leaf spot. All leaf blight diseases cause loss of green leaf tissue, resulting in fewer kernels and lightweight grain. Plants may be predisposed to stalk-rot diseases when leaf damage is severe. The amount of yield loss is usually related to the time when the plant's upper leaves become infected. The most severe yield loss occurs when the upper leaves, the ear leaf, and those above the ear, become infected at or soon after tasseling.

Yield losses will be minimal if disease does not occur on these leaves until six to eight weeks after tasseling. Leaf blight diseases are most effectively controlled by selecting hybrids with genetic resistance. Contact seed dealer for information on hybrids with resistance to gray leaf spot, Stewart's bacterial leaf blight and other leaf diseases important in the area. A one-to two-year rotation away from corn and destruction of old corn residues by tillage may be helpful if susceptible hybrids must be grown. Fungicides are also available for control of leaf diseases, but are economically viable only under severe disease pressure.

STALK ROT

Stalk rots are the most important and common diseases of corn. Annual losses are estimated at 5 to 10 per cent. There are several stalk-rot diseases, but Gibberella stalk rot and anthracnose stalk rot currently are the most prevalent. Both are fungal diseases that result in premature ripening, chaffy ears, and lodging of plants before harvest. The interior of the stalk becomes rotted, tissues break down, and the stalk is easily broken. Anthracnose stalk rot is usually associated with continuous corn and is recognized by the blackening of the outer surface of the stalk late in the season. Stalks with Gibberella stalk rot can be found in nearly any field.

Affected stalks often have pink to reddish discoloured internal tissues. Control of stalk rot diseases is based on reducing plant stress from factors such as lack of moisture, leaf diseases, insect injury, and nutritional stress. To reduce the affects of stalk rot diseases, follow as many of the following practices as possible:

- Select hybrids with good standability and resistance to leaf blight diseases.
- Adjust soil fertility to recommendations based on a soil test. Avoid excessive rates of nitrogen in relation to potassium.
- Follow a one- to three-year rotation away from corn. Soybeans forage legumes, and small grains are acceptable in the rotation. The longer the rotation away from corn the better.

- Plant at populations recommended for the hybrid grown. Overplanting leads to increased moisture, light and nutrient competition, and more plant stress.
- Harvest fields with the greatest level of rotted stalks first to avoid lost ears on lodged plants.
- Control insects, particularly root worms and stalk borer. Insects cause injuries to plant roots and stalks permitting stalk rot fungi to enter the plant.

EAR ROT

Gibberella, Fusarium, and Diplodia ear rot diseases, but Gibberella ear rot is the most important. The Gibberella ear rot fungus is the same fungus that causes Gibberella stalk-rot disease. Gibberella enters from the silk end of the ear when cool, wet weather persists for several weeks through late silking of the crop.

The occurrence of a whitish to pinkish mold on the ear tip is diagnostic, but extensive mold growth may not occur. On shelled grain, the symptoms may be seen as a pinkish colouration in some of the kernels. Even though extensive rotting does not always occur, the disease is serious because the fungus frequently produces toxins that makes the corn unfit for feeding.

Hogs are particularly sensitive to the toxins produced in moldy grain and may refuse to eat it even when hungry. If hogs refuse to eat grain, have a mycotoxin analysis run to determine the kinds and levels of toxin present. Some corn hybrids are less susceptible than others to Gibberella ear rot. Ears with tight husks which mature in an upright position often have more ear rot than those maturing in a declined position.

Diplodia ear rot appears to be more common in continuous corn under reduced tillage. Ears affected by Diplodia are covered with a thick mat of white fungal growth. Fusarium ear rot is common, but only individual kernels are affected on ears. Plant hybrids known to be less susceptible to these ear diseases. Grain with evidence of ear or kernel rot should be dried to 14 per cent moisture before storage and maintained at this level until used. Feeding less than 5 per cent moldy kernels may prevent feeding problems, but grain should be tested for mycotoxin levels prior to feeding to avoid any problems.

VIRUS DISEASES

Maize dwarf mosaic and maize chlorotic dwarf are potentially destructive diseases where johnsongrass is established. The two viruses that cause these diseases are able to survive in this perennial weed grass. Aphids and leafhoppers feeding on johnsongrass in the spring pick up the virus and inoculate nearby corn. Control is achieved by planting resistant or tolerant hybrids. Efforts also should be made to eradicate johnsongrass.

WHEAT DISEASES

Many different types of diseases affect wheat. They can be classified as seed-borne diseases, leaf and head blight diseases, crown and root rot diseases, and virus diseases.

SEED-BORNE DISEASES

Most problems resulting from seed-borne diseases have been eliminated by highly effective seed-treatment fungicides. Several seed-borne diseases are of concern to wheat growers. They are seed-borne scab, seed-borne Stagonospora (previously known as Septoria), common bunt (stinking smut), and loose smut. Seed-borne scab and Stagonospora are discussed later in the section on leaf and head blight diseases. Both diseases result in lightweight, shriveled kernels that may be moldy.

Producers should follow the recommendations listed below for proper seed cleaning and planting to reduce seedling blight and stand losses resulting from planting diseased seed. The two smut diseases, stinking smut and loose smut, can be particularly devastating. Stinking smut causes losses by giving the seed of diseased plants a foul, fishy odour, making the grain unfit for milling. Producers have been docked severely when attempting to sell smutty grain. Loose smut affects plants and yield by converting the grain and parts of the head to smut spores. Therefore, infected plants have no grain left to harvest. There are no varieties resistant to stinking smut, and numerous races of the loose smut fungus exist.

Note the following guidelines to control seed-borne diseases and seedling blights:

- Plant the highest-quality, disease-free seed possible. Seed-production fields should be inspected from the head-emergence growth stage through harvest for occurrence of scab, Stagonospora glume blotch, loose smut, and stinking smut. Do not use seed from severe smut infested fields.
- Clean seed thoroughly to remove all shriveled, lightweight kernels. This may require raising the test weight of the grain by several pounds per bushel.
- Have a standard germination test run on the seed. Use only seed with 80 per cent or greater germination percentage. If poor germination is due to Fusarium head scab, certain seed treatment fungicides can improve germination by 15 to 20 per cent.
- All wheat seed should be treated with a seed-treatment fungicide effective for control of smut fungi, Fusarium scab and Stagonospora.

Plant in a well-prepared seed bed or with a no-till drill capable of proper seed placement, when soil moisture is adequate and soil temperatures are not too high.

LEAF- AND HEAD- BLIGHT DISEASES

Major diseases in this group are powdery mildew, leaf rust, Septoria tritici leaf blotch, Stagonospora (Septoria) nodorum leaf and glume blotch, and Fusarium head scab. All can cause major yield losses, but their occurrence is essentially weather-dependent.

Cool, rainy weather from mid-April through the flowering period of the wheat plant in late May to early June favours the development of most of these diseases. They require either the leaf surfaces to be wet for a certain period of time or the relative humidity within the plant canopy to be near 100 per cent. Powdery mildew and Septoria tritici leaf blotch are the first leaf diseases to occur in the spring. Both are favoured by cool, humid, or wet weather.

Leaf rust and Stagonospora nodorum leaf blotch require slightly warmer weather, thus they follow in mid to late May. Stagonospora nodorum glume blotch and Fusarium head scab become evident in June soon after flowering, especially if wet weather persists through this time. The use of resistant varieties is the major control procedure for these disease management, leaf, and head blight diseases. Few varieties are resistant to all of these diseases. Determine which diseases cause most consistent problems in the area, and choose a variety based on its level of resistance.

The level of fungal carryover from one wheat crop to the next is minimal if a two-to three-year rotation away from wheat is maintained. Rotation is a primary control measure for powdery mildew and the Septoria and Stagonospora diseases. Spores of leaf rust are blown up from the southern states in late May; therefore, crop rotation has little effect on the incidence of leaf rust. Adequate and balanced fertility, to provide optimum nutrition for hardy plants, helps lessen the adverse effects of foliage diseases. High rates of nitrogen will favour powdery mildew and Stagonospora leaf and glume blotch.

Head scab is usually more severe when wheat is planted after corn because the fungus causing scab is the same one that causes Gibberella stalk rot. When possible, wheat should follow soybean or other legumes in the cropping sequence. Fungicides are available to control most foliar diseases of wheat. However, the use of these fungicides should be based on sound economic decisions and the level of disease in the field. Fungicides have been profitable during years when foliar diseases have been severe on susceptible cultivars or in locations where diseases are a persistent problem.

CROWN AND ROOT ROT DISEASES

Two of the more important crown- and root-rot diseases are take-all and Cephalosporium stripe. Both of these diseases are soilborne, meaning that the fungi that cause these diseases reside in the soil. Take-all can be recognized by examining the roots and lower stems of prematurely killed plants. The base of the stem and roots will have a scurfy, black appearance. Cephalosporium stripe disease is characterized by alternating yellow and brown stripes that extend the entire length of the leaf blades. Both of these diseases are favoured by planting wheat year after year in the same field. Usually a rotation sequence with a break of two years or more between wheat crops will eliminate fungal carryover.

The exception to this is when no-till is used to produce all crops in the rotation sequence and wheat residues do not decompose before the next wheat crop is planted. The other exception to this is when perennial grass weeds, such as quack grass, become established in the field. Proper rotations, tillage and elimination of grass weeds have been highly effective in managing both diseases. Additional control of the stripe disease can be achieved by maintaining a soil pH above 6.2 by proper liming according to a soil test. Adequate soil fertility will also reduce yield losses from root diseases.

VIRUS DISEASES

Wheat spindle streak mosaic (yellow mosaic) and barley yellow dwarf are the two most common virus diseases. Wheat spindle streak mosaic is a soilborne disease that is usually recognized in early May as the stems of the wheat plant begin to elongate. The upper leaves of affected plants will show short, spindle-shaped, yellow streaks. These symptoms may intensify if weather remains cool. The symptoms will tend to disappear as the weather begins to warm. Control of wheat spindle streak is achieved through the use of resistant varieties. A number of highly-resistant varieties are available. Barley yellow dwarf virus is transmitted by aphids.

Aphids arriving from the southern states transmit the virus to the newly-planted wheat crop in the fall. Severely affected plants may be stunted, have reddish or yellowish leaf tips and produce no heads. Yield losses greater than 50 per cent have occurred when entire fields have been infected in the fall. Because no varieties have an acceptable level of resistance and early-fall infections cause the greatest yield losses, wheat planting should be delayed until after the Hessian fly safe date when aphids have ended their fall flights.

RED STELE ROOT ROT OF STRAWBERRY

Many commercial strawberry cultivars are susceptible to the red stele fungus. This root rot disease has become a serious problem facing strawberry production in the northern two-thirds of the United States. The disease is most destructive in heavy clay soils that are saturated with water during cool weather when the fungus is most active.

The red stele fungus can survive in soil for up to 13 years or longer once it becomes established in the field or garden. Normally, the disease is prevalent only in the lower or poorly drained areas of the planting; however, it may become fairly well distributed over the entire patch, especially during a cool, wet spring.

Symptoms

When plants start wilting and dying in the lower portions of the strawberry planting, the cause is very likely to be red stele. Infected plants are stunted, lose their shiny-green luster, and produce few runners. Younger leaves often have a metallic, blueish-green cast. Older leaves turn prematurely yellow or red. With the first hot, dry weather of early summer, diseased plants wilt rapidly and die. Diseased plants have very few new roots, when compared with the roots of healthy plants that have thick and bushy roots with many secondary feeding roots. Infected strawberry roots usually appear gray, while the new roots of a healthy plant are yellowish-white.

The most reliable symptom of red stele is found within the roots and may be observed by gently digging up a few plants that are just beginning to wilt, taking care to preserve the root system. Plants with red stele usually have few fine lateral roots so the main fleshy roots have a "rat-tail" appearance. During intermediate stages of disease development, these fleshy roots will be white near the crown of the plant but will show a dark rot progressing upward from the tips. When the white outer portion of the root just above this rotten zone is peeled off or sliced through, the root core (or stele) will appear to be dark red. It may be necessary to examine several rotting roots before finding a red stele, but this symptom is very distinctive and is diagnostic for the disease. Reddened steles are relatively difficult to find after harvest because most infected roots have died and begun to decay by then.

Causal Organism and Disease Cycle

Red stele is caused by the soilborne fungus Phytophthora fragariae. This fungus is not a natural inhabitant of most agricultural soils but probably is introduced on nursery stock or by the movement of infested soil and runoff water from fields in which the disease occurred previously. P. fragariae is very persistent and can survive in a field for many years once it has become established, even if no strawberries are grown during that time.

The organism that causes red stele of strawberry is not known to cause disease on any other crop, with the possible exception of loganberry. P. fragariae persists in the soil as thick-walled resting spores (oospores). When the soil is moist or wet, some of the oospores germinate and form structures called sporangia, which are filled with the infectious spores of the fungus (zoospores). These microscopic zoospores are released into the soil when it becomes completely saturated with water (flooded or puddled) and use tail-like structures to swim short distances through water-filled soil pores to the tips of strawberry roots, to which they are chemically attracted.

Zoospores also may swim to the soil surface, where surface runoff water may carry them relatively long distances. Zoospore activity may occur at soil temperatures ranging from about 38 to 77 degrees F (4 to 25 degrees C), but is most significant from 44 to 59 degrees F (7 to 15 degrees C). Thus infection is most likely in the spring and fall. Once zoospores have infected the root tip, the fungus begins to grow up into other parts of the root, causing the characteristic dark rot and red stele symptoms. New sporangia are formed along the outside of infected root issue and release additional zoospores whenever the soil is saturated, thereby continuing to spread the disease. The fungus produces oospores within infected roots as they begin to rot and die, and these oospores are released into the soil when the roots decay, thus completing the disease cycle.

Control

Since significant production and movement of infective zoospores occurs only during periods when the soil is completely saturated, the key to control is drainage. Strawberries should not be planted in low-lying or heavy soils where water accumulates or is slow to drain. On marginal soils, planting strawberries on beds raised at least 10 inches high will bring much of the root system above the zone of greatest pathogen activity and the severity of red stele root rot should be significantly reduced. Strawberry varieties highly resistant to red stele should be seriously considered for planting in a marginally drained site or a field in which red stele has been suspected of occurring in the past.

Only resistant varieties should be planted in a field where red stele is known to have caused losses within the last 5 to 10 years. The following junebearing varieties are reported to be resistant to Red Stele: Allstar; Delite; Earliglow; Guardian; Lester; Midway; Redchief; Scott; Sparkle; Sunrise and Surecrop. The everbearing varieties are also reported to be resistant. All "resistant" varieties, however, are resistant only to certain common races of the red stele fungus and can become diseased if exposed to other races of the pathogen. It is important to minimize the chance of introducing the red stele fungus into a field where it does not already exist.

Buy nursery stock only from a reputable supplier, and take care not to transfer soil on farm implements from an infested field into a clean one. New fungicides active against red stele also help in controlling this disease but are most effective when used in combination with good soil water management practices.

GRAPE BLACK ROT

Black rot is one of the most damaging grape diseases. All cultivated varieties of grapes are susceptible to infection by the black rot fungus. If not controlled, some or all of the grapes within a cluster will be rotted. The disease is favoured by warm, humid weather as is found during the summer. Before good control measures were devised, vineyards along the River often were hard hit. Grape growers commonly lost most of their crop, and the grape industry was literally driven out of the area.

SYMPTOMS

Symptoms of black rot first appear as small yellowish spots on leaves. As the spots (lesions) enlarge, a dark border forms around the margins. The centres of the lesions become reddish brown. By the time the lesions reach 1/8 to 1/4 inch in diameter (approximately two weeks after infection), minute black dots appear. These are fungal fruiting bodies (pycnidia) and contain thousands of summer spores (conidia). Pycnidia are often arranged in a ring pattern, just inside the margin of the lesions. Lesions may also appear on young shoots, cluster stems, and tendrils.

The lesions are purple to black, oval in outline, and sunken. Pycnidia also form in these lesions. Fruit symptoms often do not appear until the berries are about half grown. Small, round, light-brownish spots form on the fruit. The rotted tissue in the spot softens, and becomes sunken. The spot enlarges quickly, rotting the entire berry in a few days. The diseased fruit shrivels, becoming small, hard, black and wrinkled (mummies). Tiny black pycnidia are also formed on the fruit mummies. The mummies usually remain attached to the cluster.

Causal Organism

Grape black rot is caused by the fungus, Guignardia bidwellii. Black rot survives the winter in cane and tendril lesions and fruit mummies. In the spring during wet weather, the pycnidia on infected tissues absorb water and conidia are squeezed out. Conidia are splashed about randomly by rain and can infect any young tissue in less than 12 hours at temperatures between 60-90 degrees F. A film of water on the vine surface is necessary for infection. A second type of spore, an ascospore, may also be produced in overwintered fruit mummies. Ascospores are forcibly discharged into the air and can travel considerable distances. Research has shown that ascospores are an important source of primary infections in the spring.

Control

- Sanitation is important. Destroy mummies, remove diseased tendrils from the wires, and select fruiting canes without lesions. It is very important not to leave mummies attached to the vine. Research has shown that mummies on the ground release most or all of their ascospores before the end of bloom. Mummies left up in the trellis can produce ascospores and conidia throughout the growing season, thus making control of this disease much more difficult. If only a few leaf lesions appear in the spring, remove these infected leaves.
- Plant grapes in sunny open areas that allow good air movement. Proper row orientation to prevailing winds and good weed control beneath the vines also enable plants to dry more quickly during wet weather.

APPLE POWDERY MILDEW

Damage from powdery mildew attack results in stunted growth. The foliage becomes distorted and twig growth is reduced. Also, the fruit surface may become russetted or discoloured, and dwarfed. Heavily mildewed trees are weakened, and are more susceptible to other pests and winter injury.

SYMPTOMS

Powdery mildew may be found on buds, blossoms, leaves, twigs, and fruit. Symptoms first appear in the spring on the lower surface of leaves, usually at the ends of branches. Small, whitish felt-like patches of fungal growth appear and quickly cover the entire leaf. Diseased leaves become narrow, crinkled, stunted and brittle. By mid-summer, tiny, black round specks show up on the lower leaf surface, but more commonly on the twigs.

These are fungal fruiting bodies, but their importance in the disease cycle is probably minimal. The fungus spreads rapidly to twigs, which stop growing and become stunted. In some cases the twigs may be killed back. Leaves and blossoms from infected buds will be diseased when they open the next spring. Infected blossoms shrivel and produce no fruit. Fruit symptoms are not usually seen unless the disease has built up to high levels on susceptible cultivars. Diseased fruit has a fine network type surface blemish called russetting.

Causal Organism and Disease Cycle

Powdery mildew is caused by the fungus, Podosphaera leucotricha. Powdery mildew overwinters as fungal strands (mycelium) in vegetative or fruit buds which were infected the previous season. Infected terminals may have a silvery gray colour, stunted growth, and a misshapen appearance and are more susceptible to winter kill than are noninfected terminals. Temperatures near -18 degrees F kill a majority of mildewed buds and the fungus within them. Even at lower temperatures, however, some powdery mildew survives. As buds break dormancy, the powdery mildew fungus resumes growth and colonizes developing shoots causing primary infections.

The powdery white appearance on infected shoots consists of many thousands of spores which are responsible for spreading the fungus and causing secondary infections later in the growing season.

Secondary infections are important because they produce the overwintering infected buds. Secondary infections usually develop on leaves and buds before they harden off and may reduce the vigour of the tree. Fruitlets may become infected shortly after bloom, resulting in a web-like russetting on the mature fruit. Powdery mildew infections occur when the relative humidity is greater than 90 per cent and the temperature is between 50-77 degrees F. The optimum temperature range for the fungus is 66-72 degrees F. Although high relative humidity is required for infection, the spores will not germinate if immersed in water.

Leaf wetting is, therefore, not conducive to powdery mildew development. This is quite different from most other foliar and fruit diseases caused by fungi that require free water for their spores to germinate and infect. Under optimum conditions, powdery mildew can be obvious to the naked eye 48 hr after infection. About 5 days after infection, a new crop of spores is produced. Non-germinated powdery mildew spores can tolerate hot dry conditions and may persist until favourable conditions for germination occur. It is important to remember that powdery mildew can be a problem in drier growing seasons when other diseases are not a problem.

Control

- Apple varieties vary greatly in their susceptibility to powdery mildew. Jonathan, Granny Smith, Mutsu (Crispin), Rome, Cortland, Baldwin, Monroe and Idared are very susceptible and should be avoided if powdery mildew is a problem. Most other varieties may also be infected if inoculum is present and conditions are favourable for infection.
- Plant trees in sunny locations with good air drainage. This reduces the humidity around trees and reduces the chances of disease.
- Where powdery mildew is a problem, a good fungicide spray programme is generally required for control. This is especially true in commercial plantings.

9

Economic Improvements Procedure on Indian Agricultural Sector

AGRICULTURAL ECONOMICS

Agricultural economics originally applied the principles of economics to the production of crops and livestock — a discipline known as agronomics. Agronomics was a branch of economics that specifically dealt with land usage. It focused on maximizing the crop yield while maintaining a good soil ecosystem. Throughout the 20th century the discipline expanded and the current scope of the discipline is much broader. Agricultural economics today includes a variety of applied areas, having considerable overlap with conventional economics.

ORIGINS

Economics is the study of resource allocation under scarcity. Agronomics, or the application of economic methods to optimizing the decisions made by agricultural producers, grew to prominence around the turn of the 20th century. The field of agricultural economics can be traced out to works on land economics. Henry Charles Taylor was the greatest contributor with the establishment of the Department of Agricultural Economics at Wisconsin in 1909. Another contributor, Theodore Schultz was among the first to examine growth economics as a problem related directly to agriculture. Schultz was also instrumental in establishing econometrics as a tool for use in analysing agricultural economics empirically; he noted in his landmark 1956 article that agricultural supply analysis is rooted in "shifting sand," implying that it was and is simply not being done correctly.

Growth

One scholar summarizes the growth of agricultural economics as follows: "Agricultural economics arose in the late 19th century, combined the theory of the firm with marketing and organization theory, and developed throughout the 20th century largely as an empirical branch of general economics. The discipline was closely linked to empirical applications of mathematical statistics and made early and significant contributions to econometric methods. In the 1960's and afterwards, as agricultural sectors in the OECD countries contracted, agricultural economists were drawn to the growth problems of poor countries, to the trade and macroeconomic policy implications of agriculture in rich countries, and to a variety of production, consumption, and environmental and resource problems."

Agricultural economists have made many well-known contributions to the economics field with such models as the cobweb model, hedonic regression pricing models, new technology and diffusion models (Zvi Griliches), multifactor productivity and efficiency theory and measurement, and the random coefficients regression. The farm sector is frequently cited as a prime example of the perfect competition economic paradigm. Since the 1970s, agricultural economics has primarily focused on seven main topics, according to a scholar in the field: agricultural environment and resources; risk and uncertainty; consumption and food supply chains; prices and incomes; market structures; trade and growth; and technical change and human capital;.

In terms of technical change, there have been increasingly rapid growths and innovations in the equipment designed for agricultural research. This equipment includes instruments for plant physiology research, and monitoring soil conditions and atmospheres.

IMPACT OF ECONOMIC REFORMS PROCESS ON INDIAN AGRICULTURAL SECTOR

Agricultural sector is the mainstay of the rural Indian economy around which socioeconomic privileges and deprivations revolve, and any change in its structure is likely to have a corresponding impact on the existing pattern of social equality. No strategy of economic reform can succeed without sustained and broad based agricultural development, which is critical for

- Raising living standards,
- Alleviating poverty,
- Assuring food security,
- Generating buoyant market for expansion of industry and services, and
- Making substantial contribution to the national economic growth.

Studies also show that the economic liberalization and reforms process have impacted on agricultural and rural sectors very much. The three sectors of economy in India, the tertiary sector has diversified the fastest, the secondary sector the second fastest, while the primary sector, taken as whole, has scarcely diversified at all. Since agriculture continues to be a tradable sector, this economic liberalization and reform policy has far reaching effects on (I) agricultural exports and imports, (ii) investment in new technologies and on rural infrastructure (iii) patterns of agricultural growth, (iv) agriculture income and employment, (v) agricultural prices and (vi) food security. Reduction in Commercial Bank credit to agriculture, in lieu of this reforms process and recommendations of Khusrao Committee and Narasingham Committee, might lead to a fall in farm investment and impaired agricultural growth.

Infrastructure development requires public expenditure which is getting affected due to the new policies of fiscal compression. Liberalization of agriculture and open market operations will enhance competition in "resource use" and "marketing of agricultural production", which will force the small and marginal farmers (who constitute 76.3% of total farmers) to resort to "distress sale" and seek for off-farm employment for supplementing income.

MARGINALISATION OF SMALL FARMERS

A central issue in Agricultural Development is the necessity to increase productivity, employment, and income of poor segments of the agricultural population. Among the rural poor, the small farmers constitute a sizeable portion in the developing countries. Studies by FAO have shown that small farms constitute between 60-70% of total farms in developing countries and contribute around 30-35% to total agricultural output.

Liberalisation era (1990-91) began in India when over 40% of rural households were landless or near landless, and over 96% of the owned holdings and 68.53% (over 2/3rd) of owned land belonged to the size groups (marginal, small and semi-medium). The decade of 1981-82 to 1991-92 seems to have witnessed a marked intensification of the marginalisation process-the percentage of small owners increased from 14.70% to 21.75%.

Small farmers emerged as the size group with the largest share of 33.97% in the total land, which is just doubled during this decade. As regards the Large Farmers, they were 1 % of the total owners in 1990-91 but owned nearly 13.83% of the total land. An interesting, but speculative, inference is that the changing position of the large owners represents the other side of the marginalisation process, *i.e.*, the presence, and possibly growing strength, of a small but dominant and influential group in agriculture.

Analytical reports reveal that marginalisation process could gather further momentum in the years ahead to become an explosive source of economic and political turbulence, due to the features of prevailing policy-cum-market environment in the country. Trend towards a greater casualisation (erratic and low-paid work) of the workforce that was witnessed in the 1980s appears to have continued in the 1990s. Low productivity and inability to absorb the growing labour force make the agricultural sector in India witness to a pervasive process of marginalisation of rural people. This process is likely to get intensified in the coming years, raising formidable problems in achieving sustained development of rural areas and rural people.

Both Information Technology, Genetic Engineering and Bio-Technology, which are the "drivers" of globalization with their complementarities of liberalisation, privatisation and tighter Intellectual Properties Rights, are bound to create new risks of marginalisation and vulnerability. Information Technology is able to produce a penetrating and clinical mapping of the land, encompassing the physical, chemical and biological features, and groundwater resources, and forecast of climatic conditions in a focused manner, that even small geographical segments-the small farms-can be benefited through the guidance provided by the ways in which natural and human resources can be optimally combined with appropriate technologies, inputs and options to enhance and diversify agricultural production [KVS2K]. Information Technology will facilitate dissemination of information on development, education, extension, husbandry, marketing, production, and research, to agricultural farmers.

INDIAN AGRICULTURAL SECTOR

The Indian Agricultural sector provides employment to about 65% of the labour force, accounts for 27% of GDP, contributes 21% of total exports, and raw materials to several industries. The Livestock sector contributes an estimated 8.4 % to the country GDP and 35.85 % of the agricultural output. India is the seventh largest producer of fish in the world and ranks second in the production of inland fish. Fish production has increased from 0.75 million tons in 1950-51 to 5.14 million tons in 1996-97, a cumulative growth rate of 4.2% per annum, which has been the fastest of any item in the food sector, except potatoes, eggs and poultry meat. The future growth in agriculture must come from [GBSingh2K] *viz.*,

- New technologies which are not only "cost effective" but also "in conformity" with natural climatic regime of the country;
- Technologies relevant to rain-fed areas specifically;
- Continued genetic improvements for better seeds and yields;
- Data improvements for better research, better results, and sustainable planning;
- Bridging the gap between knowledge and practice; and
- Judicious land use resource surveys, efficient management practices and sustainable use of natural resources.

IX PLAN STRATEGY ON AGRICULTURAL DEVELOPMENT

The agricultural development strategy for the Ninth Five Year Plan is essentially based on the policy on food security announced by the Government, to double the food production and make India hunger free in ten years. The Strategy to ensure food security is as follows:-

- Doubling food production
- Increase in employment & incomes

- Supplementary/sustained employment and creation of rural infrastructure through Poverty Alleviation Programmes (PAP)
- Distribution of food grains to the people Below Poverty Line (BPL)

The Ninth Plan Target is to achieve a growth rate of about 4.5% per annum agricultural output and production of 234 MT of food grains by 2001-02. The Policy thrust and key elements of Growth strategy, as proposed in the Ninth Five Year Plan Document (Volume II: PP444), are as follows:-

- Conservation of land, water, and biological resources
- Rural infrastructure development
- Development of rainfed agriculture
- Development of minor irrigation
- Timely and adequate availability of inputs
- Increasing flow of credit
- Enhancing public sector investment
- Enhanced support for research
- Effective transfer of technology
- Support for marketing infrastructure
- Export promotion

The Ninth Five Year Plan Document (1997-2002) reveals that development of the vast rain-fed areas of about 90MH would require over Rs.37,000 Crores. Further, scientific treatment for soil and water conservation for 12 MH of arable and 3 MH of non-arable land would require about Rs.7500 Crores. Development of rain-fed areas require a substantial public investment, which may not be possible due to the new policies of fiscal compression. In the coming millennium, on the basis of current trends in the consumption pattern, the estimated total requirement of food grains is likely to be around 245 Million Tons by 2006-07.

AGRICULTURAL PLANNING AND DEVELOPMENT

India is a vast country with a variety of landforms, climate, geology, physiography, and vegetation India is endowed with regional diversities for its uneven "economic and agricultural" development, on account of (i) Agro-climatic environments (15 Zones/127 regions), (ii) Agro-ecological regions (20) and 60 sub-regions, (iii) Agro-Edephic regions, (iv) Terrain mapping sub-units, (v) Natural resources endowments (geology, geomorphology, soil, ground water, surface water, & infrastructure), (vi) Human resources (Population density), (vii) Level of investments in rural infrastructure, and (viii) Level of investment in technology and its adoption.

India has a total geographical area (TGA) of 329 Million Hectares (MH) out of which, about 265 MH represent varying degrees of potential for biological production. [Dhuruva89] report reveals that more than 50% of TGA is threatened by various types of land degradation, such as soil erosion, gully & ravine formation, salinity, water logging, shifting cultivation, etc. Development of irrigation potential is considered as the key factor in the sustenance of "Green Revolution". Despite 50 years of development planning, rainfed agriculture is the largest and the most important sector of crop production in India.

Soil resources are the most precious non-renewable vital resources for growing food, fibre, and fuel wood to meet the human needs. Management of Soil Resources is essential for both the continued agricultural productivity and protection of environment. By considering various factors like population growth rate, diminishing per capita of land and water resources, and increasing land degradation problems, it is estimated that India will be required to produce an additional 5-6 million tons of food grains annually in 21st Century. This will lead to tremendous pressure on soil resources along with competitive demand for it from industrialization and urbanization. However the capacity of soil to produce is limited and its limits to production are set by its inherent characteristics, agro-ecological settings, and its use and management.

Forests are an important natural resources of India, having a moderating influence against floods and also protecting the soil against erosion. About 95% of the forests in India is owned by States and the total area under forests is about 22% of the total geographical area.

Development of livestock has been envisaged as an integral part of sound system of diversified agriculture. In animal production, the major aim is for raising ecologically adapted animals and efficient utilization of locally available feed resource. Dairy development is intimately linked with cattle population, breed improvement, cattle health and disease management, and fodder development, etc. Animal Husbandry in India is essentially a endeavour of millions of small holders (Resource-Poor-Farmers) who rear animals on "crop residues" and "common property resources" without generally allowing them to compete with man for food grains. The small holders produces milk, meat, wool, etc., for the community, with virtually no capital, resource, training and at a cost that no modern technology in the world had ever produced. Food and Fodder Resources will be crucial to the future development of "livestock resources" in the Country. There is very little scope for increasing the area under fodder production, keeping in view the priority for food grains, pulses and oil seeds. Development of Fodder Resources is basically an activity based on a multi-disciplinary approach involving the areas of agriculture, animal husbandry, environment & forests, revenue, rural development, and wasteland development.

Water Resources of India contain diverse group of flora and fauna. Agriculture is the greatest user of Water accounting for about 80% of all consumption. Animal Husbandry and Fisheries require abundant water. Development of Water Resources, since Independence, has been undertaken for specific purposes like irrigation, flood control, hydro-power generation, drinking water supply, industrial and various miscellaneous uses. Minor irrigation projects have both surface and ground water as their source, while major and medium projects mostly exploit surface water resources. The break up of the ultimate irrigation potential under the above three categories is,

- 58 M.Ha by major and medium irrigation projects,
- 17 M.Ha by minor surface water schemes, and
- 64 M.Ha by minor ground water schemes.

Fisheries Resources of India are either inland or marine. The principal rivers and the tributaries, canals, ponds, lakes, reservoirs comprise inland fisheries. The river extend about 27,200 kms, and other subsidiary water channel comprise about 112,000 kms. Marine resources comprises of about 2 Million sq.kms of EEZ for deep sea fishing, and 7,250 kms of coastline. With the diverse fish fauna, the development objectives are to judiciously & optimally utilize the resources for [NBFGR2K]:-

- Enhancing production and productivity of fishermen, fish farmers and fishing industry;
- Increasing fish production and thereby, raising nutritional standard of people;
- Earning of foreign exchange from export of marine products;
- Improving Socioeconomic conditions of traditional fishermen;
- Generating employment for coastal and rural poor; and
- Conservation of depleting species of fish.

Good infrastructure helps in raising productivity and lowering the unit cost in the production activities of the economy. "Agricultural Infrastructure" refers to "Rural Infrastructure" whereas "Industrial Infrastructure" refers to "Urban Infrastructure". Agricultural development requires (i) agricultural research and extension, (ii) rural financial institution, (iii) irrigation and drainage, (iv) agricultural inputs (fertilizers, seeds, credits), and (v) marketing and storage facilities.

Agriculture Credit is a crucial input for increasing agricultural production and productivity. Institutional finance for Agricultural credit is disbursed mainly by Commercial banks, Regional Rural Banks, Land Development Banks, and Cooperative banks. Share of commercial banks in total institutional credit to agriculture is about 48%, that of Cooperative banks is about 46%, and Regional Rural Banks account for 6% only. Short-term Credit accounts for 2/3rd of the total institutional lending to the Agriculture.

AGRICULTURE AND ECONOMIC DEVELOPMENT

As a country develops economically, the relative importance of agriculture declines. The primary reason for this was shown by the 19th-century German statistician Ernst Engel, who discovered that as incomes increase the proportion of income spent on food declines. For example, if a family's income were to increase by 100 percent, the amount it would spend on food might increase by

60 percent; if formerly its expenditures on food had been 50 percent of its budget, after the increase they would amount to only 40 percent of its budget. It follows from this that, as incomes increase, a smaller fraction of the total resources of society is required to produce the amount of food demanded by the population.

REFORMS IN AGRICULTURE

Policy reforms in the rural sector are both critical and sensitive in nature as well as in their impact because of heavy concentration of working people in rural areas. At present about 40% of total state expenditure in the rural sector is absorbed by direct subsidies, another 22% by anti-poverty programmes and only 38% goes to productivity enhancing expenditure, as opposed to 60% in 1981-82.

During the post-reform period, annual growth rate of agricultural subsidies in real terms has substantially declined. But, it remains as high as 3.6% of GDP per annum. In real terms, the food subsidy increased from Rs. 10.8 billion in 1989-90 to 14.3 billion in 1995-96 at 1980-81 prices, although food subsidy as a percentage of GDP remained constant at about 0.5%.

The revamped Public Distribution System (PDS) has been introduced since 1992, which is targeted to those poor and backward regions where the Employment Assurance Scheme (EAS) is implemented (Annual Report, Ministry of Rural Areas and Employment, 1996). However, Mr. Yashwant Sinha in his Budget, 2000-01 targeted middle and upper classes. From now on, income-tax payers would not get any commodities under PDS, and the others would not get certain commodities such as sugar.

The fertilizer subsidy as percentage of total agriculture GDP declined from 0.9% in 1990-91 to 0.6% in 1995-96. But in absolute real terms, it has been subjected to high annual variations. The fertilizer subsidy policy affected different fertilizer prices differently. The prices of phosphoric and potassium fertilisers were decontrolled in 1992, but price control on low analysis nitrogenous fertilisers continued. However, in the current year (2000-01) the subsidy price of urea is fixed at Rs. 4,600 per ton. Same for MOP (Potash) is fixed at Rs. 4,260 per ton and for Di-Ammonium Phosphate (DAP) it is Rs. 8,880 per ton. This means that there would be an increase of 15% in prices of urea and MOP and 7% in the case of DAP.

Power and irrigation subsidies, which are supported by the state governments, accounted for nearly 8% respectively of the total agricultural subsidies (as of 1994-95). During the post-reform period (1990-91 to 1994-95), rural power subsidy grew at the rate of 14% per annum in real terms, while the growth rate of irrigation subsidy remained low at 1.2% per annum (based on the Budget Estimates). But irrigation subsidy was reduced mainly on account of non-wage outlays on operation and maintenance and not because of improvement in cost recovery. Zonal restrictions on the movement of agricultural commodities have been removed since February, 1993, including the lifting of informal controls on wheat movement by private trade.

The excise duty on coffee has been removed. The role of coffee board has diminished and now there is a trend towards open marketing of coffee. Imports of all agricultural commodities other than cereals, oilseeds and edible oils and all agricultural exports (except onion) have been decannalised. India has agreed to phase out quantitative restrictions on import of 2700 items, out of which 800 are agricultural commodities by April 2003. An agreement had already been reached with European Union and Australia to remove quantitative restrictions on imports from these countries by April, 2000 (Haque, 1997:12).

Agricultural trade reforms initiated in 1991-92 relaxed quantitative restrictions on a few minor commodities. But by 1994-95, it included rice exports and imports of most edible oils, sugar and cotton. Nevertheless, quantitative restrictions on exports of most agricultural commodities except rice continue. The share of tradable agricultural production protected by non-tariff barriers on the import side, were reduced from about 96% before June, 1991 to 77% in July, 1996. With the liberalisation of sugar imports under 0% tariffs, sugar industry has now to compete with imports. Similarly, the liberalisation of cotton imports at zero percent tariff has been initiated in 1994. Edible oils are now importable at 20% tariff. The tariff on import of pulses has been reduced from 10 percent to 5 percent. In January, 1997 the U.S. and several other developed countries contended that India no longer suffers from balance of payments problems and therefore, the quantitative restrictions on imports by India would have to be removed immediately. India made an agreement with European Union and Australia to remove quantitative restrictions on many items in three phases of 3 years, 2 years and 1 year, using April, 1997 as the reference year. But the dispute with U.S. has yet to be resolved.

In the livestock sector, state controls and subsidization of dairy co-operatives continue. The Milk and Milk products Order (1992) presents competition in the dairy industry. The poultry feed manufacturing continues to be reserved for the small scale sector. The commercialization of fishing has been initiated. Agro-industries that export 50% or more of their output, have been allowed to import their inputs duty free and to import capital equipment at concessional import duty rates w.e.f. April, 1993. In 1991, tractors, combine harvesters and rice transplanters were included in the list of products for which there is now automatic approval of foreign equity of up to 51%. But several other agricultural implements and farm inputs such as plastic piping, sheeting etc. are reserved for production by small-scale firms. In the area of rural credit, the reforms include:

- Reducing target group lending from 100 percent to 40 percent in the case of regional rural banks,

- Greater freedom to the banks to rationalize their branches,
- Deregulation of interest rates of rural cooperative banks,
- Permission to urban co-operative banks to lend to borrowers in continguous rural areas and
- Relaxation of service area restrictions.

Besides, the Reserve Bank of India (RBI) and National Bank for Agriculture and Rural Development (NABARD) have initiated actions for strengthening Regional Rural Banks (RRBs). Further, the 1996-97 budget provides for doubling the paid up share capital of NABARD and establishing agricultural development financial institutions at the state level to promote investment in horticulture, floriculture and agro-processing.

Agriculture Reforms – The Way Ahead

Sustainable agriculture thus sustains rural livelihoods. This in turn is directly linked to the nation's as well as the household food security. Any development alternative to ensure long-term food security therefore has to be linked to sustainable agriculture. Let me therefore draw the outline of the sustainable farming systems that the country needs to focus on. This is the overall framework under which location-specific alterations and adaptations need to be tried.

What is needed is a fresh approach that takes the ground realities into consideration before embarking upon any policy imperatives. I am trying to make an attempt, presenting a collection of five of the important rational decisions, which would certainly initiate the revival of Indian agriculture: *Sustainable farming*: Indian agriculture faces an unprecedented crisis in sustainability. Foodgrain productivity in the food bowl, comprising Punjab, Haryana, and western Uttar Pradesh, is on the decline. The green revolution areas are encountering serious bottlenecks to growth and productivity. The dryland areas (comprising nearly 70 per cent of the cultivable lands) continue to drown in misery and apathy. Excessive mining of soil nutrients and groundwater have already brought in soil sickness. Indiscriminate use of chemical pesticides has done serious harm to environment, human health and ecology. Introducing new Centrally Sponsored Schemes or contract farming to improve production in these areas is going to be counter-productive. Banking upon genetically engineered crops to take care of the second-generation environmental impacts is sure to worsen the existing crisis. Outlays earmarked for genetic engineering in agriculture also need to be diverted to sustainable agricultural practices.

Encouraging sustainable and traditional farming practices therefore is the only way ahead. Agricultural research must reorient itself to meet the new challenges resulting from the collapse of the green revolution technology. Investments and increased outlays for agricultural research that is based on external chemical inputs like fertilizer and pesticides need to be discouraged. Instead, financial allocation should be made for reviving low-input agriculture, which uses cheap and locally available technology and in turn improves production and protects environment. This has been amply demonstrated in several parts of the world. Water productivity and efficiency has to be the hallmark of agricultural research based on the local conditions.

Local Solutions: For the past three decades, more so after the introduction of the land-grant system of education, the focus is on finding global solutions to local problems in agriculture. The World Bank/IMF, the Consultative Group on International Agricultural Research (CGIAR) and now some of the major donors like DFID and GTZ have been embarking of translocating alien approaches to agricultural improvement and have thereby exacerbated the crisis on the farm front. The Indian Council for Agricultural research (ICAR) too has blindly followed the land grant system of research and education, the negative results of which are now becoming apparent. Ignoring the traditional knowledge and time-tested technologies has created a crisis on the farm front. This process must be immediately stopped, if not reversed. Given the diversity of the agro-ecological regions, sustainable agriculture needs location-specific solutions.

International agricultural research, as well as the national agricultural research systems, should re-orient the focus of farm research based on the principles of – farmer friendly, environment friendly and long-term sustainability. Instead of the 'Lab-to-Land" approach, which has done immense damage to agriculture globally, the emphasis should be on learning from the land, meaning going back to farmers and the traditional farming systems. Technology need not always be high-tech and sophisticated. It can be simple and effective. This can only be ensured if the effort is to fit the new and improved technology to farmers need rather than asking farmers to fit into the technology package developed. This can only happen if farm research is brought back to the public sector. All technology should be freely available, and should not come with any proprietary tags.

Dryland farming: Despite the former Prime Minister Mrs Indira Gandhi's emphasis on dryland farming, agricultural scientists as well as the policy makers have failed the dryland farmers. This is essentially because the entire thrust of dryland research was to bring in an external model in which the dryland farmer, who manages to survive against all odds, would fit in. No effort was made to improve the existing technology base under numerous location-technology specifications.

At the same time, drylands continue to be plagued with recurring drought engulfing vast tracts of central and north-western India. The increased emphasis on water harvesting notwithstanding, the reduced availability of water is emerging as a major social and economic crisis. This is because much of the investment is going into a faulty technology of rainwater harvesting, called the

"Ridge to valley" system, a technology imported from the United States. In addition, the cropping pattern has to be evolved keeping in mind the water availability. At present, more the water requirement for hybrid crop varieties more is its cultivation in the water-scarce regions. This is scandalous and unless the cropping pattern is rectified no measures to protect and preserve water resources will be effective.

Improved Crops Mine Water

High-chemical input based technology has already mined the soils and ultimately led to the lands gasping for breath, with the water-guzzling crops (hybrids and Bt cotton) sucking the groundwater acquifer dry, and with the failure of the markets to rescue the farmers from a collapse of the farming systems, the tragedy is that the human cost is entirely being borne by the farmers. Green revolution was projected to have saved the country some 58 million hectares of additional land to be brought under the plough to produce more food, whereas almost twice that land mass has been rendered degraded and ecologically devastated in varying degrees in its aftermath.

Green revolution has not only gone sour, it has collapsed. The unexplained number of huge number of suicides a testimony to the entire equation going wrong. However, the fundamental issue of destruction of sustainable livelihoods is not at all being addressed. All these years, for instance, the dryland regions of the country, which comprise nearly 75 per cent of the total cultivable area, have increasingly come under the hybrid crop varieties. While the crop yields from the hybrid varieties was surely high, the flip side of these varieties – these varieties are water guzzlers – was very conveniently ignored. For the sake of comparison, let us take the example of rice.

Not only rice hybrids, all kind of hybrid varieties that require higher doses of water – whether it is of sorghum, maize, cotton, bajra, and vegetables are promoted in the dryland regions. In addition, agricultural scientists have misled the farmers by saying that the dryland regions were hungry for chemical fertilisers. The harmful combination of chemical inputs with water guzzling crops have played havoc with the drylands turning the lands not only further unproductive but also barren. The water table plummeted, the impact of deficient rainfall became more pronounced forcing farmers to abandon agriculture and migrate. As if this was not enough, Bt cotton requiring more water than hybrid cotton, was knowingly promoted so as to allow the seed industry to make profits.

Investments in rainwater harvesting need to be immediately shifted to the revival of the traditional forms of water conservation – ponds and tanks. Fodder cultivation, crop planning according to the water needs and availability and the emphasis on the local breed of cattle (and improving its productivity, rather than importing exotic breeds) need to be encouraged. Dryland crops, and that include coarse cereals, pulses and oilseeds require adequate policy measures that bring shine to these forgotten grains. Farmers in the rain-fed areas also need to be insured against drought. This can be ensured by making it mandatory for the foreign insurance companies to invest at least 40 per cent of their funds for farm insurance.

Sugar mills: Sugarcane is the biggest threat to India's food security. The unprecedented addition of new sugar mills by successive governments has created a major crisis on the agriculture front. Requiring good fertile and irrigated land for cultivation, its growth is at the cost of staple foods like wheat and rice. With the per hectare productivity of foodgrains on the decline in the frontline agricultural states, diversion of good fertile land to sugarcane is not without accompanying hiccups. What makes the switchover to sugarcane a pernicious trend is its enormous water requirement. Sugarcane, in fact, is the biggest threat to India's food security.

Since there is no shortage of sugar in the country, and with a large number of mills actually being rendered unviable over the past two decades, an immediate ban needs to be imposed on setting up any new sugar mill. All Budgetary support to the sugar industry needs to be withdrawn as it has led to a serious environmental crisis. Reduce the area under sugarcane, improve productivity, disband most of the unproductive sugar mills, and give a new lease of life to the cane areas.

Instead the focus should shift to pulses and fodder crops. Pulses are essential for country's nutritional security and fit very well into the harsh environments. Sugarcane growers in most parts of the country can easily be made to shift to pulses cultivation given the right incentive. Such a renewed emphasis will not only help farmers and consumers alike but also rejuvenate the environment and help in restoring soil health. Pulses have the inbuilt capacity to draw nitrogen from the atmosphere.

Marketing: Providing an assured and remunerative market for agricultural producers cannot be left to the market forces. The food policy imperatives of public distribution system and announcing the procurement prices before the crop season have to be further strengthened. Agri-processing too needs to be strengthened, but not at the cost of the domestic producers. Food-processing sector should be directed to use the abundant raw material available within the country. The 'rainbow' revolution that everyone talks about is actually aimed at helping the industry to exploit the farm sector. Already a number of manufacturing units, for instance, have begun to source the agricultural raw material, including oranges, grapes, popcorn, peas etc, from America and Europe. Domestic production in these crops is going waste. Farmers have repeatedly and in different parts of the country been dumping tomatoes, potatoes and other fruits onto the streets to express their frustration at the lack of adequate marketing infrastructure. Creating a global market for farm produce is the bane of modern agriculture. The seed multinationals, the food giants, and the supermarkets, have cornered the food chain in the process thereby destroying livelihoods, local markets and also drastically reducing food choices. Such a maket strategy has resulted in the disappearance of locally produced nutritious foods as a consequence of which micro-nutrient deficiency in human populations have grown manifold. Encouraging local markets will also reduce the dependence upon long distance transportation thereby minimising global warming. It will also help in bringing back the traditional and neglected crops, and help in changing the food habits.

Farm incomes: Growing indebtedness in agriculture is forcing an increasing numbers of farmers to end their lives. This unsavory phenomenon is a manifestation of the declining farm incomes and lack of farm credit. Institutional finance and credit has almost disappeared over the years. Banks are no longer treating agriculture for priority sector lending. Rural Banks and cooperatives are deep in the red, with a majority of them eating into their own reserves. Agriculture credit has to be revived. Schemes that encourage banks to provide easy credit facilities to farmers need to be spelled out. On top of it, agriculture credit has to be extended to sustainable farming systems. So far the banks are only providing credit for technology-oriented farming systems. This has to be extended to organic agriculture, for which an Organic Bank need to be created by NABARD (like the technology credit that goes through the private Robo Bank). Crop insurance should be extended to cover the entire farm sector immediately.

Food Security – The Way Ahead

Although, India is following the WTO dictates of doing away with the food procurement system, any tinkering with what is generally regarded as the "famine-avoidance" strategy, can be catastrophic. Corrective measures are needed to reduce inefficiency in the system while at the same time making it broad-based and widespread.

Multiple Cropping: Emphasis on commodities approach during the green revolution has encouraged monocultures, loss of biodiversity, encouraged food trade in some commodites, distorted domestic markets, and disrupted the micro-nutrient availability in soil, plant, animals and for humans humans. Thrust on farm commodities have also pushed in trade activities, encouraged food miles, adding to greenhouse emissions, water mining, and destruction of farm incomes. The need is to revert back to the time-tested farming systems that relied on mixed cropping and its integration with farm animals, thereby meeting the household and community nutrition needs from the available farm holdings.

Reverting back to mmultiple cropping will also provide the answer to the acute malnutrition that prevails in the countryside. The availability of nutritious crops, vegetables and fruits was once a part of the cropping pattern, abandoned in the wake of green revolution. The second green revolution that is being talked about will further exacerbate malnutrition crisis. This can only happen when the focus shifts away from encouraging cash crops.

For the past two decade at least, the World Bank/IMF and some other academicia and donors have been pressing developing countries to diversify from staple foods to cash crops in what is being projected as the right approach to added to farm incomes. This is a politically motivated advise and runs counter to the sustainable approached spelled out above. Many Latin American countries are faced with a serious land degradation crisis as a result. It also pushes farmers into a death trap since the developing countries do not have the resources to provide for adequate marketing infrastructure.

Public Distribution System (PDS) also needs to be strengthened and extended to upcoming agricultural areas in Bihar, Orissa, West Bengal and the northeast. Similarly, financial allocation must be made for assured food procurement at remunerative prices. In addition, procurement needs to be extended to coarse cereals, pulses and oilseeds to provide farmers an incentive to produce more. Food procurement operations, linked to the announcement of assured prices for agricultural commodities, were the two planks of the 'famine-avoidance' strategy that India had adopted in the wake of the green revolution. Whether the economists like it or not, the fact remains that a combination of these policies helped India to emerge from the dark days of 'ship-to-mouth' existence.

The emphasis by IMF, the World Bank and WTO to force India dismantle PDS is based on the corporate need. India's massive food procurement operations are coming in the way of the expansion of the food trade that the United States and the European Union are looking for. If the US doesn't find an assured food market in a country as huge as India, with one sixth of the world's population, the chances are that its own agriculture will collapse under the artificial weight of its own federal subsidies.

That the threat is real, is clearly evident. Take a look at the recent developments in neighbouring Pakistan. Under pressure from IMF and the World Bank, Pakistan's military government has begun lifting its decades-long support price system for key commodities – despite protests that this would be disastrous for small farmers. In India too, economists are asking the government to 'decentralise' the food procurement system, a euphemism for dismantling the PDS.Once the government withdraws from announcing procurement prices for agricultural commodities, it is under no obligation to purchase the surplus that flows into the *mandis*. Farmers would thus be left at the mercy of the trade and the market forces, and if the past experience is any indication it simply means rendering the farming community vulnerable to exploitation thereby threatening the country's food self-sufficiency, so assiduously built over the past three decades.

The biggest crisis afflicting the farm sector is the inability to manage the agricultural surpluses. It is here that the policy planning effort has to be redirected with an effort to ensure that the surplus does not become a national liability. The approach has to be different for the rural and urban areas. Since this chapter focuses on the link between agriculture, food security and hunger, a framework for rural India is hereby proposed.

Community Grain Banks: The answer to the intricately complex, economically unsound and politically sensitive issue of public distribution rests with the poorest of the poor and is a tribute to human ingenuity, cooperation and traditional knowledge. Effectively targetting the public distribution system to reach the needy and the poorest of the poor has been a serious concern. Moreover, for several years now, the exclusion of the well-to-do beneficiaries, including income tax payers, from the provisions of the PDS have been resisted by all political parties, irrespective of their ideological leanings.

While the debate goes on, Bolangir in Orissa and Kodagu in Karnataka have demonstrated that the real beneficiaries, the poor in the villages, are not dependent upon food doles. Such a system of sharing the benefits of the harvest with the village community also exist in several other parts of the country. This is perhaps the only viable path for the nation to wriggle out of the growing threat from food insecurity.

Starvation and hunger no longer stalks a cluster of 20 villages, about 150 kms away from Bolangir town. At a time when recurring drought has brought acute misery and suffering for tens of thousand people in the district, and with the latest controversy shrouding the starvation deaths and sale of children from western Orissa showing no signs of healing, hundreds of families in and around Sundhi munda village have built a food insurance system that keeps sure hunger and death at bay. That the food security system has successfully withstood varying degrees of natural calamities and has, in fact, grown and multiplied clearly demonstrates its social relevance and effectiveness.

It all began in 1990-91, when a social activist Bansi Dhar Behera, coordinator of the *Anchalika Jana Sewa Anusthan* in Sundhi munda village, was looking for a permanent solution to mitigate human suffering arising from the non-availability of foodgrains, especially at times of distress. His appeal to fellow villagers to donate surplus paddy and rice after the harvest so as to build a grain reserve brought in 22 quintals of paddy. In all, 150 families from eight villages, almost all of them marginal farmers, responded to his call. The village grain bank was thus formed.

The grain bank became a pivot of food security. Farmers have since then deposited their 'surplus' produce with the bank after each paddy harvest. They withdraw an equal quantity of paddy at the time of need without having to pay any interest. For others, who are landless or do not have any 'surplus' for the grain bank, borrowing paddy at the time of distress is a routine. But at the time of harvest, the grains borrowed have to be returned with half a bucket of paddy as interest. For those, who cannot repay the foodgrain loan, the village *samaj* decides whether the loan can be waived or not. For the villagers, the grain bank was an escape from the clutches of the money-lenders, who often gave foodgrains to the needy to be returned in double the quantity received, and that too within three months.

Sometimes, depending upon the immediate requirement of the participating villages, the beneficiaries are asked to contribute by way of human labour. In village Batharla, a community temple and a grain store house was constructed by the beneficiaries. Their wages were paid in kind from the interest (surplus grain) that builds up over the years. In Banjupadhar village, a traditional water harvesting tank was rejuvenated for which the society distributed 16 quintals of paddy as wages. The grain bank, in other words, is also being utilised for 'food for work' programmes, all depending upon the need of the village community.

In five years, the grain bank had grown in size and volume. In 1996, the society received and disbursed 220 quintals of paddy. A year later, in 1997, it got back 253 quintals. In all, the number of people donating to the grain bank had grown by almost ten times, with a thousand families depositing paddy this year. The number of beneficiaries too increased over the years reaching 1,066 families this year, in the 20 participating villages. More than the numbers what is important is to understand that these families have perfected a social model that gives them the freedom from hunger.

The ten grain banks in Kodagu district are, however, registered under the Cooperative Act. Successfully in operation for over 30 years now, these grain banks also work on the same principle. After every paddy harvest, each member brings not less than 100 kg of paddy as their contribution to the grain bank. And during the lean months of December-January, paddy can be borrowed as loan by members. The loan is normally repaid after the next harvest with an interest of 12 per cent in terms of paddy. After the harvesting season ends, the left over paddy stocks are sold in the market. Consequently, members receive dividend varying between 10 to 20 per cent of the total share capital.

Such is the underlying spirit of cooperation that like in Bolangir, each member in Kodangu district also deposits about five to ten kg of paddy every year towards what is called as the 'death fund'. The basic idea being that at times of bereavement, the village community comes to the rescue of the family in mourning. It is invariably because of the strong community ties in the villages that the grains banks have succeeded. Also, because these grain banks have remained outside the gambit of government interference. Its replication, therefore, has to be through the panchayats and the grassroot NGOs or perhaps an amalgamation of both. *Village Republics*: Focus on tackling the causes of poverty, hunger, the inequitable distribution of income and low human resource base with the objective of providing everyone with the opportunity to earn a sustainable livelihood. The green revolution areas are encountering serious bottlenecks to growth and productivity. Excessive mining of soil nutrients and groundwater have already brought in soil sickness. If the livelihood of the marginalised in the society (and that in the majority world is in agriculture) it must be secured by economic activities that are sustainable, that do not threaten the integrity of the environmental assets on which they depend. Food security and hunger are directly linked to the community's control over the natural resources, and also on the long-term sustainability of the resource base.

Contrary to commonly made projections and assessments, hundreds of villages in rural India have made their own effort to chart a different but equitable path to growth and human development. Deviating from the mainstream approach, these villages have put up sign board outside the village boundary warning government officials and private company executives from entering their village. The reason: these villages have become self-reliant.

A conservative estimate based on different reports shows that close to 1500 villages have imposed self-rule and have declared themselves village republics. In these villages the residents have taken control over their natural resources – namely forest, land, minerals and water sources – and have formed strong institutions to manage them. They plan, execute and resolve all affairs inside the village and government officials and programmes are accepted only after getting approval of the residents through *Gram Sabha* (village assembly consisting of all adult members). In many such villages, the forest department, the police and other officials just execute programmes and plans chalked out in village meetings. Self-reliant villages is the answer to India's multiple and complex problems of food insecurity, hunger and malnutrition.

ADVANCEMENT IN FARMING

This fact would have surprised most economists of the early 19th century, who feared that the limited supply of land in the populated areas of Europe would determine that continent's ability to feed its growing population. Their fear was based on the so-called law of diminishing returns: that under given conditions an increase in the amount of labour and capital applied to a fixed amount of land results in a less than proportional increase in the output of food. This principle is a valid one, but what the classical economists could not foresee was the extent to which the state of the arts and the methods of production would change. Some of the changes occurred in agriculture; others occurred in other sectors of the economy but had a major effect on the supply of food. In looking back upon the history of the more developed countries, one can see that agriculture has played an important part in the process of their enrichment. For one thing, if growth is to occur, agriculture must be able to produce a surplus of food to maintain the growing non-agricultural labour force. Since food is more essential for life than are the services provided by merchants or bankers or factories, an economy cannot shift to such activities unless food is available for barter or sale in sufficient quantities to support those engaged in them. Unless food can be obtained through international trade, a country does not normally develop industrially until its farm areas can supply its towns with food in exchange for the products of their factories. Economic growth also requires a growing labour force. In an agricultural country most of the workers needed must come from the rural population. Thus agriculture must not only supply a surplus of food for the towns, but it must also be able to produce the increased amount of food with a relatively smaller labour force. It may do so by substituting animal power for human power or by gradually introducing labour-saving machinery. Agriculture may also be a source of the capital needed for industrial growth to the extent that it provides a surplus that may be converted into the funds needed to purchase industrial equipment or to build roads and provide public services. For these reasons a country seeking to develop its economy may be well advised to give a significant priority to agriculture. Experience in the developing countries has shown that agriculture can be made much more productive with the proper investment in irrigation systems, research, fertilizers, insecticides, and herbicides.

Fortunately, many advances in applied science do not require massive amounts of capital, although it may be necessary to expand marketing and transportation facilities so that farm output can be brought to the entire population. One difficulty in giving priority to agriculture is that most of the increase in farm output and most of the income gains are concentrated in certain regions rather than extending throughout the country. The remaining farmers are not able to produce more and actually suffer a disadvantage as farm prices decline. There is no easy answer to this problem, but developing countries need to be aware of it; economic progress is consistent with lingering backwardness, as can be seen in parts of southern Italy or in the Appalachian area of the United States.

PEASANT AGRICULTURE

One characteristic of undeveloped peasant agriculture is its self-sufficiency. Farm families in those circumstances consume a substantial part of what they produce. While some of their output may be sold in the market, their total production is generally not much larger than what is needed for the maintenance of the family. Not only is productivity per worker low under these conditions but yields per unit of land are also low. Even where the land was originally fertile, the fertility is likely to have been depleted by decades of continuous cropping. The available manures are not sufficient, and the farmers cannot afford to purchase them elsewhere. Peasant agriculture is often said to be characterized by inertia. The peasant farmer is likely to be illiterate, suspicious of outsiders, and reluctant to try new methods; food patterns remain unchanged for decades or even centuries. Evidence, however, suggests that the apparent inertia may be simply the result of a lack of alternatives. If there is nothing better to change to, there is little point in changing. Moreover, the self-sufficient farmer is bound to want to minimize his risks; since a crop failure can mean starvation in many parts of the world, farmers have been reluctant to adopt new methods if doing so would expose them to greater risks of failure. The increased use worldwide of high-yielding varieties of rice and wheat since the 1960s has shown that farmers are willing and able to adopt new crops and farming methods when their superiority is demonstrated. These high-yielding varieties, however, require increased outlays for fertilizer, as well as expanded facilities for storage and distribution, and many developing countries are unable to afford such expenditures.

THE LABOUR FORCE

As economic growth proceeds, a large proportion of the farm labour force must shift from agriculture into other pursuits. This fundamental shift in the labour force is made possible, of course, by an enormous increase in output per worker as agriculture becomes modernized. This increase in output stems from various factors. Where land is plentiful the output per worker is likely to be higher because it is possible to employ more fertilizer and machinery per worker.

LAND, OUTPUT, AND YIELDS

Only a small fraction of the world's land area—about one-tenth—may be considered arable, if arable land is defined as land planted to crops. Less than one-fourth of the world's land area is in permanent meadows and pastures. The remainder is either in forests or is not being used for agricultural purposes.

General Relationships

There are great differences in the amount of arable land per person in the various regions of the world. The greatest amount of arable land per capita is in Oceania; the least is in China. No direct relationship exists between the amount of arable land per capita and the level of income; Europe has almost as little arable land per capita as Asia and less than Africa; Japan and the Netherlands have very limited amounts of arable land per capita.

The relationship between land, population, and farm production is a complex one. In traditional agriculture, where methods of production have changed little over a long period of time, production is largely determined by the quality and quantity of land available and the number of people working on the land. Until the early years of the 20th century, most of the world's increase in crop production came either from an increase in land under cultivation or from an increase in the amount of labour used per unit of land. This generally involved a shift to crops that would yield more per unit of land and required more labour for their cultivation. Wheat, rye, and millet require less labour per unit of land and per unit of food output than do rice, potatoes, or corn (maize), but generally the latter yield more food per unit of land. Thus, as population density increased, the latter groups of crops tended to be substituted for the former. This did not hold true in Europe, where wheat, rye, and millet expanded at the expense of pasture land; but these crops yielded more food per acre than did the livestock that they displaced.

As agriculture becomes modernized, its dependence upon land as well as upon human labour decreases. Animal power and machinery are substituted for human labour; mechanical power then replaces animal power. The substitution of mechanical power for animal power also reduces the need for land. The increased use of fertilizer as modernization occurs also acts as a substitute for both land and labour; the same is true of herbicides and insecticides. By making it possible to produce more per unit of land and per hour of work, less land and labour are required for a given amount of output.

Recent Trends

Crop yields have increased dramatically since 1950, with a faster rate of growth in the developing than in the developed countries. Most of this increased output has been due to gains in yields rather than to the expansion of cultivated land. In Europe as well as in North and Central America, the total area under crops has declined; in South America it has increased by more than one-half and in Asia by more than one-third. The large increase in Oceania was due to immigration. The large decrease in Africa was due to a succession of droughts from the 1970s on. Grain yields in the developed regions of the world have increased consistently over the past several decades. In the rest of the world the pre-World War II yields were not achieved again until the mid-1950s. The increases in grain production were more than twice as high in the developing as in the developed countries.

Food production and total agricultural production exhibit nearly identical trends, and changes in food production can be taken therefore as indicative of changes in total agricultural production. Food supplies per capita in developing countries have increased at nearly the same rate as in developed countries, indicating a narrowing gap between food supplies and population growth in the developing countries.

ELEMENTS OF COMMERCIAL AGRICULTURE

Although elements of the above ideal type of a competitive food system could be found in parts of the United States at various times, it never did exist in many areas of the country. For an individual farmer, the question was not how many firms were involved in the different stages of the food chain across the country, but rather how much of this commodity chain was accessible to his (sometimes her) farm. AS farmers moved west, one of their major problems was how to transport their products to markets in the eastern cities.

The government, wishing to promote increased industrialization, also perceived the problem and subsidized the construction of transportation systems, especially railroads. This often made the farmer dependent on a monopoly which could exploit him/her because of the unequal balance of economic power. If a farmer had access to only one railroad, the power relationship certainly favored the railroad. That farmer faced a monopoly regardless of how many other railroads existed in the country. Thus, many farmers faced the issue of monopoly control of capital from the time they became commercial farmers and began to be dependent on a single transportation system to move their products to the market.

Railroads in some parts of the country needed the business of farmers, but they had access to hundreds, if not thousands, of farmers. They were not dependent on any single farmer. Their only concern was that farmers might be successful in organizing a united stand against the railroads. Frank Norris' agrarian populist novel, The Octopus: A History of California (1901), was about a handful of farmers who attempted such a united stand, rising up in direct rebellion, only to be dispatched by the railroads. The whole history of the farmers' movement is largely about the unequal power balance between farmers and the railroads, and, more generally, between the farmers and all the "middlemen" they depended on for transportation, markets, and a host of inputs such as credit and farm equipment.

In southwestern Minnesota, for example, the selling of water fowl to cities to the East and later the selling of agriculture products, especially grain, all depended on the railroad for transportation. In the case of grain, the farmers also depended on the elevators (large silos) to store and to transfer it from farmers' wagons to the train. Many of the transnational corporations (TNCs) of today, like Cargill, exercised economic power in many of the local markets in which they began operating. Most farmers' movements were not successful in establishing alternative economic systems or firms which benefited the farmers, but with the help of legislation to encourage farmer cooperatives, there were some successes.

Advantages of Cross-subsidization to Concentrated Capital

In the food system, horizontal integration usually refers to expansion in the same stage of the same commodity sector. However, if one considers the sector to be meat, then horizontal integration would include the total meat sector. For example, ConAgra ranks in the top four firms in the processing of beef, pork, broilers, sheep, turkeys, and seafood (which is not on the list).

Spokespersons for the industry frequently highlight the competition for the public's dollar between different meats, such as the competition between beef and poultry. They frequently use the competition between meats to argue that the producers must make certain changes in their practices. This competition between commodities is also frequently used to justify the check-off system in which a per-animal fee paid by farmers is used primarily to support product promotion and research. The cost of the check-off-system is borne by the producers, but there is growing concern as to who is benefiting. Currently the Livestock Marketing Association is leading a petition drive to force a beef producer recall referendum on the check-off programmes. Their argument is that "after $1 billion spent in promotion and research over the first 10 years of the programme, beef demand is still declining". They suggest the check-off funds are being spent directly or indirectly on projects that benefit processors and retailers rather than beef producers, and that the results are increased concentration and integration of the industry. One can ask how much competition exists between the different meat products when key decision-makers are involved in more than one part of the meat sector.

The movement of firms into the processing of several commodities may at one level be an extension of horizontal integration, but it also represents a major qualitative change in the economic power relationships. When a firm has a dominant position in several commodity systems, it can cross-subsidize. Firms operating in more than one commodity system gain economic power because they can survive a major loss in one commodity system over a long period of time if they are making significant profits in other systems. If a loss continues very long in a single-product firm's only commodity, it faces serious financial difficulty.

Lane Poultry was the largest broiler producer and processor in the United States following its purchase of Valmac Industries in 1980, but it was still a single-product producer. Lane lost Valmac Industries and then was itself purchased by Tyson Foods because of its economic losses in nine of eleven consecutive quarters in the late 1970s and early 1980s. Being the largest firm in a commodity sector, but a single product producer, does not assure enough economic power to survive. Larger firms with profits in other sectors or systems have more economic power and may overtake them. Information we obtained from executives of a couple TNCs involved in broiler production at the time indicated that the goal of their firms was to obtain a larger share of a growing market.

Planned overproduction and selling below cost of production also occurred in the farm-raised catfish sector early in the 1980s. Two major catfish cooperatives, Southern Pride and Delta Pride, experienced the problem of competing against ConAgra, Cargill, and Chiquita, the parent company of Morrill (now owned by Smithfield). The three TNCs were able to cross-subsidize. The cooperatives survived despite the fact that the annual report of one of the TNCs showed a loss in the catfish division for two years because of "overproduction" in the sector. Conversations with some of the TNC's personnel indicated the firm was prepared to extend this loss for another year or two. We concluded that because the five firms absolutely dominated the production and processing of farm-raised catfish at the time, the low prices were the result of overproduction and an effort on the part of the TNCs to gain market share at the expense of the members of the cooperatives. In fact, Cargill, which has now exited the sector, entered the catfish sector during the time of negative profits with plans to increase catfish production. Like the broiler and catfish sectors in the past, the hog sector is currently involved in a large increase in production even when prices are low and are predicted to stay low. The issue is market share, not efficiency. Large firms that can cross-subsidize can operate in this arena, but smaller, nondiversified firms cannot survive. Economic power, not efficiency, predicts survival.

Horizontal Integration

Most food firms started as relatively small, local firms, but as they became profitable they expanded their operations into other geographic areas. The expansions occurred through building new facilities, acquisitions, and mergers. The expansion of a firm within the same stage of the food system as their original operation is called horizontal integration. For example, the increase in size and decrease in the number of farms in the United States during most of this century is an example of horizontal integration. Horizontal integration also occurs at each of the other stages of distribution and processing. Although there are great variations among the different commodity sectors regarding the ways concentration of ownership and control have occurred in processing and distribution stages, the same general pattern of fewer and larger firms in each stage has been underway during the last half of the twentieth century in the United States and has become most obvious during the last decade at the global level.

In some commodity sectors, one can point to significant concentration of the processing firms in even the first half of the century. For example, pork and beef slaughtering and processing were dominated by Wilson, Armour, and Swift as we entered the twentieth century. Opposition to their practices in the Chicago stockyards inspired Upton Sinclair's The Jungle (1906) and led to the passage of the first Food and Drug Act that same year. And their collusion to set monopoly prices was largely responsible for the creation of the Packers and Stockyards Agency of the U.S. Department of Agriculture (USDA) in 1921 to monitor predatory practices. The Swift and Armour brand names exist today, but the firms were bought by ConAgra, which also bought Miller and Monfort. Some would argue that the fact that these firms do not exist today suggests that even firms with significant economic power can themselves be eliminated. But the important point is that they were absorbed within the larger agglomeration of capital. Still it is true that with the continuing trend towards concentration and centralization of capital no firm is safe from takeover or elimination in other ways.

Forty percent or more of the processing of all agricultural commodities in the Midwest are controlled by the four largest firms. Although debate continues in the United States and in other countries on what constitutes an oligopolistic or near oligopolistic market, much of the economic literature suggests that when four firms control 40 percent of the market, they are able to exert influence on the market unlike that in a competitive system. In the meat sectors 87 percent of the beef cattle are slaughtered by the four largest firms (81 percent by the largest three) and 73 percent of the sheep are processed by the four largest firms. The control of hog slaughtering by the four largest firms increased from 37 percent in 1987 to 60 percent today. Over one half (55 percent) of the broilers (chickens produced for meat) today are produced and processed by the four largest firms, with Tyson now producing and processing almost one third of the broilers in the United States. In the crop sectors, the four largest firms process from 57 percent to 76 percent of the corn, wheat, and soybeans in the United States.

Like the narrow opening of an hour glass which controls the flow of sand from the top to the bottom, the processing firms are positioned between the thousands of producers and millions of consumers in the United States and the world. These firms have a disproportionate amount of influence on the quality, quantity, type, location of production, and price of the product at the production stage and throughout the entire food system. The only stage in which a set of firms begins to equal the economic power of the food processors is the retail stage, which is also becoming more horizontally integrated. The interface between the processing and retail stages is currently where the giants of the food system interact. Certainly, it is not an area characterized by easy entry and exit. How many firms in the world have sufficient capital to face the economic power of these two sets of firms?

Vertical Integration

The second major strategy of monopoly capital is vertical integration. Vertical integration occurs when a firm increases ownership and control of a number of stages in a commodity system. Just like diversifying into different commodity sectors (horizontal integration), this structure gives the firm more economic power. Another example of the extent of vertical integration in the food system comes from ConAgra's annual report. ConAgra indicates that it is the largest distributor of agricultural chemicals in North America, one of the largest fertilizer producers, and in 1990 it entered the seed business. (Since then it has formed a joint venture with DuPont and formal relationships with some of the seed companies involved in biotechnology). ConAgra owns 100 grain storage elevators, 2,000 railroad cars, and 1,100 barges. ConAgra is the largest turkey producer and second largest broiler producer. It produces its own poultry feed, as well as other livestock feed. It also owns and operates hatcheries. ConAgra hires growers to raise its birds and then it processes the birds in its own facilities. This broiler meat can then be purchased as fryers under the name of Country Pride or in further processed foods such as TV dinners and pot pies under the labels of Banquet and Beatrice Food. From the basic raw materials for agricultural production to the retail store, a significant proportion of the food system is owned and controlled by ConAgra. ConAgra is the second largest food firm in the United States (behind Philip Morris) and the fourth largest in the world, with operations in thirty-two countries.

In the subsistence food system, the family controlled its food from seed to plate. In the emerging vertically integrated food system, a few food companies are gaining control of the country's food system by controlling it from seed to shelf. This system is being extended around the world by many of the firms that are headquartered in the United States.

Starting in the 1950s and 1960s, when feed companies and others started hatching their own baby chicks, hiring growers to provide labour, buildings, and land, and constructing their own processing facilities for broilers, the farm press and farm community began to focus on contract production. Contract production is very different from forward contracting of a commodity product. Forward contracting is a sales agreement between a farmer and a buyer that involves an agreed upon price and other terms of the sale to be carried out at some future date.

Contract production is an industrial model in which the integrating firm outsources a needed ingredient-the agricultural raw product. In contract production, the growers are required to provide the land and the buildings, and equip the buildings to the integrating firm's specifications while providing all of the labour for the production stage of the system. The growers are thus hired workers paid on a piece rate basis. They never own the birds or the feed, and have no knowledge of the genetics or the feed ration. The integrating firms provided the birds, feed, and medication. All of the major decisions are made by the integrating firm.

The growers mortgage their land to raise the capital to build the buildings, which cost over $100,000 each. Typically their repayment schedule extends over a ten-to fifteen-year period, while the contract with the integrating firm goes from one batch of chickens to the next-a period of about six weeks. By the time the buildings are almost paid off, the equipment needs to be replaced and the buildings need to be modernized. As a consequence, few growers ever get out of debt. It is estimated that although about one half of the capital in the broiler sector comes from the growers, all of the major decisions are made by the integrating firms. The growers are well aware that they can be cut off at any time.

In the early stages of vertical integration in the broiler industry, most growers had access to several integrating firms, but over time the numbers were reduced. For example, in 1969 in Union Parish, Louisiana, there were four integrating firms. Two were locally owned feed operations, and two were operations based out of state. By 1982, the two local firms were no longer integrating firms; they were now growers. The two outside firms were owned by ConAgra and Imperial Foods, one of the largest food companies of England. Within the following year, ConAgra bought the Country Pride broiler facilities from Imperial Foods. The growers report that they have had no price increase since 1982.

Two processes occur that alter the growers' opportunities. First, as the integrating firms in a given geographic area become fewer, the power relationships between growers and the firms become more unequal. Because of transportation and other costs, most integrating firms will send trucks out only about 25 to 30 miles from the processing site to deliver feed and to pick up poultry for processing. Today there are about 40 firms producing about 97 percent of the broilers in this country. In total, they operate about 250 processing facilities. Thus, there are very few growers who live close enough to more than one processing facility to even have an option to choose between integrating firms.

The second process that limits options for growers is that as the number of firms operating in the same geographic area declines to two or three, an informal agreement evolves between integrating firms that they will not raid their competitors' growers. If a grower gets cut off from one integrating firm, they cannot enter into a contract with another. My thirty years of observing the poultry sector suggest that in early capitalism when the growers have access to several integrating firms, the growers experience financial success, but when the system moves to monopoly capital the growers find themselves in financial crisis. The courts have also found that the growers are at the mercy of the integrating firms in other ways. Errors in the weighing of both feed and poultry have become so well documented that legislation has recently been introduced to address this issue. The USDA has also made a commitment to study this problem.

ROLE OF FORESTRY SECTOR IN INDIAN AGRICULTURAL ECONOMY

India, in spite of having 2.5% of the world's geographic area and 1.8% of the world's forests, sustains 16% of the planet's human population and 18% of its livestock population. Forestry contribution is 1.7% of nation's GDP. This does not take into account unrecorded withdrawals (NWFP, fuel, wood, fodder etc.). Moreover, the environmental benefits of forests also remain to be quantified and calculated.

The forests contribute 1.7% to the GDP of the country (NFAP 1999 a & b). Due to problems associated with the valuation of forests and services, unrecorded removals, illegal harvesting, etc. the exactness of the contribution has not been established. A large part of the forest production consisting of fuel, fodder, medicine and food are removed without payment and without any record by the rural and tribal people. According to Ahmed (1997), the total annual value of India's harvest of all forest produce is estimated to be Rs. 300,000 millions (compared to the investment of Rs. 8000 in the sector). The low estimate of contribution to the GDP resulted in low priority for forestry investments in five year plans. Efforts are needed for monitoring the services provided by the forests so as to appreciate their contribution to human well being. Over 50% of the revenue earned by the forest departments comes from NWFPs. Their growth is generally 40% higher than timber (MOEF 2000).

Nearly 350 million people living in and around forests in India depend on NWFPs for their sustenance and supplemental income which is worth Rs.400 billion annually (Tewari 1994). Studies in Orissa, Madhya Pradesh, Himachal Pradesh and Bihar have indicated that over 80% of forest dwellers depend entirely on NWFPs.

Similarly 17% landless depend on daily wages related to the collection of NWFPs. 39% people are, however, involved in NWFPs collection as a subsidiary occupation. It has been estimated that many village communities derive as much as 17-35% of their annual household income from the sale of NWFPs. NWFPs provide 50% of the income to about 30% rural people. The average income realized through the sale of NWFPs by households in the state of Madhya Pradesh constituted 34 to 55 percent of their total income. As per estimates made in West Bengal, an average return of Rs 2270 ha yr-1 is obtained from NWFPs, which is 25% more than the polewood harvest, which fetches Rs 16,000 per ha after 10 years. There is, thus sufficient evidence to believe that the collection of NWFPs is a crucial part of the population's life support system, especially of the tribals.

Growing Pressure on Forests

The present ecological conflicts have created many economic compulsions and sociological stresses due to changing consumption patterns, scarce availability of land and other natural resources. Out of the total requirement for wood, 70% is for fuel wood and 30% for timber. Thus, forests have at least 5 times more pressure than what they can withstand. This is in addition to the 30% contribution to the fodder requirement of the country in the form of 178 million tonnes of green fodder and 145 million tonnes of dry fodder.

Employment Generation

Of the total wage employment in the forestry sector, NWFPs account for more than 70% of the opportunities for self-employment for the forest dwellers as farm mechanization has not developed well in India. According to an ILO estimate, one hectare of forest plantation creates nearly 630 mandays, from the raising of nurseries to the harvesting stage. 70% of the budget allocated to plantations or afforestation is spent on providing direct wages to the workers and only 30% goes towards purchase of seeds, planting materials, equipment etc. It would not be out of place to mention that 50% of the workforces on forest plantations are women and tribal. Rural women use 70-80% of the mandays in collection of NWFPs, fuel and fodder.

Activities related to NWFPs provide employment during slack periods and a buffer against risk and household emergencies. In the remotest areas, sometimes the forest is the only source of employment and income. Research is needed to evolve forest based entrepreneurial endeavours to produce multiplier effects through the forward and backward linkages.

Markets

The dependence of the producer on intermediaries and his limited access to markets has a direct effect on prices. The price of a product whether sold to consumers directly or through intermediaries, has no bearing on the expenditure incurred on the labour, inputs and transportation. Under direct sales, the localized activity for localized markets creates a supply position in excess of local demand. Traders control the market and dictate the prices during the season and in the off-season. The sale of produce during the flush season and in the off-season is different. In the case of sale through intermediaries, the producers have absolutely no control over the prices. Studies show that the poor primary producer's income always remains low. The need for market related studies has always been felt, and includes research on the market information system and the scope of value addition like bioprospecting, Intellectual Property Right (IPR) etc.

Bibliography

A A Rane and A C Deorukhkar: *Economics of Agriculture*, Atlantic, Publication, Delhi, 2004.

A C Gupta: *Business Economics*, Rawat Publication, Delhi, 2003.

A N Kapoor; V P Gupta and Mohini Gupta: *A Dictionary of Economics (Frontiers of Knowledge, Vol. V)*, Radha Publication, Delhi, 2007.

A.C. Mittal and Sanjay Prakash Sharma: *Agricultural Economics*, RBSA Publication, Delhi, 2001.

Ajit Kumar Roy and Niranjan Sarangi: *Applied Bioinformatics Statistics and Economics in Fisheries Research* , New India Publication Agency, Delhi 2008.

Ashwani Mahajan: *Agricultural Economics*, Centrum Press Publication, Delhi, 2010.

B.K. Tejpal: *Business Economics : Modern Methods and Techniques*, Ritu Publications, Delhi, 2012.

Frederic Grare and Amitabh Mattoo: *Beyond the Rhetoric: The Economics of Indias Look East Policy: Vol II* , Manohar Publication, Delhi, 2003.

G.L. Jain: *Business Economics*, Shree Niwas, Publication, 2007.

G.S. Prakasa Rao: *An Introductory Mathematics to Business and Economics*, Akansha Publication, Delhi, 2011.

Girish Saxena: *Basic Concept of Media Economics: Theory and Practice*, Vista International Publication, Delhi, 2010.

Gupta, K R: *Advanced Microeconomics, Vols. I and II*, Atlantic Publication, Delhi, 2009.

I.M.D. Little: *A Critique of Welfare Economics*, OUP, Publication, Delhi, 2003.

Ila A. Thanki: *Advanced Macro Economics*, Adhyayan Publication, Delhi, 2012.

Jai Narain Sharma: *Alternative Economics : Economic Thought of Mahatma Gandhi* , Deep and Deep Publication, Delhi, 2012.

James Leigh and Predrag Vukovic: *Beyond Oil Bust : Investigating Oil Economics Society and Geopolitics* , Atlantic Publication, Delhi, 2011.

K. Nirmal Ravi Kumar: *Agricultural Production Economics (2 Vols-Set)*, Daya Publication House, Delhi, 2015.

K.R. Gupta: *Advanced Economics of Development: Vols. 1 and 2*, Atlantic Publication, Delhi, 2011.

Kanchan Datta and Chandan Kumar Mukhopadhyay: *Applied Economics on North-East India* , Abhijeet Publication, Delhi, 2011.

M.S. Narasimha Murthy and S. Nagendra: *Business Economics*, Mohit Publication, Delhi, 2010.

Manish Jain: *Basics of Micro and Macro Economics*, Abhishek Publication, Delhi, 2011.

Mary George and P G Thomaskutty: *A Text Book of Mathematical Economics*, Discovery Publishing House, Delhi, 2008.

Mridula Mishra: *Agriculture and Food Economics*, Serials Publication, Delhi, 2010.

N.K. Behura and K.K. Mohanti: *Anthropological Economics, Tribal Development and Globalization* , Dominant Publication, Delhi, 2009.

Nand Kishore Prasad :*Advanced Macroeconomics*, ABD Publication, Delhi,

Nishant Shukla: *An Introduction to Economics of Financial Markets*, Cyber Tech Publications, Delhi, 2011.

P.K. Gaur: *A Textbook of Environmental Economics*, Dominant Publication, Delhi, 2012.

P.V. Venkatachalam: *A Text Book on International Economics* , Cyber Tech Publication, Delhi, 2012.

Pankaj Gupta: *An Introduction to History of Economics*, Cyber Tech Publications, Delhi, 2012.

Pankaj Gupta: *An Introduction to Microeconomics and Finance : Theories and Economics Methods,* Cyber Tech Publications, Delhi, 2011.

Pankaj Tandon: *A Text Book of Microeconomics Theory*, Sage Publication, Delhi, 2015.

Prakash Vohra and Rakesh Mehta: *Business Economics*, Commonwealth Publication, Delhi, 2007.

Pranav K. Desai: *Agricultural Economics* , Daya Publication, Delhi, 2010.

Premananda Pradhan and S.N. Tripathy: *Business Economics* , Anmol Publication, Delhi, 2006.

Ravi Chaddha: *Business Economics*, Sumit Enterprises Publication, Delhi, 2011.

Ruth Towse: *A Textbook of Cultural Economics*, Cambridge University Publication, Delhi, 2011.

S.S. Rana: *A Modern Hand Book of Environmental Economics*, Cyber Tech Publication, Delhi 2010.

Index